THE
BITTER YEARS

By the same author

ACROSS THE TOP OF RUSSIA
IN THE WAKE OF TORREY CANYON

THE
BITTER YEARS
The Invasion and Occupation
of Denmark and Norway
April 1940 - May 1945

by RICHARD PETROW

William Morrow & Company, Inc., New York   1974

Maps by Richard D. Kelly, Jr.

Printed in the United States of America

1 2 3 4 5 78 77 76 75 74

Book design by Helen Roberts

Library of Congress Cataloging in Publication Data

Petrow, Richard
 . The bitter years.

   Bibliography: p.
   1. Denmark—History—German occupation, 1940-1945. 2. World War, 1939-1945—Campaigns—Denmark. 3. Norway—History—German occupation, 1940-1945. 4. World War, 1939-1945—Campaigns—Norway. I. Title.
D802.D4P45   940.54′21   74-9576
ISBN 0-688-00275-7

For my son Jay

Contents

Contents

THE
BITTER YEARS

1
Rationale for Defeat

The German invasion of Norway and Denmark, which Adolf Hitler launched in April, 1940, and which was executed by his military services with lightning success, delivered to the two Scandinavian countries military and psychological blows of devastating impact. For England and France, the German invasion of the northern countries was almost as shattering. Although World War II was then in its eighth month, only Poland had felt the full force of the German war machine. Along the Western Front in France, the "twilight war" played itself out, with Allied troops waiting behind the fortifications of the Maginot Defense Line. By his attack on Denmark and Norway, Hitler served notice that more, and heavier, blows could be expected, striking at the very heart of the Western Alliance.

So one-sided was the German victory in Scandinavia that the defeated countries sought explanations to relieve their feelings of failure, impotence, and guilt. The Scandinavian countries could not have been defeated merely by stronger German forces, better German strategy, or more daring German battlefield tactics; something else must have been involved, something secret, sinister, and shameful. The explanations promulgated in the immediate aftermath of the invasion, and repeated consistently during the war years, took account of these hidden factors by crediting the success of German arms to German treachery, sabotage, and espionage, aided and abetted by the German Fifth Column, that unseen force of spies, rumormongers, collaborators, and traitors believed to have been operating within Denmark and Norway. The basic explanation for the German victory eventually incorporated a series of conspiracies and treacheries into a complex and internally logical theory of defeat that served to assuage the emotions felt in Norway and Denmark and, to a lesser extent, in England and France as well. That it was a theory with little factual substantiation did not lessen its grip on the minds and hearts of Allied citizens. It is what they believed at the time. It is what they wanted to believe. Devious reasons were advanced for simple failures of equipment, performance, or intelligence; actual events were distorted, time sequences rearranged, incidents invented. To this day, the reasons advanced in 1940 to explain away the German victory in Scandinavia are still part of the popular history of the war years.

The rationale for defeat boasts a rich variety of supporting detail, beginning with the German espionage effort that was supposedly launched against the Scandinavian states years before the actual invasion. German successes in the field, it was argued, must have been based on a staggering amount of military intelligence collected during the 1930s by officers posing as German attachés, consuls, tourists, explorers, travelers, students, and commercial agents who swarmed over Scandinavia with methodical thoroughness and outrageous arrogance. These German agents supposedly traveled widely, photographed all sensitive installations, drew detailed sketches of military defenses, and mapped every fjord and island of the Danish and Norwegian coasts.

Usually competent German pilots, it was also noted, fell victim to a strange malady. They consistently landed at military airfields even though their flight plans called for them to land at civilian airports. When questioned, the German pilots excused themselves by pleading that they had "made a mistake" or that they had been "forced" to land because of a malfunction of their aircraft.

Even Field Marshal Hermann Goering, commander-in-chief of the German Air Force, was accused of spying during a visit to Denmark in 1938. For that trip, Goering chose to travel to Copenhagen on his private yacht, which sailed close by several Danish naval and air bases. Goering, it was reported afterward, enjoyed "the landscape intensely through his field glasses." It was also reported that while Goering made his way to Copenhagen by sea, two Mercedes limousines carrying German officers followed the cruise route on shore. The obvious implication was that the Germans in the cars were busy observing from the land what Goering and German naval officers were observing from the sea.

So the picture was drawn of an arrogant and far-flung German espionage network operating actively in Scandinavia for years before the invasion. The reality was less dramatic. Germany did, of course, have agents scattered throughout Scandinavia, as it had in other European countries, but the military information available when Germany began to plan its Scandinavian attack was woefully insufficient. Belief in the efficiency of the German spy apparatus, however, was an integral part of the rationale of defeat and a basic building block for an even more elaborate structure of myth and half-truths. Once the thoroughness of the German intelligence effort had been established, another element could be added. Deceitful German commanders not only used the military information German spies had produced, it was said, but went on from there to employ the Trojan-horse trick to outwit the unsuspecting defenders. Ordinary merchant vessels were the chosen instrument.

In the days and weeks before the invasion of Norway, a flotilla of German merchant ships supposedly sailed on secret missions for Norwegian ports, innocent-looking vessels ostensibly on innocent missions of trade. Instead of industrial cargo, however, these vessels carried thousands of German stormtroopers hidden belowdecks, according to stories widely circulated at the time. The German ships aroused no suspicion as they sailed through the territorial waters of neutral Norway. Nor did they arouse suspicion when they tied up in Norwegian ports, for all the ships carried false cargo manifests which the German captains presented for inspection by unsuspecting Norwegian customs officials. Once in port, the German troops remained hidden until the hour for invasion. They then stormed forth to take over key locations in the towns. After the invasion, *The Times* of London quoted Norwegian sources as saying that some German troops had been "hidden on board ships for four weeks before the invasion."

Other myths developed to cover the Danish invasion. When German military planners addressed the question of how to sneak German troops past Danish coastal defenses, their thoughts turned not to cargo ships but to the colliers that plied between Danish and German ports, bringing coal from Germany to Denmark. Danish officials accepted the comings and goings of the colliers as everyday affairs and never bothered to inspect them. And it was in these vessels that the invasion troops that seized Copenhagen arrived, unseen and unheard, into the very heart of the Danish capital. To this day, Danish citizens remember seeing German colliers tied up on the Sunday before invasion day, lazily rocking away the hours before their planned attack.

Variations of this story were widely circulated, and widely accepted, both during the war and afterward. In *How the Resistance Worked*, Ronald Seth described the German arrival:

> Four colliers were challenged by a Danish patrol boat at the entrance to Copenhagen harbour. The captain of the patrol boat asked the Danish Ministry of Marine if he should search the German boats. No, he was told, and the weather was too bad to hold up coal by red tape. So the ships entered the harbour and tied up alongside Langelinie. They were scarcely tied up when they began to unload, not coal, but 2,000 fully equipped soldiers.

This version introduces a new element in the rationale of defeat; the failure of those holding high responsible positions to act promptly and effectively. If only the officer on duty at the Danish Ministry of Marine had ordered the captain of the patrol boat to search the colliers! The outcome certainly would have been different. And why didn't the Min-

istry of Marine take all necessary precautions? Two answers were popular. The first rested on Scandinavian innocence: the officer on duty was
a peace-loving man who could not conceive of any nation attacking
Denmark without warning. There was a second possibility, however—a
darker possibility: the officer on duty was a Nazi sympathizer, or even a
German agent who knew of the impending invasion. He might, in short,
have been a member of the German Fifth Column, in the 1940s viewed as
a powerful weapon indeed.

After the German spies had done their masterful work, after German military commanders had successfully used the Trojan-horse trick to
get troops past the first line of defenses, it was the German Fifth Column
inside Denmark and Norway—so the myth continued—that enabled
Germany to clinch its victory. The Fifth Column, it was whispered, had
been at work everywhere. Norway particularly was swept by rumors.
They told of loyal troops receiving false orders to lay down their arms, of
pro-Nazi officers who surrendered to the Germans without a fight, of
widespread sabotage throughout the country, of minefields in Oslo Fjord
being cut, of German nationals living in Norway who turned out to act as
guides and interpreters for the invading troops.

The usually reliable *New York Times* printed several stories that
fixed these images firmly in the minds of American readers. On April 17
the *Times* reported:

> German invaders today sped a Nazi packed troop train through
> Norwegian-held territory, past Norwegian-manned fortresses.
> Norwegian railway employees, supplied with false information that
> the train bore their own forces, gave right of way to the Germans.

In a later article, the *Times* reported that there was "some reason to
believe that the electrically controlled mines guarding the inner harbor of
Oslo were put out of action by a highly placed Norwegian traitor."

In June, Otto D. Tolischus summed up the Norwegian experience
in an article printed in the *Times Magazine*:

> In Norway, Germans had not only full knowledge of every inch of
> Norway's difficult terrain and the sad state of its defenses but also
> possessed hidden or disguised resident armies which seized Bergen
> before any German ships arrived and occupied Narvik with the ap-
> parent connivance of its commander.

Such an accumulation of events could be plausibly explained only if
there had been treachery in high places and this element, too, was quickly
added to the rationale of defeat. Certain events supported this interpretation. Within twenty-four hours after German troops set foot on
Norwegian soil, Vidkun Quisling, the leader of the Norwegian National
Unity Party, *Nasjonal Samling,* which modeled itself after Hitler's Nazi
Party, proclaimed himself prime minister of Norway and ordered the

nation to stop its fight. Quisling's sudden emergence into the limelight, with the ostensible support of German administrators, could only mean that Quisling and his supporters had known of the invasion beforehand and had played an active role in its success. Norway had been betrayed from within.

Commented *The New York Times*: "Quisling had been, if not actually in the pay of German Nazis, at least in close contact with them for years."

The Times of London indulged in more florid prose:

> Quisling has added a new word to the English language. To writers, the word Quisling is a gift from the gods. If they had been ordered to invent a new word for traitor they could hardly have hit upon a more brilliant combination of letters. Actually it contrives to suggest something at once slippery and tortuous.

Leland Stowe, a newspaper correspondent for the *Chicago Daily News,* had been in Oslo when the Germans arrived. Shortly afterward he left for Stockholm, where he filed what he described as "the most important newspaper dispatch I have ever had occasion to write." Stowe's article combined many of the rumors and myths that lodged themselves in the minds of the West:

> Norway's capital and great seaports were not captured by armed forces. They were seized with unparalleled speed by means of a gigantic conspiracy which must undoubtedly rank among the most audacious and most perfectly oiled political plots of the past century. By bribery and extraordinary infiltration on the part of Nazi agents, and by treason on the part of a few highly placed Norwegian civilians and defense officials, the German dictatorship built its Trojan Horse inside Norway. Absolute control by a handful of key men in administrative positions and in the Navy was necessary to turn the trick and everything had been faultlessly prepared.

Stowe's article was praised as enlightened reportage, making understandable an otherwise incomprehensible defeat. Other stories and eyewitness reports about treachery in Norway followed. British soldiers who later fought in Norway in an abortive effort to stop the Germans from overrunning the whole country were the source of many of the stories. One Scottish soldier of the Royal Engineers was reported as complaining, "The place was full of spies. Every move we made was known to the Germans almost as soon as we had made it."

Along with these tales of spies and treason, of deceit and corruption, there were other reports that produced moral outrage at German behavior. One story hinged on Norway's efforts after World War I to aid "undernourished, homeless German and Austrian orphans." Many of these children were in fact sheltered and cared for in Norwegian homes.

Norwegians were particularly shocked, then, to read that in April of 1940 these foster children, the beloved *Wienerbarn* of World War I days, had returned as members of the invasion force. Indeed, it was reported, the German Army had specially selected these former *Wienerbarn* for the assault divisions because they knew the countryside so well. *The New York Times* covered the development:

> After the last war, thousands of undernourished German and Austrian children were fed, housed, schooled and all but adopted by kindly Norwegians; the same children, now grown into Nazi youths, returned last month in the vanguard of Hitler's invaders.

When facts are separated from fiction, the Fifth Column proves to be a negligible factor in the German conquest of Norway and Denmark. It existed primarily as a fantasy which was obsessively, even lovingly, embraced by a people fallen victim in a disastrous war, and accepted almost as enthusiastically by Allied nations that failed to render effective assistance.

The five years of the German occupation of Norway and Denmark that followed produced another set of myths and propaganda images. Stories start with a picture of decent, peace-loving citizens who slowly found the courage to rise up in open rebellion against the Nazis. Once embarked on resistance, the Danes and Norwegians pressed their underground fight with sabotage attacks and raids on German units, all carried out under an occupation that rivaled any in its harshness.

Wartime mythmakers and propaganda experts also did an effective job on the Norwegian and Danish resistance. Both countries emerged from the war firmly on the Allied side: Norway was credited with one of the fiercest resistance movements in Europe, its strength and vigor mirroring the ruggedness of its mountains and windswept plateaus; tiny Denmark earned for itself the reputation of Hitler's "model protectorate"—his "pet canary"—which thwarted and frustrated Germany by its independent behavior.

Tales of the resistance in Denmark played heavily on the Danish sense of humor and what was portrayed as the country's peculiarly impudent and self-assured posture in relation to the Germans. In motion-picture theaters, it was reported, filmed excerpts from Hitler's speeches were drowned out by cries of "Who is that?" Newsreels of victorious German troops were supposedly greeted with gales of laughter.

The Danish cold shoulder was also seen as a powerful weapon. In August, 1942, *Atlantic* magazine reported:

> People turned their backs on the assailants from the very first day. Many stories attest this. There is, for instance, an idyllic little park in the suburb of Copenhagen where ducks swim among water lilies. A

Dane observes a German soldier sitting on a bench close to the ducks, apparently addressing a monologue to them. An hour later the German is still at it. The Dane's curiosity breaks bounds, he asks the soldier why he talks to the ducks. "Nobody else will listen to me."

The Danes also liked to present themselves as particularly adept at outwitting German officials. Under wartime orders handed down by German censors, for instance, Danish newspapermen were prohibited from reporting the results of Allied air raids. After one successful Royal Air Force raid on rail yards in Frederikshavn, local Danish editors were instructed to print only that the bombs fell harmlessly on a nearby field, killing a cow. Two days later, however, a Danish writer found a way to let his readers know what had really happened, provided they were able to read between the lines. "The cow that was killed in the R.A.F. raid of two days ago is still burning," he wrote. This anecdote is still related with relish in Denmark today even though it has never been authenticated.

Many such apocryphal stories involved Denmark's late King Christian X, who developed into a symbol of national independence and opposition to Nazi philosophy. King Christian's public image combined quiet heroism with regal dignity.

On one occasion, it was reported, a German officer informed the king that he had orders to raise the swastika over King Christian's castle. The king angrily declared, "If this happens, a Danish soldier will go and take it down."

"That Danish soldier will be shot," the German officer warned.

"That Danish soldier will be myself," the king replied. As a consequence, the Nazi flag never flew over his castle.

On another occasion, when the Germans supposedly ordered Danish Jews to wear yellow Stars of David on their arms, King Christian is credited with thwarting the German order by pinning a Star of David to his own sleeve and riding through the streets of Copenhagen, an action which prompted tens of thousands of Copenhagen citizens to don Jewish stars as well, thereby presenting the Germans with a united opposition to their Jewish policies.

An emotional report on these developments in the British *Evening Standard* was later reproduced in pamphlet form and given wide circulation:

> A noble voice comes out of Nazi-occupied Denmark . . . "If the Germans want to introduce the Yellow Star for Jews in Denmark," announces King Christian, "I and my whole family will wear it as a sign of the highest distinction." . . . Today, a Christian King converts a badge of shame and segregation into a symbol of pride and unity.

The Norwegian resistance was portrayed as a more active force. In the early years of the war, it is true, Norway's public image suffered because of the impact of Quisling and his followers. Some in the Allied nations viewed Norway as a "nation of traitors," but this reputation changed as the war progressed. Abroad, the stalwart Norwegian merchant marine sailed under Allied convoy commanders. At home, the growth of armed resistance in the face of a cruel occupation regime erased the taint of treason.

The Norwegian terrain favored armed resistance; Norwegian men knew their mountains and could survive where others would perish. Given the terrain and the fighting qualities of the Norwegians, it was only to be expected that German troops would face continuing guerrilla warfare in which their strength and morale would be drained in a series of lightning-swift raids by Norwegian underground fighters.

By war's end, the fierceness of the Norwegian resistance was second to none in the eyes of the world. As liberation approached, newspapers reported the existence of forty thousand highly trained and well-equipped Norwegian underground fighters, ready to battle the Germans should they attempt a last-ditch stand. With the German surrender, these underground soldiers made their public appearance at last, tommy guns held casually in the crook of their arms, to show to the world the stern face of the underground force that had beleaguered the Germans during the last years of war.

The picture of the German invasion and occupation of Denmark and Norway created during the war is still accepted today. Two peace-loving nations, expecting no harm from their powerful neighbor to the south, were invaded by deceitful enemy armies, which with the help of traitors quickly overwhelmed the brave defenders in an unfair fight. In the occupation that followed, the defeated nations, strongly pro-Allied in sentiment, built powerful resistance forces which took to the field to harass and intimidate German troops and thus contribute, by their militance, to the eventual defeat of the armies of the Third Reich.

It was not that way at all.

2
Scandinavian Neutrality

Centuries ago, in the Dark Ages of European history, the Norsemen of Scandinavia struck fear and terror throughout the continent. No coast was safe from seaborne Viking raiders, while on land Scandinavian armies cut deep into the heart of Russia and Byzantium in their search for riches and plunder. By the eleventh century, Canute the Great of Denmark had subjugated England and Norway. Later, what is now Sweden and Finland fell under his control. In the early 1660s, it was Sweden's turn to assume military supremacy. Under Gustavus Adolphus (Gustavus II), the military genius who created the world's first modern army, Swedish soldiers subjugated the entire eastern shore of the Baltic Sea, and in the Thirty Years' War fought their way south through Europe, capturing the cities of Prague and Munich during their campaigns.

From these high points, Scandinavia witnessed a steady erosion of strength and prestige as new concentrations of power formed within Europe. Sweden lost Finland to Russia in 1809. A few years later, Denmark was forced to give up Norway. In the Peace of Vienna in 1864, Denmark's territory contracted even further after her defeat by the German Confederation. By the nineteenth century the Scandinavian countries had turned their energies and thoughts inward and no longer sought to play major roles in international affairs.

Denmark, in particular, lived in the shadow of the continent's great land power, imperial Germany. As early as 1901, strong forces within Denmark advocated a *Tysker-Kurs,* or German course, in case of general war among the Great Powers.

When fighting broke out in August, 1914, Denmark quickly bowed to German pressure and mined the waters of the Great Belt, that body of water within Danish jurisdiction that constitutes one of two major nautical entrances to the Baltic Sea. By mining the Belt, Denmark provided protection for the German naval base at Kiel. Once established, the minefield was maintained by Denmark until the end of the war. King

Christian X justified his country's action by remarking that "Denmark at this moment is in such a serious condition that one cannot play banque with one's country." To ease the blow to Britain, King Christian drafted a personal message of explanation for his cousin, King George of England, in which he outlined the pressures that had influenced Denmark's decision and pleaded for understanding. Denmark remained neutral and untouched by battle through four years of World War I.

Neutrality in the First World War was somewhat more difficult to maintain for Norway and Sweden. Sweden's industrial output and iron ore from fields in northern Sweden were vital materials of war, coveted by both sides. Norway's merchant-marine fleet and her strategic coastal position were likewise of vital military significance. As the war developed, most of the vessels of the Norwegian and Swedish merchant fleets were pressed into service for the Allied cause while most of Swedish industrial production and iron ore flowed to Germany.

Both countries, nevertheless, guarded their neutrality jealously. Norway, in particular, was determined to keep her sheltered territorial waters, known as the Leads, open to all shipping. Through these waterways, ships could sail from above the Arctic Circle to the mouth of the Baltic Sea without leaving Norwegian waters. The arctic port of Narvik drew especially heavy traffic, for it was the terminal point of a railroad running from the iron-ore districts of northern Sweden.

The question of safe passage through the Norwegian Leads came up in 1918. During the winter of 1917–18, the British Navy began to lay a mine barrage across the North Sea, from the Orkney Islands north of Scotland to the Norwegian coast immediately south of Bergen. The primary purpose of the minefield was to protect Allied merchant ships by preventing German surface raiders and submarines from leaving the North Sea.

Once the minelaying was under way, British admiralty officials immediately pressed to extend the minefield into the Norwegian Leads and thus prevent German merchantmen and U-boats from slipping around the minefield's unprotected end inside Norwegian territorial waters. Diplomatic and economic pressures were applied; and in September, 1918, Norway finally succumbed and agreed to mine the Leads, but the war ended before Norway actually laid any mines.

For Norway and Sweden, the policy of neutrality—though bent and twisted by the pressures of war—brought both countries through the great conflict without their armies seeing combat and without their territories suffering the devastation of battle. All the Scandinavian countries emerged from World War I with their faith in neutrality unshaken. They firmly believed that neutrality must be a cardinal principle of their foreign policy.

Throughout the troubled 1930s, Scandinavia maintained that faith in neutrality. What had worked in World War I should work in any future world war; but the situation on the eve of World War II, while it might have appeared similar to the situation that faced Scandinavia before World War I, was only superficially the same. Adolf Hitler's Third Reich was more daring and aggressive than had been the government of the Kaiser. If Norway and Denmark hoped to duplicate their feat of World War I and remain aloof from the fight, there were pressures at work which would sweep those hopes aside.

On September 1, 1939, the day Germany invaded Poland, the German Foreign Ministry instructed its minister in Oslo to inform Norway that Germany intended to respect its neutrality, provided there was no breach of neutrality by a third party. Germany had previously given similar assurances to Denmark, with whom she had a treaty of friendship.

By the third week of September, the conquest of Poland was almost complete. In Berlin, uncertainty arose about the next step, but on September 27, when Warsaw surrendered, Hitler informed his top commanders that he had decided to launch an offensive in the west before the end of the year. All the services had doubts about Germany's ability to launch an early strike against the west. Despite Hitler's declared intentions, the German Armed Forces High Command (OKW), which had responsibilities similar to the present-day U.S. Joint Chiefs of Staff, and the high commands of the three individual German armed services immediately started to turn out alternative proposals and studies on the assumption that the invasion in the west would not take place as scheduled.

It was Grand Admiral Erich Raeder's Navy High Command that first looked to Norway as a possible sphere of action. Since the end of World War I, German naval leaders had viewed Norway as the key to German victory at sea. During the First World War, the British blockade and mines had limited the operations of the German Navy. If Germany had had bases in Norway, Britain's "hunger blockade" might have been broken and German surface ships, it was believed, could have pushed through into the Atlantic.

There was another factor which turned the eyes of the German Navy northward. Sweden provided Germany with vital supplies of iron ore. Swedish iron-ore fields were located in the Kiruna-Gällivare district of northern Sweden and ore destined for Germany was transported by rail either to the Swedish port of Luleå on the Gulf of Bothnia or to the Norwegian port of Narvik. In winter, however, the Gulf of Bothnia froze, and ore could be shipped only via Narvik. Control of the Norwegian coast, therefore, would provide Germany with year-round protection for the cargo ships loaded with vital Swedish ore sailing from Narvik for German ports.

In the days immediately following the outbreak of war, Admiral Rolf Carls, the third-ranking officer in the German Navy, suggested to Admiral Raeder "the importance of an occupation of the Norwegian coast by Germany." Certainly this was not a new concept. Raeder in response sent a confidential questionnaire to his naval war staff asking it to explore the possibility of gaining "bases in Norway." The naval staff's initial appraisal was ready by October 9, and it was not optimistic: Norwegian bases could be won only by a hazardous military campaign and, once captured, could be defended with difficulty. Britain's supremacy at sea made any such undertaking risky indeed.

Undaunted, Raeder saw Hitler the next day for one of his routine reports on naval operations. During the meeting, he mentioned to Hitler the Navy's view that bases in Norway—at Trondheim and Narvik—were necessary. Raeder presented Hitler with a series of notes to buttress his position. He later wrote:

> I stressed the disadvantages which an occupation of Norway by the British would have for us: the control of the approaches to the Baltic, the outflanking of our naval operations and of our air attacks on Britain, the end of our pressures on Sweden. I also stressed the advantages for us of the occupation of the Norwegian coast: outlet to the North Atlantic, no possibility of a British mine barrier, as in the year 1917/18.

Hitler's mind, however, was elsewhere. Only the day before he had finished a lengthy political and military analysis that reaffirmed his intention to launch an offensive in the west. Hitler's preoccupation with the invasion of the west doomed Raeder's immediate hopes of involving Hitler in his Norwegian project. Norway was obviously a matter of secondary importance to Hitler, if not an unwelcome distraction.

In London, as in Berlin, the Norwegian question occupied the minds of those involved in the prosecution of the war. Although British Navy officials were pressing most eagerly for action in the northern theater, the first move was made by the Foreign Office. Late in August, 1939, one week before the outbreak of war, Foreign Minister Lord Halifax informed the British Chiefs of Staff that the Foreign Office was considering a confidential message assuring the Norwegian government that Britain would regard a German attack on Norway as an attack on the United Kingdom. The Foreign Office did not give Norway its formal assurances until September 16, more than two weeks after the outbreak of war.

Britain's interest, when it looked northward, focused on the Swedish iron ore that poured through Narvik for German ports. In the autumn of 1939, the British Ministry of Economic Warfare thought Germany's supply of iron ore was very low, probably no more than two million tons, and estimated that Germany had to import an average of 750,000 tons of ore per month during the first year of war or risk a "major industrial breakdown." When British analysts studied the transportation picture, the importance of Narvik, which could handle 250,000 tons per month, loomed large. If the Narvik route could be cut, German industry would find itself one million tons short after the winter of 1939–40.

On September 19, 1939, Winston Churchill, who then held the post of First Lord of the Admiralty, with a seat in the War Cabinet of Prime Minister Neville Chamberlain, proposed that British ships lay a minefield in Norwegian territorial waters to force German iron-ore ships out of the Leads into international waters, where they could be stopped, seized, or sunk by the Royal Navy.

Despite Churchill's urgings, the British War Cabinet took no action. Not until the middle of November did the question of Scandinavian ore again appear on its agenda. On that occasion, Churchill presented to his fellow cabinet members a memorandum calling for a minefield stretching from the Orkneys to the Norwegian coast. Since the preparation of the mine barrage would take a minimum of six months, Churchill also suggested that Britain lay mines at once within Norwegian territorial waters to prevent the passage of ore ships from Narvik. The cabinet approved the mine barrage across the North Sea but held back from mining Norwegian territorial waters, calling instead for staff studies on the military and economic consequences of such an operation. Before these studies could be completed, the Soviet Union invaded Finland, inserting a new factor into the Scandinavian question.

The Soviet Union and Finland had been discussing Russian territorial demands since the end of the fighting in Poland, but despite Finnish willingness to go along with most Russian demands, the talks broke down in mid-November, 1939. Less than three weeks later Red Army troops attacked Finland at eight separate points along their mutual border. The heaviest attacks fell on the Karelian Isthmus, where the Finns had constructed a defensive line twenty miles deep. Fierce Finnish resistance halted the Russians in their tracks.

The Russian invasion produced instant sympathy for Finland in Allied nations and forced Britain and France to take a second look at Scandinavia. On December 11, Winston Churchill asked his colleagues in the War Cabinet what the British response should be if the Soviet Union followed up its attack on Finland with attacks on Sweden and Norway. The Foreign Office replied that the Soviet Union, after the defeat of Finland, would not press demands on Sweden and Norway for fear that those countries, Sweden particularly, would call on German assistance.

The Foreign Office evaluation failed to satisfy Churchill, who sought avenues for action in the developing Scandinavian situation. Churchill "welcomed this new and favourable breeze as a means of achieving the major strategic advantage of cutting off the vital iron-ore supplies of Germany." Five days after he first brought up the question of Russian intentions, Churchill was back with another major memorandum to the War Cabinet in which he repeated his demand that the ore from Narvik be stopped by laying minefields in Norwegian territorial waters. "If Germany can be cut from all Swedish ore supplies till the end of 1940," he wrote, "a blow will have been struck at her war-making capacity equal to a first-class victory in the field or from the air."

Churchill acknowledged that his proposal could not be carried out without violating Scandinavian neutrality, but he brushed aside all objections. "Small nations must not tie our hands when we are fighting for their rights and freedom."

Churchill's memorandum broke new ground on the Scandinavian question, but it was France which made the next move, escalating Allied plans beyond Churchill's furthest reach. France seized upon the Soviet invasion of Finland to suggest dispatching a joint Anglo-French force to Finland's assistance. Norway and Sweden, it was assumed, because of their pro-Finnish sympathies, would permit passage of the force through their territories. But France had more than Finland on its mind. In a draft memorandum, France noted:

> Our promise to cooperate with Sweden and Norway, if accepted, might be developed into the despatch of an expeditionary force which would be able to occupy Narvik and the Swedish iron ore fields as part of the process of assisting Finland. . . .

By mid-December, both England and France, reacting to developments in Scandinavia, had agreed on steps which, if acted upon, would put Allied troops into action in the northern sector.

Hitler, too, looked upon Scandinavia in a different light in December. He feared—and his fear had a basis in fact—that the Allies might use the Russo-Finnish conflict to establish bases in Norway, under the guise of helping Finland. When Admiral Raeder raised the Norwegian question again in mid-December, Hitler was more inclined to listen. Raeder not only had the Russo-Finnish war as an argument; he also had support from the Norwegian Nazi Vidkun Quisling, who was in Berlin seeking German support for a coup d'état.

Quisling, a former Norwegian Army officer who had served as a minister of defense in 1931, maintained close ties with Alfred Rosenberg, the "philosopher of the Nazi movement," throughout the 1930s. Rosenberg was impressed with Quisling. "Of all political groupings in Scandinavia," he wrote, "only *Nasjonal Samling*, led by Vidkun Quisling, deserves serious attention."

In June, 1939, Quisling journeyed to Berlin for talks with Rosenberg. He described Norway as split politically between the bourgeois parties, which had been taken in by the British, and the Labor Party, which Quisling viewed as pro-Soviet and determined to transform Norway into a Soviet Socialist Republic. Quisling asked Rosenberg for financial aid, "in support of our Pan-Germanic policy." The sum mentioned was 6,500,000 Reichmarks.

In December, Quisling made another trip to Berlin for another meeting with Rosenberg. This time Quisling proposed to take over the Norwegian government with Norwegian stormtroopers—after they had received special training in Germany. At the same time, according to Quisling's plan, the German Navy, with contingents of the German Army aboard, should put in an appearance outside Oslo. Quisling would then issue an appeal for German assistance, thus paving the way for German troops to land.

Though sympathetic, Rosenberg did not immediately introduce Quisling to others within the German hierarchy. He reported Quisling's presence to Hitler, but did not ask Hitler to meet Quisling. Quisling did get to talk to Admiral Raeder, and in Raeder he found an interested and enthusiastic listener.

Raeder recorded the substance of the talks:

> Quisling stated that a British landing is planned in the vicinity of Stavanger and Kristiansand is proposed as a possible British base. The present Norwegian government as well as Parliament and the whole foreign policy are controlled by the well known Jew Hambro. [Carl Hambro was President of the Norwegian Parliament.]

Raeder saw Hitler the next day and mentioned his meeting with Quisling. "Quisling creates the impression he is reliable," Raeder commented, and went on to tell of Quisling's "good connections" with the Norwegian Army, adding that the Norwegian was ready "to take over the government by a political coup and ask Germany for aid."

Hitler refused to commit himself. He wanted to speak to Quisling first, "in order to form an impression of him."

The first meeting between Hitler and Quisling took place on December 14. The meeting must have gone well indeed, for, although Quisling was not informed, Hitler immediately ordered staff studies of a possible Norwegian invasion. Because of security considerations, the planning would be conducted by "a very limited circle," which would submit two alternative schemes: one for a coup engineered by Quisling with minor military support by German forces, the second for a strictly military occupation of the country.

Four days later, Hitler granted Quisling another interview. This time Hitler promised him financial and moral support, but still did not mention that Germany was exploring ways and means of taking over Norway.

The task of preparing military plans for the invasion of Norway was assumed by Maj. Gen. Alfred Jodl, chief of the OKW operations staff, who conferred separately with the chiefs of the three services. The OKW report, *Studie Nord,* covered the main military and political questions that would be involved in any invasion of Norway. In mid-January it was distributed to the three services' high commands for evaluation. Of the three services, only the naval staff showed interest. On January 23, Hitler ordered *Studie Nord* recalled for further active study. Henceforth, Hitler ordered, all work would be done under his personal guidance. With this new emphasis came a change in the code name as well: *Studie Nord* became *Weseruebung*.

Specific planning for *Weseruebung* began early in February with the assembly of a special staff under Capt. Theodore Krancke, commanding officer of the cruiser *Scheer.* The Krancke staff was hampered by lack of intelligence information. Some useful intelligence had been collected on the Norwegian Army and its military installations, but the Germans had by no means conducted a thorough intelligence operation in Norway or Denmark at the time. The Krancke staff had to call for travel guides, tourist brochures, and hydrographic charts for basic information.

Eventually, an overall plan was worked out which called for simultaneous surprise landings at Norwegian ports in six strategically important areas. First-wave troops would be transported by plane and fast warship. Second-wave troops would come by air. Third and fourth waves would arrive by transport ship. The Krancke staff proposed no military occupation of Denmark, although the threat of a military occupation of Jutland would be used to pressure Denmark into granting to the German air armada the use of airfields in northern Jutland.

While Krancke and his staff put together the details of *Weseruebung*, the British and the French continued to seek support from Norway and Sweden for their plan to send troops to Finland. The Scandinavian response was negative. Norway could not believe that Great Britain would "drive a small neutral country into war." Sweden thought "that the British government had the fate of a sufficient number of smaller States on their conscience as it is."

Despite Scandinavian misgivings, the British and French pursued their Scandinavian venture. A meeting of the Supreme War Council was convened in Paris on February 5 to agree on a joint final policy. There Chamberlain argued that, as the defeat of Germany was their primary interest, the correct Allied strategy in Scandinavia was to combine aid to the Finns with a thrust at the Swedish ore fields. Chamberlain observed that such an expedition, "ostensibly and nominally assigned for the assistance of Finland, would kill two birds with one stone." The French representatives saw the wisdom of Chamberlain's remarks.

Three or four regular Allied divisions were deemed essential for the operation, although they might be disguised as "volunteers." France agreed that the Forty-second and Forty-fourth British divisions, due shortly to join the British Expeditionary Force in France, should be held in Great Britain until they sailed for Scandinavia. France would contribute an Alpine Brigade, a Polish Brigade, and two battalions of the French Foreign Legion. Other French troops would be assembled for later embarkation. The invasion forces, under British command, would make landings at Narvik and Trondheim, striking out from there for Finland. En route, the iron-ore fields of Gällivare and Kiruna would be occupied. It was agreed that the operation had to be launched no later than the third week of March.

There remained the tricky diplomatic question of Swedish and Norwegian neutrality. Chamberlain proposed that as soon as the Allied expedition was ready to sail, Finland could be advised to appeal to the world for assistance—Norway and Sweden, in particular, ought to get urgent Finnish appeals. The Allies could then send troops in response to the Finnish request and could use this request as a moral lever to overcome any Scandinavian hesitancy.

The Supreme War Council reacted favorably to this proposal. The British general, Sir Edmund Ironside, commented in his diary:

> Everybody is purring with pleasure. All is plain sailing. The French are handing the operation over to us and are sitting back pretty. But it couldn't well be otherwise because we know so much more about the North. . . .

Both London and Paris buzzed with rumors of an impending action. On February 8, British interservice staffs were ordered to accelerate military planning. On that same day, Chamberlain appeared before the House of Commons to report on the Supreme War Council meeting. Chamberlain was obviously bursting with good news which he could not reveal. All he could do was hint broadly at significant events to come. "I wish," he said, "that I could lighten the darkness and give to the House an account of our proceedings, but I know no one will desire me to be guilty of the folly of making such a generous gift to the enemy."

By the middle of February, 1940, both Germany and Great Britain, the latter with French cooperation and support, were planning military moves which would violate the neutrality of Scandinavia and bring war to the north. It was merely a question of time which side would strike first. At this juncture, an incident involving the German tanker *Altmark* took place in the territorial waters of Norway, which gave a sense of urgency to the preparations for war under way in both Berlin and London.

3
The *Altmark* Affair

The outbreak of World War II in September, 1939, caught the eleven-thousand-ton German naval-auxiliary tanker *Altmark* on the high seas, ostensibly headed home for Germany after taking on a full load of fuel oil in Port Arthur, Texas. *Altmark*'s commanding officer, Capt. Heinrich Dau, however, carried secret orders which, with the start of war, sent him racing into the South Atlantic to rendezvous with the German pocket battleship *Admiral Graf Spee*, itself operating under secret orders to prey on Allied merchant ships.

As the *Altmark* sailed south for its first rendezvous, Captain Dau, a cautious and cunning naval officer who was determined to escape detection, ordered *Altmark*'s gray hull temporarily painted a cheerful yellow and christened with a fictitious name: the *Altmark* became the Norwegian ship *Sogne*. Norwegian colors were raised aloft in place of the flag of the Third Reich. By this deception Captain Dau hoped that the *Altmark* would pass as a peaceful Norwegian tanker if sighted by British warships.

The vessel Captain Dau commanded was well suited for her task as tender and supply ship for the *Graf Spee*. The *Altmark* was powered with four nine-cylinder diesel engines capable of attaining a speed of twenty-one knots, which was fast for a vessel of her size. Speed was essential. The *Altmark* was expected to cover almost as much ocean as the *Graf Spee*, meeting the raider at prearranged positions whenever the pocket battleship needed fuel.

The *Graf Spee* went on the hunt on September 26, after receiving direct orders from Hitler, and found her first victim, a British merchant ship, four days later off the coast of Brazil. The sinking elated the *Graf Spee*'s commanding officer, Captain Hans Langsdorff. It also provided the British Admiralty with its first news that a German raider was loose in the South Atlantic, and the British Navy immediately organized a widespread search, with the *Graf Spee* as the quarry. The existence of the *Altmark*, however, was still unsuspected.

After sinking her first victim, the *Graf Spee* headed for the west coast of Africa, where between October 5 and October 15 she sank three more British ships. Compared to the disregard for civilian lives which German submarine commanders would show later in the war, Captain Langsdorff conducted his attacks with extraordinary concern for the British merchant seamen, taking pains to rescue the officers and crew before sinking their ships. In the autumn of 1939, the war was still young enough to permit the observance of certain proprieties of naval warfare.

Finding the hunting good off Africa, the *Graf Spee* continued to prowl the coast and sank its fifth victim, the S.S. *Trevanion*, on October 22. Before going down, however, the *Trevanion* flashed a distress signal; and Captain Langsdorff, fearing he would soon be hunted, steamed to the *Altmark* to refuel and transfer all prisoners to the tanker, before racing into the Indian Ocean.

Captain Langsdorff's move into a new theater of operations succeeded in outwitting the British, who continued to look for the *Graf Spee* in the Atlantic. But the pocket battleship found slim pickings in the Indian Ocean. In more than three weeks of operations, the *Graf Spee* sank only one small coastal tanker, the 706-ton *Africa Shell*. A discouraged Captain Langsdorff quickly doubled back into the Atlantic to rendezvous again with the *Altmark* and to continue to hunt off the west coast of Africa, which had proved such a productive area before. The hunting there was still good. The *Graf Spee* sank a ten-thousand-ton merchant ship on December 2 and an eight-thousand-ton vessel on December 3. On both occasions, Captain Langsdorff adhered to his policy of rescuing the crews of his victims.

Having sunk two ships in two days, Captain Langsdorff, again fearing immediate British retaliation, decided to head for the waters off Montevideo, Uruguay, and the River Plate, where merchant-marine traffic was also heavy. En route, the lethal *Graf Spee* located and sank her ninth victim. The *Altmark* meanwhile continued to sail a holding pattern in the mid-Atlantic. By then she was carrying 299 prisoners from six sunken merchant ships. Still other captured British officers and crewmen were aboard the *Graf Spee*.

Unknown to Captain Langsdorff, however, the British had anticipated his eventual arrival off the River Plate, and three British warships awaited him there, ready to pounce on the deadly raider. The British force consisted of three light cruisers, *Exeter, Ajax,* and *Achilles.* The *Ajax* sighted smoke over the horizon early in the morning of December 13, and the *Exeter,* the heaviest of the three cruisers, was sent to investigate. Minutes later the *Exeter* signaled: "I think it is a pocket battleship." Almost simultaneously the *Graf Spee* sighted the *Exeter,* and assuming the *Exeter* was alone, the *Graf Spee* turned to give battle. Two eleven-inch German shells roared across the sea toward the *Exeter.* The *Ajax* and

Achilles raced to join the fray. Captain Langsdorff found to his dismay that the *Graf Spee* faced not one but three British warships which pressed the attack like killer sharks against a whale.

Both sides held certain advantages in the fight that developed. The German pocket battleship's main armament of six eleven-inch guns fired projectiles weighing 670 pounds apiece, which theoretically could blow any one of the cruisers out of the water with a direct hit. The *Graf Spee*'s guns had the advantage in range as well, and the pocket battleship carried enough armor to protect her from all but the luckiest of hits. An armored belt four inches thick girdled her hull and up to seven inches of armor plate protected her turrets.

Ship for ship, the British cruisers were no match for the *Graf Spee*. The heaviest weapons the British could bring into action were the eight-inch guns of the *Exeter,* but the British ships were faster than the *Graf Spee,* permitting them the option of attacking from different directions, and their guns could fire more quickly than those aboard the *Graf Spee.* There was one additional advantage for the British: because of the peculiar fire-control arrangements on the *Graf Spee,* the German battleship's main armament could concentrate on only one target at a time. Regardless of which cruiser the *Graf Spee* chose as her primary target, the other two warships could maneuver with relative safety, contending only with the *Graf Spee*'s secondary armament. Nevertheless, any naval officer studying the battle as a textbook exercise would have predicted that the *Graf Spee* could easily concentrate on and destroy each cruiser one by one.

The battle began in textbook fashion. Captain Langsdorff ordered his main armament to zero in on the *Exeter,* which was gallantly attacking from the south. Shell after shell smashed into the British vessel. Within fifty minutes, the *Exeter* had been hit so often she was forced to drop out of the fight or risk being sunk. The *Ajax* and *Achilles,* however, continued to engage the German battleship from the east and scored several direct hits on the *Graf Spee,* smashing the battleship's vulnerable control tower before the giant eleven-inch guns could be turned on them. Even though the two cruisers had taken moderate damage from the *Graf Spee*'s secondary armament, they were still able to outrun and outmaneuver the German vessel.

Captain Langsdorff, fearing his vessel would suffer more damage, broke off the engagement and headed for safety in Montevideo. There he surveyed his ship and found the damage worse than he had feared. It would take weeks, if not months, to repair, and time was not on Captain Langsdorff's side. Neutrality provisions gave him only forty-eight hours in port. After that he would have to return to sea and again face the British ships. With his ship gravely wounded, with time running out, and with a

British patrol waiting to resume the battle at sea, Captain Langsdorff began to realize that defeat was at hand.

Despite the agony of the decision he had to make, Captain Langsdorff conducted himself with dignity and compassion. Before proceeding with his final plans, he ordered the release of all British prisoners on his ship. Then he maneuvered the *Graf Spee* into the waters of the River Plate, and after seeing to the safety of his men, ordered his vessel scuttled so that she would not fall into British hands or suffer the indignity of being sunk by lighter British vessels. Three days later, humiliated at the defeat which had cost Germany one of its most powerful surface raiders, Captain Langsdorff shot himself to death. He could not face the prospect of what awaited him back in Germany.

Even before his suicide, the British prisoners who had been released from the *Graf Spee* had reported the existence and character of the prison ship *Altmark,* which was still at sea somewhere in the Atlantic, its hold the home of other *Graf Spee* victims. Immediately, the British Navy, having successfully tracked down and trapped the elusive *Graf Spee,* turned its attention to locating the *Altmark.*

The British Admiralty anticipated that, with the scuttling of the *Graf Spee,* her supply ship would immediately sail northward in hopes of reaching Germany. British naval vessels consequently concentrated their search in mid-Atlantic waters. As weeks passed with no sighting of the prison ship, the search shifted northward on the assumption that, having eluded British patrols, the *Altmark* was in fact making good its plan to reach Germany.

The frantic search made headlines in the major papers of Allied nations. Day by day the suspense grew. In Oslo, Norwegian Navy officials followed the story with avid interest. They suspected that *Altmark* might enter Norwegian waters on her voyage home. In early January, 1940, the commander of the Bergen naval defense district circulated an advisory bulletin reporting that the *Altmark* was trying to cross the Atlantic with British prisoners of war on board and instructing all units to report the *Altmark* immediately if she was sighted in Norwegian waters.

Through all of January, however, the widespread search failed to bring results, and it began to appear as if the *Altmark* were a modern-day *Flying Dutchman* which had vanished from the face of the ocean. Captain Dau, however, was no legendary captain but a hard-headed officer who was fighting for the life of his vessel and who had judged his adversaries wisely. Instead of running for home after the death of the *Graf Spee,* as the British expected him to do—and as he suspected they might think—Dau purposely kept his vessel cruising aimlessly in the South Atlantic for weeks. He did not judge it safe to start his homeward journey until

January 22. By then the British did not have the foggiest idea where he was.

Once bound for home, Captain Dau moved swiftly and decisively, heading northward at top speed until he approached the latitude of Newfoundland, where he turned his ship's bow toward Iceland. In Icelandic waters he ran the risk of being spotted by a patroling British warship, but his luck held out. Bad weather reduced visibility and the *Altmark* slipped undetected between the Faeroe Islands and Iceland, then headed due east for the coast of Norway and what Dau hoped would be a safe passage through Norwegian territorial waters. Dau planned to hug the craggy, fjord-bitten coast of Norway until he reached the Skagerrak, the deep-water passage separating Norway from Denmark. Once across the Skagerrak, the *Altmark* would be in safe waters, out of reach of British surface ships.

For the prisoners aboard the *Altmark* life was unpleasant but not excessively harsh. Sanitary arrangements were primitive, water was in short supply, and the prisoners, crammed together in close quarters, were given little opportunity for fresh air and exercise, but they were not deliberately maltreated. The daily food ration consisted of one-half pound of bread, four ounces of meat, one-and-a-quarter ounces of fat, three ounces of dried peas, beans, rice or other vegetables, three quarters of an ounce of coffee, sugar, and tea, and between one and two ounces of bread-spread and dried potatoes. Certainly not a gourmet's ideal, but a diet adequate to sustain life and health. For those who fell ill, regular medical inspections were available. Captain Dau and his officers and crew looked upon the prisoners as an additional cargo that had to be safely carried to port, much as they would have looked upon any other perishable freight.

The *Altmark* entered Norwegian waters north of Trondheim early in the morning of February 14. A Norwegian Coast Guard lookout immediately spotted the vessel, and following his instructions to the letter, notified his superiors. The news shot upward through the Norwegian naval chain of command and by eight-thirty that morning, Rear Admiral Carston Tank-Nielsen, commander of the Bergen defense district, was on the phone reporting *Altmark*'s arrival to Norway's First Sea Lord, Admiral Diesen, in Oslo.

Altmark's intrusion into Norwegian territorial waters brought a quick response. Within an hour a Norwegian motor torpedo boat was hailing the German tanker to stop for inspection, and Captain Dau, determined to avoid any incident that could compromise his voyage now that he was safe inside Norwegian waters, instructed his navigator to comply exactly with Norwegian instructions. Dau himself greeted the Norwegian boarding officer and solicitously escorted him to the bridge, where he produced papers that showed that the *Altmark,* a German naval auxiliary, had been at sea for four and a half months and was now headed for a German port. Dau insisted that, as a naval auxiliary, the *Altmark* enjoyed the same immunity from search enjoyed by all warships; and he assured the Norwegian officer that the *Altmark's* twenty-millimeter anti-aircraft guns had been dismantled long before the *Altmark* had approached the Norwegian coast. His vessel, Captain Dau remarked, should be considered as a German warship making an "innocent passage" through Norwegian territorial waters.

The Norwegian officer was taken in by Dau's manner and apparent openness and did not argue the issue. Having assured himself that the *Altmark's* papers were in order, he gave Captain Dau permission to proceed southward through the Norwegian Leads. He made no comment about the length of time *Altmark* had been at sea, nor did he ask about prisoners or attempt to look belowdecks.

Captain Dau's bluff had worked. As *Altmark* sailed south at top speed, Captain Dau convinced himself that he would meet no further trouble from Norwegian authorities. But the *Altmark* was not home safe yet. The vessel still had to traverse the Bergen naval district, which was under the command of Rear Admiral Tank-Nielsen, an aggressive and suspicious officer who read the reports of the first inspection with annoyance and disbelief. The inspection had obviously been perfunctory. From the information at hand, Admiral Tank-Nielsen was not ready to accept that the *Altmark* actually was a German warship making an "innocent passage." He ordered the ship stopped and searched again.

The task fell to the Norwegian patrol boat *Snogg*, which challenged the *Altmark* near Ålesund. Again Captain Dau played his role to perfection, cordially inviting an officer from the *Snogg* to the bridge and producing the ship's papers as requested. Again the Norwegian officer was taken in by the cordial Captain Dau and left the *Altmark* without making a thorough inspection.

Still dissatisfied, Admiral Tank-Nielsen ordered a third inspection. This time the Norwegian boarding officer at least knew what question to ask: Did Captain Dau have "persons on board who belonged to the armed forces of a belligerent country or sailors of a belligerent country?"

Dau, convinced that he could bluff his way through, confidently answered no, and the Norwegian officer accepted the answer. With the *Altmark* still being regarded as a warship and claiming a warship's immunity, the Norwegian officer did not dare search the vessel. It looked as if Captain Dau might succeed in his daring plan.

Rear Admiral Tank-Nielsen, however, brooded over the boarding reports. He was not satisfied with them, and as the *Altmark* approached Bergen, the question of her status assumed critical importance. Under Norwegian naval regulations, no foreign warship could traverse the restricted zone guarding the approach to Bergen without submitting to a thorough inspection. If the *Altmark* were a warship with immunity from search, she would have to sail around the restricted zone on a course that would bring her very close to international waters, where, if British warships happened to be in the vicinity, an international incident could explode, the very thing the Norwegians wanted to avoid. At the same time, Admiral Tank-Nielsen was not ready to allow a foreign warship through the restricted zone in violation of Norwegian regulations. In his eyes the issue was crucial and not one that could be left in the hands of junior officers. He determined to conduct his own investigation, and setting sail from Bergen in the destroyer *Garm,* raced northward and soon located the *Altmark* a few miles within the northerly limits of the re-stricted zone.

Admiral Tank-Nielsen entrusted the fourth boarding to his chief of staff and to the commanding officer of the *Snogg,* giving them specific instructions to pass on to Captain Dau: If he wanted to continue through the restricted zone, he would have to allow a Norwegian party to search every deck and compartment of his tanker. Otherwise, the tanker would have to sail around the zone, regardless of the potential danger.

Dau heard the news in cold fury. On three different occasions, he complained, he had permitted his vessel to be boarded and had given Norwegian officers all the information they requested. On all three occasions, Norwegians had given him permission to proceed. The fourth boarding was too much. He was, he said, prepared to give the Norwegians his personal assurance that his vessel carried no armaments, but under no circumstances would he permit Norwegians to search his vessel. "I am sailing under the flag of the German Reich Service," Dau said, "and I am unable on principle to permit a search."

Belowdecks the prisoners, having heard *Altmark*'s engines come to a halt and, from portholes, spotting the *Garm* close by, sensed what was happening and broke into a riot to make their presence known. Some pounded on bulkheads and stanchions with pieces of wood and hammered on steel decks with short stubs of iron. Others waved from portholes to sailors on the *Garm.* Although an official Norwegian report published after the war noted that "SOS signals were repeatedly heard from the forepart of the German vessel," the two Norwegian officers on board took no notice of the uproar. Even when the *Altmark*'s winches were started in an attempt to drown out the frantic signals from the prisoners, the Norwegian officers conducted themselves as if they were on a routine boarding visit, diplomatically deaf to the turmoil about them.

Once back on the *Garm,* however, they made a full report to Admiral Tank-Nielsen, who, unable to pretend ignorance, telegraphed Oslo to inform Admiral Diesen of the situation:

> The vessel has refused additional visitation and passage through the defended area is therefore denied. Prisoners of war are likely to be aboard.

Oslo panicked at the news. Admiral Diesen personally telephoned the secretary-general of the Norwegian Ministry of Foreign Affairs, Jens Bull, to warn him that the *Altmark* affair involved more than a German vessel and Norwegian neutrality. British involvement was also assured. Bull listened to the news with growing annoyance, for he anticipated that he certainly would eventually face strong German complaints. His anger turned not toward Captain Dau, who had hidden prisoners of war on his vessel and lied to Norwegian authorities, but toward the Norwegian naval authorities who were responsible for bringing the news to his attention. Over the phone he coldly asked Admiral Diesen why a fourth attempt had been made to investigate the *Altmark* after the vessel had already been inspected three times. Admiral Diesen was apologetic. Obviously, he replied, the blame rested with subordinates in his command who had made "a mistake." But he had a suggestion. In his opinion, the *Altmark* should be allowed to pass through the restricted zone because previous inspections had failed to confirm that the *Altmark* was in fact a warship. The wisest course of action now was to treat the *Altmark* as a merchant ship and dispose of her as quickly as possible.

Secretary General Bull was delighted with Admiral Diesen's recommendation. He concurred enthusiastically. Diesen, relieved by Bull's reaction, hastened to order the Bergen command to give special dispensation to the *Altmark* to travel through the restricted zone: "Let the vessel pass. Escort."

It was not the first time Norway had bent its regulations for Germany. In November, 1939, the captain of the German tanker *Westerwald*, also flying the German state flag, had refused to permit an investigation on board and was given "special permission" to traverse Bergen's restricted zone. *Westerwald* had set the precedent and *Altmark* was the first to reap the benefits.

Unfortunately for Captain Dau, and unknown to him at the time, *Altmark*'s passage through the Bergen defense zone was noticed by an agent friendly to the British who passed the information on to the British Embassy in Oslo. From there the news was flashed to the British Admiralty in London: "*Altmark* steaming two miles off the Norwegian coast north of Bergen."

Alerted at last, the British Navy, which had sought the *Altmark* for months, moved smartly into action. Search aircraft were ordered aloft and the Fourth Flotilla Group, consisting of the cruiser *Arethusa* and five destroyers under the command of Capt. Philip Vian, was ordered to begin a surface search immediately. The British warships began their search from the mouth of the Baltic Sea, sweeping northward in hopes of intercepting the *Altmark*, which was headed south. Captain Vian, aboard the destroyer *Cossack*, worried about missing the *Altmark*, for visibility on the night of February 15 and the morning of February 16 was poor and there were an unexpected number of ships in the Norwegian Leads. Vian feared the *Altmark* might slip past him undetected. As dawn of February 16 broke, his flotilla still had not spotted its prey.

In London that morning, a worried Winston Churchill took note of developments and instructed his subordinates in the Admiralty:

> On the position as reported to me this morning, it would seem that the cruiser and destroyers should sweep northward during the day up the coast of Norway, not hesitating to arrest *Altmark* in territorial waters should she be found. This ship is violating neutrality in carrying British prisoners of war to Germany. The *Altmark* must be regarded as an invaluable trophy.

Tension built up almost to the breaking point as the morning hours of February 16 passed without a sighting report. Shortly before 1 P.M., however, a reconnaissance aircraft of the British coastal command spotted the *Altmark* sailing along an open stretch of Norwegian coastline south of Bergen. The British pilot later reported:

> I spotted a ship with funnel aft, the distinctive feature of the *Altmark*. As we dived, my eyes were riveted on the stern, searching for a name. I saw letters about a foot high. I expected that when they could be read they would spell a Norwegian name. I could not suppress a whoop of joy when I saw that they read *Altmark*.

Within two hours, the cruiser *Arethusa* and the destroyers *Intrepid* and *Ivanhoe* found their quarry.

"Steer west," *Arethusa* signaled, hoping to force *Altmark* into international waters. *Altmark* hugged the coast even closer while the British ships followed behind. So did two Norwegian Navy patrol vessels. As *Altmark* approached a narrow channel running between the coast and a scattering of offshore islands, *Intrepid*'s commander ordered *Altmark* to heave to. Dau ignored the signal. The *Intrepid,* determined to stop the *Altmark,* fired a warning shot across *Altmark*'s bow. Still the German ship failed to stop. *Intrepid* moved closer in, hoping to get between *Altmark* and the shore and thus physically force the *Altmark* into international waters. *Intrepid*'s maneuvering room was limited, however, as the Norwegian gunboat *Skarv* had interposed herself between the British warship and the German prison ship, challenging the British destroyer's decision to stop the *Altmark* in Norwegian waters. *Intrepid*'s commander replied brusquely, "I have my orders," and ignored the Norwegian protest.

Together the ships of the three nations continued to sail south, each jockeying for position. The waters ahead were becoming more and more constricted, however, and *Intrepid* was in position to take advantage of any move by *Altmark* away from land. Instead of permitting his ship to be forced into international waters, Dau turned *Altmark* hard to port and headed his vessel toward the entrance of Jossingfjord, the waters of which glistened with ice. The tanker cracked through the surface and proceeded up the fjord when suddenly the ship's luck ran out. The *Altmark* crashed into a thick layer of ice. The impact hurled sailors to the deck and threw prisoners below into struggling heaps. The *Altmark* had trapped herself in a small Norwegian fjord with 299 prisoners aboard—prisoners she had denied having—while waiting outside was a British flotilla determined to prevent her escape.

The *Cossack,* with Flotilla Commander Vian aboard, arrived off Jossingfjord "just as darkness fell." Captain Vian, hoping to avoid combat, boarded the Norwegian patrol boat *Kjell* and demanded that the British prisoners on *Altmark* be freed. *Kjell's* captain replied that the German ship had been searched three times since her entry into Norwegian waters and no prisoners had been found. Captain Vian insisted, but the Norwegian officer was unmoved. "My instructions," he said, "are to resist your entry by force."

With *Kjell's* torpedo tubes trained on the *Cossack,* Captain Vian withdrew from the fjord. Once safe outside, he informed the British Admiralty of developments and asked for confirmation of his orders "to enter neutral waters, search the *Altmark* and rescue any prisoners found aboard."

Winston Churchill personally handled Vian's query. He realized that the situation had broad diplomatic overtones, but he was convinced that the rescue of the prisoners was more imperative than any other consideration, and after conferring with the British Foreign Secretary Lord Halifax, drafted a direct order for Captain Vian:

> Unless Norwegian torpedo boat undertakes to convoy *Altmark* to Bergen with a joint Anglo-Norwegian guard on board, and a joint escort, you should board *Altmark,* liberate the prisoners and take possession of the ship pending further instructions. If Norwegian torpedo boat interferes, you should warn her to stand off. If she fires upon you, you should not reply unless attack is serious, in which case you should defend yourself, using no more force than is necessary, and ceasing fire when she desists. Suggest to Norwegian destroyer that honour is served by submitting to superior force.

The *Cossack* reentered Jossingfjord shortly after 10 P.M., ignored a challenge from the *Kjell,* and moved steadily upfjord, each minute penetrating deeper into Norwegian waters. Soon the *Altmark* came into view. She lay bows inshore, apparently encased in ice. Her great bulk, caught in *Cossack's* searchlights, loomed black against the snow-clad mountains. Suddenly the *Altmark* started moving backward in hopes of ramming the destroyer, but the *Cossack* was too quick for her. Captain Vian adroitly maneuvered his vessel away from the clumsy tanker, which, unable to stop in time, ran aground stern first. Vian, seizing his opportunity, quickly brought his destroyer around again to enable an armed boarding party to leap onto the decks of the German vessel. They overpowered the *Altmark*'s crew, seized Captain Dau on the bridge of his vessel, and sent an armed guard from the *Graf Spee* fleeing across the ice toward shore. The British were masters of the German vessel.

Down in the dark compartments belowdecks, the British prisoners had observed the approach of the *Cossack* and felt the impact as the destroyer came alongside. A few scattered shots rang out, and then the ship fell strangely quiet. Finally a prison compartment door opened and a deep voice asked, "Any British down there?"

For the prisoners, their long months of arrest were over. They shouted back in joy and relief.

"Come on up, then," the voice continued. "The Navy's here."

Captain Vian later described the scene:

> As *Cossack* came alongside for the embarkation, her searchlight trained on the *Altmark,* the scene was one to be remembered; the long shadows on the ice and snow cast by *Altmark*'s upper works; in the foreground her brightly lit decks, on to which there began to emerge the prisoners, laughing, cheering and waving in satisfaction at the turn of events, and at a breath of fresh air. They were white and debilitated after their long spell below, but not, as had been expected, stretcher cases.

By midnight, less than an hour after the first British sailor set foot on the German ship, the *Cossack* was moving out of Jossingfjord toward the open sea, headed for a hero's welcome at home. Captain Vian took no German prisoners of his own nor did he attempt to disable the *Altmark.* Such actions, he felt, would only serve to aggravate his violation of Norwegian neutrality.

Churchill and other Admiralty officials were "delighted" with the news. Churchill, who liked nothing better than to get personally involved in naval matters, drafted a message for Vian: "The force under your orders is to be congratulated on having in a single day achieved a double rescue—Britons from captivity and Germans from drowning."

The message puzzled Vian. The *Cossack* boarding party had in fact rescued a German sailor from drowning, but the German had been dead of exposure when brought aboard. And as Vian later commented, even if the *Cossack* had saved many Germans, he always thought that "Mr. Churchill wished as many German sailors drowned as possible." Churchill's message nonetheless was a big hit with the British public, for it highlighted not only the heroism of the rescue but a gallantry in action on the part of the *Cossack*'s crew that struck sparks of pride in countless British hearts.

The rescue caught the imagination of the British people. The phrase "The Navy's here" passed from lip to lip. Admiral of the Fleet Sir Roger Keyes said that Norway should be grateful to the *Cossack* "for enabling

The *Altmark* moored in ice-clogged Jossingfjord after the British raiding party had left. *(Norsk Telegrambyra)*

her to escape the shocking stigma of having condemned 300 British seamen to imprisonment in Germany." *The Times* of London called it a "dashing rescue," adding "that the battle in which the raider *Graf Spee* was scuttled would have lacked a fitting sequel if, after the lion had been destroyed, the jackal had escaped with the prey."

Norway, however, bitterly protested the action. The Norwegian Minister in London called it a "grave violation of Norwegian neutrality." Norwegian Foreign Minister Halvdan Koht called it "the grossest violation of neutrality" since the war started and demanded that Britain return the prisoners and "make due compensation and reparation."

In the United States, public opinion generally supported the British action, although *The New York Times* predicted editorially that the action was certain to have an importance far greater than the mere rescue of several hundred men, and noted, "This is the first time since the war began that the Allies have deliberately violated neutral territory."

German propaganda experts used the incident to inflame public opinion even further against the British, accusing Britain of "piracy, murder, manslaughter and gangsterism of the worst sort." Conveniently, the versions of the incident promulgated by the Third Reich failed to mention that British prisoners had been aboard the *Altmark*. "We will present an accounting," Germany thundered.

Germany also turned its anger on Norway, warning that Norway's "responsibility in the incident is still under investigation."

Norway's Jens Bull, who had feared all along that the *Altmark* would explode into an international incident, pleaded for "understanding" from the German Minister in Oslo, Curt Brauer. Bull wanted Brauer to know that Norway had "done all it possibly could" and was vigorously protesting the action diplomatically.

Brauer's response brought Bull only partial relief. The German Minister assured Bull that he realized that Norway was protesting. "That is what I have explained in my dispatch to Berlin," Brauer said. "But that doesn't mean," he continued, "that the case is not very grave."

The Norwegian Foreign Ministry official quickly agreed: "We are just as shocked as you are. We fully realize that this case is a grave one."

4

Weseruebung

The *Altmark* affair infuriated Hitler. Gen. Alfred Jodl, chief of operations for the German Armed Forces High Command and one of Hitler's closest military advisors, noted in his diary that the leader of the Third Reich was particularly enraged by the humiliating news that the armed guard aboard the *Altmark* had failed to repulse the British boarding party. Hitler complained bitterly, "No resistance, no British losses."

The incident convinced Hitler that Great Britain would no longer respect Norwegian neutrality and that Norway itself could not be counted on to oppose British violations of territorial waters. Consequently, Hitler's interest in a Scandinavian operation, which had ebbed and flowed as other plans and projects aroused his enthusiasm, suddenly heated up again. Two days after news of the *Altmark* reached Berlin, Hitler accelerated the pace of planning for *Weseruebung,* the invasion of Norway and Denmark. "Equip ships. Put units in readiness," he ordered. However, before this could be done, *Weseruebung* needed one vital ingredient which had been overlooked until then. The operation needed a commanding officer.

The OKW came up with the name of Lt. Gen. Nikolaus von Falkenhorst, a corps commander whose primary qualification for the job seemed to stem from a few months' service with German forces in Finland in 1918. Falkenhorst was unknown to Hitler except in his capacity as a battlefield commander whose troops had fought bravely and well in the recently concluded Polish campaign, but the OKW recommendation and Falkenhorst's tenuous connection with Scandinavia were sufficient to arouse Hitler's interest. He sent for Falkenhorst immediately.

Until he was summoned by Hitler, Falkenhorst had no previous knowledge of *Weseruebung* nor was he even aware of German interest in

Scandinavia. Hitler broke the news to him at a meeting that began at noon on February 21. After the war Falkenhorst described how the session began:

> Hitler reminded me of my experience in Finland, and said to me, "Sit down and tell me what you did." After a moment, the Fuehrer interrupted me. He led me to a table covered with maps. "I have a similar thing in mind," he said, "the occupation of Norway; because I am informed that the English intend to land there, and I want to be there before them."

The operation, Hitler went on to explain, would have as its primary objectives the occupation of Norway's major ports, especially the ore port of Narvik, and the subjugation by military and political means of the Norwegian government, thereby eliminating any possibility of Norway collaborating with Great Britain. As was his habit when expounding military plans, Hitler talked with passion and urgency for close to an hour and then, to Falkenhorst's dismay, ordered the general to report at 5 P.M. that same day with a preliminary operational plan for the invasion of Norway. Hitler dismissed Falkenhorst around 1 P.M., giving the general less than four hours of actual working time to put together an invasion scheme that would satisfy Hitler and win for himself the coveted post of invasion commander. To make his task even more difficult, Falkenhorst was not given access to any existing staff studies on Norway. He was left to his own devices, but Falkenhorst, a practical and resourceful officer, refused to be overwhelmed. He later described how he set to work:

> I went out and bought a Baedeker, a travel guide, in order to find out just what Norway was like. I didn't have any idea. . . . Then I went to my hotel room and I worked on this Baedeker. . . . At 5 P.M. I went back to the Fuehrer.

Falkenhorst's efforts that afternoon resulted in a plan of stark simplicity. He proposed dispatching one Army division to each of Norway's five principal harbors: Oslo, Stavanger, Bergen, Trondheim, and Narvik. Once these strong points had been secured, the occupation of the rest of the country could proceed at a more leisurely pace. As Falkenhorst later explained, "There wasn't much else you could do, because these were the larger harbors." His plan, which paralleled in its major details the previously prepared Krancke plan, obviously satisfied Hitler, for on the next day the Fuehrer confirmed Falkenhorst's appointment as invasion commander and personally urged him to press forward.

Falkenhorst began work in Berlin four days later. With the aid of a select staff he reviewed the proposals of the Krancke plan in detail. His study resulted in only a few minor changes. Falkenhorst, like Krancke before him, started with the assumption that Norway was the primary objective of *Weseruebung,* and that the occupation of Denmark was of

secondary importance, a military incidental, with only the Danish airfields in the north of Jutland around the industrial city of Aalborg considered crucial to the success of the operation. But where the Krancke plan
had called merely for the exertion of diplomatic pressure on Denmark to
secure passage of German troops through Jutland, Falkenhorst proposed a
military occupation of the territory. And while Falkenhorst would himself be content to occupy Jutland alone, he foresaw the possibility that
Danish resistance might force him to occupy the major Danish island of
Zealand and the country's capital, Copenhagen, as well. For these additional military tasks, Falkenhorst estimated that he would need two
divisions more than those already assigned to the conquest of Norway.
Gen. Wilhelm Keitel, the Chief of Staff of the OKW, received Falkenhorst's modifications of the Krancke plan on February 28 and immediately forwarded them to Hitler for his approval.

Hitler's enthusiasm for *Weseruebung* had been aroused, and he approved Falkenhorst's request for additional troops without hesitation.
Hitler demanded that Falkenhorst change only one point in his plan.
Regardless of whether the Danes resisted or not, Hitler insisted upon a
landing in Copenhagen simultaneously with the invasion of Jutland. He
instructed Falkenhorst to send a "strong force" to take the Danish capital.

Having committed himself to an armed invasion of the two Scandinavian countries, Hitler immediately began to worry about the secrecy
of the operation. For the pro-Nazi Norwegian leader Vidkun Quisling,
this meant the end of his dreams to play a role in the German takeover of
his country. Hitler was no longer interested in Quisling. The confident
Fuehrer would rely on German arms alone to accomplish the task. On
Hitler's direct orders, Quisling, who had been willing to sell out his
country in hopes of winning personal power, was kept completely in the
dark about German invasion plans.

Once these decisions had been made, Hitler moved happily on to the
preparation of his official directive for *Weseruebung*. It was ready for
distribution to all service commands on March 1.

TOP SECRET

The situation in Scandinavia requires the making of all preparations
for the occupation of Denmark and Norway by a part of the German
Armed Forces. In view of our military and political power in comparison with that of the Scandinavian States, the force to be employed
will be kept as small as possible. The numerical weakness will be
balanced by daring actions and surprise execution. The crossing of the
Danish border and the landings in Norway must take place
simultaneously. I emphasize that the operations must be prepared as
quickly as possible. All preparations, particularly those of transport
and of readiness, drafting and embarkation of the troops, must be made
with this factor in mind. In case the preparations for embarkation can

no longer be kept secret, the leaders and the troops will be deceived with fictitious objectives. The troops may be acquainted with the actual objectives only after putting to sea. . . .

[signed] A. Hitler

Field Marshal Hermann Goering, the self-indulgent commander-in-chief of the German Air Force, was furious when he received the directive. Not only had he been kept uninformed, but Luftwaffe units had been placed under Falkenhorst's control. At a meeting in Berlin on the afternoon of March 5, Goering branded Falkenhorst's planning as worthless. General Jodl commented in his diary: "Field Marshal vents his spleen because he was not consulted beforehand. He dominates the discussion and tries to prove that all previous preparations are good for nothing."

Hitler, however, had no patience for jurisdictional disputes, even if the commander pressing the dispute was Field Marshal Goering, who normally was powerful enough and persuasive enough to win almost any concession. With March 17 as his projected date for the Norwegian invasion, Hitler wanted his forces assembled by the tenth and ready for embarkation on the thirteenth. He called together his three commanders-in-chief to iron out their differences, explaining to Goering in particular that he feared Allied intervention in Scandinavia. He stressed the need for cooperation and speed. So urgent did Hitler consider the situation in the north that he ordered the commencement of *Weser-uebung* before the planned invasion of France and the Low Countries. On March 7, he designated the units which would participate in the northern operation. The disposition of forces, Hitler declared, was final and not subject to further change.

The attention of London and Paris was also focused on Scandinavia during the weeks following the *Altmark* incident, but unlike Falkenhorst's staff, which conducted its work with a sense of urgency, Allied military planners made slow and indecisive progress on plans to send a British-French expeditionary force to Finland. Norway and Sweden continued to thwart Allied plans, rejecting a February 27 Finnish plea to permit the passage of Allied troops through Norwegian and Swedish territory. A few days later, a similar request from England and France was also turned down.

The diplomatic impasse continued into early March, when, almost overnight, the Finns found themselves facing a critical military situation in the field which threatened the very basis for the Allied plan to intervene in Scandinavia. Since the beginning of February, Russian forces, having regrouped after their winter reverses, had been steadily draining Finnish strength by a massive offensive. Massed wheel to wheel artillery pounded Finnish positions, and Soviet air attacks increased in intensity. By the beginning of March, the Finnish defense system was disorganized,

Finnish troops were exhausted, key strongpoints were at the breaking point and supplies of ammunition had all but run out. To Field Marshal Baron Carl G. E. Mannerheim, whose troops had fought so bravely against superior strength, the situation seemed hopeless; and he reluctantly advised his government to open negotiations with the Soviet Union to end the fighting.

Despite clear-cut evidence that Finland was crumbling, the Allies clung to their hope that they might somehow use the Finnish crisis as a justification for the dispatch of troops to Scandinavia. With the actual situation bleak and unpromising, the British resorted to grandiose promises to bolster the disheartened Finns, as if words alone could keep the embattled nation in the fight. Britain's fussy Chief of the General Staff, General Ironside, promised Marshal Mannerheim that Britain and France would send 57,000 Allied soldiers to Finland's assistance, this though the troops were not ready for action and wouldn't be able to reach Finland if they were. Two days later, Finnish ministers in Paris and London were assured that one hundred bombers would be dispatched to Finland within two weeks in the event of an official Finnish plea for aid. In the face of continued resistance on the part of Norway and Sweden to become involved in the affair, however, the Western powers could not say by what route the bombers would reach Finland.

Marshal Mannerheim accurately read the Allied assurances as the overblown promises they were. He advised his government to sue for peace while the core of the badly battered Finnish Army remained intact. Even while the frantic Allied promises were being received, Finnish negotiators were agreeing to a peace treaty in Moscow.

German plans also hung on the Finnish-Soviet talks, for the leaders of the Third Reich were convinced that any Allied invasion of Scandinavia would have to occur while Finland was still at war, or not at all. On March 9, Admiral Raeder warned that "the British now have the desired opportunity, under pretext of supporting the Finns, to send troop transports through Norway and Sweden and to occupy these countries if they wish. Therefore," Raeder concluded, "*Weseruebung* is urgent." Three days later, Hitler himself ordered Falkenhorst to be ready for "immediate action on an emergency basis" if the Allies moved.

Germany's appraisal of Allied intentions was accurate. It was almost as if the OKW had a direct line to the British cabinet and High Command, for on the very day Hitler warned Falkenhorst to prepare for emergency actions, the Allies, still hoping for a last-minute appeal from the Finns, took the decisive step of ordering a "semi-peaceable" invasion of Scandinavia, to "test on the Norwegian beaches the firmness of the opposition."

It was a strange invasion the Allies planned, distressingly symptomatic of their entire approach to the war at that time. The securing of Narvik, the occupation of the Swedish ore fields, and the capture of the railroad between them remained the major objectives, with the plight of Finland the prevailing justification for the invasion. But while assault troops would be used to make the landing, the Allies did not anticipate fighting their way across Norway into Sweden. The Allied High Command went so far as to decree that arms would be employed by the expeditionary force only "as an ultimate measure of self defense." Regardless of the stated position of the Norwegian and Swedish governments, it was assumed by British and French planners that their troops would be welcomed as liberators and friends upon their appearance on Norwegian soil.

By the evening of March 12, however, both sides were on the verge of action. Allied troops were being assembled for their "semi-peaceable" invasion, and Falkenhorst was rushing *Weseruebung* toward the earliest possible launching date, convinced—and rightly so—that the Allies were about to move. Late that night, however, the situation was completely altered. News from Moscow revealed the critical development: Finland, on whom the Allied plans were based, had capitulated.

For the time being, at least, both sides pulled back from war in Scandinavia. Allied troops originally destined for Norway were ordered to France and British submarines (which had assembled in the Skagerrak), were dispersed or recalled. After the war Churchill wrote: "On the twelfth, the Russian terms were accepted by the Finns. All our plans for military landings were shelved and the forces dispersed."

In Berlin, the Finnish capitulation prompted General Jodl to scribble in his diary: "Conclusion of peace between Finland and Russia deprives England, but us too, of any political basis to occupy Norway." On the next day, Jodl confided to his diary that Hitler was "still looking for justification" to mount a Norwegian invasion.

Neither side had abandoned interest in Scandinavia. Britain and France were still convinced that Swedish iron ore would play a key role in the outcome of the war, and Germany, convinced that the Allies would eventually seek to occupy some Norwegian ports, viewed Scandinavia as a "permanent seat of unrest." The Finnish surrender had changed only priorities of their plans. Norway had won not a reprieve, but merely a stay of sentence.

Navy officials in both Germany and Britain were responsible for bringing Norway back into the limelight, after the shock of the Finnish capitulation had been absorbed. Admiral Raeder waited only two weeks before submitting his views to Hitler. "Sooner or later," Raeder warned, "Germany will be faced with the necessity of carrying out *Weseruebung.*" With his fleet tied up waiting to go into action, Raeder wanted *Weseruebung* to start "as soon as possible," and won a promise from Hitler that the invasion would take place during the next new moon. April 7 would then become the earliest date for *Weseruebung.*

In Britain a frustrated Winston Churchill, having been denied the opportunity to mount an invasion, returned, like a dog to a bone, to his old plan of mining the Norwegian Leads. At a meeting of the Supreme Allied War Council in London on March 28, Churchill won approval from France and his own government to proceed with the Norwegian Leads action—code-name Wilfred—set to commence on April 5.

Churchill finally had backing for one of his pet projects, but now he wanted more, and he saw in Wilfred a means to justify the occupation of certain strategic Norwegian ports. Churchill and his naval aides assumed that Wilfred would provoke a German response. Under his plan British troops would, therefore, be held ready to occupy Narvik, Trondheim, Bergen, and Stavanger at the first sign that the Germans had landed in Norway. But Churchill was not content even with this complicated scenario. He wanted British troops sent into action even if German forces did not actually land in Norway, but only "showed that they intended to do so." Britain could thus respond militarily to whatever retaliation Germany took in reaction to Wilfred, even if the German response was restricted to diplomatic rhetoric, for that could easily be interpreted by Britain as a sign that Germany "intended" to act. Churchill found himself in the happy position of anticipating two advantageous developments from one operation. Not only would Britain mine the Norwegian Leads, which he had long desired, but British forces would also seize key Norwegian ports, thereby denying "these bases to the enemy."

The plan was ready for formal presentation to the British War Cabinet on April 3. Its supporters, buoyed by prospects for action, no matter how hastily prepared, assumed that Norway would offer no resistance and underestimated the possibility of a serious German counterstroke. Five battalions were deemed sufficient for the occupation of Bergen, Trondheim, and Stavanger, plus an additional landing force of one brigade and one battery for Narvik.

The British cabinet enthusiastically seized on the plan, but postponed its implementation long enough for Winston Churchill to travel to Paris in an attempt to persuade the French to mine the waters of the Rhine River, another minelaying action the British favored. When the French, fearing retaliatory German air raids, refused to go along, the British cabinet set April 8 as the new date for the start of Wilfred.

Orders for the mining of West Fjord, the main channel leading to Narvik, were immediately issued. The battle cruiser *Renown,* the cruiser *Birmingham,* and eight flanking destroyers were assigned the task of providing protection for four minelaying destroyers which would actually carry out the hazardous operation. Troops for the follow-up invasion of Norwegian ports were assembled for embarkation on vessels of the First Cruiser Squadron. The Allies finally were on the move.

On the evening of April 5, Prime Minister Neville Chamberlain appeared before a political meeting in a mood of optimism that reflected the mood of his military advisors. He hinted broadly at large events in the making. "After seven months of war," Chamberlain announced, "I feel ten times as confident of victory as I did in the beginning." Speaking of Hitler, Chamberlain archly remarked: "One thing is certain. He missed the bus."

Hitler had not missed the bus. Even as Chamberlain spoke, last-minute preparations for war were progressing at a feverish pace in Germany—as they had been since April 1, when Hitler had conducted a full-scale review of *Weseruebung,* calling for reports from General Falkenhorst, his senior naval and air officers, and the individual commanders of the landing teams. That day's briefings had indicated that all was in readiness for the operation. Hitler confessed in a short speech to his officers that the days until the invasion would impose upon him the greatest strain of his life, but he concluded with an announcement of his firm confidence in victory.

Hitler had made a last-minute check with his air and naval commanders the next day, April 2, and had been assured that satisfactory flying conditions could be expected and that ice conditions in the Baltic Sea would not obstruct naval operations. Satisfied with these reports, Hitler had set the date for the invasion of Norway and Denmark. The Germans would strike before dawn on April 9, a Tuesday. Hitler had given his commanders exactly one week to put *Weseruebung* into effect.

Falkenhorst perceived no difficulty in complying with Hitler's timetable. Relying on previously prepared detailed plans and the availability of assembled troops and equipment, Falkenhorst could look north with confidence. The conquest of Denmark, in fact, appeared ridiculously easy. The flat and open character of Denmark's terrain invited mobile troop operations. Even in the face of a well-prepared national defense, which was nonexistent in Denmark at the time, the offense would naturally be favored over the defense. Falkenhorst planned to deploy two Army divisions, a motorized rifle brigade with Mark I and Mark II tanks, three motorized gun battalions, two batteries of heavy artillery, and three armored trains. The German Air Force was called upon to supply one company of parachute troopers, anti-aircraft artillery, and a special motorcycle company from the General Goering Regiment. Falkenhorst anticipated that Denmark would fall before the German onslaught like a ripe plum buffeted by a high wind.

Norway, however, appeared a more hazardous venture. The Norwegian High Command had assigned full divisions for the defense of the country's six most important military and civilian centers. Oslo, the country's capital and heart of its major industrial and agricultural region, was defended by the Second Norwegian Division. The key naval base at Kristiansand was the headquarters of the Third Norwegian Division.

Other divisions were assigned to the coastal cities of Bergen, the country's second largest city, and Trondheim, the medieval capital of Norway and a major port with facilities for handling vessels of any size. A fifth division stood guard above the Arctic Circle near Narvik, while a sixth was stationed at Halden in the populous southeastern corner of the country. All Norwegian divisions were under strength, poorly equipped, and weakened by decades of neglect and inactivity; but in Norway, unlike Denmark, a mountainous terrain favored the defense over the offense.

Falkenhorst and his staff realized that the success of *Weseruebung* hinged upon the rapid capture of the Norwegian cities with an almost immediate neutralization of defending forces. With this accomplished, the fall of the rest of the country would follow almost automatically. Any setbacks in the initial assaults, however, would present critical difficulties. The German timetable would be delayed, permitting the Norwegians to regroup in the interior, allowing the Allies time to equip an expeditionary force, and thereby threatening the entire German operation. Success, for the Germans, depended on quick strikes against the key cities scattered along the long Norwegian coastline.

Of necessity, the size of the initial seaborne landing force would be small. The ships that would carry the troops to their destination could accommodate no more than 8,850 men. However, during the first three days, an additional eight thousand troops would arrive by air.

For the Germans, these first three days were the crucial period. To support the landings, the German Air Force assigned to *Weseruebung* 1,000 planes: 500 transports, 300 bombers, and 200 dive bombers, fighters, and reconnaissance aircraft. The Germans did not intend to throw their main bomber force against the Scandinavians, however, but to keep it in readiness for action against British naval forces.

And it was at sea that the Germans were most vulnerable. The British Navy outnumbered and outgunned the Nazi fleet. Germany had to rely on surprise, speed, and split-second timing to achieve success. Warships, not transports, would be used to carry the initial landing forces to their destinations, sailing on a staggered schedule so that they would all arrive at their destinations simultaneously at *Weser* hour. Because the warships were unable to carry heavy equipment and would exhaust their fuel on the long runs to Trondheim and Narvik, special tanker and supply fleets were established to transport these needed supplies to the chosen invasion sites. Ships assigned to these units were disguised as ordinary merchant vessels and dispatched to arrive in Norwegian ports in advance of *Weser* day. If all proceeded smoothly, they would be waiting in port when the German warships arrived.

The first supply ships sailed for Narvik on April 3, six days before the invasion was scheduled to begin. They traversed the Skagerrak safely and entered Norwegian territorial waters without incident. As they made their way northward through the Leads, they were sighted by Norwegian observers on several occasions but were never challenged. All observers took the ships for what they appeared to be, innocent merchantmen on routine business. No one suspected that the German ships, safe from British attack inside Norwegian waters, carried in their holds the machinery of war and the fuel needed for the invasion of Norway.

Tight secrecy was imposed on all sailings. One transport fleet given the code name *Ostpreussen Staffel* (East Prussian Relay) left port in the belief that its destination actually was East Prussia. Only after the vessels were at sea were the captains given new instructions diverting them to their true destination.

Extraordinary measures were adopted to camouflage the mission of the warships in the invasion fleet. Before sailing, all captains received secret orders to masquerade as British vessels when entering Norwegian ports.

MOST SECRET

The disguise as British craft must be kept as long as possible. All challenges in Morse by Norwegian ships will be answered in English. In answer, something like the following will be chosen: "Calling at Bergen for a short visit. No hostile intent." Challenges to be answered with names of British warships. Arrangements are to be made to enable British war flags to be illuminated.

Warships headed for Narvik and Trondheim sailed at midnight on April 6. Other warships followed in short order. As more and more invasion vessels put to sea, German fears mounted. If any one vessel assigned to *Weseruebung* was sunk and German troops captured or observed, the entire operation could be compromised. Tension gripped Berlin. Their forces had been committed and their fate was no longer in German hands.

London, too, maintained a close radio vigil, anxiously awaiting reports from the fleet dispatched to mine the waters off Narvik. Good news from Narvik would send other British warships to sea, carrying troops earmarked for the Allied occupation of Norwegian ports.

By April 7, the offensive timetables of both opponents had meshed, producing a strange race in the waters of the North Sea, where war fleets of both Germany and Great Britain sailed, each unaware of the other. Both nations pursued plans of action that they hoped would secure for them control of Norway and thereby deny that country's strategic coastline to the enemy. At this point in time, no one could have predicted the ultimate victor. Everything depended on how the battle developed.

The morning hours of April 7 passed without news for either side. The afternoon hours passed as well. On the evening of April 7, however,

British reconnaissance aircraft sighted German warships off the coast of southern Norway, steaming north at top speed. It was the first news that either side had that the other side was on the move.

Assimilating the information, British intelligence and operations officers set about the task of evaluating its meaning. The information at hand was scanty and could not answer certain key questions. Where were the German vessels headed? What were their intentions? Was the German movement northward the start of a major sortie or was it simply a feint designed to test the British response? The British naval staff could not be sure. The consensus was that the German vessels would turn back, but the possibility that Germany had launched a major thrust could not be ignored. To guard against this eventuality, the British home fleet, built around the battleships *Rodney, Repulse,* and *Valiant,* sailed from Scapa Flow at seven-thirty that night. Warships of the Second Cruiser Squadron were ordered to sail from Rosyth, Scotland, while ships of the First Cruiser Squadron that had been embarking troops for the anticipated Allied occupation of Narvik, Trondheim, Bergen, and Stavanger were told to march their soldiers ashore and to join the fleet at sea at the earliest possible hour. Although the British were unconvinced that Norway was the target of an all-out German naval effort, every available ship was ordered out against the chance that just such an emergency was developing.

Churchill had news of substance to report when the British War Cabinet met on the morning of April 8. Only a few hours before, the Admiralty had received confirmation that British destroyers had successfully laid a minefield off Narvik. This was news that the cabinet had anticipated, and it was received enthusiastically, but Churchill still had a bombshell to drop. A current of electric excitement swept through the assembly as Churchill went on to reveal that a German war fleet had been sighted at sea, its destination unknown, and that the British home fleet had sailed to give pursuit. It was Churchill's opinion that the German vessels were headed for Narvik, which they could reach at ten o'clock that night, April 8, unless intercepted first. But the situation at sea did not displease the bellicose Churchill. The German fleet seemed caught between two superior British forces. The battle cruiser *Renown* and the cruiser *Birmingham* with their escorting destroyers were standing north of the Germans at Narvik while the home fleet raced up from the south. Churchill believed that a major action would take place very shortly.

"It is impossible to forecast the hazards of war," Churchill remarked, "but such an action should not be on terms unfavorable for us."

As for the intended victims, Norway and Denmark, they passed their last hours of peace blind to the dangers around them. It was as if the two Scandinavian countries, dead set to maintain their neutrality at any cost, unconsciously refused to give credence to the gathering evidence that Germany was preparing a knockout blow. And despite Germany's efforts to maintain tight secrecy, there had been leaks. By late March, both Oslo and Copenhagen were receiving cables warning what the Germans had in mind.

Norwegian officials in Berlin, after filing several specific memoranda reporting German troop concentrations in northern ports and unusually heavy German naval activity in the North Sea and the Baltic, concluded that Germany must be preparing a strike toward the north. Without exception these reports were discounted and ignored by the Norwegian government.

Denmark received even more detailed information. It originated with Maj. Gen. Hans Oster, who was chief assistant to Admiral Wilhelm Canaris, head of the German intelligence and counterintelligence service, the Abwehr. Both men belonged to a small group of anti-Hitler officers, and Oster had on many occasions leaked military intelligence of major importance to friendly military attachés in Berlin, including the Dutch attaché Col. G. J. Sas. Sometime before the first of April, Oster informed Sas that Germany was planning to invade Denmark and Norway and possibly Sweden as well. Sas in turn alerted one of his friendly contacts, the Danish naval attaché in Berlin, Captain Kjolsen, who immediately passed the warning on to his superiors in Copenhagen, giving Sas as his source for the information. To Kjolsen's amazement, his report met with silence from Copenhagen. Finally, an angry Kjolsen traveled back to Denmark to repeat the information in person and to stress its reliability. Kjolsen arrived in Copenhagen on April 4, five days before the invasion, only to be summarily informed that his information could not be correct considering the circuitous manner in which it had come to his attention.

On the same day that Captain Kjolsen's information was being discounted in Copenhagen, another Danish intelligence officer, Maj. Hans Lunding, who was stationed in southern Jutland, and who ran a network of agents in northern Germany, reported Wehrmacht units advancing toward the Danish border. In his report filed at midnight, April 4, Major Lunding advised his superior, Col. Einar Nordentoft, that he was forced to the conclusion that Denmark would be invaded. Again the Danish government took no action.

On April 8, Lunding filed another urgent message. He had just learned from a Danish agent in Rendsburg, Germany, that German divisions were scheduled to cross the border "at four o'clock." There was but one point of ambiguity in Lunding's report. He could not say if the border crossing was scheduled to take place at 4 P.M. on April 8 or 4 A.M. on April 9. Time answered the question. When the Germans had not crossed into Danish territory by 4 P.M. on April 8, Lunding called

Copenhagen again to report that the Germans would certainly advance at four o'clock the following morning.

By this time the Danish General staff could no longer ignore the warnings from its intelligence officers, and it urgently requested permission to mobilize, but the Danish Cabinet, locked into peacetime ways, refused. Only after repeated telephone calls from Danish Army officers did the Cabinet relent, authorizing a state of alarm for southern Jutland but still refraining from total mobilization, in fear of provoking the Germans.

Norway, however, was denied even this excuse. On the afternoon of April 8, the Polish submarine *Orzel* sank the German transport *Rio de Janeiro* off the coast of southern Norway. Although there was heavy loss of life, there were some survivors: Wehrmacht soldiers in full combat dress. Once safely ashore in Norway, these German troops ingenuously told their Norwegian rescuers that they had been on their way to Bergen to aid the Norwegians against the British.

When reports of the sinking reached Berlin, a glum German naval staff assumed that the element of surprise had now been lost and that the German invasion fleet would meet resistance at all points along the Norwegian coast. Within hours, however, the German naval attaché in Oslo provided what must have seemed incredible news to Berlin. There were "reliable signs," the attaché disclosed, that the Norwegian Admiralty had not been alerted. Certainly the Norwegian Navy was not conducting itself as an organization faced with imminent danger. The chief communications officer of the Norwegian Admiralty staff was spending the evening along with other important guests at the home of the German air attaché in Oslo. The Norwegian officer was not called away from his social engagement until eleven-thirty that night. And it wasn't until one o'clock on the morning of April 9—*Weser* day—that the Norwegian Admiralty at last issued orders for the activation of mines in Oslo Fjord. The move came too late. German ships had already entered the fjord.

The Royal Norwegian Army was also caught napping. On the night of April 8–9, Lt. Col. R. Roscher Nielsen, chief of the operations section of the Norwegian General Staff, was at home asleep. Shortly after 1 A.M. he was awakened by a telephone call from the Army Chief of Staff. Nielsen was informed that fortresses at the mouth of Oslo Fjord had been attacked, and he was ordered to black out the city as a precaution against German air raids. The lights went out in Oslo at 1:58 A.M.

The Norwegian government, holding clear evidence that Norway was coming under attack, reacted even more slowly. By 2:30 A.M. government leaders were still debating whether to order the mobilization of Norway's four reserve divisions. Even at this point, the government appeared reluctant to accept the urgency of the situation. With a German invasion fleet approaching Oslo and with the possibility of air raids blacking out the capital, the Norwegian government continued to approach mobilization as if the country were still at peace. When it finally did act, immediate mobilization was ruled out. Instead, April 11 was designated as mobilization day. A delay of two full days was thus created before Norway could even begin to respond with all its strength to the German attack.

The Danish government also refused to accept the possibility that its country was in danger until it was too late. On the evening of April 8, the conversation at the royal table in Amalienborg Castle in Copenhagen centered on the sinking of the *Rio de Janeiro*. The consensus that an invasion of Norway was imminent was expanded by one of the guests to the possibility that Germany would invade Denmark as well. With a smile, King Christian X replied that he didn't "really believe that." Then he set off, in a "confident and happy mood" as a member of his personal body guard remembered, to attend a performance of *The Merry Wives of Windsor* at the Royal Theater.

While the king attended the theater, other Danes along the border between Jutland and Germany were receiving a preview of the greater drama that Germany was preparing for Denmark. Borge Outze, a newspaper correspondent for *National Tidende,* telephoned the paper's chief editor in Copenhagen to report that he personally could hear the rumble of German tanks and armored vehicles moving into position.

Major Lunding also heard the German preparations, but he could do no more. By midnight, it was simply a matter of waiting for what he knew was coming. Lunding's information had been inexact by only a few minutes. He expected the enemy to cross the border at 4 A.M. The first Germans came at four-ten.

5
The Invasion of Denmark

On the eve of the German invasion, no military analyst would have given tiny Denmark the slightest chance of withstanding a German assault. Militarily, psychologically, and geographically, Denmark's position was hopeless. Her government and her people, terrified by the might of Hitler's Third Reich, pinned their hopes for peace not on the strength of the country's armed forces but on repeated declarations of neutrality and on a determination to avoid even a hint of provocation to the German dictator. With the outbreak of war in September, 1939, Denmark actually began to reduce the number of troops on active service and succeeded, in the following six months, in cutting its ground forces by more than 50 percent, thereby earning the dubious distinction of being the only country in Europe to weaken its defenses at a time when danger to the country was growing. By April, 1940, Denmark's armed forces numbered less than fifteen thousand men, most of them untrained recruits, scattered throughout the country in isolated posts where they passed their time plodding through peacetime drills, lulled by the passivity of their officers and government. Nor did Denmark's terrain provide help for the defense. The gently rolling Jutland countryside offered ideal conditions for the German panzers that General Falkenhorst planned to throw against Denmark, and the country's two major islands, Zealand and Fyn, each weakly defended, lay ready for the plucking by an aggressive force. Even Winston Churchill recognized Denmark's hopeless position. In a meeting with Scandinavian journalists in February, 1940, Churchill remarked: "I could not reproach Denmark if she surrendered to Nazi attack. The other two Scandinavian countries, Norway and Sweden, have at least a ditch over which they can feed the tiger, but Denmark is so terribly near Germany that it would be impossible to bring help. Personally, I would in any case not undertake to guarantee Denmark."

Despite Denmark's apparent vulnerability, Germany prepared its attack with meticulous care, as if the Wehrmacht were up against an opponent worthy of the effort. And, in fact, Denmark, weak though it might be, had the potential of delivering a decisive setback to German invasion plans. General Falkenhorst was acutely aware that a determined Danish defense, even of short duration, would threaten his finely tuned offensive timetable. If his panzers did not cut through Jutland like a hot knife through butter, reaching the strategic airfields in northern Jutland within a few hours, and if the Danish government refused to capitulate, Falkenhorst feared that the chances for success in Norway would be seriously jeopardized. Much depended on how the individual Danish soldier reacted in combat, a factor Falkenhorst could only surmise, and on the thoroughness of German preparations, a factor which Falkenhorst could insist upon.

Five days before the invasion, therefore, the German battalion commander given the responsibility for the capture of Copenhagen arrived in the Danish capital on a personal reconnaissance mission. Dressed in civilian clothes and posing as an ordinary businessman, the German major moved easily through the port district, selecting a suitable landing area for the troopship *Hansestadt Danzig,* which would carry his battalion ashore, and reconnoitering the Citadel, an ancient fortress overlooking the harbor and the site of the Danish General Staff headquarters.

Bored Danish soldiers on guard duty at the Citadel welcomed the German officer with cordial hospitality. A kindly Danish sergeant was so taken with the visitor's obvious interest and curiosity that he escorted the German major around the Citadel grounds, knowledgeably pointing out the General Staff headquarters, the communications center, the barracks which housed a unit from the Guards Regiment, and the two main gates leading into the fortress itself. The German major returned to Germany confident that his assigned objective could be taken. Everything he had seen convinced him that Copenhagen would quickly fall before his battalion's assault.

An even higher ranking German officer arrived in Copenhagen a few days later for a last-minute survey. Gen. Kurt Himer, chief of staff of the task force for Denmark, wanted to see with his own eyes the state of Danish defenses and the condition of the harbor. Himer, also dressed in civilian clothes, reached the Danish capital by train on the afternoon of April 7. On April 8, after reconnoitering the city, he reported to corps headquarters in Hamburg that the harbor was ice-free and that Denmark had taken no steps to bolster the capital's defense. The invasion could proceed as planned. Later that night, General Himer called on the German Minister to Denmark, Cecil von Renthe-Fink, with instructions that Renthe-Fink deliver an ultimatum to the Danes as the hour of invasion struck. For Renthe-Fink, an old-line diplomat with close ties to the Danes, the instructions were shocking. He had had no idea his country was preparing to invade Denmark, but immediately after his meeting with General Himer he began to think how he could most effectively present his government's ultimatum to the Danes, using his knowledge of the Danish political situation to Germany's best advantage. Renthe-Fink had less than six hours' advance warning. His meeting with General Himer took place at 11 P.M. on April 8, and his ultimatum was supposed to be delivered at four-fifteen the following morning.

German units fell upon Denmark exactly on schedule, delivering simultaneously timed attacks against Jutland, Copenhagen, and the strategic island of Fyn. In Jutland, advance elements of the Eleventh German Motorized Rifle Brigade and the 170th Infantry Division smashed across the border on a broad front. They met only scattered resistance. Danish defenses along the border were nonexistent. No preparations had been made to block the roads or mine the bridges, and Danish troops, who operated under orders to oppose "with all available means" any direct action against Danish territory, quickly showed they had no appetite for combat. Danish forces assigned to the defense of the border near the town of Tønder retreated northward at the first sight of German armor and artillery without firing a single shot. German panzer units broke through so rapidly that they captured the Danish colonel in command of the district in his barracks. At other points along the Danish-German border, Danish units offered only token resistance before they fell back before the German assault. Within one hour all Danish forces assigned to southern Jutland had either been routed or had retreated without firing a shot. The German advance was aided by pro-German Danish citizens who stationed themselves at crossroads to direct German units to their destination. Many of these self-appointed guides wore swastikas on their arms and greeted the German invasion forces with flowers and shouts of *"Heil Hitler."*

On the island of Fyn, German assault forces landed without opposition on both the west coast at Middelfart and on the east coast at Nyborg. Danish forces on the island laid down their arms without a struggle, enabling a single motorcycle patrol to complete the occupation of the entire island.

The capture of Copenhagen proceeded almost as smoothly.

The troopship *Hansestadt Danzig,* carrying a German assault battalion, arrived off Copenhagen before dawn, passed the coastal forts without challenge, and tied up at Langelinie Pier in the heart of the city. Three combat companies disembarked and set off toward the Citadel, their passage through the darkened, deserted streets going unnoticed and unopposed. A few minutes before 5 A.M. German forces swarmed into the Citadel through an unguarded gate, quickly overpowered the two sentries on duty, and captured the Danish garrison of seventy men without firing a shot. No casualties were suffered on either side.

The German forces barely missed capturing the commander-in-chief of the Danish Army, Gen. W. W. Prior, who had left the Citadel at 4:50 A.M. to attend an emergency meeting of the Danish Cabinet in the king's palace at Amalienborg Square, where he had found the king and his cabinet members in a turmoil. A half-hour before Prior's arrival, the German Minister Renthe-Fink, following instructions delivered by General Himer, had presented the German ultimatum to Denmark's Foreign Minister Peter Munch. The ultimatum acknowledged that German troops were moving across the border into Jutland and were landing on the principal Danish islands, but excused these actions as necessary to "forestall a British invasion." Denmark's government was called upon to capitulate immediately. If Denmark agreed, Germany would be happy to respect Danish territorial integrity and political independence.

While King Christian conferred with his ministers, scattered rifle shots could be heard outside Amalienborg. German troops, having secured the Citadel, were moving on to the king's residence. Inside the castle, the king's top ministers, including Premier Thorvald Stauning and Foreign Minister Munch, urged a quick capitulation. Only General Prior pleaded that the Danish Army be allowed to fight on. He begged the king and his ministers to leave Amalienborg while there was still time and go to the nearest military camp to continue the struggle. King Christian appeared agitated and confused. He had been rudely awakened earlier that morning to the sight of his palace guards taking up defensive positions. Now, with shots echoing in the streets outside the palace, King Christian asked General Prior whether "our soldiers had fought long enough." Prior replied that they had not.

While the ministers conferred, German bombers zoomed over Copenhagen, coming in so low that early risers could clearly identify the Luftwaffe insignia on the aircraft. The German planes refrained from bombing the capital, but their presence over Copenhagen served the intended purpose of forcing "the Danes to accept" the ultimatum. A few minutes before six, the Danish king agreed to surrender his country without further struggle. An officer who saw King Christian shortly after the capitulation reported that "despair and concern" were written across the king's face. By six-twenty that morning, the Danish capitulation was in German hands and was being broadcast to all Danish units by means of a German transmitter transported into Copenhagen aboard the *Hansestadt Danzig*. General Himer later reported to his headquarters that the bombers "roaring over the Danish capital did not fail to make their impression."

Throughout the country Danish units laid down their arms in compliance with the cease-fire order. Only in Jutland, where some units were cut off from their headquarters, did the fighting continue for a time longer, but even there all resistance ended by 8 A.M., with the last shots being fired against the Germans by small patrols in the town of Haderslev, in southern Jutland. In less than four hours, German troops had seized all of their primary objectives, including the airfields around Aalborg which were captured by German paratroopers early in the morning, and had crushed all Danish resistance. In those few hours of fighting, the Danish Army put up just enough resistance to escape complete dishonor. Its casualties totaled thirteen killed and twenty-three wounded, against twenty killed and wounded for the Germans. This show of resistance on the part of the Danish Army was deemed sufficient for General Prior to issue an official proclamation thanking his troops for their "attitude and conduct" and assuring them that they could "look everybody in the face, with head erect, well knowing that you have done your duty."

The Danish Navy, however, could not point to even a semblance of resistance. For reasons never satisfactorily explained, no Danish naval vessel or shore battery opened fire on invading German vessels, even when German troopships were directly in range of Danish guns, a performance so unbelievable that it stained the reputation of the Danish Navy for years.

By the time most Danes awoke on the morning of April 9 and sat down to their traditional hearty breakfast, their government had capitulated, the conquest of their country was almost complete, and they faced an uncertain future as an occupied nation. In Copenhagen, the sound of German bombers overhead reinforced the dread news that came over the radio. For the civilized Danes, the news brought with it a sense of numb disbelief. Confused and uncertain how they should act, the great majority huddled around their radios or wandered into the center of Copenhagen in an attempt to make sense of the unexpected dramatic developments.

Their government, too, struggled with the question of what to do next. Under the terms of the capitulation agreement, Denmark had been forced to accept the occupation as an accomplished fact, and had agreed to surrender its military installations to the Germans, to break off relations with the Allied countries, and to permit German control of the press, radio, and external communications. In return, the Germans promised that the Third Reich would respect Danish neutrality and would refrain from interference in internal Danish affairs. As a final sop to Danish sentiment, the Third Reich magnanimously announced that the defeated nation would be permitted to maintain its Army and Navy on active-duty status. It was a *quid pro quo* arrangement that Germany hoped would persuade Denmark to fall happily within the orbit of Germany's New Europe, delivering its excess agricultural and light-manufacturing products to a Third Reich girding for a long war. But how would the Danes react?

On the afternoon of April 9, two events took place which convinced the Germans that they could expect no trouble from the Danes. In the afternoon, the Danish government, in its first official act after capitulation, urged all citizens to conduct themselves as good law-abiding Danes, obeying orders and acting "correctly" toward the German invaders. The government's proclamation also offered an apologetic explanation for its capitulation:

> The government have acted in the honest conviction that we have saved the country from an even worse fate. It will be our continued endeavor to protect our country and its people from the disasters of war, and we shall rely on the people's cooperation.

A few hours later, General Himer, accompanied by the German Minister Renthe-Fink, requested an audience with King Christian. The two German officials wanted personally to gauge King Christian's reaction to the events of the day and to ensure that the king did not have in mind any attempt to flee the country. The meeting reassured them that they had nothing to fear from the Danish king. As General Himer later reported in a secret message:

> The seventy-year-old King appeared inwardly shattered, although he preserved outward appearances perfectly and maintained absolute dignity during the audience. His whole body trembled. He declared that he and his government would do everything possible to keep peace and order in the country and to eliminate any friction between the German troops and the country. He wished to spare his country further misfortune and misery. . . . During the course of the audience the King became more at ease and at its conclusion addressed General Himer with these words: "General, may I, as an old soldier, tell you something? As soldier to soldier? You Germans have done the incredible again. One must admit that it is magnificent work."

Denmark, led by its government and king, had embarked on a road that would earn for the country the reputation of Germany's "model protectorate." Nevertheless, fear and anger seethed beneath the outwardly calm exterior. The invasion sent a hard knife edge of terror through the country's eight thousand Jews, and among thousands upon thousands of patriotic Danes the performance of the Danish Army and Navy was cause for shame and humiliation. In the days immediately following the invasion, Danish servicemen met expressions of scorn and derision from civilians whenever they took to the streets in uniform.

6

The Attack on Norway

The attack on Norway posed far graver and more complex problems for German military leaders. Every factor that made Denmark such an easy conquest appeared to be lacking in the Norwegian equation. Norway's mountainous terrain, its poor internal communications which could hinder a rapid advance, and the potential combat effectiveness of the Norwegian fighting man all combined to create an air of tense uncertainty in Berlin. One fear, however, overshadowed all others as the German invasion fleet sailed north. Once on the high seas, the German warships faced the threat of interception and destruction by heavier units of the British Navy. In any quantitative measurement of naval strength, Great Britain had the power to crush the German invasion before the first Wehrmacht soldier set foot on Norwegian soil, if that sea power could be concentrated in the right spot at the right time. Admiral Raeder was well aware of the risks the German Navy ran, but he counted on the unexpectedness of the attack to catch the British fleet off guard. He insisted, however, that his warships return to German bases as soon as they had landed the invasion troops. In a secret report to Hitler, Raeder revealed his fears:

> The most difficult operation for the ships is the return voyage which entails breaking through British naval forces. Not one destroyer may be left behind, let alone a cruiser, either in Narvik or in Trondheim, at a time when the fate of the German fleet is hanging in the balance.

The first battle for Norway, therefore, shaped up as a sea battle between British and German fleets, with the fate of Norway itself hanging in the balance. It was a battle that Admiral Raeder anticipated with trepidation, but one which Winston Churchill looked forward to with eagerness, believing as he did that the "action should not be on terms unfavorable to us."

The main German war fleet assigned the task of ferrying troops to the northern ports of Trondheim and Narvik sailed from Schillig Roads off Wilhelmshaven shortly after five o'clock on the morning of April 7, after loading troops and matériel during the previous days in the ports of Wesermünde, Cuxhaven, Swinemünde, and Wilhelmshaven. The fleet itself was divided into two warship groups. Group One was built around the powerful pocket battleships *Gneisenau* and *Scharnhorst,* escorting ten destroyers headed for Narvik, while Group Two consisted of four destroyers bound for Trondheim under the protection of the heavy guns of the cruiser *Hipper.* The two warship groups planned to sail together until it was time for Group Two to detach itself from the main fleet for the run to Trondheim.

Once in the North Sea, the senior German commander, Vice Admiral Guenther Luetjens, whose flag flew from the *Gneisenau,* ordered the vessels under his command to race northward at twenty-nine knots, trusting to a combination of speed, surprise, and poor visibility to elude observation by British units.

Luetjens' hopes were doomed. British reconnaissance aircraft sighted his vessels within five hours of their departure. Three hours later, twelve Blenheim bombers attacked the German formation—without effect, but the bombing confirmed Admiral Luetjens' worst fears: the British knew he was at sea.

Despite the early British sighting and bombing, the British Admiralty reacted slowly. Nearly seven hours elapsed before the British home fleet, built around the battleships *Rodney* and *Repulse* and the battle cruiser *Valiant,* sailed from Scapa Flow under the command of Admiral Sir Charles Forbes to give chase to the German vessels. The British fleet constituted a naval force far superior to Admiral Luetjens', for in addition to the three major warships, it included four other cruisers and twenty-one destroyers.

The home fleet's sailing was routinely noted by the German naval command which, on the basis of increased wireless traffic between home-fleet vessels and British naval commands on shore, flashed an urgent warning to Admiral Luetjens at sea, advising him that an enemy force had sailed to overtake him. While the exact strength of the British force was unknown to the Germans, Admiral Luetjens had to assume that it was superior to his, for the combined British and French navies had at their disposal a total of seven battleships or battle cruisers. Luetjens could only conclude that the odds at sea were heavily stacked against him and that hope lay in eluding the vessels that were pursuing him from the south up the coast of Norway.

The odds were even more heavily stacked against Luetjens than he feared, for at the time no one within the German naval command suspected that another British force, consisting of the battle cruiser *Renown* and eight destroyers, was far to the north of the German fleet and headed for the same objective as Warship Group One of Admiral Luetjens' force—namely, Narvik. The British aimed to mine the waters of the Norwegian Leads and the Germans to invade and occupy the town of Narvik itself. Although unplanned as such, a nautical pincer movement was developing that could trap and crush the German vessels between two British forces and thereby doom the German invasion of Narvik and Trondheim as well.

The weather turned fierce on the night of April 7, with gale-force winds sending the waters of the Norwegian Sea into a fury. The German destroyers of the warship groups, striving to keep station with the big ships, were battered and driven into disorder. On several occasions they narrowly missed colliding with one another; and when dawn broke on April 8, the destroyer captains reported to Admiral Luetjens that they had lost ten seamen, swept overboard by the mountainous seas. With his force scattered and unable to maintain top speed, Luetjens reluctantly ordered the speed of his flotilla reduced to twenty-two knots.

The storm had also battered the British destroyers with the *Renown.* One of the British ships, the *Glowworm,* had lost a seaman overboard and had been given permission to fall behind to conduct a daylight search. In the early morning of April 8, the *Glowworm* and one of the German destroyers from Group Two, the *Bernd von Arnim,* found each other in the waters west of Trondheim. A running fight developed, with each ship inflicting minor damage on the other but with neither ship able to strike a knockout blow. The *Hipper* soon appeared on the scene to help the *Bernd von Arnim,* and she hit the *Glowworm* with her first salvo, setting the British vessel on fire.

The crippled *Glowworm* laid down a smoke screen and appeared to turn away in an attempt to escape, while the *Hipper,* eager to finish off the British vessel, followed into the smoke at top speed, not anticipating that on the far side, the commander of the *Glowworm,* Lieutenant Commander Roope, had decided to ram. As the *Hipper* emerged from the smoke, her engines racing at top speed and her lookouts alert to pick up the *Glowworm* in the distance, the British ship appeared at close range on her starboard bow, headed on a collision course. Now the *Hipper* too decided to ram, but her helm did not respond quickly enough and *Glowworm*'s bow sliced into her side, ripping a 120-foot hole in her hull. Then the British ship fell away, on fire from the hits she had sustained, to blow up and sink a few minutes later. The *Hipper* stopped to pick up survivors, among them Commander Roope, but the exhausted British officer fell back into the sea as he was being hauled on board the German cruiser and was lost. He later was awarded a posthumous Victoria Cross for his actions that day. *Hipper,* though damaged, was still maneuverable and returned to rejoin Admiral Luetjens' force. The first skirmish in the naval battle for Norway had cost the British one destroyer sunk against one German capital ship damaged.

In London, British Admiralty officials had followed the action closely through messages from the *Glowworm*. At 8:30 A.M. the destroyer reported that she had engaged with an enemy destroyer. A few minutes later she reported sighting another German vessel ahead of her, then that she was engaging a "superior force." This was the *Hipper*, although the identity of the "superior force" was not known to London. At nine-forty-five that morning, *Glowworm's* signals stopped abruptly, and London knew that she was lost.

For the rest of that morning and into the early hours of the afternoon, neither side received further news of the strength or disposition of opposing forces. Then, within a period of a half-hour, two reconnaissance sightings were made—one by a long-range German Dornier 26 aircraft and the other by a British flying boat—that provided information to the respective naval commanders at sea which was to affect their immediate decisions and the ultimate outcome of the battle.

Admiral Luetjens received the first news. A few minutes before two a German reconnaissance pilot reported to him that powerful British units were south of the German war fleet and steaming northward at twenty-five knots. This was the British home fleet. The sighting confirmed the intelligence evaluation passed to Admiral Luetjens the previous day, and the German admiral took steps to disperse his force. With his ships already partially scattered by the storm, he released the *Hipper* and its four destroyers with orders to head for Trondheim, while the *Gneisenau* and *Scharnhorst* continued north, escorting the remaining ten destroyers toward Narvik.

A half-hour later, a British scout aircraft sighted the *Hipper* with her destroyers, headed on a westerly course, and reported their position and direction to Admiral Forbes, the commander-in-chief of the home fleet. The westerly course of the German ships at the time of sighting forced Admiral Forbes into a wrong conclusion. Since the *Hipper* and her destroyers were headed west, away from Trondheim, Forbes assumed that they were in fact headed for Narvik; and he altered course of the vessels under his command to the northwest in an attempt to intercept. In reality, Warship Group Two was merely maneuvering at sea until it was time to turn east for the run to Trondheim. By discounting this possibility, however, Forbes left the approaches to Trondheim undefended.

Admiral Forbes was also hindered in his evaluation of the developing situation by incomplete information on German strength. He knew only of the relatively small *Hipper* group, but had no details of the larger Group One, with the *Gneisenau* and *Scharnhorst*, which was one hundred miles north of Group Two, and which actually was headed for Narvik. In midafternoon Admiral Forbes received fresh reports that further confused the situation in his mind. British submarines related the presence of additional German surface vessels to the south of the home fleet. These German ships actually comprised light units headed for Bergen and Kristiansand, but Admiral Forbes, lacking knowledge of the *Gneisenau* and *Scharnhorst* group, believed that the German vessels to the south could be the main German fleet. Acting on the information at his disposal, Forbes took the fateful decision to split his force in two. He ordered the battleship *Repulse* and the cruiser *Penelope* to continue northward to reinforce the *Renown* off Narvik, while he on the *Rodney* and the bulk of the home fleet turned south to confront the German warships reported by British submarines. By this decision, Admiral Forbes effectively reduced the odds against the Germans, because the strongest vessels of the British home fleet were now headed away from where they were most needed.

As darkness closed in on the evening of April 8, British and German naval units were strung out along the whole length of the Norwegian coast, each aware that the enemy was at sea, but each uncertain of the enemy's precise strength, position, direction, or intention.

By the early hours of the ninth, as the German invasion fleets began to enter the fjords leading to their target cities, the major elements of the British home fleet were steaming south about sixty miles off the coast. In the far north, the battlecruiser *Renown* and her destroyers battled the force of a full gale. In the darkness and heavy seas, with visibility reduced almost to zero, and with the whereabouts and intentions of opposing forces unknown to either side, it was merely a question of chance if contact was made. And contact was made in the waters off Narvik early in the morning of April 9.

Shortly after midnight Admiral Luetjens ordered the destroyers under his command to run for Narvik while he on the *Gneisenau,* accompanied by the *Scharnhorst,* broke northwest in a diversionary move designed to draw the British fleet away from the landing area. The Germans' course led them directly into the waters being patrolled by the *Renown.*

German radar operators aboard the two pocket battleships maintained constant watch on their screens as the *Gneisenau* and *Scharnhorst* lumbered through the heavy seas at a safe seven knots. But it was a lookout on the *Renown,* which did not have radar, who made the first sighting, spotting the German warships through a snow squall shortly before 4 A.M. The *Renown*'s gunners sprang to their battle stations and prepared to open fire. Two minutes later, German radar operators alerted Admiral Luetjens to the presence of the British warship, and the German commander also ordered his gunners to prepare for action. The three ships commenced firing within seconds of each other. The *Renown*'s escorting destroyers also opened fire even though they were out of range and barely able to maneuver in the mountainous seas.

The battle was fraught with danger for both sides. The *Renown*, although heavier than both German vessels and armed with a main battery of six giant fifteen-inch guns, found herself confronting two newer, faster, more heavily armored German warships which could direct a total of eighteen eleven-inch guns against her. If Admiral Luetjens had turned to the attack, the *Gneisenau* and *Scharnhorst* could have maneuvered separately against the *Renown* much as the *Ajax* and *Achilles* had maneuvered against, and overcome, the *Graf Spee*. Instead, it was the slower *Renown* which proved more aggressive, increasing speed in an attempt to close the distance between herself and the German warships; while Admiral Luetjens, seeking to avoid battle, increased speed to twenty-five knots and fled northward. Gradually the German vessels pulled away from the *Renown*, but before they disappeared into the snow and fog, the *Renown* managed to score several direct hits on the *Gneisenau*, wrecking the ship's fire-control system and blasting the German's forward turret out of action. The *Renown* suffered only minor damage from German shells, while the *Scharnhorst*, although not hit, had her forward turret flooded as she plowed through the swells in her hasty retreat.

By fleeing the scene of action, Admiral Luetjens missed a chance to destroy one of Britain's heaviest and most important warships. Later, when confronted with this charge, he explained that gun flashes from the destroyers accompanying the *Renown* had misled him into believing that other heavy ships were present. Despite his failure to sink the *Renown*, Admiral Luetjens had nevertheless carried out the vital task of diverting the British fleet from the landings at Narvik which were taking place even while the guns of war were flashing at sea.

For the twelve hundred German troops of the Third Mountain Division who were aboard the ten destroyers of Warship Group One, the trip to Narvik was a misery. Overcrowded in their nautical quarters, unaccustomed to the sea under any circumstances, battered and thrown about by the violent movement of the destroyers, the soldiers were bitterly cold, miserably seasick, and apprehensive of the landings to come.

The captains of the destroyers faced other problems. The storm itself posed hazards to their ships. One destroyer had already been forced to drop behind the main force. But beyond the hazards of the sea, there was another potential danger: the destroyers were running short of fuel. In any protracted action they would be in critical trouble. The destroyers reached the southern tip of the Lofoten Islands late at night on the eighth and maneuvered in the lee of the islands without being discovered. The relative calm of the sea off the Lofotens gave the troops time to recover.

Shortly after 2 A.M. on the ninth, Commodore Fritz Bonte on the *Wilhelm Heidekamp,* commanding officer of the destroyer group, gave the order for the destroyers to begin their final approach to Narvik. The Germans were right on schedule.

A Norwegian patrol vessel on station at the entrance to Ofotfjord, leading to Narvik, flashed the first alert, warning naval headquarters in Narvik that German destroyers were on their way. Captain Askim, the senior naval officer in Narvik, immediately ordered two ancient iron-clads, the *Eidsvold* and *Norge,* to action stations. Captain Askim knew the weaknesses of his vessels in both gunpower and maneuverability, but the clumsy, forty-year-old ironclads constituted the main Norwegian naval strength in the fjord. Askim ordered both captains to resist any attack by force and sent the *Eidsvold* to intercept the incoming destroyers. At 3:15 A.M., the *Eidsvold* sighted and fired a warning shot across the bows of the *Wilhelm Heidekamp.*

In the next few minutes a strange scene played itself out in the waters of Ofotfjord. In response to the warning shot, Commodore Bonte brought his vessel to a halt and sent a launch with two officers and a signalman aboard to the Norwegian vessel. Captain Willoch of the *Eidsvold* greeted the German officers on his quarterdeck. Naval etiquette was carefully observed as the officers saluted each other smartly. Then the senior German officer explained to Captain Willoch that they had come as friends to protect Norway from Great Britain and suggested that Captain Willoch surrender his vessel, considering the hopeless odds against him. Uncertain what his action should be, the Norwegian officer requested time to consult his superiors. The Germans understood his concern and pleasantly agreed to return to their launch to await his answer.

The answer from Captain Askim, when it came, was unequivocal: The Norwegians would resist any attack by force; the *Eidsvold* should open fire.

Captain Willoch, still observing naval etiquette, called the German officers back to his quarterdeck and informed them of his instructions. Again the German and Norwegian officers saluted one another, but while the Germans returned to their launch, the Norwegian captain ran to the bridge, ordering his gun crews to man their positions.

"We are going to fight," he shouted.

Once on the bridge, he gave the order "Full speed ahead," and his ship got under way, heading for the *Wilhelm Heidekamp.*

Commodore Bonte on the *Wilhelm Heidekamp* had kept a close watch on the Norwegian warship during the intervening minutes. He could see the German launch pull away from the *Eidsvold.* Then, once the launch was clear, he saw a red flare burst in the sky. (This had been the signal agreed upon beforehand to warn him if the Norwegians refused to surrender.) Almost simultaneously Bonte saw the *Eidsvold* gather speed and head for his vessel.

With danger imminent, Commodore Bonte conferred with Gen. Eduard Dietl, commanding officer of the invasion troops, and together they decided to blast the Norwegian ship out of the water. When the range reached three hundred yards, a salvo of six torpedoes leaped from the destroyer toward the oncoming Norwegian vessel. Three torpedoes smashed into the hull of the *Eidsvold,* which split in two and sank almost immediately. Only eight men of a crew of 184 survived. Captain Willoch was among those lost.

The German destroyers, with the *Wilhelm Heidekamp* in the lead, moved on toward Narvik's inner harbor. There the *Eidsvold*'s sister ship, *Norge,* opened fire, and was quickly sent to the bottom by a second torpedo attack, again with heavy loss of life.

The way was thus open for a landing in Narvik that was defended by units of the Norwegian Army.

These units, though operating under orders to resist any invasion with all available force, were weak, poorly trained, poorly armed, and diffidently led. One Norwegian battalion had arrived only that night, and its men were cold and tired after the long march through the snow. The garrison commander, Col. Konrad Sundlo, ordered the reinforcements to rest for the night, as he intended to place them in defensive positions at dawn. That decision left Sundlo with only four hundred troops to man the perimeters of the town and the key machine-gun and anti-aircraft emplacements, and these troops failed to perform when the crucial time arrived. Some observers did spot the incoming German force, but visibility was poor; and the Norwegians, confused and half expecting the strangers to be British, held their fire, enabling General Dietl and his men to walk ashore unopposed after tying up their launches along Narvik's waterfront.

To a Norwegian officer who approached the Germans on the quay, Dietl called out: "I greet the Royal Norwegian Army. The German Army has come to protect Norway and her neutrality." Other officers with Dietl saluted the befuddled Norwegian officer warmly. At General Dietl's insistence, he agreed to escort the German general to Colonel Sundlo's headquarters, and to a short truce that would remain in effect while the meeting was in progress. Then General Dietl and the Norwegian officer, accompanied by the German consul in Narvik, who had been on hand to greet the invading force, rode off in a taxi to see the garrison commander.

The German troops who were already ashore used the truce time to their advantage, mounting machine guns in positions superior to those of the Norwegians and effectively shouldering some leaderless Norwegian troops out of their own entrenched positions. By the time Dietl met Sundlo in town, his men already held the upper hand along the waterfront without a single shot having been fired. The Norwegians, however, still had forces at their disposal. Danger still threatened the Germans.

Dietl greeted the elderly Colonel Sundlo cordially, as if he were the host and the Norwegian the unexpected arrival. The German described himself as a "friend" who had come to aid the Norwegians against the British; he pleaded with the garrison commander to avoid useless bloodshed and surrender his forces; and he advised Sundlo that the rest of Norway had welcomed German troops as friends and protectors. This last was an assertion that was not correct. Even if it had been, Dietl would have had no way of knowing it. The whole argument, however, was an effective one to use with Sundlo, who was a longtime supporter of Vidkun Quisling and a friend of the Third Reich. Nevertheless, Sundlo called his superiors at Sixth Division Headquarters at Harstad, north of Narvik, for instructions. Again, the Norwegian High Command's answer was firm: Sundlo was ordered to fight with all his strength and to throw the invaders back into the sea. Shaken by his instructions, Sundlo warned General Dietl that Norwegian troops would have to open fire in thirty minutes.

But General Dietl, reluctant to give up the opportunity of taking Narvik without a fight, renewed his argument that resistance would mean useless bloodshed, a point that further impressed Sundlo as he realized that the Germans were ashore and consolidating their positions with every passing minute. The outlook for his Norwegian forces would have appeared bleak even if his inclination to resist had been strong. Sundlo hesitated, torn between direct orders from Harstad and the counterpressure from Dietl. Finally he capitulated. "I hand over the town," he said.

Having made his decision, Sundlo reported again to Harstad to inform the Norwegian command that he had surrendered Narvik without firing a shot. After the war, Sundlo faced court-martial charges for surrendering Narvik but was exonerated by his fellow officers, who preferred to believe his actions better explained by incompetence than by treason.

By seven o'clock that morning German forces were in total control of Narvik. General Dietl could report a successful mission to General Falkenhorst in his headquarters in Hamburg. While Dietl's news was welcome in Hamburg, the German position in Narvik was not strong. Some guns that had been on the destroyers had been lost during the stormy passage. More crucial was the failure of cargo ships and tankers to arrive in port before the invasion force. Only one tanker had reached Narvik, from Murmansk, but the rest of the supplies the Germans had expected were not available. Nor did the Germans capture the coastal batteries that military intelligence had informed them were in place along the fjords and which General Dietl, hoping to capture by surprise attack, had counted on for his own defense against a British counterattack. German intelligence officers had erred; no coastal batteries existed. That fact had assured the German destroyers a relatively easy entry into Narvik, but now that Narvik was in German hands, the absence of the batteries meant that British vessels could traverse the same waters without peril as well.

The initial German gamble at Narvik had been a superb success, but there were more hands still to be played in the game. General Dietl feared what would come next, for his force was relatively weak, poorly equipped, and a long way from home; while at sea, the proud British fleet, once eluded, could be expected to be actively on the prowl.

Trondheim, Norway's second most important city, located halfway down the long Norwegian west coast, fell to the German invaders even more easily. Four troop-carrying destroyers, led by the damaged heavy cruiser *Hipper,* approached the entrance to Trondheimfjord early in the morning of April 9, increasing speed to twenty-five knots once they reached the sheltered waters of the fjord itself. As they raced for the inner harbor, a tiny Norwegian picket boat challenged them, but the captain of the *Hipper* replied in English: "Have orders from the government to go to Trondheim—no hostile intentions." The Norwegian patrol boat watched without making another challenge as the German ships passed by.

Further on, Norwegian shore batteries failed to fire when the *Hipper* came within range. The German destroyers, following in the cruiser's wake, did draw Norwegian fire, however, but even then the aim of the Norwegian gunners proved poor and the destroyers suffered no hits. All vessels reached the heart of Trondheim without further incident, tying up at the city's piers as if they had been on a pleasure cruise. And when the first assault troops dashed ashore at 4:25 A.M.—only ten minutes behind schedule—they found the town undefended by the Norwegian Army. The soldiers fanned out quickly to occupy all of Trondheim without a fight. In one incisive stroke, Germany had conquered a magnificent harbor capable of accommodating the largest warships of the German Navy and a vital railhead for the line running across Norway into Sweden.

Bergen, lying some three hundred miles south of Trondheim, presented special problems to the Germans because of its proximity to the British Isles. British warships could reach Bergen from Scapa Flow in eight to nine hours' sailing time, and the Germans fully expected that the British fleet would be off Bergen in strength when they made their invasion run. For this reason, German naval authorities considered the mission of the Bergen-bound Warship Group Three, led by the cruisers *Koln* and *Koenigsberg,* especially dangerous.

But the German luck held. While en route to Bergen, Group Three came within sixty miles of stronger elements of the British home fleet late in the afternoon of April 8 without being observed. Nor did the British, confused as they were about what was developing, have the foresight to station warships off Bergen itself. The German ships were thus able to make their run toward their target unopposed by any British naval unit.

Other dangers awaited Group Three, however, for the Norwegian defense forces at Bergen, led by Rear Admiral Tank-Nielsen, were alert and in good defensive position. A strong fortification guarded the entrance of the fjord leading into the heart of the city. And Tank-Nielsen, unlike other Norwegian commanders, had a premonition of danger. Early on the morning of April 8, when he learned that British warships had mined the waters off Narvik, he assumed that the British move would trigger a German counterresponse; and when later that day he heard from naval intelligence in Oslo that German ships had been observed heading north, he concluded that a large-scale action against Norway was a clear possibility. He discounted as wishful thinking Oslo's suggestion that the German vessels might be headed "for another address." Regardless of what might or might not develop, Tank-Nielsen was convinced that the danger to Bergen was potentially great enough for him to take strong defensive action. He ordered his small force of torpedo and patrol boats to guard the two narrow passages of Byfjord, one to the south and the other to the north, which led from the sea to the heart of the city, and he ordered two of his minelayers to prepare to lay mines in the same waters. Coastal forts were alerted and all coastal lights were ordered extinguished in an attempt to confuse any attacking force. The local Army commander was asked to supply infantry for the defense of the town, and reconnaissance aircraft were ordered into the air at "first light" to survey the offshore waters. Bergen itself was blacked out.

Admiral Tank-Nielsen had taken all the steps he could think of; and when, shortly after 1 A.M. on April 9, a coastal lookout reported that a German invasion fleet was headed toward Bergen from the south, he felt satisfied that the forces under his command had a chance of stopping the invasion. At this crucial point, Tank-Nielsen's precautions started to unravel because of an uncanny mixture of mischance, inefficiency, and timidity on the part of some Norwegian officers. One torpedo-boat captain, finding himself in position to attack the German ships, held back in the face of the overwhelming firepower the German vessels could deliver. And when the German ships came within range of the guns of the main fortification, the Norwegian commandant ordered the fort's searchlights turned on only to discover, to his dismay, that they were inoperable. Too late he realized that his main searchlights drew their electrical power from the same circuit that provided power for the other coastal navigation lights. Tank-Nielsen's order to black out Bergen had extinguished his searchlights as well.

Even without searchlights, the fort's gunners were able to pick out the silhouettes of the German warships. But at the opportune moment for firing, two cargo ships sailed into the zone of fire and the Norwegians held their hand out of consideration for the lives of the civilian seamen aboard the merchant ships. In the interlude, the cruiser *Koln* and her supporting vessels slipped past the fort and sped safely toward Bergen. Only after the *Koln* had passed out of range did the Norwegian gunners open fire on the German ships bringing up the rear, scoring hits on the support ship *Bremse* and inflicting heavy damage on the cruiser *Koenigsberg*. But the main body of the German assault force successfully reached the heart of the city and stormed ashore. Again the Germans were in luck, for the Norwegian infantry requested by Admiral Tank-Nielsen had failed to arrive. The city, undefended by organized units, fell with only a few scattered shots being fired.

Further south, Sola Airfield, near the port of Stavanger on the southwest coast, was taken by German parachute troops who quickly silenced the few Norwegian machine-gun emplacements assigned to the defense of the airfield. The capture of Sola Airfield not only placed in German hands Norway's largest airport but one which was of utmost strategic importance to the Luftwaffe, for German planes based at Sola could strike at British vessels patrolling the Norwegian coast and were within range of key targets in northern Britain as well. Even more important, with Sola in German hands, Luftwaffe supremacy of the air over

Norwegian civilians in Trondheim observe Wehrmacht invasion troops assemble. *(World Wide Photo)*

German fighter crews at Sola Airfield. The Luftwaffe's supremacy in the air was never challenged. *(World Wide Photo)*

Norway was assured, a factor which promised to play a vital role in the fighting to come. The town of Stavanger fell soon after without a hitch.

Kristiansand, on the southern coast, the site of a major Norwegian naval base, put up a stiffer fight. On two occasions, Kristiansand's shore batteries drove off the German Warship Group Four, which was spearheaded by the cruiser *Karlsruhe,* and on two other occasions heavy fog prevented the cruiser from breaking through. Frustrated and angry, the German naval commander called on the Luftwaffe to bomb the two forts guarding the entrance to Kristiansand harbor. The attack, carried out by a full bomber group, silenced the Norwegian guns. The port was occupied soon after.

By midday, therefore, the Germans could report a string of successes from Narvik above the Arctic Circle to Kristiansand on the southern coast. All major objectives along more than fifteen hundred miles of Norwegian coastline had been taken. German losses were light. *Weseruebung* had worked even more smoothly than its most optimistic supporters had dared hope. Everywhere German arms had carried the day, almost without opposition. There remained but one additional target—the Norwegian capital of Oslo, which was the pivot point on which the German conquest of Norway hung. And it was this vital attack on Oslo, meticulously planned as a joint air-sea operation, that came close to bringing disaster on the Germans.

The German attack on Oslo ran into trouble from the start. The German invasion squadron, headed by the brand-new heavy cruiser *Bluecher* (the flagship of the squadron) and the pocket battleship *Luetzow* (formerly the *Deutschland*) entered the mouth of Oslofjord at midnight. The squadron was immediately spotted and challenged by the Norwegian patrol boat *Pol III*, an armed whaler, which raised the alarm before being sunk by gunfire from a German torpedo boat. A short way farther upfjord, the German ships approached two small island forts which also attempted to engage the German warships, but heavy fog hindered the Norwegian gunners and the German squadron passed unscathed. Both forts, nevertheless, flashed messages warning the Oslo sea defense district headquarters that an invasion was under way, thus confirming the first urgent warning from the *Pol III*. Oslo, in short, received at least four hours' advance warning in which to organize a defense of the capital. But the Norwegian government and military leaders, immobilized by fear and uncertainty, frittered away the time in fruitless discussions. By 2:30 A.M. the Norwegians still had not ordered full mobilization, even though the Norwegian Foreign Minister Halvdan Koht could in a telephone call to the British Minister in Oslo remark fatalistically, "So, we are now at war," before returning to his colleagues for further discussions.

The decades of peace had left their mark on the Norwegians, making them incapable of reacting with the urgency and decisiveness demanded by war. Shortly before 4 A.M., when the Norwegians finally brought themselves to order full mobilization, the gravity of the situation was still beyond their grasp. Instead of mobilizing on an emergency basis, the Norwegians decided to utilize previously arranged mobilization plans which called for the country's reserves to be alerted for active duty not by telegraph or telephone but by ordinary mail.

The Norwegian government was still in troubled session when the German Foreign Minister Dr. Curt Brauer arrived promptly at 4:20 A.M. to present his government's ultimatum. Brauer, a fussy diplomat of the old school, had troubles of his own. His arrival was timed to coincide exactly with the first military attack on Oslo. The German Foreign Minister, along with the German naval and air attachés in Oslo, had spent the early morning hours eagerly awaiting the arrival of the German fleet and troop transports. They had waited in vain, however, and when Brauer presented his ultimatum to Koht there were no German warships in the harbor and no German planes roaring overhead to back up the German demands with military power.

Koht rejected the ultimatum out of hand. "We will not submit," he told Brauer. "The battle is already in progress." Dejectedly, the German envoy withdrew to await the arrival of the big warships.

The warships never came. They had run into serious trouble at the

Drøbak Narrows below Oslo, where the Norwegians had their main defensive batteries in the ancient fort of Oscarsborg.

When it was built, at the time of the Crimean War, Oscarsborg was the strongest fortress in northern Europe. Early in this century, giant twenty-eight-centimeter Krupp-built guns (Krupp model 1905) and an Austrian-built torpedo battery had been installed. These weapons, though considered old and slow to reload in 1940, still packed a deadly punch when the German warships arrived below the narrows in the early morning light of April 9. Oscarsborg, moreover, was commanded by a determined and patriotic Army officer, Colonel Eriksen, who instructed his men to fire "for effect" on any German warship that dared to force the narrows, at that juncture no more than six hundred yards wide.

The German squadron approached the fort shortly before 4 A.M. with the *Bluecher,* carrying Gen. Erwin Engelbrecht and one thousand troops of the 163rd Infantry Division, gallantly in the forefront. No lights showed from Oscarsborg Fort, and the German squadron commander, Vice Admiral Oscar Kummetz, assumed there would be no resistance. Kummetz kept his ship's main armament aligned fore and aft in a gesture of disdain for the Norwegian fortifications he had to pass.

From the opposite shore a lone searchlight flared into brilliance, outlining the *Bluecher*'s silhouette for the Oscarsborg gunners. The fort's twenty-eight-centimeter guns immediately opened fire. Within seconds, the proud *Bluecher* was a flaming, stricken vessel, torn by explosions of its own ammunition, and weaving erratically in the waters of Drøbak Narrows.

Beyond the fort itself, the Norwegian torpedo battery waited. When the crippled cruiser came within range, the battery fired. Two torpedoes smashed into the warship, leaving her a helpless hulk, ablaze and doomed. Two hours later a giant explosion racked the vessel. The *Bluecher* rolled over and sank, with the loss of more than a thousand soldiers and crewmen. Rear Admiral Kummetz and General Engelbrecht managed to swim ashore, where they were made prisoners by the Norwegians. Ironically, Germany's newest heavy cruiser had been sunk by guns built in Germany and torpedoes manufactured by an Austrian firm in Fiume at the turn of the century.

After the loss of the *Bluecher,* command of the warship squadron passed to the commanding officer of the *Luetzow,* who ordered the rest of the fleet to turn back and land their troops further down the fjord, some fifty miles from Oslo.

The naval assault on Oslo had been a complete fiasco. The fate of the Norwegian capital now rested on the performance of the German parachute and airborne troops as well as on the defense the Norwegians would put up inside Oslo itself.

The German cruiser *Bluecher* had expected no resistance from Norwegian guns and torpedoes. *(Norsk Telegrambyra)*

The German air assault started as badly as the naval attack. At Fornebu Airport outside Oslo, Captain Spiller, the German air attaché, waited impatiently for the first German paratroopers to descend out of the morning haze, wipe out the few Norwegian defenders, and secure the airfield for the transport planes which were scheduled to land later in the morning with additional troops. The paratroopers, like the warships, never arrived. Unknown to Spiller, the commanders of *X* Air Corps had ordered the paratroop planes to land at Aalborg, Denmark, because of heavy fog over southern Norway. Only German bombers and fighters, assigned the mission of covering the parachute assault, arrived over Fornebu Airport as scheduled. Spiller could hear them circling overhead, drawing desultory fire from Norwegian anti-aircraft guns. Three German aircraft crashed in flames before German bombers knocked out the airfield's AA guns, but Fornebu still remained in Norwegian hands.

As late as three hours after the scheduled *Weseruebung* invasion, no German soldier had landed in or near Oslo, either by air or by sea, and the German timetable, as well as the invasion itself, stood in grave danger. Early German failures had given the Norwegians a golden opportunity to mount a determined defense of the capital. And if Oslo—the center of the country's transportation network—could be held, the entire German invasion of Norway would be jeopardized.

But it was not to be. Norwegian authorities in Oslo, with limited information available, viewed the situation from their own distorted perspective and to them developments appeared bleak indeed. Reports coming in from coastal cities brought catastrophic news of German victories at all points. To the south of Oslo, artillery fire could be heard as troops from the *Luetzow,* which had landed below the capital, advanced on Oslo. The German ultimatum, coupled with the artillery fire and later the bombing of Fornebu Airport, convinced the Norwegians that danger was imminent. The Norwegian army command, fearing the worst, moved out early, first to a hotel in the suburb of Slemdal, then to the town of Eidsvoll. King Haakon, his government, and members of the Norwegian parliament fled soon afterward, scurrying to a special train that left Oslo at 7:30 A.M. for the town of Hamar, seventy miles inland. A fleet of twenty-three motor trucks roared out of town at the same time carrying Norway's precious supply of gold from the Bank of Norway as well as sensitive papers of the Foreign Office and other government ministries.

The government's escape and the early retreat of the Army High Command left Oslo in a vacuum, its citizens confused and frightened, and the few Army units in town bereft of effective leadership. By eight o'clock on the morning of April 9, Oslo was a city without a government and without an organized defense. It was soon to fall to a handful of German troops ferried in on Luftwaffe transport planes which arrived

German troops parade peacefully down Oslo's main thoroughfare, Karl Johan Gate, on the afternoon of *Weser* Day. *(Norsk Telegrambyra)*

over Fornebu with the field still in Norwegian hands. The commander of the transport squadron refused to believe that paratroopers had not landed and brought his Junkers 52 in for a landing, only to be driven off by Norwegian machine-gun fire. Minutes later, a lone Messerschmitt 110 fighter, its fuel dangerously low, swooped down for a landing and for reasons that have never been ascertained drew no hostile fire.

Other German fighter pilots followed the first ME 110, landing with speed and precision and quickly positioning their aircraft so German machine guns could cover the perimeter of the field. Behind them came the heavily laden transport planes to disgorge combat-ready assault troops on the runways of Fornebu. By noon eight infantry companies had landed without opposition. With the airport securely in German hands and with no resistance in sight, these German troops formed into units and marched, as if on parade, into the heart of Oslo behind a hastily organized military band to capture, in the name of the Third Reich, Norway's capital and its quarter million confused inhabitants.

Thus the last and most vital German objective fell without a fight.

7
The Conquest of Norway

The Germans had conquered all of Norway's major ports, but not the country itself, and once the feeling of numb disbelief had passed, Norway's spirit of resistance grew.

On the morning of April 9, Nils Orvik, a twenty-one-year-old student of veterinary medicine, was amazed to see German warplanes over Oslo and hear the angry answering rumble of Norwegian anti-aircraft guns. Despite the evidence at hand, Orvik could not believe that war had come to his native land. Mentally and emotionally he was unprepared to accept reality. By late afternoon, when Orvik ran into German soldiers marching down Karl Johans Gate, Oslo's main street, the strange sense of unreality still persisted. More in wonder than in anger, Orvik asked a German soldier what he was doing in Oslo, and the German replied, "We were sent here to help you against the English." The soldier's response left Orvik deep in thought on the streetcorner.

Oslo was a city rent by rumors that day. Along with reports which exaggerated, if that was possible, the facts of crushing German victories, other reports were circulated describing in vivid detail a nonexistent "iron ring" the Norwegian Army had supposedly thrown around Oslo and the stunning counterblow the Norwegians were preparing. For Orvik, these conflicting reports served to create confusion and uncertainty in his mind, and he wandered the streets of Oslo late into the afternoon, observing and questioning all who would stop to talk. Finally, he settled on a course of action: he would break out of Oslo to join the "iron ring" around the capital and thereby help beat back the invader. With skis borrowed from a friend's house, Orvik made his way through Nordmarka, the woods north of Oslo, until he reached a suburban railroad station where a train composed of makeshift cars was about to depart with a cargo of panicky refugees. Orvik hopped aboard and rode northward until the train reached a hamlet some distance from the capital. There Orvik saw a

Norwegian troop detachment, to whose commanding officer he offered his services.

The officer was unimpressed and inquired if Orvik had had military training. When Orvik replied that he had not, the officer cut him off curtly. "Sorry," he said, "but we can't use you." At a second stop further on, the same scene played itself out and Orvik's services were again rejected. Not until his third attempt to enlist did Orvik succeed and then only by assuring the officer who questioned him that he had had military training with a reserve unit. Once accepted, Orvik received the only military training he would ever undergo. As he described it later, it consisted solely of "running around the woods and hitting the dirt."

Thus one Norwegian responded to the German invasion of his homeland.

Alv Johnsen, another university student, who unlike Orvik actually had had military training with a volunteer company, had been awakened by air-raid sirens on the morning of April 9. When no bombs fell on the city, Johnson made his way into the center of Oslo expecting to ask military officers there what to do. To his astonishment, he found no one who could advise him, for most officers had long since fled. Johnsen, like Orvik, then decided to leave Oslo, setting out on skis through Nordmarka until he reached open country to the north. Eventually, still traveling cross-country on skis, he ran into a Norwegian scouting party and was escorted to the patrol's field headquarters, where his previous military training set him apart from other young Norwegians seeking to serve their country. Without further training or indoctrination, Johnsen was assigned to a combat ski patrol and sent out on a reconnaissance mission against the Germans.

Thus another Norwegian answered his country's muted call for help.

Others were less successful. Construction worker Knut Haukelid, having completed work on a project in Narvik, was traveling south toward Oslo when the war caught up with him in Trondheim. He awoke on the morning of April 9 to find German troops in control of the city. Without a moment's hesitation, Haukelid changed his travel plans and slipped into the countryside outside Trondheim hoping to join a Norwegian military unit that was still fighting. His search proved fruitless. Undaunted, Haukelid attached himself to a party of other young men who were also seeking to enlist. Together they made their way south by train, seeking Norwegian units along the way. They were never successful, being turned away by unit after unit, for in the spring of 1940 the Norwegian Army was incapable not only of absorbing untrained volunteers but even of effectively utilizing its regular and reserve troop units.

A century and a half of peace had turned the Norwegian Army into an inefficient and inflexible fighting machine. It was not always so. For more than 150 years after its establishment as an organized military force in the year 1624, the Norwegian Army created a brave heritage as it held its own in bitter border wars against the ascendant Swedes; but in 1814 the two countries united and Norway laid down its arms. Throughout the remaining years of the nineteenth century, the prestige of Norwegian military men declined as the country's peasantry as well as its intellectuals adopted a pacifist, antimilitaristic outlook. Norway's successful effort to avoid World War I only served to reinforce this attitude. And in the Depression-torn 1930s, open hostility erupted between segments of the working-class population, often Left-wing in outlook, and members of military units, who were scorned for their elitist attitude and conservative politics. As one officer on active duty at the time of the German invasion remarked, "It was very difficult to be a military man in pre-war Norway."

It was this Norwegian Army, without combat-experienced officers or men, maintained during peacetime by a country with no enthusiasm for war, and looked upon with suspicion and antagonism by a large segment of the population, which now tried amid the confusion of the German invasion to regroup and organize a defense of the country.

But first the Norwegian government and Army had to withstand a two-pronged diplomatic offensive by German civilian authorities and by Norway's own homegrown Nazi, Vidkun Quisling.

The Germans, having failed to capture King Haakon and his government in their attack on Oslo, moved to neutralize them by negotiations. On the afternoon of April 9, Minister Brauer broadcast a German appeal for the government to halt all resistance. At the same time, Brauer demanded an immediate audience with the king, who was by then safely established with his government at the town of Elverum, a few miles east of Hamar. When suitable arrangements for a meeting that night could not be arranged, Brauer reluctantly agreed to put off the confrontation for a day, a decision that infuriated his immediate superior in Berlin, Foreign Minister Ribbentrop, who was convinced that King Haakon would quickly acquiesce to *force majeure* if only Brauer could get to see him.

Quisling also made his move on April 9. Contrary to what was generally believed after the war, Quisling (who in December, 1939, had invited German troops to take over his country) did not have a minute's advance notice of the German invasion. Hitler's warnings to his generals not to take Quisling into their confidence had been strictly heeded. But once German troops were in Oslo, Quisling acted on his own.

In the early afternoon, he ventured into Oslo to gauge conditions at first hand. One of his first stops was the War Office, where a handful of functionaries still lingered. A few who knew Quisling from his Army

days saluted as he entered. Quisling returned the salutes joyfully, inter-
preting them as indications of support.

From the War Office Quisling moved next to the offices of his own
Nasjonal Samling Party where he conferred with party associates and
with Hans Wilhelm Scheidt, a personal emissary of Alfred Rosenberg,
one of Quisling's longtime German backers. There is some evidence that
Scheidt, on Rosenberg's orders, led Quisling to believe that Germany
would be sympathetic if Quisling were to form a new government. And
that, apparently, was exactly what Quisling wanted to hear.

With Scheidt's support, Quisling drafted a personal message to the
Norwegian people, and using Scheidt's identification papers to gain entry
to the main Oslo radio station, he went on the air at 7:30 P.M.:

> Norwegian men and women. England has violated the neutrality of
> Norway.... The German government has offered the Norwegian
> government its help.... In reply to this offer, our Government has
> carried out general mobilization and given aimless orders to all
> Norwegian military forces to oppose German help by armed
> force.... The Government itself has fled.... Under these circum-
> stances, it is the duty and right of the *Nasjonal Samling* movement to
> assume the powers of government, with Vidkun Quisling as its head
> and as Minister of Foreign Affairs.... All Norwegians are hereby
> called upon to keep the peace.... I add that resistance is not merely
> useless but directly synonymous with criminal destruction of life and
> property. Every official and every municipal employee is duty bound
> to obey orders from the new National Government. Any deviation
> from this will involve the utmost personal responsibility on the part of
> the offender....

Quisling's speech burst on an unsuspecting Norway which had long
held Quisling in disdain, considering him an eccentric and egocentric
politician without popular support. It also caught Minister Brauer by
surprise. He now had two Norwegian prime ministers to deal with—
Prime Minister Johan Nygaardsvold, who was with the king in Elverum,
and the new, self-proclaimed Prime Minister in Oslo, Vidkun Quisling.

Brauer, with long and close ties to many Norwegian politicians, was
well aware of Quisling's lack of support among the Norwegians, but he
could not ignore the surprise development. Dutiful diplomat that he was,
Brauer telephoned Quisling's secretary and invited the Norwegian Nazi
to a conference in his office. When Quisling heard of the call he reacted
with the arrogance that was to typify his actions throughout the war.

"Tell the German minister," he instructed his secretary, "that if he
wants to meet the Norwegian Prime Minister he must come and see me."
And Brauer complied!

He found Quisling ensconced with his staff in a suite on the fourth
floor of Oslo's plush Continental Hotel. The conference, however, did
nothing to increase Brauer's estimate of Quisling.

On his return to his own office, Brauer immediately telephoned Ribbentrop in Berlin with a harshly belittling assessment of Quisling's power, competence, and political future. Both Ribbentrop and Brauer agreed that Quisling should be ignored, if for no other reason than his close ties to Rosenberg, who was a bitter rival of Ribbentrop's for power within the Nazi hierarchy. Such a decision, however, could not be made on their own initiative, and while Brauer waited on one telephone, Ribbentrop got through to Hitler on another.

The call caught Hitler in a euphoric mood. All military news flooding in from Norway was better than he could have anticipated and, in a spur-of-the-moment decision, Hitler brushed aside Ribbentrop's reservations about Quisling. "Why not Quisling?" Hitler demanded.

To Brauer's dismay, he soon heard Ribbentrop repeating Hitler's instructions: Brauer was to support Quisling fully and to insist, in all negotiations with King Haakon, that Quisling remain as the country's Prime Minister.

Hitler's decision was an astonishing gift for Quisling. Twenty-four hours earlier he had been an isolated figure in Norwegian political life destined to play no role in the German invasion and occupation of his country. By the night of April 9, he had Hitler's enthusiastic support.

Quisling responded to the news in characteristic fashion, marching at the head of an entourage to the Norwegian Parliament (Storting)

Vidkun Quisling in office . . . always the striving for effect.
(Norsk Telegrambyra)

building, where he haughtily demanded that German troops who had taken up positions inside move out as quickly as possible. As the new Prime Minister of Norway, Quisling demanded that the Parliament building be available for use by the new Norwegian government he planned to organize. The German officer in charge brushed aside Quisling's demands and the Norwegian walked away in a huff.

One more surprise development was brewing that evening of April 9, unknown to either Brauer or Quisling. The German air attaché in Oslo, Captain Spiller, who had waited so long at the Fornebu Airport for the arrival of German parachutists, decided on a dramatic move to seize the Norwegian king and government by force. Spiller approached the commander of a company of paratroopers who responded enthusiastically. "With this company I could get the devil out of hell," he confidently assured Spiller.

The German troops set out in commandeered buses, moving rapidly northward over narrow Norwegian roads as if on a routine training maneuver. The Germans expected no resistance; none had been offered at Oslo. Below Elverum, however, they ran into a roadblock that had been hastily organized by Col. Otto Ruge, the inspector-general of infantry, who had traveled north with King Haakon's party and who was determined to protect his king from capture. Ruge, informed of the German advance, threw a force numbering no more than a hundred men into defensive positions. It was a motley group to throw against the superbly trained German parachute troops, consisting of one company of King's Guards that had just completed its basic training and a group of officers from various Norwegian divisions who had been attending an experimental course in tactics at the infantry school in Elverum. The heaviest weapon available was a lone machine gun manned by Lt. Odd Øyen. Otherwise, the Norwegian defenders were without hand grenades, without mortars, and without hand-held automatic weapons.

The German troops hit the Norwegian roadblock shortly after 1 A.M. on April 10, debussed quickly, and went on the attack. Lieutenant Øyen was surprised to note that the Germans did not bother to take time to aim but relied on the intensity of their firepower to overwhelm the defense psychologically. But the Norwegians, inspired by Ruge's leadership, held their ground, and in the skirmish that followed Spiller was mortally wounded and other Germans hit. Demoralized by the unexpected resistance, the Germans pulled back toward Oslo, leaving Spiller in a Norwegian hospital along the way. There he died, as did his plan to capture the Norwegian king.

During the day on April 10, Brauer traveled the same road to Elverum to meet King Haakon, whom he insisted on seeing alone. Once secluded with the Norwegian king, the German minister used all the arguments suggested by Ribbentrop to persuade the king to capitulate, to accept a new government under Quisling, to return to Oslo. The Germans, Brauer insisted, had not come to Norway as enemies of the Norwegian people or government but to protect the country against the English. Germany, he continued, was willing—even eager—to maintain King Haakon's dynasty as it was willing to preserve the dynasty of Haakon's brother, King Christian of Denmark. If Haakon accepted the German demands, he would continue to enjoy the honors and perquisites of his position and would be assured that his action had saved his country from needless bloodshed. If he refused to accede to the German demands, however, the full weight of the Wehrmacht would be unleashed against Norway, crushing the country by military might.

King Haakon, a resilient, determined monarch, responded coldly. The issues raised by Brauer, he noted, were so important that he could not think of deciding them without first consulting his government, as the Norwegian constitution and his own understanding of the Norwegian political process demanded. Haakon assured Brauer that his answer would be telephoned to the German envoy during his trip back to Oslo.

When the German envoy had left, Haakon retired to a modest inn outside Elverum where members of his government had gathered to await news of the meeting. Haakon was as formal and correct with his own government leaders as he had been with Brauer, presenting his views in written form so there could be no misunderstanding or doubt in their minds where he stood.

> I am deeply affected by the responsibility laid on me if the German demand is rejected. The responsibility for the calamities that will befall people and country is indeed so grave that I dread to take it. It rests with the government to decide, but my position is clear. For my part, I cannot accept the German demands. I have carefully examined my mind and my position, and I find that I cannot appoint Quisling Prime Minister, a man in whom I know neither our people as a whole nor its representatives—the Storting—have any confidence at all. If, therefore, the government should decide to accept the German demands—and I fully understand the reasons in favor of it, considering the impending danger of war in which so many young Norwegians will have to give their lives—if so, abdication will be the only course open to me.

It was a message of defiance to the Germans and rejection of their demands. Faced with the king's courage, the government quickly followed his lead. Even those members who had been willing to accept the German ultimatum refrained from pressing an opposing view. Their king had shown the way and as loyal subjects they could do nothing else but follow.

Norway's decision to fight on reached Brauer at Eidsvoll, halfway back to Oslo, where he took a telephone call from Foreign Minister Koht. Brauer immediately telephoned the substance of the decision to the

German legation in Oslo before continuing with his own journey, now soured by a sense of failure. From Oslo the news flashed to Berlin:

> The King will name no government headed by Quisling and this decision was made upon the unanimous advice of the Government. To my specific question, Foreign Minister Koht replied: "Resistance will continue as long as possible!"

Norway, unlike Denmark, had refused to capitulate. The Norwegian population heard the news later that day in a radio message broadcast in the name of the government from a rural radio station. The king formally associated himself with the announcement which rejected the German demands and called on all Norwegians to resist the invader with all their might.

The battle for Norway was on. Before it was over, it would involve not only German and Norwegian troops but British, French, and Polish forces as well; and it would range over all parts of the country, with two major theaters developing almost simultaneously—one in the south-central part of the country and the other in the far north, where the port city of Narvik, although in German hands, remained a coveted prize of war.

First, the Norwegian Army needed a new commander-in-chief. Sixty-five-year-old Maj. Gen. Kristian Laake was persuaded to retire "because of age" and Colonel Ruge, who had organized the defense at Elverum, was promoted to general's rank and appointed to replace him.

The new general wasted no time taking over his command. Ruge reached Army headquarters at Rena, a small community in the Øster Valley, early on the morning of April 11. He was immediately struck by a sense of confusion and despair that affected most of the officers there. Nor did he find much to cheer him when he reviewed the military situation. He had at Rena effective combat command of only the Second Norwegian Division, which was still in the process of mobilization in the area north of Oslo, but the mobilization was proceeding erratically, and the division had no armor or air support and almost no artillery. Though communications with other Norwegian units in the field were poor, General Ruge knew that their combat readiness was no better than the Second's. Ruge possessed only one ace in the hole—the hope and expectation that Britain and France would send reinforcements to help him stem the anticipated German offensive. It was a slender hope on which to base his country's future. In the meantime, Ruge determined to make the Germans pay for every foot of Norwegian territory and to slow their advance by every means possible.

The Norwegian government also remained adamant in its determination to continue the fight. Early on the morning of the eleventh, while Ruge was arriving in Rena, Minister Brauer made another effort to reach the king. Ribbentrop had curtly ordered him to "give the Norwegian people one last chance of a reasonable agreement," but the Norwegians again turned Brauer away. The Germans reacted violently to this second rebuff. Within hours, German warplanes arrived over the village of Nybergsund, where Haakon and his government were holed up, having fled from Elverum. The Germans hoped to kill the stubborn king and his followers and the Luftwaffe pilots returned to their base apparently convinced that they had succeeded. One pilot noted in his diary after the raid: "Nybergsund. Oslo government. Completely wiped out."

King Haakon and his key advisors, however, had escaped in time. At the first sound of the approaching bombers they had retreated to a nearby forest where, standing silently in deep snow, they watched the German planes smash the hamlet to splinters. When the German planes had disappeared toward the south, in the direction whence they had come, the king and his government continued their northward retreat, hoping to rally their countrymen along the way.

At Rena, meanwhile, General Ruge was presiding over his first formal staff conference. Many of the divisional and headquarters officers gathered before him were obviously discouraged, some to the point of demoralization, and Ruge seized on the events of the day to impress upon his officers the government's determination to fight on, a determination he sought to instill in his officers. He told his officers of the king's refusal to bow to the German demands, and he stressed the fact that Norway was at war and must fight with every ounce of her strength. All officers were required, both by their military code of conduct and by their loyalty to king and country, to reject any plea to capitulate, either from the Germans or from Quisling.

Then Ruge set about issuing specific orders. All bridges north of the capital were to be destroyed and all communication lines cut. Units to the east and west of Oslo were instructed to seal off the capital, while the Second Division was ordered to do the same in the north. Thus, belatedly, Ruge sought to throw an "iron ring" around Oslo.

But General Ruge realized that with the troops at his disposal he could not keep the Germans bottled up. What he feared most was a German thrust northward along the twin Øster and Gudbrands valleys to link up with the Germans in Trondheim. If the Germans could accomplish this, the heart of southern and central Norway would be in their hands. Ruge also knew that the Trondheim area offered the best possibilities for an Allied counterinvasion.

It was from Trondheim that a combined Allied and Norwegian force could most easily counterattack toward Oslo. Whatever else he did, therefore, Ruge had to prevent the German forces in Oslo from joining the German forces in Trondheim. But Ruge could not risk his troops in all-out battles with the Germans. Instead, he ordered them to hold their defensive positions as long as they could but to withdraw before they were overwhelmed. In this way he hoped to slow the German advance long enough for the Allies to land in the Trondheim area, join with his own Norwegian forces, and then, together, counterattack to reconquer southern Norway.

Ruge had judged the German intentions perfectly. General Falkenhorst arrived in Oslo in the afternoon of April 9, only hours after his troops had secured the city. He was determined to press the attack as quickly as possible. Oslo had fallen, but not as rapidly as Falkenhorst had wished. For a few days he was off balance, but he soon recovered. By April 11 his forces were ready to strike. Falkenhorst's primary objective was Trondheim—he too realized its strategic importance—but he wanted his flanks cleared first, and he ordered German units to smash southeastward and southwestward from the capital at the earliest possible date. His strike forces were motorized, mainly by the use of requisitioned Norwegian trucks and busses, and Falkenhorst ordered his troops to attack not in division strength but in tactical groups, on the assumption that smaller, self-contained groups could move and fight with greater flexibility. The German troops performed even better than Falkenhorst hoped.

Units of the 196th Infantry Division attacked toward the southeast on April 12, and in three days of lightning warfare they overran the entire southeastern part of the country. The Germans captured eight hundred

German infantry advances through a Norwegian village.
(Wide World Photo)

Norwegian troops in their advance. Another three thousand Norwegian troops were so demoralized by news of the German onslaught that they marched into Sweden in orderly formations without ever seeing combat. The Swedes promptly interned them.

Units of the 163d Infantry Division launched their attack, also on April 12, to the west and southwest of the capital. Everywhere Norwegian resistance crumbled at the sight of German units. The city of Kongsberg, fifty-five miles southwest of Oslo, fell on the same day. Fifteen hundred newly mobilized Norwegian troops laid down their arms in the countryside outside Kongsberg the next day.

At Kristiansand, on the coast, Norwegian forces surrendered without resistance. The German invasion of the key naval port had been followed by a slow retreat of Norwegian forces under the overall command of Major General Liljedal. With each Norwegian retreat, the Germans advanced until contact was established, and then the Norwegians retreated again, without either side firing a shot. This incredible series of battlefield maneuvers went on until the Norwegians reached a position that precluded further retreat. General Liljedal immediately telephoned General Ruge for instructions. Liljedal wanted to capitulate. He described one of his key units—the First Battalion of the Telemark Regiment—as "unfit for battle" because of "overstrain" and described the German forces opposing him as "overwhelming." He neglected to mention that the battalion had yet to see any action.

General Ruge was furious. "The defeat or captivity of her forces is better for the nation than their voluntary capitulation. That is my order."

But the battalion surrendered anyway, as did other troops in the area. One observer who watched the men of the First Battalion march into captivity noted that their bearing and military presence were good, and the men looked as if they "would have been prepared to do their duty for their Fatherland, but if ordered to surrender, they would obey that order as well." By April 15 the Germans were in complete control of the Kristiansand area.

Norwegian forces defending the area between Oslo and Bergen put up stiffer resistance. The Norwegian Fourth Brigade surprised the Germans by mobilizing rapidly on the outskirts of Bergen, and then surprised the Germans a second time by conducting a well-organized fighting withdrawal from Bergen toward the east. The Fourth Brigade eventually hoped to join General Ruge's forces north of Oslo and thus strengthen the front where the danger was greatest. But General Falkenhorst perceived the threat early enough and acted promptly. He ordered German troops in Bergen to pursue the Norwegians from the west, while he dispatched a strong force from Oslo to confront the Norwegians from the opposite direction. The pincer snapped shut near the mountain town of Bagn. Unlike Norwegian troops at Kristiansand, the Norwegians at Bagn fought fiercely against superior German units, beating back repeated

German attacks in two days of heavy fighting. Strong attacks by German dive bombers eventually broke the Norwegian resistance, however, and all Norwegian forces at Bagn, including the Fourth Brigade's 300 officers and 3,200 men, surrendered on May 1. The next day German forces met each other along the Bergen–Oslo railroad, clearing the overland route between these two vital cities and concluding the capture of Norway's south-central area.

German forces attacked north of Oslo on April 14, less than a week after the city's capture. Their immediate objectives were the entrances to the Østerdal and the Gudbrandsdal, the valley approach routes through the mountains to Trondheim. A major road and railway line ran through the Gudbrandsdal connecting Oslo with the junction town of Dombås. From Dombås, major lines branched off to the port of Åndalsnes and to Trondheim to the north. The Østerdal, while without a rail connection to Trondheim, offered an alternate overland route to that city. General Falkenhorst knew that to complete the conquest of Norway south of Trondheim he would have to take both valleys.

German panzer battalions, motorized machine-gun battalions, and an elite battalion of the General Goering Regiment fanned out north of Oslo and easily swept aside the first defenses of General Ruge's forces. Motorized infantry columns, operating independently of larger formations, proved particularly effective. Norwegian strongpoints fell before the fast-moving columns as much from surprise at their appearance as from the superiority of German arms. On those occasions when Norwegian defenses held, German panzers and artillery deployed rapidly to wipe out the pockets of resistance. The gently rolling and sparsely wooded terrain south of the valley mouths also favored the Germans, providing ideal ground for German motorized units. The unmotorized Norwegians, forced into static defense positions without tanks or effective antitank weapons, fell back all along the line. Within eight days, Falkenhorst's troops advanced 130 miles from Oslo to Rena in the Østerdal, the site of General Ruge's first headquarters, and 120 miles from Oslo to Lillehammer in the Gudbrandsdal, where Ruge had established his second headquarters.

Here Norwegian resistance stiffened. The terrain was now mountainous. Deep snow still covered the ground, forcing the Germans to keep to the roads. The German advance lost momentum, slowed not only by the sudden change in climate (the Germans had left Oslo in early spring and suddenly found themselves fighting under winter conditions) but also by the stubborn defense thrown up by the Norwegians. Here, where the valleys narrowed and where undergunned defenders held the upper hand, General Ruge had built his main defenses. He hoped to hold the line at Rena and Lillehammer to buy time for the continued mobilization of additional Norwegian forces and for British and French reinforcements to arrive.

German troops in action against Norwegian mountain forces near Bagn. A German patrol in a cleaning-up action in Hönefoss. *(Photos from World War II Collection of Seized Enemy Records in The National Archives)*

In view of their prior preparations to land troops in Norway under one pretext or another, the British were inexcusably slow in reacting to the German invasion, which, as Churchill admitted, had "completely outwitted" them. On the morning of the invasion, the British Minister in Oslo did assure the Norwegians that Britain would extend her full aid and would fight the war in close association with Norway. The British Minister specifically informed the Norwegians that his country was taking steps to deal with the German occupation of Bergen, Trondheim, and Narvik. But these British assurances were not followed by immediate action.

London was gripped by conflicting emotions. Despite the humiliating German victories, Britain managed to find reasons for optimism. The termination of Norwegian neutrality was considered a particularly favorable development. Now at last Britain and France could act militarily without having to consider diplomatic obstacles. Time too was seen as favoring the Allied cause. The British fleet, although outwitted during the actual invasion, could be expected to dispose of the German landing parties "in a week or two."

The British military establishment, responding to an internal time clock more in keeping with the trench warfare of World War I than to the new *Blitzkrieg* pace of German operations in World War II, began reassembling its expeditionary force, which had precipitously disembarked from its ships on April 8; in a slow and leisurely fashion. Overlapping British commands and poor coordination with the French further slowed the effort. A few days after the invasion, Churchill complained to Prime Minister Chamberlain that "there are six Chiefs of Staff . . . [and] three Ministers . . . who have a voice in Norwegian operations. But no one is responsible for the creation of military policy." Final decisions were made by the War Cabinet on the advice of the individual services, which true to tradition operated independently of one another.

Three major objectives presented themselves for possible counterattack. Narvik in the far north was crucial because of its iron-ore traffic. Trondheim further south offered the best avenue into the heart of Norway. And Bergen, still further south, was considered an important objective on political grounds, the British and Norwegians in the Bergen area sharing a long and warm history of close commercial and cultural ties. In the immediate aftermath of the invasion, the British contemplated counterattacks on all three cities.

Narvik, at first, ranked as the primary objective, but as news of the German advance up the Gudbrandsdal and Østerdal reached London, Trondheim became the more urgent target. London observers watched the retreat of General Ruge's forces with growing concern. If the heart of Norway was not to fall, action had to be instituted against Trondheim. The plan eventually worked out called for two landings, one at the small

port of Namsos, 127 miles northeast of Trondheim, and the other at
Åndalsnes, 100 miles to the southwest. Once firmly established on
Norwegian soil, troops from both beachhead areas would launch a giant
pincer movement to encircle Trondheim, capture the German forces
within the city, and thus deny Trondheim to Falkenhorst's forces moving
up from the south. At least that was the plan.

The northern landings at Namsos began well. By April 19, approximately six thousand British and French troops were ashore—a
350-man naval landing party arriving first, followed by the British 146th
Brigade and finally by the crack mountain troops of the French Fifth
Demibrigade of Chasseurs Alpins. The Allied force joined with
Norwegian troops that had assembled north of the city and struck out for
Trondheim, rapidly expanding their bridgehead in the first days of the
advance. The Allied force outnumbered the four thousand Wehrmacht
soldiers in Trondheim by better than two to one.

Hitler panicked at the news of the British landings. He ordered
reinforcements rushed to Trondheim by every available plane and ship
and instructed Brig. Gen. Kurt Woytasch, the Trondheim commander,
to counterattack and seal off the peninsula on which the Allied force had
landed. It was a difficult time in Berlin. General Jodl noted in his diary:
"Chaos of leadership is again threatening. Fuehrer is increasingly worried
about the English landings."

Hitler's fears soon eased. The German buildup proceeded rapidly
(by April 30 an additional 5,500 men had joined Group Trondheim) and
German commanders made effective use of the Luftwaffe, which controlled the skies over the battlefield. German aircraft reduced Namsos to
ashes in a devastating raid and pounded Allied ground positions at will, for
the Allies were forced to fight without air support and without anti-aircraft guns. British fighters could not reach the scene of battle and through
an incredible logistics blunder, the British and French troops had landed
without artillery of any sort, an oversight which left the expeditionary
force helpless against German air attack. As a result, the Allied advance
ground completely to a halt and both sides dug in—the Allies incapable of
advancing in the face of German air supremacy; the Germans, once the
Allied attack had been blunted, content to hold the defensive positions
they had consolidated.

London lost heart almost immediately. By April 23 the British were
openly discussing evacuation and even though some anti-aircraft guns
arrived on the twenty-seventh, the decision to withdraw had already been
made. By the morning of May 3, all British and French troops had fled
Namsos, leaving two thousand discouraged Norwegian officers and men
to surrender to German forces, which entered the still smoking town on
the evening of May 4. The Namsos arm of the pincer against Trondheim
had been cut off.

The southern arm of the planned British pincer also met with difficulties. Troops of the 148th Brigade under the command of Brigadier Morgan, stepped ashore at Åndalsnes on April 18. Their landing was unopposed but the British troops were ill prepared for combat from the start. They had no artillery. They were short of ammunition for the weapons they did carry. And because they had sailed from Britain intending to land in Namsos, only to have their destination switched while at sea, they arrived in Åndalsnes without detailed maps of their new operational area.

The brigade nevertheless found its way to the rail junction at Dombås, where it expected to turn north for an assault on Trondheim. Brigadier Morgan had received orders soon after sailing to "operate northward and take offensive action against the Germans in the Trondheim area." At Dombås, however, Morgan heard from General Ruge, who pleaded with him to turn south instead. Ruge informed Morgan that Norwegian troops were still clinging to positions below Lillehammer, but that German infantry backed by artillery and tanks was massing for a new assault. General Ruge feared that the Norwegian position would collapse unless Morgan and his troops rushed south to the assistance of the embattled Norwegians. "My men are near exhaustion," Ruge warned.

Brigadier Morgan, unable to communicate directly with his headquarters back in Britain, faced a lonely and difficult choice. Although his orders directed him to "operate northward," he realized that the danger of a possible Norwegian collapse overrode all other considerations. A German breakthrough would not only eliminate General Ruge's forces as an effective battlefield component but threaten his own force as well. Without waiting for confirmation from London, Morgan ordered the brigade to turn south at Dombås, to meet General Ruge and his Norwegian soldiers.

Morgan's first meeting with Ruge started awkwardly. General Ruge thought the British had landed "in great strength" and could not contain his disappointment when he learned that Morgan's forces consisted of only one-and-a-half battalions, without artillery and without adequate supplies. Norwegian officers were also disappointed at their first sight of British troops. They had anticipated first-line combat troops, but the men under Morgan looked to them like poorly trained Territorials, which in fact they were, no more prepared for combat than had been their own Norwegian troops. Lt. Col. Roscher Nielsen, a member of General Ruge's staff, looked down upon the British troops as "untrained steel workers from the Midlands."

Despite Norwegian disappointment, General Ruge ordered Morgan's men into action immediately. The British troops moved toward the front in lorries driven by Norwegian civilians who spoke no English, and took over forward positions just as Norwegian defenses broke down.

An emergency Luftwaffe airlift rushed men and war materiel to Trondheim.
(World War II Collection of Seized Enemy Records)

There, to the south of Lillehammer, the first engagement of the war between British and German troops took place. The outcome was never in doubt.

The British infantrymen, in combat for the first time and fighting under Norwegian officers they did not know, armed with only rifles and machine guns against German artillery and tanks, and subjected to repeated attacks by German dive bombers, bravely held out for almost twenty-four hours before they too broke under the weight of the German attack and joined the Norwegians in a precipitous retreat. It was the start of a disastrous 140-mile withdrawal up the Gudbrandsdal. The British, with the Norwegians fighting alongside them, were forced back from position after position. By the afternoon of April 21, they had retreated to the north of Lillehammer and on the 22d they were beaten back again from their new positions. On April 23, the British dug in at the village of Trettin, determined to hold the line while the Norwegian troops regrouped. A German attack led by three tanks smashed through the British roadblock and scattered the British infantrymen into the mountains. Groups of confused British soldiers wandered aimlessly through the Norwegian countryside for days after the battle seeking to escape capture. Some eventually made their way to Sweden, but the great majority found themselves taken prisoners of war by the Germans. Even the arrival of French reinforcements on April 24 failed to halt the advancing German panzers. The French troops, under Maj. Gen. Bernard Paget, promptly joined the retreating Norwegian and British units.

With the Allies in retreat, General Falkenhorst ordered German ground forces to follow closely on the heels of the routed force. German warplanes pounded the demoralized troops incessantly. So heavy was the German air attack that for one whole day the bulk of Brigadier Morgan's battered British force hid in a railway tunnel to escape detection by German planes.

Norwegian civilians turned against the retreating soldiers with a vengeance. One British soldier complained that Norwegian resentment was "as strong against the British for letting the country be ravished by the Germans as against the Germans for doing it." Norwegian officers who sought to place their troops in defensive positions along the Gudbrandsdal were repeatedly asked by farmers to move elsewhere. "If you fight here," the farmers pleaded, "we will lose our barns and our homes."

By April 24, London was also beginning to have second thoughts about the Allied effort south of Trondheim. Gen. Sir Edmund Ironside, Chief of the Imperial General Staff, noted in his diary:

> . . . the situation of the poor old Norwegians on their Oslo front, so called, is very poor. They have gone back a long way and show no signs of being able to stand at all. . . .

A column of British infantry, defeated near Trondheim, march off to imprisonment. *(World War II Collection of Seized Enemy Records)*

Three British soldiers captured near Lillehammer during their first encounter with the Germans. *(World War II Collection of Seized Enemy Records)*

On the 25th, Ironside was even more pessimistic:

The wretched Norwegians are withdrawing as fast as they can. . . . It looks more and more likely that we will have to contemplate some evacuation of our troops.

By April 26, less than one week after British troops first went into battle, the British military coordination committee, after consultation with the Chiefs of Staff, decided to withdraw. Government ministers were duly informed, and agreed wholeheartedly. Ironside observed in his diary:

I have now issued the orders for the eventual evacuation of the Central Norway force on a military basis. . . . All the Ministers were impressed with the gravity of the decision and they had no arguments of a controversial nature. . . . Rather a welcome change. They all, including the Prime Minister, began making up stories they could tell the public. I dare say they will make a story that will pass muster. . . . The thing that troubles me is that we have not taken the French into account, nor called a Supreme War Council to consider it.

As Ironside had anticipated, the French were shocked by the decision. They had agreed to send reinforcements only a few days before and were concerned that news of the early withdrawal would adversely affect morale at home. Churchill also worried about the consequences of the withdrawal on civilian morale. For a time Churchill even argued that the British troops should be ordered to remain in Norway to carry on the fight as irregular guerrillas, but no other military leader wanted to sacrifice the remnants of Morgan's force in the interest of civilian morale. Eventually Churchill was won over to the withdrawal on "military grounds."

But the British, having made the decision without consulting the French, left to Major General Paget the onerous task of informing the Norwegians. Even though he had arrived late on the battlefield, Paget was the senior Allied representative attached to General Ruge's headquarters and, as the senior Allied officer, he was responsible for transmitting the Allied decision to General Ruge.

The news stunned the Norwegian. "So Norway must go the way of Czechoslovakia and Poland," he commented. "But why? Why withdraw when your troops are still unbeaten?"

General Paget shrugged his shoulders and made no response.

The evacuation began on the night of April 30. French troops and what was left of Brigadier Morgan's battered 148th Brigade boarded British cruisers in the port of Åndalsnes and the nearby city of Molde. German aircraft attacked the evacuation fleet repeatedly, mounting the first night attack of the war on April 30.

The night before, the king of Norway and members of his government were taken aboard the British cruiser *Glasgow* at Molde. The captain of the *Glasgow* had to bring his vessel alongside a burning quay, with his ship's hoses playing on the flames, to receive the royal party. General Ruge embarked on a British destroyer the next day. Both king and general were taken to the arctic town of Tromsø, where, in the frigid north, the battle of Norway was still continuing, with Narvik as the prize. Norwegian troops left behind at Molde and Åndalsnes scattered through the countryside or were captured by German units. By the night of May 1 no organized resistance remained in the field to confront the advancing Germans. It had taken the Germans less than one month to conquer the heart of Norway.

There remained only the far north, and Narvik. Narvik was the grand prize of the Norwegian campaign, for the Germans as much as for the British. For Germany to lose Narvik while capturing the rest of Norway was, in effect, to lose the campaign. For the British, to win Narvik while losing the rest was really to win the battle.

Narvik itself was an attractive arctic town sitting on a stubby peninsula flanked by the waters of two fjords. In summer, when the arctic grass and moss and wildflowers burst into color, there is a narrow fringe of green where land meets water. A few scattered, stunted birch trees cling precariously to the rocky soil. Away from the water, however, the terrain is immediately harsh: gray rocks and windswept plateaus, cold and forbidding under the best of climatic conditions.

When the Germans came in early April the land lay under a blanket of snow and glistening ice, three feet deep in Narvik itself and up to eight feet in the inland valleys. As a naval base, Narvik was of minor importance. German warships could indeed find refuge in its harbor, but the town was too far from Germany for easy fueling. Nor was Narvik a vital industrial center. Its location above the Arctic Circle placed it on the periphery of Norwegian commercial and industrial concern. Only in one way was Narvik important. A single-track railway line ran from Narvik into Sweden and her northern iron-ore fields. To cut this route had been an uppermost objective in British planning. To safeguard the route had been only slightly less important to the Germans.

The British Navy reacted sharply to the German occupation. On the morning of April 9 five British destroyers under the command of Capt. B. A. W. Warburton-Lee received orders to counterattack immediately. That same afternoon after arriving off Narvik, Warburton-Lee learned from a Norwegian pilot that there were ten German destroyers inside Narvik, to his five, and that the German ships were heavier than his. Undaunted, Warburton-Lee advised his superiors that he intended "attacking at dawn high water"—dawn for surprise, high water for protection against mines.

The attack took place early on the morning of April 10, twenty-four hours after General Dietl and his troops had stepped ashore, and it was a smashing success. In two separate runs, the British destroyers sank two German destroyers and damaged three others. Six merchant ships were also sent to the bottom. Only the tanker *Jan Wellem* escaped. The first British raid caught the Germans so completely by surprise that for a time the German sailors thought they were coming under air attack. In this action, Commodore Bonte, the senior German naval officer in Narvik, was killed when his destroyer *Wilhelm Heidekamp* was torpedoed.

The British destroyers ran into trouble, however, leaving the harbor after their second attack. The five other German destroyers which had been at anchor in a side fjord arrived on the scene and opened fire. In the running battle that developed, one British destroyer was sunk and two others severely damaged, including Warburton-Lee's vessel, the *Hardy*, which beached itself in a last-ditch effort to save some of its crew from drowning. Warburton-Lee himself was critically wounded and died a few hours later.

Two of the German destroyers were also hit in this encounter, and the German ships broke off the battle, primarily because they were running low on fuel.

In terms of numbers alone, the British had outscored the Germans significantly. The Germans had two destroyers sunk and five destroyers damaged, as well as six merchant ships sunk in the inner harbor; and the ammunition vessel *Rauenfels* was sunk by the battered British destroyers as they reached the open sea. Against this number the British lost two destroyers and had a third damaged. Even more significantly, the remaining German destroyers were still bottled up in Narvik while heavier British reinforcements were steaming to the scene of action.

At noon on April 13 the British returned to mop up those vessels left afloat by Warburton-Lee on the tenth. This time the British force was built around the battleship *Warspite,* a thirty-thousand-ton vessel that had seen action in the Battle of Jutland in World War I. Risking the *Warspite* was a daring move by the British. Never before had they sent a battleship into such confined waters. But the gamble paid off. The *Warspite*'s fifteen-inch guns made quick work of a German destroyer that came within range and pounded the city of Narvik at close range. The rest of the ships in the flotilla finished off the remaining German warships inside Narvik harbor. In all, eight German destroyers and one submarine were either sunk or forced to beach themselves in the upper reaches of a fjord, there to be pounded to bits by British guns. When the *Warspite* and her escorting destroyers steamed out of Narvik they could exultantly report that all effective German naval strength in Narvik had been crushed.

Vice Admiral W. J. Whitworth, the commanding officer of the flotilla, in radioing the results of his mission to the Admiralty, predicted that the city could easily be captured. "Narvik," he reported, "can be taken by direct assault without fear of meeting serious opposition on landing."

But Whitworth, although a daring officer at sea, held back from putting ashore a landing party from his own vessels. His excuse: his troops—which had yet to see any action—would be too tired to oppose the highly trained Germans known to be in the Narvik area. Whether the small force that Whitworth had with him could have taken Narvik on the thirteenth cannot be answered, but it seems likely that the town was ripe for capture. Certainly the Germans on land thought the naval bombardment by the *Warspite* signaled the start of an Allied counterinvasion, and they had taken to the hills to escape the attack. No one was more surprised than General Dietl to see the British warships withdraw without mounting an assault. He promptly moved back into town when the British ships left.

London nevertheless absorbed the news of the second naval battle of Narvik with joy, more pleased with the results of the naval action than upset by the thought of opportunities lost. Even General Ironside, generally jealous of the good name of British ground forces, had praise for the Navy in his diary:

> The Navy have had a very fine effort in Narvik. . . . They went right up the fjord with nine destroyers and the battleship *Warspite*. Not very much resistance was made. . . . The enemy appears to have evacuated the town. There may still be 3,000 Germans there, but their centre has now gone and there should be not much difficulty in mopping up the remains of the force.

News of the British attack sent Hitler into "a state of frightful agitation." General Jodl's diary talks of "terrible excitement" inside Hitler's headquarters, with the Fuehrer himself the most excited. Without waiting to hear of any British follow-up invasion, Hitler demanded that General Dietl be given orders to withdraw from Narvik and begin a retreat southward, over harsh arctic terrain, to join with the German forces near Trondheim. German Army officers, less prone to hysteria than their leader, persuaded him to drop the idea for the time being.

Hitler's fears, although exaggerated, were based partially on a realistic appraisal of conditions at Narvik. General Dietl's position was not strong. On April 14, the day after the *Warspite* attack, Dietl had at his disposal 4,600 men, only 2,000 of whom were combat-trained infantrymen. The remaining 2,600 were sailors from the destroyers that had been beached during the British attack, and they were practically useless as ground forces. To add to his difficulties, Dietl's troops were critically short of heavy weapons and ammunition and there was little hope of receiving shipments of these vital items from Germany. British naval

German photo shows harbor at Narvik after British destroyers had done their work.
(World War II Collection of Seized Enemy Records)

General Eduard Dietl found his German forces outnumbered and outgunned at Narvik. *(World War II Collection of Seized Enemy Records)*

forces off Narvik would see to that. Dietl in effect was cut off from help from home and hemmed in by a hostile British fleet.

On April 14, an advance party of British troops—two companies of the Twenty-fourth Scots Guards—landed at Harstad to the north of Narvik, joining forces with the Norwegians there and adding one more element to General Dietl's long list of difficulties.

The arrival of British troops increased Hitler's fears to the breaking point. On April 16 he again insisted that General Dietl's force either withdraw into Sweden or be evacuated by air. General Jodl argued against a withdrawal into Sweden on political grounds and pointed out to Hitler that evacuation by air was "impossible"—Germany did not have enough long-range aircraft for the job. Hitler remained unsatisfied. On the afternoon of April 17, against the advice of his Army commanders, he signed an order giving General Dietl authority to withdraw into Sweden. This time the Army had to act more subtly to thwart the Fuehrer's will. Hitler's message was delayed long enough for Gen. Walther von Brauchitsch, the Army commander-in-chief, to dispatch his own message to Dietl, in which he congratulated Dietl on his promotion to lieutenant general and expressed his confidence that Dietl would manage to "defend Narvik even against a superior enemy." General Jodl, meanwhile, was arguing with Hitler that withdrawal would be disastrous for the morale of the entire Army. In the end, a worried Hitler agreed to a new order advising Dietl to hold Narvik as long as possible.

With evacuation ruled out, the Germans moved to reinforce Narvik by air. Ten Junkers 52s landed on the ice of a nearby lake and disembarked a battery of mountain artillery. Negotiations were also started with Sweden for permission to use the Swedish railway to reinforce Narvik. Sweden at first refused, arguing that such a request violated her neutrality, but eventually Sweden buckled to German demands. The first train reached Narvik from Sweden carrying rations, medical supplies, and a group of German radio technicians. More than 230 specialists of various kinds were brought to Narvik through Sweden in the month of May and close to eight hundred German merchant sailors and injured servicemen were evacuated from Narvik over the same route.

The British ground attack against Narvik gathered momentum slowly and was marked by disputes between the senior naval officer, Admiral of the Fleet, the Earl of Cork, and the senior Army officer, Maj. Gen. P. J. Mackesy. Lord Cork wanted to stage a landing at Narvik on the morning of April 15 with 350 Scots Guards and 200 sailors but was forced to abandon the idea because of objections from General Mackesy. On the next day General Mackesy again rejected a proposal to attack Narvik directly on the grounds that it would be difficult to land weapons on beaches covered with deep snow, and he did not feel his troops were equal to the task of taking on German defenders.

Within days the Admiralty and the War Office in London were pressing for an immediate assault, but General Mackesy continued to have serious misgivings. On April 19, after a reconnaissance of Narvik, General Mackesy reported that any attempt to land in Narvik would involve the destruction of the Twenty-fourth Guards Brigade. Instead of a direct assault, General Mackesy conceived a plan to induce the Germans to surrender by means of a naval bombardment. If the Germans surrendered under bombardment, General Mackesy was prepared to land troops. Otherwise he would not risk an assault.

The bombardment took place on April 24 with the battleship *Warspite* again leading the attack, supported by two cruisers and eight destroyers. General Dietl, convinced that the bombardment heralded an Allied landing, informed General Falkenhorst that if his troops could not hold the city they would fall back along the railroad toward Sweden. But there was never any thought of surrender, and after a bombardment lasting three hours the British vessels withdrew, having accomplished little more than the razing of several buildings in the town.

Winston Churchill was appalled by Mackesy's lack of aggressiveness. Even General Ironside, Mackesy's immediate superior, grew disillusioned with Mackesy's performance. When Mackesy had been appointed to command the Army forces in Narvik Ironside had drafted a personal letter in which he had instructed Mackesy that "boldness is required." By April 25, Ironside was scribbling in his diary, "I think that Mackesy is not doing very much in the way of pushing."

Mackesy did, however, have a plan for seizure of Narvik. It called for a deliberate and scientific campaign of encirclement and eventual assault which, he hoped, would bring Narvik falling "like a ripe plum" into Allied hands. The first major land engagement took place on April 24—the same day of the second bombardment of Narvik by *Warspite*—and it pitted four Norwegian battalions that had placed themselves under General Mackesy's command against German defenders to the north of Narvik. It was a bloody beginning for the Norwegians. German troops beat back the Norwegians easily, killing almost half of the Norwegian troops and an especially large number of company commanders. But Mackesy's forces were growing daily and the Allied advance pressed on, although progress was painfully slow. In more than two weeks of fighting to the north of Narvik, Mackesy's forces advanced a mere five miles while British troops that had landed to the south of the city were practically stalled in their tracks. Mackesy blamed "climatic difficulties" for his slow advance, complaining that "the country was covered with snow up to four feet or more in depth. Troops who were not equipped with and skilled in the use of skis or snowshoes were absolutely incapable of operating tactically at all. I had no such troops at my disposal when I first landed."

Three battalions of French Chasseurs Alpins, arriving late in April, gave Mackesy some troops trained in mountain warfare. They were followed in early May by two battalions of the French Foreign Legion and by four battalions of Polish troops who, although styled *chasseurs du nord,* had received no training in mountain warfare. The battlefield effectiveness of the Allied force improved only marginally as the campaign ground on. At all times Allied troops were severely hampered by the terrain and weather. Even the Chasseurs Alpins performed poorly in the arctic mountains. The Allies had to rely on sheer weight of numbers to beat back the Germans. Eventually the pressure grew great enough to worry General Dietl. On May 13 he warned General Falkenhorst that his troops were close to exhaustion. On the fifteenth, he warned that his northern front would break unless reinforcements arrived immediately by air. By May 21 German troops were near rebellion. Units resisted orders to move from one position to another and some were so tired that they fell asleep under machine-gun fire. It remained for the Allies to press their attacks one more time and Narvik would assuredly fall.

The final attack came on May 28. An Allied force numbering 25,000 men fell on Narvik from all sides and seized the town, but failed to prevent General Dietl and his troops from slipping out of the city at the last minute. Dietl retreated along the railway to Sweden, determined to hold a bridgehead along the Swedish border for as long as possible.

Relief was coming for Dietl, however, from an unexpected quarter. The Allies themselves, having captured Narvik, the prize that had loomed so importantly in their thinking, now abandoned the city because of the

French mountain troops strike confident pose before seeing action in Narvik.
(Norsk Telegrambyra)

need for reinforcements to bolster the defense of Britain. The German *Blitzkrieg* against France launched on May 10 had placed once important Narvik far down on the list of priorities. By the end of May Winston Churchill, who had taken over as Prime Minister, was calling for the urgent return of all Allied troops in Norway.

The evacuation of Narvik started on June 3 as the first of 15,000 soldiers climbed aboard troopships for the trip back home. The vessels carrying these men sailed on June 7. A second group of troopships took on the remainder of the Allied force, numbering 9,500 men, on June 8. King Haakon and his government, after a last-minute effort to neutralize Narvik under Swedish supervision, sailed for England as well, departing on the British cruiser *Devonshire*.

The Norwegians in Narvik were particularly disillusioned by the Allied decision to withdraw and by the manner in which they were informed. The decision had been kept from them until after Narvik itself had been captured, because the British, always suspicious of their Norwegian allies, assumed that the Norwegians would lay down their arms if they knew beforehand about the planned withdrawal. General Ruge did not hear the news until the morning of June 2, at a time when he and his staff were planning their last drive to push the Germans out of Norway into Sweden. The withdrawal left many of the Norwegians convinced of British duplicity and betrayal. General Ruge, although offered the chance to escape to England, chose to remain with his soldiers.

The evacuation of Narvik caught General Dietl completely by surprise. He didn't discover that the Allied forces had left until late in the afternoon of June 8, but then he responded quickly. By the evening of the same day Dietl's troops were back in Narvik. Two days later a member of General Ruge's staff signed an armistice which ended the fighting between German forces in the area and the men of the Sixth Norwegian Division.

So Norway was taken. In view of the massive killings that took place later in the war on other fronts, it was a minor campaign. The cost to Germany was 1,317 killed and 2,375 lost at sea. The Allies suffered heavier losses. The British lost approximately 4,400 men on land and at sea. The Norwegian losses numbered 1,335 men, while the French and Poles lost another 530 men.

Losses at sea were heavy, for there had been naval engagements up and down the Norwegian coast throughout the campaign. Britain lost her aircraft carrier *Glorious* (sunk by the pocket battleships *Scharnhorst* and *Gneisenau* during the final days of the evacuation of Narvik), the cruisers *Effingham* and *Curlew*, as well as four submarines and nine destroyers. Germany lost her new heavy cruiser *Bluecher* in the waters of Oslo Fjord, as well as two other light cruisers, the *Koenigsberg* and *Karlsruhe*, ten destroyers, one torpedo boat, six submarines, and fifteen small naval aircraft. More important, many of Germany's major vessels were damaged. The pocket battleship *Scharnhorst* was torpedoed and damaged on June 9 by a British destroyer. Her sister ship *Gneisenau* was torpedoed on June 20 while returning to Germany from Trondheim. The warships *Luetzow, Hipper,* and *Emden* were also damaged in sea engagements during the campaign.

At the end of the fighting, Germany had only one heavy cruiser and two light cruisers fit for action, a fact which Churchill said was "of major importance, potentially affecting the whole future of the war."

Considered in its totality, the German invasion and capture of Norway was a superb success for German arms. It was the first joint operation involving all three branches of the armed services. Despite rivalries and bickering, they functioned effectively on most occasions. The campaign won for Germany control of the supply line for Swedish iron ore and several new naval bases from which German warships could break out into the Atlantic.

Hitler was pleased with the success of his armed services. The Norwegian campaign was, he boasted, "not only bold, but one of the sauciest undertakings in the history of modern warfare."

For Great Britain, the Norwegian campaign revealed critical flaws in the Allied command structure and weaknesses in combat effectiveness of British commanders and troops. Lack of coordination between services, hastily planned and poorly equipped expeditions, and cautious commanders all contributed to the Allied defeat.

Hitler's comment on Britain's performance in Norway was biting. "From the military point of view," Hitler observed, "it can only be described as frivolous dilettantism."

For Norway, the campaign was a disaster. Her armed forces had been crushed. Her king and government had fled to London. German military commanders were in control of the country. The ease of the German victory, coming on the heels of her successes in Austria, Czechoslovakia, and Poland, gave Germany an air of invincibility. German victories in Holland, Belgium, and France, coming at the tail end of the Norwegian campaign, wiped out all hope that the Allies would or could return to Norway's aid. By any objective standards of evaluation, the future certainly belonged to Hitler and Germany.

Against this background of despair and defeat, a crushed and demoralized Norway entered, in the summer of 1940, the darkest period of her existence.

8

The Civilian Front in Norway

While the battles for Norway flared, one after the other, throughout the length of the land, another struggle began to take shape behind German lines that had as its objective the hearts and minds of the Norwegian people. More subtle than the clash of arms, yet equally important in the long run, this struggle was destined to continue through the entire occupation and to color even the postwar years with its bitter psychological legacy.

Vidkun Quisling, the arrogant and dogmatic Norwegian Nazi, threw himself into the political fight immediately after receiving Hitler's surprise endorsement on the evening of April 9. By the morning of the tenth, Quisling had embarked on a series of meetings with leading Norwegian businessmen, trade-union leaders, and public officials seeking support for a *Nasjonal Samling* government with himself at its head. To Quisling's shock, he met rebuffs at almost every turn instead of the enthusiastic acceptance he had anticipated. Even Hitler's backing proved ineffectual in winning public support. Oslo's intellectual elite snubbed him, its labor leaders scoffed at him, and almost all men of repute recoiled from close affiliation with him, spurning his offers of government posts. Two high Army officers who had been undecided on the course they should follow quickly rejoined their units after hearing Quisling publicly name them as prospective government officials.

Quisling emissaries sent to negotiate with King Haakon returned empty-handed and the Norwegian press, with the exception of his party's own paper, *Fritt Folk*, found him an object of ridicule and derision. Quisling gained support only from a few staunch reactionaries and from a small band of opportunists who saw in the German invasion the start of a New Order for Norway, but those who rallied to his banner had such little standing among Norwegians that the German military attaché in Oslo, Gen. Bruno Uthman, described Quisling's proposed cabinet as a "gangster government." Uthman thought Quisling himself nothing more than a common "criminal."

Quisling's prestige evaporated almost overnight. Even those Germans who first looked with favor upon Quisling as a promising puppet began to have second thoughts. A German officer who asked the clerk of the Storting how many *Nasjonal Samling* members had been represented in the preinvasion Parliament could hardly believe the answer, "None at all." When German authorities gained access to a list of Quisling supporters, they were dismayed to learn that his followers included a heavy percentage of young people still in school, but very few men or women of influence or power.

The German Army soon became totally disillusioned with Quisling. When, on April 12, three days after he had proclaimed himself Prime Minister, Quisling sought to assert his personal power by dismissing the Oslo police chief, Army officials to whom the police official turned for guidance shrugged off Quisling disdainfully. "Ignore him," a high German officer advised. "He does not matter in the least."

The next day a frantic Quisling sent a personal emissary to Berlin to plead his case with Hitler, but already it was too late. Hitler had turned against him. Two days later the Germans kicked him out of office, publicly stripping him of his title. German infantrymen hustled an enraged Quisling and his supporters out of their headquarters in the Continental Hotel. Only in one way did Hitler ease Quisling's humiliation. He insisted that Quisling be given an "honorable position" and "held in reserve" against the day when his services might be needed again. The exact nature of Quisling's new post was left to the German minister in Norway, Curt Brauer, whose opinion of Quisling had sunk even lower since their first encounter. Brauer gleefully named Quisling to a newly established position as Norway's Commissioner of Demobilization, a meaningless post without duties or power.

Quisling's reign as Prime Minister had lasted only six days.

But he put up a good front. His party paper *Fritt Folk* boldly commented, "We have taken a step backward, but we shall soon take two steps forward."

It was Brauer's turn next to run afoul of Hitler. Having failed in his negotiations with King Haakon and having supported the ouster of Quisling, Brauer found himself under pressure to provide a Norwegian government with whom Germany could negotiate. He was, therefore, most receptive when a group of influential Norwegians led by Paal Berg, the chief justice of the Supreme Court, and Bishop Eivind Berggrav, the leader of Norway's Lutheran Church, proposed the establishment of a civil Administrative Council which would handle the practical problems of life in the occupied areas.

The chief justice, a stickler for legal detail, warned Brauer that the council did not intend to involve itself in questions of national policy, for that was the domain of King Haakon and the legal Norwegian government. The council, Berg said, would deal only with the administration of necessary civilian services, out of concern for the well-being of innocent Norwegian civilians. Brauer quickly agreed, but while assuring Berg that he understood and accepted the limitations of the council's functions, he secretly nursed the hope that the council could in time be transformed into an alternative government around which the Norwegian people could rally.

Consequently, Brauer filed enthusiastic reports on the proposed council to Berlin and made the grave mistake of describing the council as a "government council," a distortion he hoped time would validate. On the basis of these glowing but inaccurate reports, Ribbentrop and Hitler became convinced that Brauer had accomplished his task of establishing a viable Norwegian government and gave their approval to the council, which came into existence on April 15, the same day Quisling was ousted from office. It took only two days for Hitler to learn of Brauer's deception. When he did, he angrily recalled the envoy and dismissed him from the Foreign Service. Brauer never again held a diplomatic post, and eventually was sent to the Western Front as a soldier.

But Hitler had his Administrative Council, and for a time it appeared as if it would provide him with the alternate government he urgently sought. Council members, loyal supporters of their king as they were, proved willing to work with German authorities for the benefit of the Norwegian population. Chief Justice Berg took it upon himself to inform King Haakon what had happened. His message reached the king, who was then retreating up the Gudbrandsdal with his government, via the Norwegian legation in Stockholm.

> The Supreme Court has considered it necessary to be instrumental to the institution of a Council of Administration to carry on the civilian administration in the occupied areas. . . . Confident that the King of Norway under the present extraordinary circumstances will approve. . . .

And King Haakon did approve. For a day or two the council found itself in a strange twilight position, working under German authorities with the blessing of the king of Norway. The arrangement could not last, however. The council soon succumbed to intense German pressure and called on the Norwegian crown prince to appeal to his people to "abstain from all acts of sabotage and violence."

It was too much for King Haakon, who angrily chastised the council for interfering in the war. "Nobody," he commented, "can expect that I or the crown prince should admonish the people to obey German orders."

The king's rejection of the council caught Hitler at his shakiest. British troops had just landed at Åndalsnes and Namsos and Hitler feared the outcome of the battle. On top of these military considerations, Hitler realized that he had no Norwegian government to deal with. He reacted sharply, deciding to appoint a *Reichskommissar* for Norway who would hold supreme command in the country with complete authority over all civilian matters.

As *Reichskommissar* of Norway Hitler chose an old-line Nazi, the forty-one-year-old Joseph Terboven, a functionary known for his loyalty to the party. Terboven had been a flier in World War I and had joined the Nazi Party in the 1920s, rising up the ranks by his strong-arm tactics as the leader of street-fighting gangs who battled in "Red" strongholds of the Weimar Republic. By 1927 he was an important member of the party, and by 1933 he had become *Gauleiter* of Essen, a post from which Hitler plucked him for his Norwegian assignment.

The title *Reichskommissar* had a long and honored place in German history, having been used to designate special representatives of the central German government who were assigned to deal with emergency situations that normal governmental agencies could not handle. In the Third Reich, Hitler added political functions to the job, making the post an exceptionally powerful one. As *Reichskommissar* in Norway, Terboven represented not only the German state but the Nazi Party as well.

Terboven, a short, thin, humorless man with an icily cold manner, arrived in Oslo on April 24 and immediately issued a proclamation to the occupied districts: "By order of the Fuehrer, I have, as *Reichskommissar,* taken over for the duration of the Occupation. . . ." Norway's master had arrived. Throughout the long years of the war, Terboven wielded ultimate power in Norway, with an authority greater even than that of General Falkenhorst or of the German secret police.

Terboven came to Norway with two major objectives in mind. He was determined to advance Germany's total war effort by all possible means and he was determined, like Minister Brauer before him, to organize a government inside Norway that would be pliable to German pressure and capable of controlling the Norwegian population. First Terboven had to consolidate German control over the civilian population, and he began his efforts by moving against the Norwegian press.

Direct censorship was imposed on Norwegian newspapers and radio stations, and Nazi journalists were installed to head both the Norwegian Telegram Bureau, the agency which handled news from abroad, and the news department of the Norwegian Broadcasting Company. Even before Terboven's arrival, one Norwegian newspaper pleaded for understanding in its editorial column: "Our readers must understand that the job of a newspaperman is not easy nowadays." Under Terboven, all press freedoms were wiped out. By early June he had detailed rules ready for the guidance of reporters and editors: All reports of German losses or British victories were forbidden. There could be no coverage of any speeches by the king or members of the Nygaardsvold government, nor any pictures of the king. There could be no criticism of German authorities and official German communiqués had to be given prominent play. All foreign news was to be commented on in the "German spirit," and only good economic news of "progress" and "improved conditions" could be printed.

With the press under control, Terboven moved next to break the ties between the Norwegian people and King Haakon and his government, by then in exile in England. The campaign against the king began in the press on June 10. All major newspapers published that day carried editorials accusing the king of betraying his patriotic duty by fleeing the country, and demanded his dethronement and the elimination of the exiled Nygaardsvold government as the legitimate government representing the country.

The next day Terboven called representatives of the four major Norwegian political parties to his office to discuss the formation of a new government sympathetic to Germany. Negotiations began on the day Paris fell. To soften up the Norwegians, Terboven warned that if they were not cooperative, the Germans would impose a Government of Commissars who, he warned, would "rush at you like bulls." On the other hand, he assured the Norwegians that "Hitler is a friend of heroic conduct. If I tell him that it has been a great sacrifice for the Norwegian people to depose the king and the government, the Norwegians would, by this sacrifice, win from him something essential."

In less than a week, the Norwegian politicians and public leaders, with the exception of Chief Justice Berg, who withdrew from the talks, adopted a German proposal calling for the establishment of a special governmental State Council, the *Riksrad*, and the ouster of the old government. In its first proclamation the *Riksrad* announced:

> The Nygaardsvold Government can no longer be recognized as the Government. As the King is resident outside the frontiers of the country, he is unable to exert his constitutional functions.

The *Riksrad* followed up with an "urgent demand" that King Haakon abdicate "in consideration of the welfare of the nation and the future of the country."

But Haakon, safe in London, had no intention of resigning. Even though Norway was under German occupation, Haakon managed to follow the negotiations in Oslo closely, obtaining daily and precise reports via the Swedish capital of Stockholm. He was ready with his reply when he received the *Riksrad* message requesting his abdication. It was broadcast over the British Broadcasting Corporation Radio:

> If I was persuaded that at this time I would serve best by abdicating, or

if I was certain that back of the request stood a majority of the
Norwegian people, I would, deeply as it would hurt me to separate
myself from Norway, grant the request you present to me.

Haakon went on to argue, however, that the request for his abdication was unconstitutional and had been drafted under pressure from a
foreign power. "The Norwegian people's freedom and independence,"
he continued, "is for me the constitution's firm command and I intend to
follow this firm command and guard the Norwegian people's interest best
by holding fast to the position and duty a free people conferred upon me."

Under Terboven's instructions Norwegian newspapers refused to
print the text of the king's response. Instead, the newspapers unanimously
condemned King Haakon for failing his nation in its hour of need. But the
news of the king's declaration spread by word of mouth. Those with
radios who heard the original broadcast on the BBC passed the news on to
neighbors, who in turn told friends and acquaintances, until almost everyone in Norway knew the reasons given by the king for his refusal to
abdicate. The king's declaration clarified the political issue for thousands
upon thousands of Norwegians. By rejecting the demand that he abdicate,
the King provided a rallying point for those Norwegians who despaired at
the thought of collaborating with the Germans.

Churchgoing Norwegians resorted to chain letters, which had seized
the fancy of the country in the 1930s, to mobilize opposition to collaboration. One letter began:

Thou shalt obey King Haakon . . . thou shalt detest Hitler . . . thou
shalt regard as a traitor every Norwegian who keeps company with
Germans or Quislings at home . . . thou shalt despise treason and
remember that its punishment is death. . . .

The letter continued in this vein until a litany of ten political commandments was completed. It was, in the summer of 1940, all that sustained the
hope of many Norwegians.

That summer and the autumn that followed were a depressing time
for Norway. The Germans, with most of Europe at their mercy, applied
constant pressure on Norwegian politicians. Terboven kept insisting that
ties with the king be cut. In September, a docile Norwegian Parliament,
convened at the summons of the *Reichskommissar,* complied with his
wishes by declaring the Royal House had ceased to reign for the duration
of the war.

Terboven moved quickly to consolidate internal control. In late
September he established by fiat a new commissariat government staffed
completely with Quisling supporters. Surprisingly, Quisling himself was
not one of the new commissar-ministers, for Terboven was still not sure
how the public would respond to him. But Quisling remained as leader of

the *Nasjonal Samling* Party and Terboven, despite his doubts about Quisling personally, banked heavily on the *Nasjonal Samling* Party for the future. After naming his new ministers, Terboven, again by decree, abolished all political parties in Norway with the lone exception of the *Nasjonal Samling* Party and then, in a crowning touch, he rewarded the Norwegian Parliament for its previous compliance with his wishes by abolishing it as well. From the end of September onward, Norwegians had no elected representatives in Oslo, they had only one legal party to which they could belong, and they found themselves ruled by fifteen pro-German ministers, all of whom held their office by appointment of the *Reichskommissar.*

The machinery for control was thus in Terboven's hands. It remained only for him to use it wisely to assume control over other Norwegian institutions and, through them, over the rank and file of the Norwegian people.

It appeared an easy task. Norway was an extraordinarily structured society. Almost every Norwegian belonged to one or more national organizations representing various professions, businesses, labor unions, and social and athletic groups. Teachers had their own organization, as did the clergy and the doctors. Telephone and telegraph workers were organized; so were transport workers and farmers and bankers. And it was these organizations, numbering close to fifty throughout the country, that Terboven planned to infiltrate and intimidate until they too went along with the New Order. In this effort the new Quislingite commissar-ministers proved willing accomplices.

The first attack came on the legal front. In November, 1940, the new minister of justice, Svere Riisnaes, decreed that he alone had the right to appoint or dismiss jury members and other court officials. Riisnaes followed up with a second decree threatening that any judge, including those presiding over the nation's highest courts, could be forced into early retirement if the minister of justice believed that retirement would be for the good of the country. As most of Norway's most eminent judges were already close to retirement age, they quickly perceived that they faced immediate dismissal if they refused to bow to Riisnaes' authority. Alarmed, the judges appealed directly to Terboven, but he backed up his handpicked minister. In a haughty letter to the Supreme Court, he bluntly told the judges that they should not presume to question any decree issued in his name. Only the German *Reichskommissar* had the authority to decide what measures had to be taken to assure public office in Norway. Faced with Terboven's ultimatum, all members of the Supreme Court resigned. It was an act of symbolic opposition to Terboven's rule which shocked the Norwegian people, but it nevertheless left the court without any judges, and it was exactly what Terboven had desired. Under his direction, Minister Riisnaes promptly named judges sympathetic to the new regime to fill the vacancies. The highest court in the land had been taken over.

Terboven moved next against the clergy of Norway's established Lutheran Church. Acting on Terboven's instructions, the minister of culture demanded that the Norwegian state radio make time available in its regular religious programming periods for "sympathetic sermons" and that clergymen make broadcasts sympathetic to the regime. The first clergyman to volunteer opened his sermon by "thanking God for men like Quisling." He continued: "Now the day dawns. Quisling and his men have found a field in which to work and work in peace. I call upon you to give thanks and praise."

Terboven wanted more than mere verbal support from the Lutheran priests, however, for he fully understood the close ties that existed between the clergy and their parishioners. And he knew that in the privacy of confessional meetings many secrets were shared, of both a personal and political nature, that clergymen were prohibited from divulging by the strictures of the Church's traditional oath of silence. What passed between priest and worshiper was, by the traditions of the Church and the custom of the country, inviolable by secular authorities. And it was this oath of silence that Terboven attacked next, abolishing by decree and authorizing the imprisonment of any priest who refused to divulge details of a confession when called to do so by "competent authority."

It was too much for the Norwegian Lutheran Church. In January, 1941, the Lutheran bishops protested not only what they saw as an attempt to coerce the Church but also the general oppression inflicted on the people of Norway, citing acts of terror by Gestapo agents, violence by members of Quisling's stormtrooper organization, *Hird,* the tampering with Norwegian justice, as well as the arbitrary abolishment of the oath of silence.

The Church protest went into specific detail on individual cases of brutality: In November, a band of *Hird* youths had forced their way into the Oslo School of Business and had attacked pupils and teachers with fists and clubs. In December, a sixteen-year-old Oslo youth had been seized for wearing a paper clip in his lapel, then a symbol of national solidarity, and taken to the cellar of the *Hird* headquarters, where he was stripped and lashed with his belt. That same month, the head of the student association in Trondheim had been beaten repeatedly for refusing to post placards for the *Nasjonal Samling* Party. "Can the church sit quietly by," the Church protest concluded, "while the commandments of God are set aside?"

Fifty thousand copies of the protest were run off and even though German authorities confiscated twenty thousand of them, the remainder were delivered to churches throughout the country. From there they were distributed to parishioners.

The bishops' protest reinforced the impact of the resignation of the Supreme Court justices. Two of the most respected institutions of the land had come out in opposition to the Nazis.

At this point the struggle intensified. Additional Norwegian organizations became involved. The medical association protested the appointment of *Nasjonal Samling* members to positions for which they were not qualified. Athletes refused to participate in sporting competitions under the *N.S.* banner.

Organizations began to cooperate with one another. When the minister of the interior set up a special bureau to check the political attitude of civil-service workers, twenty-two organizations of civil servants protested directly to Reichskommissar Terboven. Their letter produced no change in the regime's policies—members of the *Nasjonal Samling* Party still received preferential treatment—but it sent Terboven into a fit of anger. He was enraged not only by the fact that twenty-two organizations had banded together in anti-Nazi solidarity, but also by the fact that the text of their message had been broadcasted by the BBC's Norwegian desk even before the letter reached Terboven's desk.

The Norwegian organizations, emboldened by the joint action of the twenty-two national groups, intensified their protests. In mid-May, no fewer than forty-three national organizations, with a combined membership of 750,000—approximately one-quarter of the total Norwegian population—filed a written protest with Terboven denouncing the policy of Nazification and attacking all Nazi-inspired proclamations and decisions as "openly contrary to law."

The protest posed an open challenge to Terboven's rule and stung the *Reichskommissar* into action. Gestapo agents interrogated the most prominent leaders of the various organizations in their offices and homes. Three of the most outspoken were arrested and disappeared into Gestapo headquarters in Oslo. The rest were summoned at short notice to the Parliament building in Oslo for a personal dressing down by Terboven. Armed German guards lined the walls of the meeting room as the Norwegian leaders entered. Terboven marched in soon after, quivering with rage, his manner particularly abusive and menacing. He warned those assembled before him of the consequences of their protest and threatened that he would not tolerate any resistance from the organization leaders. To reinforce his warning, Terboven had guards seize six more leaders and place them under arrest in the assembly hall while the others looked on in terror. Then he dismissed those who remained with a final warning not to "create trouble."

New decrees followed soon afterward. Several national organizations were dissolved while those that were permitted to continue in existence received new directors, all of them *Nasjonal Samling* men whose primary allegiance was to their party and not to the organizations they now headed.. Terboven left untouched only the trade unions, out of fear of disrupting the Norwegian economy.

Terboven's angry crackdown touched off a strange transformation in the organizations involved. The arrival of Quislingite leaders at the offices of the groups that were permitted to remain in existence sparked mass resignations from the membership, leaving the organizations empty shells of what they had once been, with few members, discredited leaders, and little influence with the public. Those organizations that were dissolved simply went out of existence, or so it appeared on the surface.

Beneath the surface, however, all national organizations continued in operation as illegal underground groups. Throughout Norway, a network of "B," or illegal, organizations developed, with a membership drawn from those men and women who had resigned from the official organizations. By the summer of 1941, these "B" organizations, with their "B" leaders, came to hold far more power than did the legal organizations with their Quislingite directors. In time the "B" organizations would develop into the framework for an organized civilian resistance. During the summer of 1941, however, the groups were hard pressed to maintain contact with their members in the vague terrain of the underground. What was needed was a major incident of oppression to propel the organizations into action. And Terboven, with the help of a resurrected Quisling, soon provided the incident.

From the first days of the occupation, the German authorities, with the backing of Quisling and his *Nasjonal Samling* leaders, recognized the importance of the Norwegian school system as a potential instrument for the propagation of Nazi philosophy.

On taking office as minister for church and education in the fall of 1941, Ragnar Skancke, a close associate of Quisling and an ardent Nazi, sought to introduce the New Order into Norway's educational system. Skancke ordered revisions of all textbooks on constitutional law and European history to bring them into harmony with the new philosophy. He ordered the immediate elimination of all English-language texts and substituted the German language for English as the country's second language, which all schoolchildren were required to learn. Portraits of Quisling were hung in schools and disciplinary measures imposed against any student or teacher who dared take them down. Most distasteful to Norwegian teachers, however, was Skancke's insistence that the teachers use the classrooms to indoctrinate students in the Nazi philosophy, a directive that the majority of teachers saw fit to ignore. Throughout the country, the teachers met regularly in underground "B" organization cells to discuss how they could best oppose the policies of Skancke and his henchmen who were being placed in local control of the schools. At best, it was a standoff, with Skancke's men in control of the school administration and the bulk of the country's anti-Nazi teachers in effective control of the students in the classrooms.

By early 1942 Terboven was ready for a more determined effort to break the resistance of the teachers. Once again, Quisling entered the picture.

Since his ouster from power in April, 1940, Quisling had devoted himself to building the membership rolls of the *Nasjonal Samling* Party, which before the invasion numbered no more than four thousand. The presence and power of German occupying forces helped him gain new recruits. Seven thousand Norwegians joined in the month of October, 1940, following the formation of the commissariat government. By the end of 1940 *Nasjonal Samling*'s membership stood at 26,000 and it was still going up.

Quisling was overjoyed. When his membership topped thirty thousand, he contacted Berlin to inform the Chancellery that his party's membership in relation to the Norwegian population "was approximately the equivalent" of Hitler's party's "strength when it came to power." Quisling's not-so-subtle reminder was unnecessary. The growth of the party had been noted in Berlin. Hitler was beginning to look more sympathetically upon Quisling again, and Alfred Rosenberg, Quisling's old friend from the 1930s, continued to be a strong supporter. Rosenberg advocated a second chance for Quisling at every opportunity. German

Norwegian Nazis—members of the *Nasjonal Samling* Party—meet in Oslo in February, 1941. Sign reads, "With Quisling for Norway." *(Wide World Photo)*

officials in Norway, however, remained unconvinced that Quisling could handle the task. But by January of 1942 a combination of events and trends combined to persuade Terboven that possibly he could make use of Quisling after all. Terboven's attempt to take over Norwegian institutions through his commissariat government had proved less than successful. He needed a new approach. When the membership of the *Nasjonal Samling* Party hit the forty-thousand mark, Terboven decided that the time had arrived for Quisling to play a public role in Norwegian politics. He acted quickly, summoning Quisling to a meeting, where he informed the startled Norwegian that he would be allowed to form a new government.

Quisling, momentarily set back by Terboven's abrupt change, recovered quickly and tried to capitalize on the unexpected developments. He wanted to assume office with the appearance of autonomy, and he suggested to Terboven that Norway and Germany sign a preliminary peace treaty before he took over as Minister President. Such a treaty would enable Quisling to appeal to the Norwegian people from a position of strength. He also demanded a reduction in the number of German administrators in Norway, another move that he was sure would be popular with the people. In Quisling's mind a heady picture was forming: He would head a united nation, which, while aligned both militarily and philosophically with the Third Reich, would otherwise be independent. Under Quisling, Norway would offer Germany friendly cooperation within the framework of the greater Germanic ideal, equal nations committed to the same goals and aspirations. At least that was Quisling's dream.

Terboven, however, saw in Quisling a political tool of questionable efficiency who was being offered the chance to consolidate pro-German opinion in Norway, if he could. The *Reichskommissar* brushed aside Quisling's demands, placating the Norwegian's ruffled feelings by promising to take the questions up with Hitler after Quisling assumed office.

Quisling could not resist. He capitulated immediately, agreeing to take office on Terboven's vague promises that the matter would be settled in the summer.

Quisling assumed his new post as Minister President on February 1, 1942, in a colorful ceremony in Oslo's Akershus Castle, where the Norwegian Army had its headquarters. The guest list glittered with top Nazis. Hitler's confidant, Martin Bormann, came from Berlin for the occasion. Terboven was there as was Police General Rediess. Representatives of the German Navy and the Wehrmacht attended, and so did members of all German administrative units. Quisling wore his gray *Hird* uniform for the occasion and stood at attention as an honor guard representing seven Norwegian regiments marched by. The Norwegian flag was raised over Akershus Castle and the Parliament building to indicate to the country in symbolic fashion that Norway had a government of its own. In the evening, Quisling gave a banquet for those who attended the ceremony in Villa Grandi, a large mansion in the suburb of Bygdo which Quisling took over for his own use. Eventually he renamed the villa Gimle (Home of the Gods) in honor of its new inhabitants.

Quisling moved almost immediately against the teachers. On February 5, he established a new Teachers' Front, with membership obligatory for all teachers, and appointed Orvar Saether, the former chief of staff of the hated *Hird* strong-arm force, to become the organization's first leader.

Fritt Folk, Quisling's official organ, declared that the Teachers' Front "will serve as a straight jacket for all those who are unwilling to do their duty to the State and to Norwegian youth."

Membership in the *Nasjonal Samling* was strongly advised. Saether warned in a speech that while individual teachers would not be compelled to join the party, they would in time "no doubt find it appropriate to do so."

Quisling had other innovations in mind. On the day after he issued his decree establishing the Teachers' Front, he issued another decree establishing a *Nasjonal Samling* Youth Movement, modeled after the Hitler Youth Movement in Germany. Membership was compulsory for all Norwegian youngsters between the ages of ten and eighteen. "The Youth Movement," Quisling explained, "gives us control of 400,000 young people from whom we shall select those who are to be trained for membership in our party."

Both measures, if implemented, would eventually give Quisling extraordinary powers to influence the minds of young Norwegians. The Youth Movement would provide control over students; the Teachers' Front would provide control over the teachers who taught them. Both decrees worked hand in hand.

But the drive against the teachers was only Quisling's first foray of a much wider battle. Victory over the teachers would set a pattern by which he could win control over other professional and trade oganizations and thus build for himself a framework for even greater political power.

For the teachers, however, the time for decision was at hand: whether to bow to the demands of the Norwegian Nazis and join the Teachers' Front or reject membership and lose their jobs. The leaders of the underground "B" organization thrashed over the issues for days before deciding to organize the teachers throughout the country and in a mass action reject membership in the Teachers' Front. The letters of rejection were to be drafted in the same words and mailed on the same day—February 20—to heighten the impact of the action. With this decision made, the leaders of the "B" group, using a secret communications system organized the year before which bypassed the German censors, dispatched letters to teachers in all towns and hamlets of the country, instructing them in the precise words to use in their letter of protest.

The results surpassed even their wildest hopes. Twelve thousand out of Norway's fourteen thousand teachers rejected the Teachers' Front in identical words. Quisling faced an organized civilian resistance. Within a week, when the teachers refused to back down, arrests began. Under Saether's personal direction, three hundred teachers, among them many of the most prominent in their communities, were sentenced to compulsory manual labor "as an example to others."

Three weeks later, when the great majority of the country's teachers still refused to join the Teachers' Front, Saether ordered another series of sweeping arrests: 290 in Oslo, 200 in Bergen, 100 in Trondheim, hundreds more in other smaller cities and towns throughout the length of the land. By the end of March, Quisling had more than thirteen hundred teachers in custody. Most were penned in the Grini concentration camp outside Oslo while Quisling used the threat of forced labor in the arctic alongside Russian prisoners of war in an attempt to break their will.

"Since they are so fond of Bolshevism," he gloated, "they can now find out what it is like to share the conditions of their Bolshevik friends."

The Grini camp commandant sneered at the teachers. "Filthy Norwegian schoolmasters," he remarked, "cannot oppose the New Order in Europe."

Close to seven hundred teachers were selected for transport to the arctic. They left Grini packed in railway cattle cars, headed first for a rural concentration camp at Jorstadmoen, where they underwent an exhausting program of physical harassment: gymnastic exercise at the double, belly crawls through slush, and constant work details on meaningless tasks. Conversation was forbidden. The teachers could neither write nor receive letters. Food parcels were banned. Camp officials made it clear that those who could not withstand the pressure could win freedom merely by joining the Teachers' Front. At the end of fourteen days, fifty teachers out of 687 at Jorstadmoen had a change of heart. They broke down, joined the Teachers' Front, and were freed. One hundred and fifty others, mostly elderly and ailing, were transferred back to Grini. The remaining teachers, numbering close to five hundred, were marched onto unheated cattle cars and transported to Trondheim, where they were packed aboard the S.S. *Skjerstad,* an old wooden coastal steamer built in 1904 which had room for a normal complement of 250.

One teacher later gave this description of conditions aboard the ship: "Twenty-five of my colleagues were stowed away right at the bottom, on the keelson. They could not stand upright, the height being only three feet."

Conditions appalled even a *Nasjonal Samling* physician who was permitted aboard the vessel. He complained to the county governor, who in turn sent a personal message to Quisling apprising him of conditions:

> S.S. *Skjerstad*, with some 500 teachers, and guards and crew on board, is due to leave Trondheim. Many cannot even lie down at night but must stand, as the ship has only room for 250 persons. Many of the teachers are very ill with pneumonia, gastric ulcers, asthma, bronchitis, hemorrhage, and mental derangement. There are only two closets [toilets] for everybody. The cookhouse can only provide for 250 and cannot supply sufficient food for the journey. The water supplies are totally inadequate. Several of the teachers are willing to join the Teachers' Front.

Quisling, unmoved, commented that "the measures which are being taken against Norway's teachers are a direct consequence of their treasonable activities." When local clergymen appealed to Terboven, he replied that the teachers had been given their last chance to recant at Jorstadmoen. He ordered the ship to depart as scheduled. The *Skjerstad* sailed on April 14, headed for the arctic port of Kirkenes, close to the Finnish border. En route the prisoners received only one hot meal a day—usually a thin soup, served in the morning and cooked in installments during the night. Crowded conditions made life a misery. One teacher who was forced to spend much time in the hold wrote: "A tiny gleam of light shone from above, but there was no fresh air. There was a fearful stench, and one heard the despairing moaning of the sick."

Conditions improved once the teachers reached Kirkenes. Wehrmacht officers in charge of work details housed the teachers in barracks and barns, provided regular food rations, and assigned the teachers to the easier tasks on the docks or on construction projects. The Germans were content to leave the Norwegians to their own devices provided the work was done. Throughout the rest of the country, however, the deportation of the teachers aroused a wave of sympathy among Norwegians who thought it particularly demeaning that educated men should be forced to labor alongside Russian prisoners of war under what were thought to be brutal arctic conditions.

Nor did the deportation break the teachers' resistance. Despite the example supposedly set by the deportation, only a few more teachers joined the Quisling Front. The schools remained closed for close to two months until, by the beginning of May, even Quisling was forced to accept his failure to coerce the teachers. He ordered all schools reopened and permitted teachers back into their classrooms without mention of the Teachers' Front.

It was a bitter defeat for him. Appearing before an assembly of teachers in mid-May, Quisling berated them for their resistance, complaining, "You have destroyed everything for me."

Five months later, in the fall of 1942, Quisling gave orders to free the teachers imprisoned at Kirkenes. They returned home as transportation became available to be greeted as heroes by those they had left behind. Quisling ignored their homecoming, partly because of his frustration and partly because he was by then busy taking action against another Norwegian group that was far weaker than the teachers and far more vulnerable to threats and intimidation.

By the autumn of 1942, Quisling was moving against the defenseless Norwegian Jewish community, which had always been small, unsophisticated, and relatively detached from the mainstream of the country's business, cultural, and professional life. For centuries there had been no Jews in the country at all and their immigration was discouraged by law and custom. The first Norwegian constitution, drafted in 1814, barred the entry of Jews (as well as Jesuits) to the country. They were viewed as threatening strangers whose arrival and presence would be unwelcome to the isolated northerners.

The restriction against Jewish immigration was lifted in 1851 after a long campaign for reform by the Norwegian patriot-poet Henrik Wergeland. The first Jews arrived the next year, from Lithuania. As late as 1880, however, there were only fifty Jews in the whole country.

The first spurt of Jewish immigration came in the late 1880s, when pogroms in Russia and Poland sent a horde of Jewish refugees seeking haven throughout Europe and in the United States. Some of these displaced persons found their way to Norway. By 1892 the Jewish community had grown large enough to establish a synagogue in Oslo. A second synagogue was established in Trondheim in 1905. But even then the Jewish community was not large—approximately one thousand men, women, and children—and it had little impact on the country at large. The Jews lived quiet lives in the cities, where they were primarily engaged in family businesses or in the small-scale manufacture of shoes and tobacco products. By April, 1940, when the German invasion took place, the Jewish population still numbered less than fifteen hundred. Of that number more than 350 were Jewish political refugees who had escaped from Hitler's Germany during the troubled 1930s.

Norway in the 1930s was one of the few islands of peace for the Jews of Europe. Even members of Quisling's *Nasjonal Samling* Party expressed no open anti-Semitism. With the coming of the German troops the situation changed. Within days of the invasion, German troops slashed out at visible signs of Jewish life. In Trondheim, German soldiers smashed into the synagogue, where they replaced Stars of David with swastikas, demolished all holy objects, and pockmarked the interior walls with bullet holes after using the synagogue's large religious lamps for target practice. From that point on the injustices inflicted on the Jews continued day after day, increasing in severity as the war progressed.

In May, one month after the invasion, German authorities ordered Norwegian police to confiscate all radios belonging to Jews. Jewish travel was curbed and permission to leave the country was canceled. German authorities demanded membership lists from the Jewish communities.

In the spring of 1941, Quisling police arrested a handful of Jewish refugees from mainland Europe on a variety of charges and imprisoned them in the Grini concentration camp. Because the number of those arrested was small and because those imprisoned had not been native Norwegian Jews, the regular Jewish community chose to interpret the arrests not as the beginning of a widespread persecution against all Jews but as isolated incidents based on specific case histories. Even the deportation of one outspoken anti-Nazi Norwegian Jew to Germany was viewed as a lone affair portending no danger for the community as a whole.

But in June of 1941, a few days before Germany invaded the Soviet Union, all Jews living in northern Norway were arrested and sentenced to forced labor in arctic camps. Later that year, Quisling police began selective arrests of Jewish store owners, confiscating their businesses in the name of the Norwegian government. At the same time, the Norwegian minister of justice called on provincial governors to submit inventories of Jewish-owned real estate. All Jews and half-Jews were ordered to file reports on their property and income.

In February, 1942, the letter *J* was stamped on all identity papers held by Jews and all Jewish adults were required to fill out detailed questionnaires on their jobs, education, professional and organizational affiliations, details of self-employment, details of any bankruptcy, jail records, and bank accounts.

The following month, Quisling, with the full support and urging of Reichskommissar Terboven, set the groundwork for the legal persecution of Norwegian Jews. That portion of the old Norwegian Constitution which had forbidden the entry of Jews into Norway and which had been rescinded in 1851 was now—in March of 1942—reinstated as national law. Once again Jews were forbidden to enter Norway and those in the country were considered illegal aliens.

The Jewish persecution grew steadily harsher. In the summer of 1942, four Jewish residents of Trondheim were executed without trial for "spreading news" about the war based on BBC broadcasts. Listening to the BBC was a crime for all Norwegians, but the death penalty was not meted out to non-Jews.

In September, Norwegian police began arbitrary arrests of Jews in Oslo based on flimsy political charges. News of arrests sent a few hundred Jews fleeing across the border to Sweden, but the majority, neither fearing deportation nor knowing of the existence of the death camps in Germany, hesitated to leave their homes and jobs. Despite the anti-Semitism that appeared in all Quisling publications, the majority of Jews conducted their lives in the expectation that conditions would continue as they had in the past, uncomfortable but not unbearable. By the end of September, however, events were approaching a climax. The next month, a Norwegian policeman was shot by the leader of a group of Jews trying to escape to Sweden. Nazi papers seized on the incident to demand "an end to the Jewish problem in Norway."

Four days after the incident, Quisling's government introduced legislation confiscating all Jewish property; that same day, Norwegian police began arresting Jewish males over sixteen years of age. In November, Quisling decreed that all Jews, including those considered "quarter blood Jews," had to register their whereabouts with the police. With an excess of bureaucratic zeal, even those Jews already in prison were methodically given forms to fill out, asking them to state where they could be found. Jews outside prison had two weeks in which to comply. When that time period was up, Norwegian police swept Norway to complete their roundup of all Jewish men, women, and children. More than five hundred were thrown into Grini concentration camp.

The action set off protests by Norwegian clergymen and educators. A group of Norwegian bishops and professors sent a personal petition to Quisling begging him to intervene on behalf of the arrested Jews, and in a pastoral letter to the clergymen sought to arouse public opinion against the arrests, denouncing anti-Semitism as unethical and contrary to the tenets of Christianity.

Quisling's answer came in the first week of December. By then the fate of the Jews had been sealed: all were slated for deportation to Germany. Quisling argued the question directly:

> There are many who say that a Jew cannot be expelled simply because he is a Jew. In my opinion, no such reasoning could be more superficial. A Jew is not Norwegian, not European, he is an Oriental. Jews have no place in Europe. They are an internationally destructive element. The Jews create the Jewish problem and cause active anti-Semitism. When the eastern ghettos were opened, Germany was overrun by Russian and Polish Jews like grasshoppers. . . . It was the same in France, Hungary and Bulgaria. So one sees the depth of this problem, which stems from a world problem. For us, there can be no compromise.

The first mass deportation of Jews followed closely after Quisling's public statement. Five hundred and thirty-two Jewish prisoners were jammed aboard the troopship *Donau*, which sailed for Germany. There the Jews were loaded onto trains headed for the death camp at Auschwitz. Among those deported were an eight-week-old infant and an eighty-two-year-old woman. Quisling radio commentators gleefully reported that the "Jewish problem in Norway had reached a definite conclusion as the Jews had been taken on board the *Donau*."

Additional transports were needed, however, to complete the deportation. These took place in early 1943. By the end of February, a total of 760 Norwegian Jews had reached German ports and had been sent to Auschwitz. Once inside the death camp, women, children, and men too old to work were sent to the gas chambers almost immediately. Able-bodied males were put to hard labor. Most died of mistreatment, hunger, or sickness in 1943. Of the 760 Norwegian Jews deported to Germany, only twenty-four survived the war, a survival rate of 3 percent.

9
Resistance

Three months after the German invasion of Norway and within weeks of the final Allied evacuation of Narvik, Prime Minister Winston Churchill drafted a memorandum to his War Cabinet calling for the establishment of a unique military organization to carry on the war against Germany in occupied Europe, using the resistance movements in German-occupied countries as part of the overall war effort. In his official memorandum, Churchill asked for the coordination of "all action of subversion and sabotage against the enemy overseas." In a later informal pronouncement, Churchill described the mission of the new organization in more colorful terms: "to set Europe ablaze" by unconventional and "ungentlemanly" tactics. For a country such as Great Britain, it was a concept without precedent and it elicited more than its share of criticism from those who preferred a tightly structured military approach to warfare and who had little sympathy for or understanding of irregular warfare behind enemy lines. The organization, however, on Churchill's urging, was duly established on July 19, 1940, given the rather misleading name of Special Operations Executive, and ordered to bring the war home to the Germans by whatever means possible, the more irregular and aggressive the better.

Dr. Hugh Dalton, who was the director of the Ministry of Economic Warfare, which involved itself in intelligence, sabotage, propaganda, and subversion and which administratively was the parent ministry for the SOE, spelled out his views on the new organization in a message to the British Foreign Secretary Lord Halifax:

> We must organize movements in enemy-occupied territory comparable to the Sinn Fein in Ireland, to the Chinese guerrillas now operating against Japan. . . . We must use many different methods, industrial and military sabotage, labour agitation and strikes, continuous propaganda, terrorist acts against traitors and German leaders, boycotts and riots.

In Norway, while the SOE was being organized in Britain, a military resistance was developing, albeit slowly and uncertainly. It started with groups of young men who had known each other before the occupation and got together with the idea that they should "do something" against the Germans even if they lacked means and training.

In Oslo, members of the Student Athletic Association formed action groups that conducted physical and military drills in the fields. They had no weapons, only a few qualified instructors, and they did not know what other groups around the country were doing. Those who participated thought of themselves as involved in resistance, but in public referred to themselves as "ski and football clubs."

Such informal groups formed in most Norwegian cities. In Bergen, Capt. Mons Haukeland, who had seen action against the Germans with the Fourth Brigade, talked with former soldiers and began to organize an underground army without arms. Since Haukeland thought the war would last for years, he was content to "plan for the long pull," to build up a secret army slowly and cautiously and to avoid initiating actions that would attract the attention of the Germans.

Lt. Odd Øyen, who had participated in the Norwegian defense of Elverum against the German paratroopers seeking to capture King Haakon, found it difficult to hold a group together. Øyen recruited thirty men and held weekly drills in Vestmarka, the woods to the west of Oslo. His men tried to keep in top physical condition, hiking in the summer and skiing in winter, and Øyen, as a former officer, instructed them in basic tactics; but it was difficult to train men without weapons, for missions that never materialized. They had no contact with other groups and lacked overall leadership to give meaning to their activities. Nor did the Norwegian public support overt actions against the Germans. Except for excesses by SS and Gestapo personnel, the typical German Wehrmacht soldier in Norway was on his best behavior, a Nordic in a Nordic country. Many arrived in Norway expecting to be welcomed as "friends," and conducted themselves accordingly. Throughout the occupation German discipline was excellent. Mons Haukeland described the behavior of German troops as "perfect." Odd Øyen viewed the occupation as "mild." At times German troops reacted with surprising tolerance to individual acts of provocation by Norwegians. When the Germans came to the tiny fishing village of Ulstein, south of Ålesund, a twenty-year-old student by the name of Ragnar Ulstein decided to "get to know the enemy" and volunteered as an interpreter for troops manning a gun battery in his village. German soldiers put up with him with amused forbearance when with youthful bravado he played the British and Norwegian anthems on the piano in the German soldiers' lounge.

By the end of 1940 there was communication between the informal military groups active in various parts of the country, but this contact was sporadic. The groups were poorly organized, and the leadership was in the hands of former military officers, steeped in traditions of service protocol and table-of-organization charts, and incapable of conceiving how a guerrilla campaign could be waged against the Germans.

Maj. Haneborg Hansen, one of the early leaders of Milorg, as the Norwegian military resistance was called, even opposed the idea of receiving arms by air from England on the grounds that such an air drop would place the men of Milorg in jeopardy. Hansen suggested instead that no arms be dropped in Norway until the Allies were ready to mount an all-out invasion of Norway, at which time arms should be dropped throughout Norway on a massive scale. Hansen clearly failed to understand the problems of receiving arms by air, and that men without training in specific weapons could not effectively use those weapons in combat. Nevertheless, his suggestion was warmly received by other Milorg leaders who, like him, favored a "passive" buildup of a Norwegian underground army and a "go slow, lie low" posture against the Germans.

The early Milorg suffered severely from poor security as well. Their leaders were not accustomed to secrecy or the ways of underground life. One Norwegian Army colonel named Dannevig, for instance, was forced to go underground after his involvement in Milorg became known to the Germans. He moved from his regular residence into a friend's apartment where he thought he was safe from arrest, but he continued to walk the streets of Oslo wearing only a pair of sunglasses as a disguise. When friends who met him on the street asked what he was doing, he would reply confidentially, "I've gone underground—don't tell anyone."

Dannevig was picked up a short time afterward and eventually died in prison under Gestapo control. British SOE officers who later worked with Milorg considered the Norwegians too open and too talkative, warning that they would have to learn "the hard lesson of security in the bitter school of experience." A few aggressive and sophisticated Norwegian resistance leaders agreed. As the occupation continued, they remarked among themselves that the "Gestapo is a bad enemy, but the Norwegians are even worse."

A handful of Norwegians, however, was determined to take a more active role in the fight against the Germans. During the summer of 1940, groups of young Norwegian men arrived in England by sea, after perilous voyages from Norway in fishing smacks or private boats. British officers working in SOE's Scandinavian section selected a few with outstanding abilities and unquestioned motivation for special training as British agents. By September, 1940, SOE had seven Norwegians trained as agents and awaiting missions that would take them back to Norway. Among them was a former actor, Lt. Martin Linge, who became the prime mover in the Norwegian section of the SOE. Eventually the group of seven agents grew into the Norwegian Independent Company No. 1, with Linge as its leader. In its early days, Company Linge, as it soon was commonly called, was an aggressive combat outfit that fully accepted SOE's view of how the war should be fought.

Through the autumn of 1940, SOE moved slowly to implement its Norwegian policy. An SOE section opened in Stockholm to coordinate activities and intelligence, and SOE participated in gathering a nucleus of a fleet of fishing boats which, it was planned, would carry agents and refugees between the Shetland Islands, north of Scotland, and Norway.

SOE also sought to formalize its Norwegian policy. In a document dated December 11, 1940, SOE predicted that the liberation of Norway would come about as the result of an Allied invasion, although it conceded that this development would take some time to materialize. SOE's long-term program nevertheless called for the secret buildup of an underground army inside Norway that would see action when an Allied invasion materialized. On paper this objective meshed finely with the aims of the Norwegian military resistance, Milorg.

But SOE was more interested in its short-term program, also spelled out in the December 11 document, which called for sabotage and propaganda and "hit and run landings and air raids" inside Norway to let the Norwegian people know they had not been forgotten and to inhibit Norwegian acceptance of German rule. "Norway must become and remain a thorn in the German side," the document concluded.

SOE's first move came a few weeks after the release of its Norwegian policy document. On December 22, 1940, the first SOE agent landed successfully on the Norwegian coast from a submarine and established the first SOE wireless station in Norway. He also began organizing a local resistance group around his base, near the southernmost part of the country. This was followed by a small hit-and-run raid in Sognefjord.

In March, 1941, came the first large-scale raid against Norwegian territory, a Combined Operations and SOE mission against the Lofotens, a group of islands off the coast near Narvik, separated from the mainland by the waters of Vestfjord. The islands are rugged, and so are the Norwegians who live upon them, fishermen mainly, going after cod and herring, supplementing their livelihood by some marginal farming during the short and cool summers.

As a group, the Lofoten Islanders probably represented a good cross section of Norwegian public opinion, certainly of those who lived along the coast and whose contact with Britain had always been strong. H. George Mikes, a journalist who operated the *Lofoten Folkeblad* at the time of the invasion and saw his newspaper closed down after the Germans arrived, described the attitude of the islanders:

> The majority sympathized with the Allies. Our love for Britain is deep-rooted; we are sea-going people as well as the British, and our livelihood depended on Great Britain to a great extent.

Before the German occupation, there was not a single *Nasjonal Samling* member to be found on the Lofoten community council. With the coming of the Germans, however, some local residents publicly announced their support of Quisling and took over civil posts on the islands. Mikes described the reaction of the islanders:

> Our relations are much better with the Germans than with the Quislings. After all, it was not the decision of these soldiers who walk about on the Lofoten Islands that they should invade Norway. . . . But the Quislings chose their way for themselves. They joined the enemies of the country . . . in order to obtain power, to achieve material results.

Militarily the Lofotens held little importance, but the islands were held by only a weak German force and the seas around could be controlled by British naval units. They were a tempting target for victory-starved Britain.

On March 4, 1941, an attack force of 450 British Commandos, accompanied by fifty-two men of Company Linge, led by Martin Linge (by now promoted to captain), landed on two major islands in the Lofotens. They surprised the small German garrisons there which surrendered meekly, and proceeded systematically to blow up German and Norwegian ships in the harbors and to destroy four fish-oil factories that produced 50 percent of Norway's total fish-oil output. Six ships totaling nineteen thousand tons were sent to the bottom and 213 Germans and a dozen Norwegian *Nasjonal Samling* sympathizers were arrested. Among the prisoners was Norwegian Chief Police Inspector Birkeland. A British officer, accompanied by two commandos and a Norwegian interpreter, confronted Birkeland in his office and informed him that the British Army were taking prisoners at the moment. Would the chief inspector oblige and follow them?

"Where to?" Birkeland asked.

"To London," the officer replied.

The Lofoten Islanders turned out en masse to welcome the invading troops. Mikes described events in his hometown of Stamsund:

> Loudspeakers started to make a proclamation: "The British Navy is here. The population should remain calm. We are your friends. People who want to should gather in the main street." Before five minutes had passed, the population of Stamsund was crowded in the main street. Villagers competed with each other to guide the commandos and were almost ready to fight each other as to who should answer the British officers' questions.

When the attack force, its work done, prepared to depart from the islands, 314 native Lofoteners insisted on boarding the British vessels as volunteers to join the fight against Germany. Once in Great Britain, many enlisted in Company Linge. The raiders also brought back with them captured German documents which provided British intelligence with an inside look at conditions in Norway as seen through German eyes. One document had been issued by General Falkenhorst in December, 1940, warning that "the temper and attitude of the Norwegian population have recently stiffened against our endeavours." Falkenhorst recommended "restraint and caution" in order to win over the Norwegians and warned the Wehrmacht not to become involved in domestic Norwegian political controversies and to report to Norwegian and German police any instances of provocation or insult.

> Intervention by the German Wehrmacht must only occur in order to ensure the security of the Occupying Force and its property, but where action is taken it must be ruthless and employ the severest measures.

Falkenhorst's conclusions about the political climate within Norway made happy reading for the British. "With the exception of the *Nasjonal Samling* Party," he wrote, "all other organizations and parties, and particularly the representatives of commerce and industry, remain now as before pro-English and, consequently, anti-German."

British newspapers and propaganda experts exploited the victory, calling it "an unqualified success." The government called it a "perfect example of Allied collaboration." Churchill and the military leaders involved were well pleased with results. Churchill sent his personal congratulations to the Chief of Combined Operations who had been responsible for the planning and execution. SOE saw the raid as certain to result in better morale among Norwegian resistance leaders. The success of the raid encouraged the SOE to release in mid-April another document on Scandinavian policy which optimistically reviewed the possibilities of further raids against the Norwegian coast.

On the Lofotens themselves, however, the initial elation was soon followed by depression and fear as German troops resumed command. The Germans burned homes in reprisal and imprisoned leaders from among the non-Nazi Norwegians. Arrests were particularly heavy in the town of Svolvaer. Seventy persons from seventeen to seventy years of age were arrested and sent to Grini concentration camp.

The Norwegian government in exile in London reacted angrily to the raid. Its leaders had not been consulted beforehand. They felt slighted and humiliated by what they regarded as high-handed action on the part of the British.

Milorg leaders also objected. The German reprisals, they argued, were too high a price to pay for the fruits of victory. Milorg viewed the destruction of Norwegian ships and oil facilities not as a blow against Germany's war effort but as destruction of Norwegian property, pointing out that the local population depended on the fishing trawlers and oil factories for its livelihood.

By June, 1941, Milorg leaders were worried enough to appeal to the Norwegian government in exile in London. In a wide-ranging letter designed to clarify Milorg's cautious philosophy, the Norwegian resistance leaders stated their opposition to further British coastal raids and to what they called "hazardous sabotage actions." They expressed fear of German reprisals and pleaded that the Norwegian people were "not immunized against German threats and Gestapo terror." They protested SOE's leadership, insisting instead that "every action should be carefully thought out with our cooperation." At the same time, they reiterated their intention to avoid any actions and clashes with the Germans that could result in reprisals.

The letter, addressed to King Haakon personally, was sent by courier to a liaison officer on the Shetlands. There it was intercepted by SOE officers, who after reading its contents promptly dubbed Milorg the "military Sunday school" and decided to answer the message directly instead of passing it on to King Haakon. The SOE tried to soften its response by diplomatically praising Milorg's intentions, but went on to insist that there was an immediate and pressing need for active training, arms drill, and sabotage within Norway and to reject Milorg's claim that any action should have Milorg's prior approval. In SOE's view all Milorg activities must be subordinated to the British military authorities.

The exchange of letters aggravated the distrust between Milorg and SOE. By the terms of its assigned mission, SOE was determined to "set

A British soldier displays a souvenir of the successful raid against the Lofotens. *(Wide World Photo)*

Europe ablaze," not only to bring the war to the enemy but to justify its own existence, but this was exactly what the Norwegian resistance leaders sought to avoid. The conflict between the two opposing views plagued relations between SOE and Milorg for the greater part of the war.

The third party in the dispute, the Norwegian government in exile, harbored suspicions of both groups, resentful of SOE for its high-handed tactics, but wary of backing Milorg, which the government in exile feared was seeking to establish a countergovernment to take over power after liberation and thus prevent members of the exiled Norwegian government from resuming office.

The situation could not continue in this fashion. In October, 1941, two leaders of Milorg reached London to discuss with Norwegian government leaders the misunderstandings between them. The Milorg representatives assured the London ministers that Milorg was not building a rival government inside Norway, and they convinced them that SOE was pursuing its own war in Norway with little regard for or consultation with Milorg. As a result of these consultations, the Norwegian government in exile formally acknowledged Milorg as part of the Norwegian armed forces. Milorg had struck a good bargain. By pledging support of the Norwegian government in exile, Milorg gained not only a degree of legitimization from that government but also support for its view of how the resistance should be conducted and an ally in its dispute with SOE.

Soon afterward, the Norwegian government reached a meeting of minds with the SOE as well. In a memorandum titled "Anglo-Norwegian Collaboration Regarding the Military Organization in Norway," both sides pledged to work toward harmonious cooperation and mutual confidence between British and Norwegian resistance leaders. The memorandum accepted the propositions that the British could not mount an effective resistance inside Norway without Norwegian help and that Norwegian resistance forces could never hope to gain strength without British support. A *rapprochement* had been reached, at least on paper. But events in December, 1941, tore into shreds the well-meaning sentiments that had been put on paper.

A second British Commando raid on the Lofoten Islands took place shortly after Christmas, 1941. Actually there were two separate operations—one against the Lofotens itself, Operation Anklet, and the other against the coastal towns of Målöy and Vågsöy, Operation Archery. SOE Norwegians from Company Linge accompanied the British Commandos on both raids.

The Norwegians looked forward to combat with eagerness. After more than a year of training they were ready for action, and most of the

Norwegians assigned to the assault on the Lofotens were convinced that this would not be a hit-and-run operation like the first Lofoten raid. The men of Company Linge were equipped for a three-month campaign; they had drawn pay for three months; and their ID cards were issued for the same period of time. Before departure their commander, Martin Linge —again promoted, to major—had called his company together and in an emotional speech told them that the "raids were the fulfillment of our dreams."

Major Linge was placed in command of a force of sixteen Norwegians that was part of a larger Commando force of fifty-one officers and 525 men scheduled to make the assault on the towns of Vågsöy and Målöy. Again, as in the first Lofoten raid, their objectives were fish-oil factories and shipping. The Norwegians under Major Linge went in with the Commandos against Målöy.

The attack began on the morning of December 27 with an intense ten-minute bombardment by four destroyers and the cruiser *Kenya,* which smashed the German barracks and knocked out three of Målöy's four coastal guns. A flight of Royal Air Force Hampdens followed up the naval bombardment with a low-level smoke-bomb attack to screen the assault troops coming ashore. The soldiers hit the beach without drawing counterfire from the Germans. In the assault on the German headquarters, however, the joint. British-Norwegian Commando force suffered some casualties. Among those killed was Major Linge, who was struck by a German bullet as he led his men in the attack. He died immediately. Minutes later, the German garrison surrendered. They had resisted less than ten minutes.

The British considered the attacks—Vågsöy was captured almost as easily as Målöy had been—a superb success. At Målöy the Commandos destroyed every German installation and every gun emplacement that survived the naval bombardment. At Vågsöy the Commandos demolished German offices and barracks, several fish-oil factories, a wireless station, and a lighthouse. Nearly fifteen thousand tons of shipping in the two ports were sunk. One hundred fifty German troops were killed and ninety-eight captured. And when the naval force sailed away that same afternoon, the ships carried an additional seventy-one Norwegian residents who had volunteered to go to England so they could better fight the enemy.

For the Norwegian Commandos, the mission, though successful, was a bitter blow. The death of Major Linge left them demoralized and depressed.

The simultaneous attack on the Lofoten Islands also began smoothly. A landing force of three hundred men, including seventy-seven Norwegians, seized the towns of Reine and Moskenes almost without opposition and settled down to what they thought would be a prolonged stay.

Operation Anklet had in fact been originally conceived as a means of establishing a permanent naval base in northern waters for British warships, but the difficulties of supplying such a remote base soon became apparent and by the time of the attack itself the objectives had been significantly reduced. Rear Admiral Louis Hamilton, the commanding officer of the British naval force, was under orders to inflict as much damage to local shipping and factories as he could and to maintain a toehold on Norwegian territory for as long as possible. When the assault troops landed on December 27 it was Admiral Hamilton's intention to hold onto the Lofotens at least for several weeks. He even harbored the hope of establishing a semipermanent base in the southern Lofotens, if the military situation indicated that this was feasible.

The Lofoten population, still strongly pro-British, welcomed the British and Norwegian troops warmly. "You are heartily welcome if you come to stay," the Commandos were told, "but we don't want another Svolvaer."

Convinced themselves that they were in the Lofotens for a prolonged period, the soldiers assured the local population that they had nothing to fear. Norwegian troops of Company Linge gave particularly glowing promises of Allied intentions. Once again the Lofoten Islanders turned out to help the invading troops identify and arrest local Nazis and indicated their support of the Allied cause in public demonstrations.

Their joy lasted less than a day. On the morning of December 28,

British and Norwegian assault troops easily captured Vågsöy, but there were casualties. *(Wide World Photo)*

German bombers raided the Lofotens, barely missing hitting the cruiser *Arethusa*. At the same time British signalmen intercepted German radio traffic which was interpreted as indicating that a German counterforce was forming in Narvik.

Alarmed, Admiral Hamilton ordered his troops back aboard their ships, and planned on an immediate retreat. As the British and Norwegian troops began marching toward the loading areas, the realization that they were leaving hit the Lofoten Islanders, who turned out into the streets in angry groups. Terrified by what the Germans would do in a second round of reprisals, the islanders turned their fear and rage on the departing troops, cursing and spitting at them as they marched, directing their most emotional outbursts against their fellow countrymen, the Norwegians of Company Linge.

Two weeks later, an SOE officer recapitulated the political repercussion of Operation Anklet:

> The population had been told that the British Force had come to stay.... The local population was very patriotic-minded; the town of Reine was nicknamed London. All these people were hoping that the moment had at last come when the fight would be taken up once more.... None were prepared for the news that the forces were to flee without even having tried to fight; therefore, when the notice came about retreat it not only caused deep disappointment, but also indignation and fury. The general feeling was that once more propaganda had been successfully achieved with nearly 100 per cent security for the military, whereas the landing would once more bring upon the heads of the remaining population the horrors of German reprisals....

German reprisals, as feared, came quickly. SS squads sped to the area to arrest those who had helped the British and Norwegians. Relatives of those who had volunteered to go to Britain were arrested and sent to concentration camps, even if they themselves had been inactive.

Milorg and the Norwegian government in exile were especially bitter. Despite the memorandum signed only a short while before that provided for mutual collaboration, the Norwegians knew nothing of the raids until after they had been carried out. A Norwegian report called Operation Anklet a "milestone" in the history of SOE's Norwegian operations that caused the year 1941 to "end on a sad note."

The British could ignore Norwegian protests no longer. A special Norwegian section was established within SOE to work solely on Norwegian affairs. Lt. Col. J. S. Wilson was named head of section and ordered to ease the tensions then existing between the Norwegians and the British. The Norwegian government, for its part, established a Norwegian High Command to work with SOE's Norwegian section. The first meeting between representatives of these two groups took place in the middle of February. After close to two years of war, the top leaders of the two nations, supposedly working together in alliance against the Germans, finally had an administrative instrument through which they could communicate and cooperate. It was, optimistically, named the Anglo-Norwegian Collaboration Committee.

If 1941 ended "on a sad note" for the Norwegian resistance, 1942 proved even more disastrous. Only in one area of activity did the British and Norwegians succeed in outwitting the Germans, and that was at sea, where a small fleet of Norwegian fishing vessels began making regular runs between Norwegian ports and the Shetland Islands, lying one hundred miles northeast of the northern tip of Scotland.

The seas are rough between Norway and Great Britain and in winter they are among the stormiest in the world, with fog, extreme cold, and continuous darkness adding to the hazards. But as early as the winter of 1940, British intelligence officers noted that Norwegian fishermen, carrying volunteers who sought to fight against the Germans, were arriving in the Shetlands in increasing numbers. Some of these Norwegian fishermen, after their arrival in the Shetlands, were asked by British intelligence officers to return to Norwegian waters on special missions. When these trips proved successful, Maj. L. H. Mitchell of British Army Intelligence was ordered to the Shetlands to organize a base to handle continuous traffic between the two countries, carrying agents, saboteurs, and arms to Norway and volunteers and refugees back to the Shetlands.

Mitchell established his base in a secluded cove at Lunna and re-cruited a mixed force of British Army officers and enlisted men, Shetland natives, and about forty sea-wise civilian Norwegian seamen to run the ferry service, which started operations with four small fishing vessels. The Norwegians were paid a wage of four pounds a week, with a ten-pound bonus for each trip, good money for the time.

The first trip took place in August, 1941, when the fishing boat *Askel,* under the command of a young fisherman familiar with Norwegian coastal waters, sailed for the coast of Norway north of Bergen with an SOE agent hidden belowdecks. The *Askel* dropped off the agent at the appointed spot and returned home having successfully eluded German patrols. This first voyage was followed by another, using the smallest vessel in the fleet, the fifty-foot *Igland.* It too was successful. The trips continued through the winter of 1941–42. The hardy Norwegian sailors welcomed the darkness of winter for the protection it provided and purposely chose the worst weather for their trips on the assumption that German naval patrols would be tied up in port during stormy periods. Lt. Comdr. David Howarth, one of the British officers assigned to the Shet-lands home base, commented after the war that "in all the history of man's seafaring no other series of journeys has been undertaken deliberately in such bad weather in such small boats."

By late spring of 1942, when the lengthening daylight made further crossings too hazardous, the fishing boats had completed more than forty round trips, had landed forty-nine SOE agents in Norway, had delivered 150 tons of arms and equipment, and had brought back to Britain forty-six Norwegians, including resistance fighters fleeing from the Germans and some Norwegian VIPs who wanted to reach London for consultations with the government in exile.

The sailings between the Shetlands and Norway continued until 1945. In the later years of the war, after German patrols became aware of the traffic and began to threaten the slow fishing boats, speedy American sub chasers were put into service; they ran in and out of Norwegian waters with little trouble. In time, Norwegians began to refer to the boats that plied the waters of the North Sea as the "Shetland bus," an acknowledgment of the safety and regularity with which the trips were made. By the end of the war, the "Shetland bus" had transported nearly four hundred tons of arms and equipment and hundreds of SOE agents to Norway and had rescued more than 350 Norwegian refugees. Psychologically as well, the service was a boost to Norwegian morale. When the Gestapo was close at hand, almost everyone in Norway knew that if he could get to the coast, he stood a chance of riding the "Shetland bus" to safety.

Inside Norway during 1942, however, the resistance forces met with setback after setback, for the men of the Gestapo and German counterintelligence were active, capable, and adept at playing "in the negative sector" and infiltrating resistance groups.

In the Ålesund area, a Norwegian informer named Henry Oliver Rinnan proved an especially productive counteragent for the Germans. Posing as an anti-Nazi, Rinnan infiltrated an "export" group in Ålesund which sent refugees and volunteers across the North Sea in fishing vessels. On February 23, 1942, the Gestapo, acting on information from Rinnan, seized a fishing vessel with twenty-three persons aboard minutes before it was scheduled to sail. During interrogation the twenty-three implicated others in Ålesund, and another twenty persons were arrested the following days. One man considered the ring leader was executed immediately, the others held in jail where they were subjected to repeated interrogations.

The Ålesund incident was followed by an even more tragic affair at Televaag, a small fishing village near Bergen. The coast near Bergen was an especially active area for illegal landings and departures, for Bergen was the closest large city to the Shetlands, it boasted good transportation eastward to Oslo and southward to the cities along the southern coast, and its population was strongly pro-British. As a result, many of the first agents to land in Norway set foot on Norwegian soil near Bergen. The arrival and departure of these strangers, however, could not be kept completely secret and the movements of the undercover agents soon became general knowledge to local inhabitants.

Eventually the information reached German ears. In March, a Televaag woman reported what she knew to the local police chief, who was a member of Quisling's *Nasjonal Samling* Party; he, in turn, passed on the information to the Gestapo chief in Bergen. At the same time, another Televaag resident, himself pro-British, was overheard bragging to friends that he had seen weapons, ammunition, and radio sets in the farmhouse of a local merchant who was the Milorg leader for the area. In April, the Germans learned that two Company Linge Norwegians who had received special-agent training from the SOE had arrived in Televaag and were hiding out in the Milorg leader's barn.

Troops attached to the Sicherheitsdienst (SD), the intelligence service of the SS, swooped down on the farmhouse on the morning of April 26, surprising the two agents in the barn loft. With their retreat cut off, the SOE agents opened fire and killed two German officers before they themselves were captured. Both were wounded. One died immediately, while the other was taken away for interrogation.

When the fruits of that interrogation were sent to Reichskommissar Terboven, he ordered widespread reprisals against Televaag as an example to the rest of the country. German troops burned more than three hundred houses to the ground, killed or confiscated all cattle, and sank all local fishing vessels. Then the Germans moved against the population itself. Seventy-six Televaag men between the ages of sixteen and sixty-five—almost the entire male population—were deported to concentration camps in Germany. Most of them perished in prison before the end of the war. The rest of the population—260 women, children, and elderly men—were arrested and interned in Norway. When the Germans were finished, the village of Televaag had been wiped off the map. The wounded SOE agent and the local Milorg leader were tortured and finally executed.

Still Terboven was not satisfied. He ordered the execution of eighteen young men who had been arrested in Ålesund, even though they had had no connection with the Televaag underground. Then, acting on information obtained from the Televaag and Ålesund prisoners before their execution, he ordered the Gestapo to "roll up" all Milorg leaders known to be operating. During May and June of 1942, German police and Gestapo agents, assisted by Norwegian Quislingite police officials, seized resistance leaders in Bergen, Stavanger, Oslo, Drammen, and Kongsberg. By the early summer of 1942 the entire Milorg organization in the southern half of Norway had been destroyed. Those leaders who escaped arrest either fled to Sweden or, completely demoralized, went into hiding inside Norway. They blamed the SOE for the disasters that had befallen them, and they lived in constant terror that they would be arrested and subjected to interrogation by the Gestapo. Despite the "good behavior" German troops showed to the general Norwegian population, the men of the Norwegian underground knew that they could expect little mercy in the dungeons of Norwegian prisons and in Gestapo interrogation rooms. By 1942 the full scope of Nazi brutality was becoming generally known. A Swedish newspaper noted that "these reports of violence are so fearful that at first one shrinks from believing them." In a series of quasi-legal hearings conducted by the royal Norwegian government in London, Norwegians who had managed to escape to England testified about Gestapo behavior toward prisoners.

One witness told of the interrogation of a fellow prisoner:

He was taken down into the basement after having denied that he had been engaged in espionage. Here he was burned with a soldering iron on a couple of less sensitive points on the inside of the hand. Afterwards it was explained to him how much more painful it would be to be burned in a more sensitive place. As he still refused to confess, he was first burned on the inside of one of his wrists, which made a wound about the size of a florin, and then burned with the same iron on the other side of the artery.

Another witness, housed in the same cell with a resistance fighter, testified:

He found great difficulty in talking. . . . I had to feed and wash him. The policemen had broken four of his fingers and had pulled out the nails from two of them. Afterward they had hit him with sticks wrapped in cloth until he collapsed. They then turned him on his back and jumped on his stomach. He stated that he had asked his tormentors to shoot him. I myself saw that he was bleeding through the mouth and the rectum and that four fingers had been broken and were bent backwards. I also noticed that two nails were missing. . . .

The main German prison in Oslo was located at No. 19 Møllergaten. It was used primarily as a holding institution before prisoners were transferred to the Grini concentration camp outside the city or to the Gestapo headquarters on Victoria Terrasse, a four-story brick building with a large courtyard, where all important political prisoners were interrogated. During the war years even Quisling supporters passed the curtained windows of the building on Victoria Terrasse with fear.

By the autumn of 1942 a viable resistance movement existed only in the northern half of Norway, and disaster was coming for Milorg there as well, in part because of Churchill's continued fascination with northern Norway as a theater of operations, in part to Hitler's fears that he was particularly vulnerable in the north.

Even after the British defeat in Norway in 1940, Churchill looked upon Norway as a promising theater for offensive action. In late 1941, he considered mounting an invasion against Trondheim, but was dissuaded by his naval and air advisors, who pleaded the impossibility of providing adequate air support. In the spring of 1942, Churchill's thoughts turned to northern Norway. He proposed to land a self-contained British Expeditionary Force in the northernmost part of Norway. The immediate objective would be to wipe out German airfields used by the Luftwaffe to launch bombing raids on Allied convoys to the Russian ports of Murmansk and Archangel, but Churchill had larger hopes for the operation, which was code-named Jupiter. In a memorandum to Gen. Sir Hastings Ismay and his Chief of Staff committee, Churchill wrote:

> If we could gain possession of these airfields and establish an equal force there, not only would the northern sea route to Russia be kept open, but we should have set up a second front on a small scale from which it would be most difficult to eject us. If the going was good we could advance gradually southward, unrolling the Nazi map of Europe from the top.

The British Chiefs of Staff were unanimously opposed. Churchill had mentioned only two German airfields that had to be captured, but when the Chiefs of Staff conducted a detailed study of the area they learned that there were ten German airfields that would have to be captured, not two. The British Navy feared heavy losses; the British Air Force cited the difficulty of providing air cover; and the British Army thought that Churchill's estimate of the ground forces needed for the operation—"a storm force" of divisional strength that would land in the Pechenga area, near the Norwegian-Russian border, and an additional brigade group that would take the airfield at the head of Porsangerfjord—was far too modest. In the Army's view, the entire northern arctic coastline from Pechenga to Narvik would have to be occupied, at the expenditure of far more men and materials than Churchill envisioned.

Churchill was unconvinced. In June he wrote another memorandum in which he vigorously put forward his arguments for Jupiter:

> Once we have established ourselves with growing air-power in the two main airfields, we can attack by parachute the airfields to the southward. With the spring of 1943, other landings could be made, Tromsø and Narvik taken, then Bodø and Mo. . . . The population would rise to aid us as we advanced. . . . The reactions upon Sweden and Finland might be highly beneficial. . . .

In his enthusiasm for Jupiter, Churchill swept aside military warnings. He challenged the axiom that it was impossible to land anywhere against opposition without superior air strength. "It is a question," he argued, "whether it is better to land without fighter cover at a point where the enemy are very weak in armour and troops, or with fighter cover at a point where the enemy are very strong in armour and ground troops."

He also confronted head on the possibility of heavy losses to shipping. "It seems unlikely," he argued, "that more than one-fifth or one-sixth of the transports and covering craft would be sunk. A military attack is not ruled out simply because a fifth of the soldiers may be shot on the way, provided the others get there and do the job."

British military planners remained skeptical of Jupiter. They scoffed at the idea that Hitler's European map could be unrolled from the top, noting the extraordinary difficulties of transportation from northern Norway into the country's southern heartland. Even if Jupiter were successful, they argued, it would pose no threat to Germany's war effort.

Churchill, frustrated by his own military, turned to the Canadians. After the war he wrote:

> I still hoped for Jupiter. Little or no progress had been made with its planning. I thought that this operation would give a glorious opportunity to the Canadian Army, which had now for two years been eating its heart out in Britain, awaiting the invader.

In a long talk with Lt. Gen. A. G. L. McNaughton, the Canadian commander-in-chief in England, Churchill outlined his thoughts and hopes for Jupiter and asked McNaughton to conduct a "personal inquiry into the scheme." He assured McNaughton that Canadian troops could be used as the main assault force, thereby reaping all honor for the victory. General McNaughton promised to do his best, but his report wasn't ready until the middle of September and it too highlighted the hazards of the operation and minimized the potential benefits.

Churchill wryly responded the next day, commenting in a memorandum that McNaughton "certainly does not err on the side of underrating the difficulties before us."

For all practical purposes, the McNaughton report ended serious discussion of Jupiter as an actual operation. Churchill, however, urged continued planning of Jupiter to provide "cover" for the planning of Operation Torch, the Allied invasion of North Africa, which in the early autumn of 1942 was close to completion, as well as to have plans ready for use if the developments of war would so change the situation as to make a northern operation both feasible and desirable.

General McNaughton, obedient to the Prime Minister's wishes, continued planning work; but his effort was conducted in the belief that Jupiter, despite Churchill's obsession with northern Norway, would never come off. In Norway, however, SOE agents operated on a different set of assumptions; they pushed with vigor their preparations for what they thought was a coming invasion.

SOE activities in northern Norway had begun in early 1942, concurrently with Churchill's first Jupiter proposal, when three operational groups were landed in the district around Mosjøen, approximately half-way between Trondheim and Bodø. Their orders were to build a military organization of guerrillas that would be ready to "cut Norway in half" in the event of an invasion farther north. The SOE agents, all Norwegians attached to Company Linge, were ordered to mobilize their forces as quickly as possible and to avoid contact with Milorg units in the area. The SOE agents thus were forced to start fresh, impelled to haste as spring turned to summer and as the hints of the possibility of a forthcoming operation began to reach Norway. The agents found recruitment easy among the men of the district. The sense of urgency that spurred the activities of the SOE groups produced expectations of an early invasion. So did the arrival of tons of arms and ammunition, which the resistance volunteers transported on their backs from landing zones to hiding areas. More than twenty-four tons of equipment were brought in during the first half of 1942, an insignificant amount by usual wartime standards but large enough to convince the Norwegians who were unused to war or the requirements of combat that an invasion was actually in the making.

The sudden spurt of underground activity could not be kept secret for long. Henry Oliver Rinnan, whose information had resulted in the arrest of twenty-three Norwegians in Ålesund early in the year, suc-cessfully infiltrated one of the new resistance groups and provided the Germans with information on the whereabouts of an SOE radio trans-mitter and a large arms dump near Lake Majavatn. In October, Reichs-kommissar Terboven, sufficiently worried about signs of Allied military activity in a strategically important area, declared a state of emergency from Majavatn in the north to Røros in the south, including the city of Trondheim.

As a cover operation, Jupiter was a superb success, meshing smoothly with Hitler's fears and fantasies, which were the mirror image of Churchill's hopes and dreams. From the time of the German invasion, Hitler was obsessed by the idea that Britain was planning a reinvasion of Norway. He took steps to avert this possibility, often against the advice of his own military leaders.

In March, 1941, Hitler ordered reinforcements sent to Norway against the wishes of Gen. Franz Halder, Chief of the Army General Staff, who was then juggling masses of men and equipment for the coming invasions of Greece, Yugoslavia, and Russia, and who thought he had none to spare for Norway.

Later in 1941, Hitler ordered the German fleet to concentrate its main units in Norwegian waters, again against the advice of his naval commanders. Hitler told Admiral Raeder: "If the British go about things properly they will attack northern Norway at several points. In an all-out attack by their fleet and ground troops, they will try to displace us there, take Narvik if possible, and thus exert pressure on Sweden and Finland." Such a move, Hitler believed, could be "of decisive importance for the outcome of the war."

To protect against this development, Hitler demanded that the German Navy concentrate all its battleships in Norway. The German Navy had formidable units in Norway already. The forty-thousand-ton *Tirpitz*, a warship more powerful than any vessel in the British Navy, was berthed at Trondheim, a constant threat to the British, who had to assign major units to guard against her breaking out into the Atlantic. The pocket battleship *Scheer* and the cruiser *Hipper* were also in Norwegian waters. Even this naval concentration did not satisfy Hitler. He insisted that the battle cruisers *Scharnhorst* and *Gneisenau* and the cruiser *Prince Eugen*, at the time ready for sea in Brest, break through the English Channel into the North Sea. Raeder opposed the move but Hitler was adamant. On a foggy February day in 1942, the three German ships sailed from Brest and slipped through the Channel into the North Sea, successfully reaching Norwegian ports against the efforts of the British Navy and Air Force.

Hitler's interest in Norway provided rich rewards for him at sea. U-boat activity in the North Atlantic proved particularly catastrophic for the Allies in the spring of 1942. In March, German U-boats sank ninety-five ships totaling 534,000 tons, most of them on the run for Russian arctic ports. But his obsession with Norway prevented him from taking fuller opportunity of other targets. For instance, after the United States entered the war, the entire eastern coast of the United States became an open shooting gallery for U-boats. During the first three months of 1942, U-boat commanders could pick and pluck their targets almost at will, often with the lights of Miami or New York glimmering in the background. Despite the availability of targets, however, the German Navy never sent more than eighteen U-boats to United States coastal waters at any one time; usually their number was half this total. Hitler continued to be more interested in the far north. In mid-March, 1942, convinced that the British were about to invade Norway, he ordered intensified U-boat activity in the arctic, transferring submarines from other areas of the sea. By strengthening his efforts in the north to protect against an invasion that never came, Hitler reduced his strength in other areas where targets were available for German torpedoes.

Nothing, however, could shake Hitler's conviction that Norway was the "zone of destiny in this war." To some extent General Falkenhorst agreed. He thought it was possible that the Allies would mount a major offensive in the spring of 1942 and was promised reinforcements numbering eighteen thousand men.

By late spring of 1942, when Churchill first began to press seriously for Operation Jupiter, Hitler was conditioned by his own fears to expect and prepare for what Churchill hoped to deliver. Throughout the summer and autumn of 1942, Hitler lived with what he saw as a "constant threat of an enemy invasion" in Norway.

Even after Churchill had given up all hope for Jupiter, Hitler remained worried about Norway. In October, Falkenhorst warned that British landings were absolutely certain. In November, Hitler declared that he regarded "unqualified security in the Northern area" as more important than a new spring offensive against the Soviet Union, and stopped all troop exchanges with the Eastern Front. In December, Hitler and Falkenhorst started worrying afresh after receiving intelligence reports about an Allied plan to land on the narrow "neck" of Norway, between Trondheim and Narvik, and thus split the German forces in two.

Against this background of German fears, the Norwegian underground as well as the SOE-trained Norwegian agents who were operating independently of Milorg stood little chance. In October and again in December, Gestapo units cracked down on all underground groups, arresting hundreds in the north of Norway, where twenty-four agents and Milorg leaders were executed, along with ten other influential citizens, killed strictly as a reprisal measure. Hundreds more were arrested in the south of Norway around Kristiansand, where more than fifty were executed, including the Milorg district leader.

By the end of 1942 German action had rolled up all existing Milorg organizations as well as most of the SOE units in the field. For all practical purposes, the Germans could look at the internal situation in Norway with satisfaction: it was a country without a military underground.

Within two months, however, the Germans in Norway, confident and assured of control as they were, would be hit by one of the most damaging sabotage operations of the war, an operation that may well have played a part in shaping the final outcome of the conflict.

10
Heavy Water and the Atomic Bomb

The conquest of Norway delivered into German hands a remarkable power plant and manufacturing facility—the Norsk Hydro Electric Company plant at Vemork, dug deep into the mountains of southern Norway, and in 1940 the only firm in the world producing on a commercial scale the substance known as heavy water. For Germany, the Norsk Hydro plant loomed as a prize of war beyond compare, for heavy water was the key element in the Third Reich's secret effort to produce a German atomic bomb.

Heavy water is a variation of ordinary water in which the hydrogen atoms of ordinary water are replaced by atoms of heavy hydrogen, or deuterium, giving heavy water the chemical formula of D_2O, rather than the familiar H_2O which runs from our taps. The physical characteristics of heavy water also differ from those of ordinary water. It freezes at a higher temperature, boils at a higher temperature, and when concentrated weighs approximately 11 percent more than ordinary water. These physical characteristics of heavy water attracted the attention of the German atomic scientist Dr. Hans Suess when he began searching for a nuclear "moderator" to control an atomic reaction that German scientists hoped to produce in the laboratory.

For research and development purposes, a controlled nuclear reaction in the laboratory was a prerequisite before German scientists could even think of producing an atomic bomb which would unleash an uncontrolled nuclear explosion, so the search for a moderator, or braking agent, was crucial to their work. Dr. Suess's suggestion that D_2O might be the sought-after moderator was followed by small-scale experiments that proved that his faith in heavy water was valid. Heavy water could indeed be used as the moderator for a nuclear reactor built around a uranium pile.

Having settled upon heavy water as their moderator, German War Office planners confronted the problem of supply. They estimated that five tons of heavy water would eventually be needed to control chain reaction in a uranium pile, but the amount of heavy water available in Germany was barely sufficient for experimental purposes, and none was available from any country within its sphere of influence. Germany had to look abroad to the Norsk Hydro plant at Vemork, which in late 1939 was producing ten kilograms (twenty-two pounds) of heavy water per month, woefully under German needs but still the largest supply source available. Hopefully Norsk Hydro could be persuaded to increase its output.

In January, 1940, therefore, a representative of the giant German industrial combine, I. G. Farben—chosen because Farben held a financial interest in Norsk Hydro—visited the Norwegian plant for confidential talks with Norsk Hydro officials. The Farben representative came on what must have seemed a mysterious mission to the Norwegians. He wanted to buy Norsk Hydro's entire supply of heavy water, which then amounted to 185 kilograms, and he wanted Norsk Hydro to increase its production to enable Germany to buy an additional hundred kilograms (220 pounds) of heavy water each month.

How long would Germany want one hundred kilograms per month?

The answer astonished the Norwegians. There was no cut-off date to the order. It would continue indefinitely.

But why, the Norwegians wondered, did Germany need so much heavy water? To this question they received evasive replies.

In private conferences, Norsk Hydro officials agreed to postpone any decision. The Farben representative had to return to Germany with Norsk Hydro's assurance that the matter would receive sympathetic consideration but without a definite commitment from the Norwegians.

One month later, another foreign visitor arrived on the same mission—Jacques Allier, a lieutenant in the French Secret Service and an influential figure in the French bank that held a commanding financial interest in Norsk Hydro. Allier wanted Norsk Hydro's supply of heavy water for his country, but unlike the Farben representative, Allier confided the reason for the French interest to Dr. Axel Aubert, Norsk Hydro's managing director. He explained that French scientists under the world-renowned physicist Frédéric Joliot-Curie were experimenting with an atomic pile. Allier was a persuasive advocate. He appealed to Dr. Aubert's judgment and political sentiments and won from the Norwegian his promise to deliver Norsk Hydro's total supply of heavy water to France at the earliest possible date. "And tell your Premier," Aubert added, "that Norsk Hydro will accept not one centime for the product you are taking if it will aid France's victory."

France accepted delivery of the heavy water late in February, 1940. Almost concurrently, Farben in Germany was informed by Norsk Hydro that, while distressed at the news it had to impart, the company found it impossible to fill Germany's order.

Germany did not learn the true reason for Norsk Hydro's decision until German troops captured the plant in early May. Intelligence officers who went through the company records immediately afterward discovered to their dismay that the entire supply of heavy water had been sent to France. The loss to Germany, while disappointing, was overshadowed by a happier thought. One hundred and eighty-five kilograms of heavy water may have slipped from Germany's grasp, but the Third Reich now had control of something much more valuable: the Norsk Hydro heavy-water plant itself.

In May of 1940, Norsk Hydro was still producing only ten kilograms of heavy water a month, or a projected annual production of 120 kilograms, far short of Germany's potential needs. Soon a covey of German scientists descended upon the plant determined to increase production more than tenfold, to an annual output of 1,364 kilograms, or three thousand pounds. Throughout the summer and autumn of 1940, German scientists made frequent visits to the Norsk Hydro facilities, continually urging the Norwegians to step up production. In the close-knit community of Vemork and the neighboring town of Rjukan the comings and goings of the German scientific parties attracted strong local attention. Among those curious about German activities were a few Norwegians with ties to British intelligence.

The first message mentioning heavy water reached the desk of a British scientific-intelligence officer who, realizing its significance, brought it to Lt. Comdr. Eric Welsh, then head of the Norwegian section of British intelligence. Welsh had managed the International Paint Company's factory in Norway between the two world wars and had some scientific background, but the message meant nothing to him. The scientific-intelligence officer soon filled him in on its significance. Welsh's immediate response to the heavy-water report—after learning of its importance—was to request more detailed information from the Norwegian agent, Professor Leif Tronstad, a thirty-six-year-old chemist who had worked on the construction of the plant in the 1930s. Tronstad refused to supply additional information. Instead, he inquired if Imperial Chemical Industries of Great Britain, a peacetime competitor of Norsk Hydro, was not the organization interested in the information. "Remember," Tronstad added, "blood is thicker even than heavy water."

From then on, however, Welsh was alert for any mention from Scandinavia of heavy water, and by the summer of 1941 the reports were pouring in. Swedish scientists heard through the scientific grapevine of German pressure on Norsk Hydro to increase production. Tronstad, overcoming his initial hesitation, filed ominous bulletins reporting that production actually was increasing rapidly. Other agents confirmed his news. Reports from other sectors filled in the intelligence picture. The international scientific community was aware of the atomic experiments under way in Germany, and this knowledge filtered down to Allied intelligence officers. American scientists working on the United States atomic project confirmed that heavy water could in fact be used as a moderator. From all available information, therefore, it was becoming clear that Germany was basing its atomic development on heavy water, and the Allies in turn understood the importance of Norsk Hydro.

In the spring of 1942, the Norwegian coastal steamer *Galtesund* arrived in England, having been seized by a group of Norwegians trying to escape their occupied homeland. Among those on board was Einar Skinnarland, a hydroelectrical technician from Rjukan. Skinnarland was closely questioned by British intelligence officers who for some time had been seeking an agent to operate in Vemork itself. Skinnarland, an expert skier, an amateur radio operator, and a rugged outdoorsman, seemed a likely candidate. Neither his friends nor his family knew he had escaped to England, for Skinnarland had told them merely that he was going on a skiing vacation. And he was willing to work for British intelligence.

Time was short, however, for the longer Skinnarland remained away from home the greater was the danger that he would be missed. Within a few days, Skinnarland mastered the intricacies of the radio set he would carry back to Norway, rushed through basic parachute training, and sat through lengthy briefing sessions with Leif Tronstad, who had himself escaped to England only a few months before. Tronstad, by now a major assigned to Norwegian espionage operations, reviewed the layout of the Vemork plant in detail and instructed Skinnarland on the information that was most important to the Allies.

An RAF bomber dropped Skinnarland over Norway in the early morning of March 29, 1942, only eleven days after he had landed in Britain. Skinnarland touched down in predawn darkness at a spot twenty miles from his home, a distance he easily covered on skis before dawn broke. He had breakfast with his mother at daybreak. None of his neighbors or friends connected him to the *Galtesund* affair nor did they suspect that his skiing vacation had been spent undergoing training by British intelligence experts.

Skinnarland moved quickly into action. Through his brother, an influential merchant in Rjukan, he obtained work with a construction team inside the Vemork plant. Once established as a regular worker, Skinnarland contacted Dr. Jomar Brun, the chief engineer for the heavy-water concentration plant, and other engineers known to be sympathetic to the Allied cause. From them he obtained detailed reports of actual week-by-week production figures for heavy water.

Finally, Skinnarland provided London with the clincher they needed. On one of his many visits to Norsk Hydro, the German scientist Hans Suess had dropped an unguarded reference directly connecting heavy water with Germany's nuclear-energy program. Skinnarland's report of this incident wiped out any remaining doubts in London.

The intelligence picture was complete. It was now up to London to determine the means by which the heavy-water plant could be destroyed, thereby aborting Germany's race to build an atomic bomb. A bombing raid was considered but was ruled out after the British conferred with Major Tronstad, who feared the bombs would hit liquid-ammonia tanks in the area, endangering the civilian population. Tronstad suggested a ground assault against the heavy-water installation itself.

The British War Cabinet agreed with his suggestion and turned over the planning responsibility to the Combined Operations Staff, which in turn called on the Norwegian section of Special Operations Executive for its advice. The attack plan eventually worked out by Combined Operations called for a one-two punch: First, a four-man advance party would drop near Vemork to prepare a landing area for a volunteer assault force, which would land by glider near Vemork and then shoot its way into and destroy the heavy-water plant. SOE was called upon to provide the four men for the advance party and information on the desolate Hardanger plateau northwest of Vemork, which Combined Operations had chosen as its landing area.

SOE saw no difficulty in providing the four-man advance party, which they believed would have a good chance to accomplish its assigned task. But SOE warned that the gliders carrying the assault troops would run into trouble, that the Hardanger plateau, with its giant boulders and deep-cut fissures, was no place to land gliders packed with troops and explosives.

Despite SOE objections, Combined Operations moved ahead. News from Norway spurred them on. In September, 1941, production at the Norsk Hydro plant had reached 130 kilograms and was expected to continue to increase. Staff planning received added impetus with the arrival in Britain of Norsk Hydro's chief engineer, Dr. Jomar Brun—who had escaped with his wife to Sweden and from there to London. Brun brought with him disquieting information. The year before, he reported, he had visited Germany and had learned details of Germany's progress toward the manufacture of an atomic bomb. This information dovetailed exactly with intelligence reports the British had received from other sources.

For operations behind the enemy lines in occupied Norway, the British could draw on a remarkable body of Norwegians, all highly motivated members of Company Linge, the volunteer company of special action troops. Their rigorous training in hand-to-hand combat, signaling, sabotage techniques, map reading, advanced weapon handling, silent killing, boat handling, survival techniques, and parachute operations under the direct supervision of SOE officers—as well as the special training in code, security, cover stories, and special-agent techniques of a few members—well fitted them for the daring task. The company, though trained to razor sharpness, had seen little action, with the result that internal strife and discontent adversely affected its morale. The death of their leader Captain Linge in the British raid on the Lofoten Islands had aggravated the demoralization. By the autumn of 1942, the company had a solid core of frustrated men who had been trained to operate on their own ("Remember," their British instructors had told them, "expect nothing. There will be no one to help you in action") and who believed that they were superbly equipped to handle any situation they could conceivably face in combat. It was from these men that the SOE chose the four-man advance party, code-named Swallow, that was scheduled to drop into Norway sometime in October.

Chosen to command Swallow was Lt. Jens Poulsson, a tall, lanky native of Rjukan with a matter-of-fact approach to combat. Poulsson's second-in-command was Sgt. Arne Kjelstrup, an Oslo plumber in civilian life. To round out the group, Poulsson selected two other natives of Rjukan, Claus Helberg, an experienced outdoorsman whom Poulsson planned to use primarily as a scout and hunter, and Knut Haugland, the unit's radio operator. Poulsson knew Helberg and Haugland well from the days when all three were young men growing up in Rjukan. He had gotten to know his second-in-command, Sergeant Kjelstrup, during their escape to England in 1941. Both men were part of a group of Norwegians who, after crossing into Sweden, spent the next five and a half months making a roundabout journey to England. Their route took them through Finland, Russia (just ahead of invading German armies), and Egypt into India, where they eventually boarded a vessel headed for the British Isles by way of Nova Scotia. During those long months, the two men became fast friends, each respectful of the other's attitudes and abilities.

This tight-knit group parachuted into Norway shortly before midnight on October 18, 1942, landing far from their designated drop zone. The countryside, which strangers would consider hostile, offered a friendly environment to the men of the Swallow mission, each of whom had spent many years in civilian life skiing and camping in the wilderness. Although they had no idea where they were, they did know that they were alone, and comforted by the knowledge that the rugged mountain terrain was their greatest protection against German patrols, they wrapped themselves in their parachutes and went to sleep in the open.

They awoke to one of the finest mornings they could remember—a brilliant sun shone down on a layer of new snow that had fallen while they slept. However, their spirits sank as soon as they consulted their maps. They had landed one hundred miles off target and their trip to Vemork would have to be made over some of the most difficult terrain in southern Norway.

It proved a grueling experience. Temperatures at the four-thousand-foot altitude at which they traveled often fell below zero, and the men labored under heavy loads. One hundred and twenty pounds of equipment had been assigned to each man, but the maximum load that any individual could carry under the conditions that prevailed was only sixty pounds, so the party had to cover a distance of three miles in order to achieve an actual advance of one mile: first forward with part of the equipment, then back to the original starting point, and then forward again over the same ground with the remaining equipment. In this way the party advanced toward Vemork, buffeted by high winds, chilled by numbing temperatures, and forced to take two extra steps for every one step forward. Nevertheless, they pushed ahead with grim determination. A good portion of the equipment they struggled with would be needed to light a landing zone for the assault gliders. The success of the mission depended on their labors.

The Swallow party finally reached the Vemork area on November 9, far behind schedule, and made contact with Skinnarland, who had been alerted to expect their arrival. He had discouraging news for them. The local German commander had recently added extra troops to guard the Norsk Hydro plant. Any attack was certain to meet with stiff resistance.

That same night a worried Haugland raised London by radio to report the party's arrival on the scene and to deliver his first situation report. London liked neither the news it heard nor the manner in which the message was transmitted. Something in Haugland's transmission aroused suspicions that the party had been captured by Germans and that a German counterintelligence agent, not Haugland, was sitting at the sending key. Using special prearranged check messages, London eventually succeeded in confirming to its satisfaction that it was Haugland at the other end. What they did not realize was that the bitter cold had stiffened his fingers and changed his normal touch.

There remained the news Haugland had reported, and this could not be dispelled. An increase in the number of German guards raised the danger level for the assault troops. The enemy now had much more firepower available, while the British were limited in the number of men they could throw against the target. Without question the odds for success had dropped sharply, but Combined Operations was not about to call off the mission. After only a short reconsideration, London gave the go-ahead signal for the actual assault, using the code name Freshman for the operation. Thirty-four specially trained sapper volunteers under the command of a British lieutenant were ready for action ten days later.

Two Halifax bombers, each towing a Horsa glider packed with heavily armed troops, took off from Wick Airfield, Scotland, on the evening of November 19. The Halifax pilots were tense. They had had only limited experience towing gliders and the weather was bad. Thick cloud cover was expected for most of the four-hundred-mile run to Norway. Trouble started almost immediately. Telephone links that were supposed to provide communication between each glider and its towing aircraft failed to operate, leaving the crews in the air without any means of talking to each other.

One bomber-glider unit hit the coast of Norway near Egersund, coming in low in hopes of creeping under the cloud cover. But the pilot, unfamiliar with the Norwegian terrain, came in too low. Both bomber and glider crashed into a mountainside ten miles from the coast.

The other bomber-glider unit crossed the Norwegian coast at a safe ten-thousand foot altitude and made what seemed good progress toward the drop zone, but once near the designated area, the bomber pilot could not locate the landing lights set out by the Swallow party. With fuel running low, he turned for home with the glider still in tow. As he neared the Norwegian coast on the homeward run, the towline connecting glider and bomber snapped, sending the second troop-laden glider on a slow descent toward the sea.

German troops found the wreckage of the bomber and glider that had crashed near Egersund the following morning. From the position of the two wrecked aircraft, and the distance between them, it was evident that the bomber pilot had set the glider free at the last minute in an attempt to save his own aircraft. But all six crewmen of the Halifax were dead when German troops arrived at the scene, while fourteen soldiers who had been in the glider survived the crash.

German officers at the glider crash also found explosives, small arms, and radio transmitters amid the wreckage and correctly concluded that the British troops had been on a sabotage mission. The fourteen surviving soldiers were rushed to Egersund, where, after a brief and superficial interrogation, they were taken out and executed by a German firing squad. The German battalion commander in Egersund was more obedient than intelligent. He had followed Hitler's Commando order literally:

> On account of the increased number of cases in which aircraft are used for landing saboteurs, who do serious damage, I order that personnel from sabotage aircraft shall be immediately shot by the first persons who come into contact with them.

When news of the executions reached Reichskommissar Terboven and Gen. Wilhelm Rediess, head of the German secret police in Norway, they could not believe what they heard: the British soldiers had been executed without any attempt having been made to determine the nature of their intended target. General Rediess complained bitterly to Berlin:

> A British towing aircraft and its glider have crashed near Egersund at about 3:00 A.M. on the 20th. Cause of accident not yet known. As far as has been ascertained, towing aircraft's crew is military, all dead. There were seventeen men in glider, probably agents. Three of them

were killed, six badly injured. Glider's crew was in possession of large quantities of Norwegian money. Unfortunately the military authorities executed the survivors so explanation scarcely possible now.

General Falkenhorst, the German commander-in-chief of Norway, was equally infuriated, for the action of the Egersund battalion commander reflected adversely on his command. Falkenhorst immediately ordered all army units to delay any future Commando executions until the men could be interrogated by security police, noting that Hitler's Commando order made specific provisions for delay in execution for the purpose of interrogation. No sooner had Falkenhorst's order been distributed than an Army unit near Stavanger received word that Norwegian police had arrested three British soldiers and were seeking to turn them over to an appropriate German command.

Under questioning, the British soldiers confessed that they were survivors of the second glider and gave their captors the location of the downed aircraft. Search parties quickly rounded up other survivors.

Given a second opportunity to question British glider troops, the Germans did not repeat their first mistake. Gestapo agents alerted to the capture subjected the British soldiers to a lengthy and brutal interrogation. Only after the survivors had revealed all that they knew, including details of their objective, did the Gestapo release them from their torment and permit the German Army to execute them in compliance with Hitler's Commando order, as amended and interpreted by General Falkenhorst.

General Falkenhorst was pleased with the outcome. "The interrogation," he proudly reported, "provided valuable admissions of the enemy's intentions."

Even General Rediess was placated. In a memorandum to his superiors in Berlin, he indicated that before they were killed the British troops had indicated "that the British placed great importance on the planned destruction" of Vemork's heavy-water plant.

In London, the Combined Operations Staff passed on what little they knew to Jens Poulsson and his men, who had maintained a vigil for the gliders throughout the appointed time. "Stand by," London ordered. Poulsson noted in his diary that it was "a hard blow." Kjelstrup remembered it as "a sad night." The men of Swallow, however, had a critical predicament of their own to solve.

Exactly one month had passed between the time they had landed in Norway and the unsuccessful glider mission. Their food was running out, and they faced the dread prospect of trying to survive the winter in the wilderness. And they were on their own, with no help available from any quarter, as their SOE instructors had warned them they might be. By background and temperament, however, the men of Swallow were ideally equipped for the task at hand. Poulsson led them first to a hut deep in the mountains where he had previously passed time on skiing trips. There they dug themselves in and set about providing for their two greatest needs: food and warmth. Wood was scarce, but somehow they found enough of it under the snow to fuel their fires. And Helberg, who had been taken on as hunter and scout, came through superbly. Under his skilled guidance, the men of Swallow tracked down and killed thirteen reindeer, eventually devouring every edible morsel, including unborn fetuses, eyeballs, and the contents of the reindeer's stomachs, which they forced themselves to eat for the vegetable matter they provided. Though weakened by malnutrition and a lack of vitamins, the Swallow party held on through the long winter while London planned its next assault on the heavy-water plant at Vemork.

11
The Raid on Norsk Hydro

The failure of Operation Freshman was not only a disaster in itself but it imposed grave difficulties on any second attempt to destroy the Norsk Hydro heavy-water plant. Before Freshman, London and Washington were fully aware of the significance of heavy water to Germany's atomic development and had known what the Germans were up to in Vemork, while the Germans, on their part, were unaware of Allied interest. The first attack, therefore, was planned with the expectation that surprise could be achieved.

When British staff officers began planning a second attack, however, they were forced to assume that the worst possible set of circumstances actually existed. Although information about the fate of the glider and bomber crews was not immediately available, London had to consider the possibility that some of the crewmen had survived the crash, that they had been picked up and interrogated by the Germans, and that Germany knew of Allied interest in Norsk Hydro, all of which had in fact occurred. The advantage now seemed to rest with the Germans, who, once alerted, would certainly be on their guard against a second attempt. Surprise could no longer be considered a factor.

As a second attack in force, based on surprise, was no longer feasible, there remained two possibilities: a bombing attack on Vemork or a special sabotage operation. When the British War Office again rejected bombing, the responsibility for planning a sabotage attack fell to the Special Operations Executive, under Col. Jack Wilson, head of the SOE's Norwegian section. Much to its relief, Combined Operations was taken completely out of the picture; the fiasco of Freshman had soured the staff on the whole project. SOE was now totally responsible.

The plan decided upon by Colonel Wilson, in consultation with Major Tronstad and Dr. Brun, both of whom were intimately familiar with the layout of the heavy-water plant, called for dropping another small team of agents on the Hardanger plateau, where they would join forces with the men of Swallow to carry out a sneak sabotage raid on the facility. It was a plan fraught with danger, but it was the best one available to Wilson and his Norwegian associates.

To command the sabotage raid, SOE chose one of the most highly trained Norwegian officers of Company Linge, Lt. Joachim Ronneberg, a native of the Norwegian coastal city of Ålesund who had escaped to Great Britain in 1941 and who had subsequently become an officer-instructor training other Norwegian volunteers for "special actions," as the no-holds-barred SOE raids were euphemistically called. Ronneberg was itching for combat. On his arrival in Britain in 1941, he had told British interrogators that he had escaped from Norway "to fight the Germans."

By every possible indicator Ronneberg seemed the perfect choice for the assignment, which went under the code name Gunnerside. His outlook, his training, his ability to lead men, and his personal inclination on how the war should be fought fitted him for the role.

Ronneberg selected five good skiers from Company Linge and reported with his men to London for briefings with Major Tronstad, who informed the Gunnerside force of their target and told them about the failure of Operation Freshman. Major Tronstad was not reassuring. Norwegian agents by then had reported what had happened to the captured glider troops and Tronstad warned that if the Gunnerside mission failed, Lieutenant Ronneberg and his men could expect the same fate that had befallen the men of Freshman.

By December 15, 1942, the Gunnerside operation order was ready for review. Classified "Most Secret," the order instructed the Gunnerside force to "attack the storage and producing plant at Vemork with high explosives, so that present stocks and fluid in the course of production are destroyed." The most reliable information available at the time indicated that the Gunnerside force would have to contend with one hundred German troops, most of them Gestapo, stationed in Rjukan, and a regular German unit stationed at Vemork itself. Other German units were scattered around the area at key points.

The Gunnerside force completed its training by January 1, 1943, using a dummy plant built to duplicate specifications of the real Vemork facility. The men knew their target so well they could, in practice, set explosive charges in the dark, identifying the important tanks and machinery by touch alone. Their information covered all items that could conceivably be useful. Ronneberg and his men were even told where to find a key which, if the situation arose, they could use to lock any watchmen in the plant's washroom.

Departure day was set for January 23, the Swallow force alerted to expect Gunnerside, and Ronneberg and his men were moved from their holding area near Cambridge to Scotland for the flight that would take them back to Norway. On the appointed day, Major Tronstad and

Colonel Wilson flew up from London to brief the men for the last time. Tronstad was concerned both for the safety of the men and the success of the mission. He stressed the importance of the target they would be attacking and assured the men that if they succeeded in their mission, Norway would remember their deed and their names for hundreds of years.

The Gunnerside force knew they were embarking on an exceedingly dangerous mission. They had already written last letters to their next-of-kin; these would be held by the SOE in case they did not return. As they boarded the RAF bomber that would carry them over their drop zone, each man was issued a last piece of equipment—a small brown cyanide capsule—confirming in their minds that few expected them to return safely.

The RAF bomber roared aloft and headed northeastward to Norway and the Hardanger plateau. It crossed the coast at a high altitude and then descended rapidly, hoping to elude the eyes of German observers. Difficulties arose over the Hardanger. The pilot, not being able to spot the lights of the advance party below, brought his aircraft back to the coast for fresh bearings, but still could not find the drop zone. After cruising aimlessly over Norway for two hours, he headed for home, refusing to let the "heartbroken" Norwegians jump in the dark. As the plane neared the coast, alert German anit-aircraft gunners opened fire, damaging the aircraft so badly that it barely managed to limp back to Scotland. It landed with one engine inoperative and another on fire. The first attempt at Gunnerside had failed, but the operation was promptly rescheduled for the next full moon, on February 16.

A different drop zone was chosen for the second attempt—Lake Skryken on the Hardanger plateau, thirty miles from the factory, and a geographical landmark that could be identified from the air even in the absence of marker lights. The second flight went well. The outline of Lake Skryken came into view exactly on schedule. Inside the aircraft, the green jump lamp flashed and Lieutenant Ronneberg dropped through the open hatch, followed by the other Gunnerside men. On the ground the men formed up and began to gather the weapons and equipment. Operation Gunnerside had successfully landed in Norway after a perfect flight and a safe jump unobserved by German patrols. But soon an unanticipated danger faced them.

The weather, which had been good for the drop, turned suddenly fierce. Even as the Gunnerside force struggled to pack their equipment, a winter blizzard swept across the frozen surface of Lake Skryken, making work impossible and sending the men racing for the edge of the lake, where they crept into an uninhabited mountain shack. Ronneberg later commented that it "was problematical if we could have survived without shelter."

For six days the wind blew so strongly that movement was impossible. Not until February 22 did conditions improve enough for travel. "The weather turned fine," Ronneberg wrote in his diary, "and I gave the order to prepare for departure." The Gunnerside force set out to make contact with the Swallow force, six days behind schedule but otherwise in excellent shape and with all their equipment in hand.

The Swallow force, however, had about given up hope that Ronneberg and his men had survived. On the day after the drop, London assured the advance party that Gunnerside had had "a successful drop," a message which was greeted with skepticism by Swallow's commanding officer, Lieutenant Poulsson. The Gunnerside force may indeed have left the plane successfully, but conditions on the ground were so bad that Poulsson was convinced the party had perished. "Successful drop," Poulsson commented sarcastically to his companions, "but unfortunately the party died upon landing." Nevertheless, when the weather eased, he permitted Sergeants Kjelstrup and Helberg to start searching for Ronneberg's unit on the chance that they were still alive.

After searching one day without success, Kjelstrup and Helberg came upon the Ronneberg party the following day, February 23. "Wild yells of pleasure" sounded over the snow-covered Norwegian countryside as the men, most of whom had trained together in England, greeted each other with enthusiastic bear hugs. To the Gunnerside force, the two Swallow men appeared gaunt and weak from malnutrition, and before moving on, Ronneberg distributed chocolate bars and raisins "imported directly from England" as emergency rations. That evening the combined party reached the Swallow hut where another joyful reception awaited them. "Tongues were loosened over reindeer meat and porridge," Ronneberg wrote in his operation report. "The lads were in wonderful spirits."

The next morning, February 24, the men of Swallow and Gunnerside tackled the problems at hand. How should they approach their target? How should they make their escape? Before deciding, Ronneberg and Poulsson sent Sergeant Helberg, the best scout available, on a reconnaissance patrol to the Vemork plant for the latest information. Once Helberg had left, the remaining force set out after him, following in his footsteps at a slower pace. Only two radio operators, Einar Skinnarland, who had been the first agent dropped in the Vemork area, and Knut Haugland, who had dropped with the Swallow mission, were left behind at the Swallow hut. After the mission, a man from the assault force would be sent back to inform them of the outcome. Their job then would be to report the news to England.

On the morning of February 27, the main party reached another hut less than two miles north of Vemork. Here they settled in to await the return of Sergeant Helberg. Helberg returned later that morning with up-to-the-minute information on the state of German defenses at Ve-mork. Two sentries, he reported, stood guard at a narrow suspension bridge spanning a gorge that lay between the attacking force and their target. Twenty more German soldiers were stationed inside the com-pound itself, but they could be expected to be in their barracks at night. In addition, two Norwegian watchmen patrolled the main building while two more guarded the main gate.

Despite the odds against them, Ronneberg's force was not unduly worried by the news Helberg brought back. It was, in fact, fairly en-couraging. From all their specialized training, they knew that men standing sentry duty could be counted on to be bored and disinterested in their duties. Unless specifically alerted, sentries could normally be sur-prised or bypassed by an aggressive force operating with stealth and speed. Unless special circumstances arose, Ronneberg anticipated no trouble getting around the sentries.

One major problem remained, however. The Gunnerside force still had not decided on a route into the factory itself. The plant rested like an eagle's eyrie high up on a mountainside, on the opposite side of a deep ravine cut by the waters of the River Maan. Ordinary traffic used the suspension bridge that spanned the ravine, but the Gunnerside force had to rule out this approach because of the bridge sentries. Even if the sentries could be overcome, which the Gunnerside force believed possi-ble, they would certainly have time to raise an alarm, which would alert the German troops inside the heavy-water plant and doom the mission. The Gunnerside force needed an alternate route to their target, one which would bring them into the plant unobserved. From Helberg's report there was but one alternate route . . . down a steep, snow-covered mountain slope to the valley of the River Maan, across the river itself, and then up the opposite side of the gorge to the factory. But Helberg and the other men in the party who were natives of Rjukan ruled out this approach as well. To the inhabitants of the area, the gorge was considered too steep to climb. Lieutenant Ronneberg, however, disagreed. Aerial photographs of the area, which he had studied back in Britain, showed clumps of trees and foliage in an irregular line, clinging up and down the cliff. Where trees grow, Ronneberg argued, man can climb. Helberg was sent out on another mission specifically to check out the cliff at the point where the aerial photographs showed there might be a possible route. He returned four hours later with good news: the cliff could be climbed. The attack route was settled.

The nine-man Gunnerside force, led by Lieutenant Ronneberg, moved out on skis for the final approach to the heavy-water plant at 8 P.M. on February 27, a Saturday. Their schedule called for an attack shortly after the changing of the guard at midnight. The time of the attack and the day of the week were considered auspicious. For the majority of

The Norsk Hydro power complex at Vemork. *(Wide World Photo)*

German forces in Norway, Saturday nights were given over to whatever revelry and relaxation they could find. The Gunnerside force assumed that troops unlucky enough to be on duty at the time of the attack would be less alert than usual.

The party made quick headway after leaving their last rendezvous hut. On their backs they carried explosive charges that had been prepared in England. The rifles slung across their shoulders, on Ronneberg's specific instructions, were unloaded. Fearing any premature firing could alert the German garrison, he had instructed his men that they were not to load their weapons under any circumstances unless they were absolutely certain that they would have to fire.

Two thousand yards below the hut the woods thickened, forcing the party to take off their skis and proceed on foot toward a winding road running along the valley. Weather and snow conditions were on their side. A brilliant moon lighted the landscape and hard-packed snow on the road enabled the party to travel for more than a mile and a half without leaving tracks.

The attacking force heard the factory before they saw it. A faint mechanical hum reached them from a far distance as they made their way along the road. Moving on, they came to a curve in the road where they caught sight of their target for the first time. It was an awesome view. The factory, perched on an outcropping of rock on the far side of the ravine, loomed ominous and forbidding. Lights flickered inside the heavy-water plant and the steady hum of its generators carried across the ravine with increased intensity.

For a few seconds the men of Gunnerside paused to let the scene sink in, as if to etch in their memories their first view of the plant and of the precipice they would have to scale to reach it. Then they pushed on along the road until they came to a cluster of farmhouses standing dark and silent in the fields. Silently, Sergeant Helberg motioned the party to leave the road and reenter the deep woods through which they would have to pass to reach the bottom of the ravine. Their descent proved slow and difficult, for the terrain grew more rocky and the descent steeper the farther they advanced down the mountainside. Deep in the woods the party halted again in a tiny open clearing to pull off their white camouflage uniforms. Underneath they wore the khaki combat uniforms of British soldiers, for it had been decided in London that the Norwegian unit would make its attack dressed as British soldiers and thus deny the Germans any justification for taking reprisals on the civilian population should they be captured. Once in combat dress, the Gunnerside force hid their skis and rucksacks and set off for the final descent down the steep and slippery north face of the gorge. If the attack went well, they hoped to return to the same spot, recover their equipment, and make their escape over the same route they had just traveled. They took with them on their final descent only their precious explosive charges, their weapons, and a pair of armorer's shears which Sergeant Kjelstrup planned to use to cut a way into the compound.

The party crossed the River Maan over a convenient ice bridge, covered with only a few inches of rushing water, and approached the precipice on the south bank of the river. A fierce southwesterly wind whistling through the valley made conversation difficult. They climbed in silence, seeking out footholds where hardy bushes and stunted trees gripped the mountainside. Yard by yard they crawled and clawed their way upward. Almost imperceptibly their pace increased as they gained ground toward the top, for each man had the feeling that his comrades were climbing more rapidly than he and consequently prodded himself to greater effort. In this way they reached the top, exhausted by the exertion and gasping for breath, but ahead of schedule and optimistic about what was to come. The mission so far had proceeded exactly to plan. They had conquered a cliff some feared could not be climbed, they had not been detected, and they were in time to observe the changing of the guard at midnight.

Having successfully overcome one critical obstacle, the Gunnerside force took shelter behind a small building a few hundred yards from the plant to regain their strength and to review for the last time their plans for the attack. The nine-man party was divided into a four-man demolition team under the command of Lieutenant Ronneberg and a five-man covering unit under the command of Lt. Knut Haukelid, which would provide protection for the demolition party in case the Germans were alerted. The demolition team was further broken down into twin two-man units, each capable of blowing up the plant and each prepared to act independently of the other. In effect, the operation had two demolition parties.

Promptly at midnight, as anticipated, two German soldiers assumed their posts on the bridge while the two sentries who had been relieved of duty strolled nonchalantly back toward the German barracks. Ronneberg waited what he thought was a sufficient time to enable the two sentries to get to bed before ordering Sergeant Kjelstrup to advance toward the factory fence. Crouching low and clutching his armorer's shears in one hand and his rifle in the other, Kjelstrup raced forward, snipped a man-sized hole in the wire-mesh fence, and waved the rest of the party into the compound. Within seconds the attacking force scattered to their assigned positions. Lieutenant Haukelid, carrying a pistol and satchel of hand grenades, and Lieutenant Poulsson, armed with a tommy gun, stationed themselves within twenty yards of the German barracks. Once in position, Haukelid and Poulsson could talk without fear of being heard—the hum from the electric generators drowned out their words. If German troops responded to an alarm, Poulsson planned to riddle the wooden barracks with automatic small-arms fire while Haukelid attacked with grenades.

Other men of the covering party took up positions at vital approach routes at the plant. As they slipped into position, they were cheered by the fact that they had heard no shooting. Sergeant Kjelstrup, a member of the covering force, recalled later that he thought at the time the operation had to succeed. With the Norwegians in position at strategic points, nothing could stop the operation.

The demolition teams, meanwhile, moved rapidly toward the heavy-water plant, seeking a cable tunnel which they had been told would provide them with an access route into the factory. The first team missed the tunnel, however, and continued on around the exterior of the plant, while the second team, composed of Lieutenant Ronneberg and a sergeant, located the tunnel and started to crawl through to their objective. Their passage went smoothly and the two men soon found themselves inside the plant, in position to look into the room where the tanks of heavy water stood invitingly before them. A lone Norwegian watchman sat in the room, writing on a table. He was completely unaware of the eyes upon him.

Ronneberg and the sergeant burst into the room with their weapons at the ready, surprising the watchman at his work. "He seemed frightened," Ronneberg later wrote, "but otherwise was quiet and obedient."

Ronneberg noted that the heavy-water plant was an exact duplicate of the plant in England, and then had to correct himself mentally, for the plant in England was a duplicate of the real plant, not vice versa. Ronneberg nevertheless felt that he was on familiar ground. He set to work assembling his explosive charges and fuses, placing them around the tanks of heavy water. As he worked, the sound of shattering glass brought him whirling around in fright, but it was only the two men of the other demolition team who, having failed to find the cable tunnel, had broken into the heavy-water plant through a ground-floor window. Together, Lieutenant Ronneberg and the leader of the second demolition team completed the job of setting explosive charges on the heavy-water tanks, placing two two-minute charges and a single thirty-second fuse on each cell, thus providing a double backup system to ensure that no cell escaped undamaged.

Before lighting the fuses, the Norwegian saboteurs scattered around the room unofficial calling cards which had been specifically chosen to anger and humiliate the Germans. The calling cards were authentic British parachute badges. When all was in readiness, Ronneberg ordered the fuses lit, and the four men of the demolition team, closely followed by the frightened Norwegian watchman, fled for cover. They had barely left the room when the charges went off with a dull rumble. Ronneberg later wrote that for a moment after the explosion he "looked back down the line and listened. But except for the hum of machinery that we heard when we arrived, everything in the factory was quiet."

The men of the covering party outside heard the explosion as an even more muted rumble, "astonishingly insignificant," as one recalled later. So did the Germans. Seconds after the explosion, a lone, bareheaded German soldier peered out of the barracks hut for a few seconds, disappeared quickly inside, and then reappeared with a helmet on his head and a rifle and a flashlight in his hands. Lieutenants Haukelid and Poulsson watched silently as the German guard began to examine the exterior of the heavy-water plant, the circle of yellow from his flashlight weaving erratic patterns on the frozen ground. His curiosity may have been aroused, but the German still had no idea what had happened. He disappeared from view around the corner of the plant as Haukelid and Poulsson retreated from their posts toward a previously-agreed-upon assembly point where Lieutenant Ronneberg and the other Gunnerside men were waiting. Ronneberg could hardly contain his joy. The mission, he proudly told them, had been a complete success. It was now time for the Norwegians to look after their own lives and withdraw.

The Norwegians slipped away quickly and silently, khaki ghosts in the night, and made their escape over the same route they had taken on their approach. Mystifiedly, they heard no sounds of alarm from the heavy-water plant. They had scrambled down the precipice on the south side of the gorge and had reached the River Maan before the factory's air-raid siren signaled the alert, and they were well up the far side of the mountain before the factory's searchlights flared into life, crisscrossing the night with sharp beams of light. But by then the fast-moving Norwegians were out of range, under cover of the woods and close to the spot where they had hidden their skis and supplies. The Norwegians had every reason to be pleased with their night's work.

Their mission completed, the Gunnerside and Swallow forces split up. Lieutenant Ronneberg led four members of his unit on a four-hundred-mile trek to Sweden, a journey they successfully completed in eighteen days. Sergeant Helberg, who had performed so admirably as a scout, hunter, and reconnaissance expert for both the Swallow and Gunnerside parties, went into hiding in the Rjukan area. London wanted him "in place" for future assignments. Lieutenant Poulsson, who had successfully commanded the Swallow team, headed for Oslo to take up other resistance work. The remaining two members of the assault team, Lieutenant Haukelid and Sergeant Kjelstrup, were given the responsibility of reporting the outcome of the operation to the two radio operators who had been left behind. They in turn flashed the good news to London:

OPERATION CARRIED OUT WITH 100 PERCENT SUCCESS. HIGH CONCEN-
TRATION PLANT COMPLETELY DESTROYED. SHOTS NOT EXCHANGED SINCE
THE GERMANS DID NOT REALIZE ANYTHING. THE GERMANS DO NOT
APPEAR TO KNOW WHENCE THE PARTY CAME OR WHITHER THEY DISAP-
PEARED.

The attack team had indeed done its job extremely well. When German authorities inspected the damage the day after the raid, they found that explosive charges had destroyed all heavy-water cells, permitting approximately two thousand pounds of the precious substance to spill out over the floor. Shrapnel from the explosions had also punched holes in the pipes and tubes of the installation, compounding the damage. German authorities were appalled. On a visit to the factory, General Falkenhorst became so enraged at the sight of the inept German garrison that he personally berated the unit's officers and men before a group of interested Norwegian onlookers. Afterward Falkenhorst conceded to an associate that it was "the best coup I have ever seen."

News of the raid created intense excitement throughout Scandinavia even though the importance of the Vemork plant to Germany's atomic program was not public knowledge. A Swedish newspaper described it as "one of the most important and successful undertakings the Allied saboteurs have carried out as yet during the war."

In the weeks following the raid, British intelligence received additional information about the damage inflicted. A secret message sent by an agent in Oslo via an undercover contact in Stockholm concluded that damage at the plant was "not extensive except at the place where the attempt was made and there the devastation was total." From these reports, Britain estimated that Germany's heavy-water production program had been set back by two years.

Nine Norwegians had dealt a crippling blow to Germany's efforts to build an atomic bomb.

12
Occupied Denmark

Denmark is, in essence, an accommodating country, its people stirred by no grand passions. At one time in history it was different. For centuries the Danes were a warlike people, battling their way south into Italy and east into Estonia, overrunning England and later consolidating their hold on Norway and Sweden to the north. But the days of the Vikings were a millennium ago. As early as the 1500s, Denmark's power was in decline, her people no longer feared throughout Europe.

An English traveler who visited Denmark in 1692 described the country in terms that could be used today. "The face of the land," he wrote, "is pleasant in the many places, abounding with little hills, woods and lakes in a very agreeable diversity." The Englishman found the Danish women "exceeding fruitful" and described all Danes as living for "today, as the poet advises." The Danish language has a word to define the country: *hyggelig,* cosy, comfortable, agreeable.

Into this *hyggelig* country the German Wehrmacht arrived like a slash of iron. The German ultimatum delivered to the Danish government on the morning of April 9 assured the Danes that acceptance would not mean submission.

> In accordance with the good spirit which has always prevailed in Danish-German relations, the Reich Government declares to the Danish Government that Germany does not intend now or in the future to interfere with Denmark's territorial integrity or political independence.

And Gen. Leonhard Kaupisch, the German commander-in-chief for Denmark, sought to allay the fears of the average Dane, dropping leaflets by air and broadcasting appeals over the Danish radio:

> Strong German military forces have this morning taken possession of the principal military points in Denmark and Norway. These measures are the subject of agreements which are at present being made

Germany defended the coast of Jutland against an invasion force that never came.
(Nordisk Pressefoto)

between the German Government and the Royal Danish Government . . . to secure the continued existence of the Kingdom, the maintenance of the Army and Navy, respect for the freedom of the Danish people and the full security of the future independence of this country.

Denmark, faced with the presence of German military strength, set about finding ways to accommodate the invader as well as to assure the safety and continued comfort of her own citizens. The Danish government called on its population to remain calm and obedient "to all persons in authority." Denmark's King Christian X, in a personal appeal to his subjects, called on them "to show an absolutely correct and dignified behavior." And the Danish Foreign Minister, Peter Munch, seized on German assurances that Germany did not intend to interfere with Denmark's independence to suggest a "policy of negotiation" with the Germans, a suggestion endorsed by all Danish officials. The alternative to negotiation—resistance—was never considered. The presence of German military units inside Denmark, and the widely held belief that Germany would win the war, precluded any thought of it.

The Germans also favored negotiation. The German Foreign Minister in Denmark, Cecil von Renthe-Fink, a diplomat of the old school and personally sympathetic to the Danes, was convinced that a close working relationship between the two countries would give Denmark some degree of sovereignty while assuring Germany of Danish foodstuffs, Danish manufactured goods, and Danish support for the German war effort.

For three years, Denmark succeeded in its efforts to maintain a degree of independence. From April, 1940, until the summer of 1943, a crucial period in Danish history, Denmark remained an island of plenty and relative peace in war-torn Europe. Denmark's farms produced more than enough food for her population, while increasing agricultural exports to Germany. From October, 1941, to October, 1942, Denmark shipped 93,000 tons of meat and 31,000 tons of butter to Germany; the next year the exports increased to 100,000 tons of meat and 33,000 tons of butter. For the average Dane life under German occupation continued near normal. Schools remained open. The Danish Army and Navy were not disbanded. Church, business, and social groups operated freely. Jobs were available. Even Danish Jews were permitted to lead lives free from fear of harassment or arrest.

But there was a price to pay. German demand followed German demand. The Danish Constitution came under attack almost immediately. In July, 1940, the Danish government under pressure from the Germans curtailed the country's free press. After that, any Danish editor printing a story considered detrimental to Danish foreign relations could be jailed for one year. In the same month, King Christian X personally summoned the pro-German Danish politician Erik Scavenius to head the Danish Foreign Ministry. Scavenius had served as Danish Foreign Minister during World War I. On taking over the post again in 1940, he issued a declaration of policy which drew a parallel between World War I and World War II:

> Denmark should not under any circumstances come into conflict with its great neighbor to the south. This policy has met with German understanding and support alike during the World War and during the present war. The Great German victories which have struck the world with astonishment and admiration have begun a new era in Europe, which will bring with it a New Order in political and economic spheres under Germany's leadership. It will be Denmark's task herein to find its place in mutual active cooperation with Greater Germany.

Scavenius' statement, with its strong pro-German bias, attracted wide attention among both Danes and Germans. German Minister Renthe-Fink wrote in his diary that "with this statement Denmark accepts an economic and political reconstruction under German leadership." Highly placed Danes supported Scavenius' initiative. A few weeks after Scavenius took office several leading Danes, including the editor of Copenhagen's most prestigious newspaper, *Berlingske Tidende,* and the general manager of the Danish State Railways, established a Danish-German Association designed to foster better relations with the invading forces. The association scheduled lectures and social gatherings where the beer and schnapps flowed freely. Danes highly placed in the country's business and professional life were easily persuaded to accept membership in the association. Other Danes developed friendly contacts with German officials on their own. Carl Popp-Madsen, an assistant undersecretary in the Ministry of Justice who had been accepted into Hitler's Academy of German Jurists because of his pro-German speeches during the late 1930s, became a frequent visitor to the home of Renthe-Fink, whom he considered an "amiable and intelligent man" devoted, as he himself was, to peaceful relations between Denmark and Germany.

Denmark also had its own version of Hitler's Nazi Party—the Danish National Socialist Workers Party (DNSAP) headed by Dr. Fritz Clausen, a provincial Jutland practitioner with no political experience. Clausen had taken over the DNSAP leadership in 1933 but had failed, throughout the 1930s, to gather appreciable support from the Danes. In the national election of 1935, the DNSAP received only fifteen thousand votes. In the elections of 1939, its vote increased to 31,000, sufficient to send three members to the Danish Parliament, Clausen among them; but even so, the DNSAP received less than 2 percent of the total vote. In April, 1940, the hopes of the Danish Nazis ran high. Members of the DNSAP turned out in Jutland to assist the invading German troops, and once the occupation was secure, Clausen was available to push German policies in Parliament and in the party's newspaper, *Faedrelandet* (Fatherland). Renthe-Fink began to funnel financial aid to the DNSAP, averaging 600,000 kroner per month. But the Danish Nazis were badly splintered, and the Danish public, even those who looked with favor upon Germany, did not rally behind the Danish Nazis. Circulation of *Faedrelandet* never rose over ten thousand. A Danish joke popular during the early years of the occupation asked: "What is a Danish National Socialist?" The answer: "One who sells *Faedrelandet.*"

In November, 1940, the DNSAP, with German support, sought power itself, joining with the small Right-wing Danish Peasant's Party in an attack on the government. While they approved of Foreign Minister Scavenius, they denounced as anti-German all other members of the government, including the highly respected Premier Thorvald Stauning. Stauning's resignation was demanded, "since the Germans prefer a government of loyalists to one of Marxists." The DNSAP newspaper *Faedrelandet* demanded that King Christian form a new government which "understood the new era."

When King Christian rejected suggestions that he take Danish Nazis into the government, Clausen's supporters, five hundred strong, turned out to demonstrate in the streets of Copenhagen, where they were met by a counterdemonstration of citizens who broke up their line of march and forced the DNSAP to disperse. From that point on there was no serious German effort to help the Danish Nazis gain positions of power. Nor was there any need, for the Danish government cooperated fully with German officials on most issues or bowed under protest to German pressures on others.

In 1941, the Danish government amended its criminal law again to make the circulation of rumors inimical to Danish foreign relations a crime subject to imprisonment. The law applied even to two individuals holding a private conversation. There were even more drastic revisions of Danish law coming. New statutes were passed authorizing life imprisonment for entering the service of "enemies of the Occupying Power," eliminating the defendant's right to select his own counsel in cases involving state security, and imposing prison terms for demonstrating against German forces in Denmark.

In January, 1941, Denmark turned over six new torpedo boats to the German Navy, an act which the British Foreign Office attributed to a "lack of guts in the Danish Navy," and in June, 1941, after the German invasion of Russia, Denmark broke off diplomatic relations with the Soviet Union. Danish police arrested hundreds of Danish Communists, and in August, the Danish Parliament outlawed the small Danish Communist Party. One member of the conservative People's Party, Ole Bjorn Kraft, conceded that the bill "regrettably clashes with the usual Danish

Danish Nazis hold a public rally in a Copenhagen square.
(Danish Ministry for Foreign Affairs)

sense of justice," but argued that the Communists were perpetrators of "terror and sabotage." And in a move that shocked the sensibilities of many Danes, three Communist members of Parliament were also arrested under an authorization voted by more than half of their Parliamentary colleagues.

Danish men of military age were recruited for the volunteer *Frikorps Danmark,* which was destined for service on the Eastern Front. Lt. Col. P. C. Kryssing of the Danish Army Artillery, the unit's first commanding officer, assured all officers and men of the regular Danish Army that their regular positions would be held open for them if they volunteered, and appealed to Danish men between the ages of seventeen and thirty-five to sign up.

> Men of Denmark!
> With the Government's approval I have been given the command of the *Frikorps Danmark.* The corps will fight against the Bolshevik world enemy. I call upon you to join up in the columns of *Frikorps Danmark* so that we can make a combined contribution against Bolshevism.

Frikorps volunteers went first to Germany for combat training. There they received regulation SS uniforms and weapons as well as pay and allowances. Then the unit, numbering about a thousand men, was thrown into action on the Russian front near Lake Ilmen, south of Leningrad. It suffered heavy casualties. Lieutenant Colonel Kryssing was killed in one of the first battles, and the officer appointed to succeed him, Christian Schalburg, a Russian-born Dane who held the rank of lieutenant captain in the Danish Royal Guard, was killed within two weeks.

As the fighting in Russia continued, Germany moved to consolidate the political front against Bolshevism inside occupied Europe. In the autumn of 1941, Hitler "invited" Denmark to join the Anti-Comintern Pact aimed at the Soviet Union. In a special emergency meeting called to consider the invitation, Scavenius urged that Denmark join the pact, but ten of the other eleven top Danish governmental ministers viewed the invitation as an infringement of Danish neutrality. Renthe-Fink, informed of the Danish position, sought instructions from Berlin, and on November 23, 1941, handed Scavenius Berlin's answer:

> Denmark must immediately sign the Pact. If not, Germany will cancel the agreement of the 9th of April, 1940, and Denmark will be regarded as an enemy country and must face the unavoidable consequences.

That same night, the Danish State Council, headed by King Christian and composed of the twelve senior ministers, bowed to German pressure. Scavenius traveled to Berlin the next day and signed the Pact on November 25 along with other European satellite nations: Finland, Bulgaria, Rumania, Croatia, and Slovakia.

German newspapers hailed Denmark's signing as a victory in the fight against communism, noting that Denmark had shown its support for a "New Europe." In Great Britain, a leading member of the pro-Allied Danish community in London went on BBC radio to denounce the signing:

It is clear to Free Danes abroad that Denmark's participation in the conference in Berlin puts Denmark in the eyes of the world, not so much as an enemy-occupied country, but as a country which has now accepted what Hitler aims at, the New Order in Europe.

The Danish Ambassador in London, Count Edouard Reventlow, a "little gray man in a little gray suit" who was personally loyal to his king and government, resigned his office because of the pact. In a telegram to King Christian, Reventlow complained that the pact was "likely to seriously damage Denmark's reputation in Great Britain and to endanger the traditional good relations" between the two countries. Reventlow remained in London to continue diplomatic relations with the British government in the name of "Free Denmark."

In Washington, the Danish Ambassador to the United States, Henrik Kauffmann, also protested Denmark's signing of the Anti-Comintern Pact, but by November, 1941, Kauffmann no longer had ties with the government of King Christian. Kauffmann had been in Washington at the time of the German invasion of his homeland and had immediately declared himself a representative of "Free Denmark," who was not bound by orders coming from Copenhagen. Even before the Anti-Comintern crisis, Kauffmann, acting on his own initiative, had signed a formal treaty with the United States placing the Danish colony of Greenland under U.S. protection and had resisted, with the support of U.S. Secretary of State Cordell Hull, an angry order for him to give up the Danish Embassy in Washington and return to Copenhagen.

The most violent reaction to Denmark's signing of the Anti-Comintern Pact came on the streets of Copenhagen where widespread demonstrations, led by students, broke out on November 25 when news of Scavenius' signing reached the Danish capital. Protesters gathered in Amalienborg Square and marched from there to the office of the Danish Nazi newspaper *Faedrelandet* and to the House of Parliament. *The Times* of London carried this report:

The crowd numbered several thousands. They swept the police aside and demonstrated in many parts of the town with cries of "Down with Scavenius" and "Down with the traitors." They sang patriotic songs and carried Danish, Norwegian, Swedish, Finnish and Icelandic national flags. The demonstration continued after darkness had fallen. The police used searchlights, charged the crowd with truncheons and fired a number of blank shots, successfully barring the way to the

Hotel d'Angleterre, where the German headquarters were established.

So tense was the situation in Copenhagen that Scavenius, returning from Berlin on November 26, sneaked into the city under conditions of utmost secrecy to avoid the outbreak of another round of demonstrations that his presence would likely touch off.

A few days later a special Danish governmental committee chastised the demonstrators, calling the riots a "disservice to our fatherland" and noting that the Anti-Comintern Pact had been signed on the "authority of his Majesty the King." The riots troubled both the Danish government and the Germans, for they indicated that there was a well of discontent inside Denmark that could under proper circumstances be tapped for resistance work. Despite Denmark's official policy of negotiation with the Germans, a body of public opinion had actively opposed the German occupation from the first hours of the invasion.

On the morning of April 9, Jens Lillilund, the tall, taciturn, thirty-five-year-old owner of a tool-manufacturing firm, rode into the center of Copenhagen on his bicycle to check out the news that the Germans had arrived. He saw his first German soldiers on Langelinie Pier, nonchalantly guarding the waterfront. Pedaling home that afternoon, Lillilund came across a group of German troops on the street, singing Nazi songs. The scene enraged Lillilund. He attempted to wheel briskly through the Germans and, when ordered to halt, spat disparagingly onto the pavement. German officers placed him under arrest, almost as a matter of routine, and turned him over to Danish police, who after questioning Lillilund for two hours released him with a warning not to provoke the Germans again. That evening Lillilund reflected on the events of the day. He concluded that his actions had been immature and nonproductive. If he was opposed to the Germans, he would have to do more than make meaningless gestures of personal disapproval. During the following days and weeks Lillilund speculated on what action he could take. His first overt act of resistance was to set fire to a truck that had been left unattended in Kongensgade Square. It had been loaded with hay for the German barracks at the Kastellet.

On April 9, 1940, Pastor Harald Sandbaek was in Finland as military chaplain to approximately six hundred Danish volunteers. The Danes had volunteered to help the Finns fight the Russians but had seen no action, and in April they were awaiting transportation back home. Sandbaek viewed with dismay the failure of the Danish Army and Navy to defend the country. He returned to Copenhagen with the rest of the Danish volunteers later that summer and took up a rural parsonage in the small community of Hersom in Jutland. Sandbaek found the Danes in

Hersom living "too good a life." Food was plentiful. German troops were seldom seen; when they were, they were on their best behavior. Life went on as it had before, with the only difference being the lack of news from abroad. In such a situation Pastor Sandbaek found it difficult to know how to oppose the Germans. As a clergyman he could only preach against them, which he did, telling his congregation that "dictatorship is against Christianity," and wondering all the time how long the Germans would continue to permit him the freedom of the pulpit.

In the autumn of 1940, Jorgen Barfod, an enlisted man in the Danish Army, was accepted for officer training in the Danish infantry school. Upon successfully completing the one-and-a-half-year course, Barfod could expect appointment to the rank of *kornet,* or subofficer, and assignment to active duty with the Danish Army, which, under the terms of the Danish-German agreement of April 9, continued in existence. Barfod considered himself a loyal Dane and an obedient officer candidate, but he disapproved of the "policy of negotiation" the Scavenius government had adopted. So did many of his friends. Throughout 1940 and 1941 he participated in informal *daglistue,* or "living room," meetings to discuss what could be done to bring Denmark into active opposition. Many who attended called for "Norwegian conditions" in Denmark, arguing that it was preferable for the country to break openly with Germany and to bear the brunt of whatever oppression would follow than to work in cooperation with the enemy.

Similar meetings took place throughout the country. In Copenhagen anti-Nazi journalist friends of Stig Jensen, a former executive of *Berlingske Tidende,* met secretly in private homes to assess the political situation. Their reading of the political climate inside Denmark in 1940 convinced them that it was unwise to express their view publicly. Too many Danes thought Hitler had done a good job in Germany; too many backed the policy of negotiation. Frustrated and angry, the journalists looked to the Allies for help. Stig Jensen took it upon himself to travel to Stockholm, where he hoped to meet with Allied representatives.

Another journalist, Svenn Sehusen, a nationalistic member of the Young Conservatives who had urged that Denmark fight if invaded and who was a bitter opponent of the Danish Nazis, established in July of 1940 a national press service, *National Presse-tjeneste,* which concentrated on the activities of Nazis in Denmark and in Norway. One of the earliest issues carried photographs taken during the German invasion of Denmark showing Danish Nazis in uniform on the roads of Jutland helping direct German units. The headline over the picture read: "Fritz Clausen Shows the Way to a New Denmark." Sehusen took care not to attack the Germans directly, but in the confused situation during the early days of the occupation, he could attack the Danish Nazis in a news service operated in the open, with his name and address on the masthead.

Twenty-five-year-old Mogens Staffeldt, a bookseller in a shop on Köbmagergade, also began his resistance work using the printed word as his weapon. When official censors circulated lists of banned titles to all the city's bookstores, thus cutting off the supply of those books from Danish distributors, Staffeldt began to import the same titles from Sweden in defiance of the censorship regulations.

In the small community of Holstebro in Jutland, a group of former Danish Boy Scouts met regularly through the autumn and winter of 1940–41 under the leadership of their old leader, Anton Jensen, a former lieutenant in the Royal Danish Life Guard. The group spent the hard winter crawling over the frozen ground in military training exercises and climbing up telephone poles in preparation for the day when they would be called upon to perform acts of sabotage and resistance against the Germans.

Capt. Niels Bjarke Schou, an officer of the Second Danish Field Artillery Regiment assigned to the sleepy provincial town of Holbaek, west of Copenhagen, was standing duty watch in the regimental barracks on the afternoon of April 9 when a German light motorized column drove up. The Second Regiment had seen no action that day; the capitulation order had reached them hours before. The German major in command of the motorized column saluted sharply and informed Schou that he "wanted to report himself and his force to the garrison commander." Schou returned the salute and escorted the German officer to the stable where the Danish commanding officer was exercising his horse. After a short conference between the two senior officers, Schou received orders to secure all equipment and ammunition and to provide the Germans with a complete inventory. Schou dutifully carried out his orders that same day. Two days later, however, Schou made an unofficial journey to the nearby town of Ringsted, where, he knew, a battalion had drawn a supply of hand grenades for training purposes which it had not used. He backed his pickup truck close to the battalion storeroom, loaded four boxes of grenades onto the vehicle, and drove back to Holbaek without arousing the suspicions of the Germans. Captain Schou had in his possession four boxes of grenades that were not on any German inventory; he had no idea when or where he could use the grenades, but as an anti-German Army officer, he felt more comfortable knowing that there was a secret cache which he could get to in case of need.

Newspaperman Ebbe Munck had covered Berlin in the late 1920s, London in the early 1930s, and middle Europe during the years before the outbreak of war. The German invasion of Denmark and his country's capitulation occurred while he was on assignment in Finland. From his experience as a foreign correspondent, Munck realized that Denmark's international reputation was grievously impaired by the capitulation, especially in view of the continued fighting in Norway. He hurried back to Copenhagen for conferences with a group of sympathetic editors at *Berlingske Tidende* and for secret talks with officers of the Danish military intelligence who shared his views. The outcome of these conferences was an assignment in Stockholm, where Munck was expected to play two roles—one overt and the other covert. As a correspondent affiliated with *Berlingske Tidende*, he would be expected to file regular journalistic reports from the Swedish capital, while in his undercover role he would pass on to British sources in Stockholm information on military developments inside Denmark supplied to him by pro-Allied Danish intelligence officers.

Munck quickly established himself in Stockholm and began to feed information on German shipping activity to the British Embassy. During the first months of his operation, Munck received this information from Denmark disguised as journalistic assignments. He knew that a message informing him to "write twenty paragraphs for tomorrow" on a preselected subject meant that twenty German vessels were due to sail the next day. Munck's information proved so reliable that in late autumn of 1940 the head of SOE's Western European section, Charles Hambro, visited Stockholm for a personal meeting with Munck to size up the man and plan for the future. In the meeting it was the Dane who proved the more aggressive and Hambro the more cautious of the two. Munck, concerned about Denmark's political image, sought SOE help in mounting a campaign of sabotage within Denmark, to show the world that Denmark was doing its part in the war; while Hambro, whose organization was only then gearing for action, argued that the time was not yet right for sabotage, nor could SOE provide much help. "It would not be in the interests of Denmark or Great Britain," Hambro remarked, "if sabotage were to break out in Denmark." But Munck's arguments must have impressed Hambro, for shortly after his return to London he set in motion a series of steps to strengthen the Danish section of the SOE.

The Danish section had been established before Hambro's trip to Stockholm, with Comdr. R. C. Hollingworth of the Navy, who had served as assistant to the British naval attaché in Copenhagen, as its head. With Hambro's return the pace of activity in the Danish section increased. Hollingworth got an office on Baker Street and began recruiting staff members. In February, 1941, SOE agent Ronald Turnbull was sent to the British legation in Stockholm as the regular SOE contact for Scandinavia. Turnbull, like Hollingworth, was familiar with Denmark; he had served as press attaché in the British legation in Copenhagen before the German invasion. Later that spring, the SOE began to train parachute agents for missions inside Denmark.

Before the first of the agents dropped in Denmark, however, the BBC launched a propaganda campaign based on the letter *V* which was destined to become famous throughout occupied Europe, with a special impact on Denmark. Credit for the *V* campaign goes to the Belgian section of BBC's European service. The BBC had an avid listening audience in German-occupied countries, and, in the early months of 1941, BBC controllers were seeking some means to rally those listeners against Germany. In pondering the problem, the men in the Belgian section took note of certain developments. They knew that mischievous Belgian boys irritated German soldiers by chalking the letters *RAF* on walls and signs. They had also heard of the Danish "cold shoulder," a method the Danes had adopted to show their contempt for the Germans. *The Times* of London reported: "To the Danes belongs the credit of inventing a new order, unthought of by Hitler—the Order of the Cold Shoulder, D.K.S., standing for Den Kolde Skulder—and it expresses the feelings towards the Germans of about 90 per cent of the Danish population."

The Belgian section eventually came up with an answer to the problem it had posed itself which proved to be a deft device. It urged the Belgian people to draw the letter *V* whenever and wherever possible—*V* for the Flemish word *vrijheid,* *V* for the French word *victoire.* The letter could be scrawled quickly on walls and posters and would stand as a sign of victory to come for the Allies.

The campaign reached Denmark in June of 1941, when Leif Gundel, a Danish-speaking member of BBC's Danish section, broadcasted a special program to his native country. It ended in rousing fashion.

> *Vi har V'et, det gode, gamle, danske V, der staar for Vilgen til at Vinde—for Vejen til Sejr—for Varslet om arvefjendens endelige sammenbrud—for den gamle Vikingeaand—V'et der betyder at VI VIL VINDE.*
> [We have the V, the good old Danish *V,* which stands for the Will to Win, for the Way to Victory, for the warning of the enemy's final collapse, for the old Viking spirit, the *V* that means WE WILL WIN.]

The Danes seized upon the *V* campaign with enthusiasm. The letter began appearing wherever there was a blank space on an open wall. Radio announcers subtly highlighted the letter *V* when it normally appeared in approved and censored radio copy. Beethoven's Fifth Symphony became a favorite selection in Denmark, for the opening bars of the symphony duplicated in musical terms the Morse code for the letter *V*—dot, dot, dot, dash. *V*'s were scribbled on discarded newspapers and fingered in the dust of German vehicles. Painted *V*'s appeared on trees and tiny *V*'s were scratched on Danish coins. Some Danes went even further, writing out the Danish phrase *Vi Vil Vinde,* or the English word "victory" on walls and bench seats. Danish newspapers carried on the campaign in their pages. Shortly after the start of the *V* campaign, the conservative paper

National Tidende printed an advertisement for a commercial business headline that read:

> *Vi Vil Vinde*
> *mange kunder i kraft af vore billige*
> *priser og vor extra prima Expedition*
> *DEN HVIDE FLIP*

The Germans could not officially object to the advertisement for the copy merely read: "We Will Win many customers through our low prices and first-rate service. The White Collar."

The Germans, however, understood the political power of the symbol and took steps to suppress it. One Dane was imprisoned for forty days for writing "victory" on the wall of a building occupied by German officials. But the BBC had chosen its symbol well. The *V* was not to be stopped. For every Dane caught in the act, thousands succeeded in scribbling their *V*'s without danger. In a program beamed to Denmark, the BBC commented: "The Nazis are completely clear how ominous a sign this is of the spirit of the oppressed peoples. They know that the *V* sign is the first ripple in the sea of resistance which will gradually become a deluge, and which will wash the last Nazi up on the shore of defeat, like a dead body."

Despite the stirrings the *V* campaign raised in Denmark, and despite other signs of an incipient resistance—the secret private meetings and individual acts of minor sabotage, the cold shoulder, the military intelligence passed to Stockholm—Denmark itself was not ready to come out openly against the Germans. Even after the demonstrations that followed Denmark's signing of the Anti-Comintern Pact, the nation as a whole still accepted a policy of negotiation. Nor were the first parachute agents dropped in Denmark able to accomplish much.

The first two-man team of British-trained Danish agents dropped onto Danish territory in September, 1941, landing on the island of Zealand. One of the agents, Thomas Sneum, had reached England only three months before in a tiny two-seater airplane which he had patched together in a barn near the city of Odense. The other agent was a former ship's radio operator by the name of Christoffersen. Both men underwent special training by the British Secret Intelligence Service and were dropped into Denmark with orders to establish a secret radio transmitter and report to England whatever intelligence information they could get. They landed safely, set up their transmitter, and raised London; but before they could begin to provide information of substance, German counterintelligence agents learned of their operations and closed in. Alerted to the danger, Sneum and Christoffersen separated and fled, Christoffersen into hiding in Denmark and Sneum to Sweden. The first pair of agents had been neutralized even before they started operating.

The second two-man team, both SOE-trained Danes, jumped from an RAF plane two days after Christmas, 1941, aiming for a forest area near the town of Haslev, sixty miles south of Copenhagen. The team leader, Dr. Carl Bruhn, was an especially intelligent and competent Dane who had impressed his superiors while undergoing special-agent training in England. Bruhn's parachute, however, failed to open and he plummeted to his death, carrying with him to destruction the team's only radio transmitter. The second man in the group, Mogens Hammer, landed successfully, but after searching for Bruhn for several hours, he made his way into Copenhagen without a radio transmitter, without the list of contacts that had been entrusted to Bruhn, and without a clear indication on how to proceed.

In Copenhagen Hammer visited his family, although forbidden to do so by his SOE superiors, and was introduced by relatives to anti-German politicians, including Christmas Moller, the chairman of the Danish Conservative Party, who had been forced out of his cabinet post because of his anti-German views. Hammer also met with a group of Danish Army officers who called themselves "the Princes" and who were feeding military information to Ebbe Munck in Stockholm, by coded journalistic messages and couriers. Hammer inserted himself into this communication chain, taking over as liaison man between the Princes and Munck. Eventually this link provided Hammer with a radio to replace the one lost with Dr. Bruhn on the initial drop, but it wasn't until April 26, 1942, that Munck was able to record in his diary: "First direct radio communications from Arthur" (Hammer's code name).

That same month, three more SOE agents dropped into Denmark, led by twenty-four-year-old Christian Rottboll, who had helped Sneum build his airplane. Rottboll himself had fled from Denmark to England via Sweden shortly before Sneum's flight. Once in England, he was quickly recruited by the SOE, given special-agent training, and then, despite his youthfulness, sent back to Denmark as SOE's senior representative. Rottboll's age, however, worked against him. Hammer refused to take orders from the young SOE representative, and the Princes looked down on him as a "civilian amateur."

Despite the difficulties under which he worked, Rottboll helped arrange the escape of Christmas Moller to England, on the invitation of the British government. Moller reached London in May, 1942, and was awarded a warm reception. The Ministry of Information arranged a press conference which was attended by more than one hundred journalists from England, America, and other Western countries. The BBC reported Moller's arrival as a "great and happy event for the Free Danes in London."

Moller set to work to explain Danish attitudes and conditions to the British and Americans. He wrote articles for the British press, gave speeches before mixed Anglo-American audiences, and spoke personally to many leading British statesmen, his former position as a Danish government minister opening diplomatic doors to him. To his dismay, however, he found that his scripts for the BBC were subjected to tight censorship. Only innocuous topics were permitted, such as "Danish Seamen," "What England Thinks of Denmark," and "A Visit to a Machine Gun Factory." Moller, who had hoped to arouse his country in a fight against the Germans, expressed his bitter disappointment in a letter to Commander Hollingworth, head of the Danish section of the SOE: "I neither can nor will work in this way."

What Moller did not know was that the Danish Army officers known as the Princes had forwarded details of their own mobilization plan to London prior to his arrival there. This was the so-called *P* Plan, which called for the formation of an underground military army which would be held in readiness for instant mobilization when needed. In the meantime, the Princes wanted no sabotage within Denmark, no SOE agents in the country, and no BBC propaganda against the existing pro-German Danish government.

The British pondered the plan for a long time and finally accepted the Princes' argument. In April, 1942, a month before Moller's arrival in Britain, Ronald Turnbull, the SOE representative in Stockholm, wrote to the Princes:

> London will modify its radio propaganda to avoid upsetting the status quo inside your country, and steps are being taken to bring American propaganda into line. In the future all unnecessary incitement to sabotage will be avoided and unnecessary attacks will not be made upon the present Government.

It was a decided shift in British attitude, for only weeks before the BBC had been attacking specific "Quisling rats" in the Danish government and warning that the Allies were considering how best to deal with the "Danish quislings" after the war.

Throughout the summer of 1942, Christmas Moller remained a disillusioned man, restricted in his BBC broadcasts to even more harmless topics, such as a "Tribute to King Haakon" and "Cooperation Amongst the Northern Countries."

In August, 1942, despite the opposition of the Princes, the SOE dropped three more agents in Denmark. They landed safely in Jutland but were quickly brought under surveillance by German counterintelligence agents and forced to go into hiding. In Copenhagen, meanwhile, Rottboll faced serious political problems with Hammer and the Princes. The German Abwehr also was aware that Rottboll's radio operator was making regular transmissions to London. German direction-finding vans cruised the streets of Copenhagen searching for the location of the radio.

They found what they were looking for early in September. German troops and Danish police sealed off the area. In the subsequent raid Rottboll's radio operator was killed. Information uncovered compromised Hammer, who fled to Sweden. Later that month, Abwehr agents discovered Rottboll's whereabouts and he too was killed in a raid. By the end of September, 1942, the SOE organization inside Denmark was completely shattered. Two agents had been killed; one had been forced to flee. The remaining four were young, without leadership potential and without radio contact with England. They posed no problems for the Germans. Instead, they faced the problem of survival inside occupied Denmark where an aggressive and efficient Abwehr knew of their existence.

Danish journalists played a more effective early role in developing a resistance against the German occupation. Having enjoyed freedom of the press under the Danish Constitution of 1849 and having developed over the decades a continental viewpoint, the Danish press was generally regarded as the most cosmopolitan in all the Scandinavian countries, equally comfortable with issues of big-nation politics as with questions of Denmark's local agricultural output. In terms of its political sophistication and its traditional influence with the Danish public, the press of Denmark was a force to be reckoned with by the Germans and their Danish collaborators.

Shortly after the invasion had been consolidated, therefore, the German press attaché, Dr. Meissner, personally visited the press bureau of the Danish Ministry of Foreign Affairs to suggest to Danish diplomats what Germany would consider appropriate behavior on the part of the country's newspapers. All foreign news had to be cleared through the press bureau. All editorials touching on internal developments also had to be cleared in advance. News from Norway was sharply curtailed. No criticism of German occupying forces would be permitted and no military news of any kind could be published without prior approval. But given the special relationship that existed between Denmark and Germany, Meissner himself was content to act behind the scenes, leaving to Danish officials the task of implementing German wishes by installing a board of censors to check the performance of the Danish press and radio.

Danish journalists reacted to the censorship by an often humorous campaign of passive resistance, becoming adept at writing between the lines. Suggestive headlines appeared in print and layout editors placed German reports in ironical juxtaposition, thus inviting readers to draw their own conclusions. The provincial press, in particular, out of immediate touch with the censors in Copenhagen, often ignored regulations and played up the few Allied victories and played down the continuing string of German victories. Even Copenhagen newspapers carried on a running though hidden struggle with the censors and their German mentors. The flashy afternoon newspaper *Ekstrabladet* once printed an entire article with double spacing between the lines, thus making it easier for readers to read between them.

Announcers for Radio Kalundborg, the country's main long-wave transmitting station, and for Radio Copenhagen, the medium-wave station, could rely only on the inflection of their voices to indicate their opposition to the German regime. Many Danish listeners believed they often heard intimations of sarcasm and disbelief in the voices of news announcers when they read the standard opening for the mandatory censor-approved war news, "Here is the latest German communiqué," and the standard closing, "That was the latest German communiqué."

The anti-German attitude of the Danish press was so pronounced that in April, 1941, Dr. Meissner abandoned his behind-the-scenes role and summoned a number of leading Danish journalists to a meeting in Copenhagen's Hotel d'Angleterre, where he complained of their "negative attitude" and warned that "it is steadily becoming more and more evident how spiritual influences from the West are working against a logical and sensible mode of thought." As good journalists, the Danish newspapermen took copious notes of what Meissner had to say. These notes found their way into the hands of a Swedish writer who reproduced them in a book on Denmark under the occupation, which eventually became available in Denmark. There it enjoyed wide readership, infuriating Meissner even more.

While criticism of German occupying forces was forbidden, non-Nazi journalists were free to attack Danish Nazis in print, and a running journalistic battle developed. Late in 1940, when five hundred followers of Fritz Clausen moved into the streets to demand the resignation of the Danish government, only to have their march broken up by a larger group of noncollaborationist Danes, Borge Outze, a reporter for *National Tidende,* commented: "Yesterday Copenhagen showed Fritz Clausen its loathing of him." Clausen's newspaper, the *Faedrelandet,* counterattacked, calling Outze a provocator and inviting him to inspect a German concentration camp "from the inside." Non-Nazi journalists began calling the Nazi newspaper *Faedrelandet* the *Forraederlandet,* substituting "Traitorland" for "Fatherland." The nickname caught on with large segments of the public.

As the occupation continued, however, most journalists found it increasingly difficult to report the news fully and fairly. An editorial in the dignified newspaper *Borsen* commented on the problem:

> It is frequently said that the people have not the same confidence in the Danish press as before. We do not deny that there are things happening which confirm this; they are mainly due to the present circumstances to which the press, cut off from some normal sources of information, is subjected.

Two outside sources of news *were* available to the Danes, however, even during the early occupation years. Several pro-British Swedish newspapers circulated legally in Denmark during the early years of the occupation. And because of the special relationship between Germany and Denmark, German authorities did not prohibit Danes from listening to the BBC, nor did they confiscate radios as they did in Norway and other occupied countries. One Nazi publication complained that Danes who "listen to the British radio are convinced that only there can they hear the truth, and that the German announcements are only propaganda."

What the average Dane lacked was an accurate picture of internal events and informed comment on international events by independent Danes. To fill this need, Danish journalists launched a number of illegal underground papers. The first clandestine paper, *De Frie Danske,* began publication in the autumn of 1941 and was followed in the spring of 1942 by *Frit Danmark,* which had been established by representatives of all Danish political parties opposed to the Germans, including the Communists. The illegal press grew rapidly in size and number. One paper, *Danske Tidende,* attracted a readership of ten thousand within a few months. The Communist underground paper, *Land og Folk,* also was influential.

From their earliest issues, Denmark's illegal papers pushed an "active" line against the Germans, against the policy of their own govern-

Denmark's underground press actively opposed German authorities and collaborators. *(Danish Ministry for Foreign Affairs)*

ment, giving support and respectability to those who advocated sabotage and strikes. The Germans branded all illegal papers as "Communist," ordered the arrest of all editors and the confiscation of all duplicating machines. Despite the threat of arrests, the Danish underground press became one of the most active in occupied Europe, achieving a relatively larger circulation than in any other German occupied country. By 1945 a total of 538 illegal issues were printed, with a combined circulation of more than 24 million copies.

Denmark, a nation of readers, also specialized in publishing illegal books. Resistance-minded students working with bookseller Mogens Staffeldt turned out books by mimeograph machine, bound the copies in cardboard, and distributed the copies informally. John Steinbeck's *The Moon Is Down* was an early best seller, followed closely by the Danish *White Book,* which reprinted documents detailing the attitude of the Danish government and Army General Staff in April, 1940, and which contained revelations so sensational to most Danes they eagerly bought more than twenty thousand copies within a few weeks of publication.

Because of the difficulties of printing books by mimeograph machine, resistance workers sought regular printers willing to put their presses to work on illegal projects despite the danger that the Gestapo could trace the printer of unauthorized books and periodicals by the typefaces used. Wendell Willkie's *One World,* the first illegal book published by a regular printer, hit a first run of ten thousand copies. Readers snapped up all available volumes before the Gestapo identified the printing plant and arrested the printer. Other illegal books came off the presses soon after, including Howard K. Smith's *Last Train from Berlin,* Harold Nicolson's *Why Britain Is at War,* and Carl Hambro's account of the German invasion of Norway, *I Saw It Happen.* By the war's end, more than seventy-five titles had been turned out by various printing houses.

One book in particular—a critical collection of excerpts from the speeches of Hitler—aroused the anger of German officials. Resistance workers mailed two thousand copies of the book *Führerworte* to German military field post-office addresses, free of charge. Its cover showed Hitler in knight's armor, mounted on a white horse and carrying a banner with the swastika prominently in view. A determined Gestapo tracked down the printer, placed him under arrest, and brought him to trial in a Danish court. The examining judge agreed with the prosecution and called the cover a "vulgar caricature" of Hitler and an "insult" to the Fuehrer. The printer, in his defense, produced a postcard purchased in pre-war Germany, showing the picture from which his illustration had been copied. The original painting was the work of a German artist living in Hamburg.

In the late spring and summer of 1942 the first signs of widespread disquiet began to appear inside Denmark. The small Communist-led underground group BOPA carried out its first sabotage raid against an industrial target and followed this initial raid with other minor scale actions. Organized by a handful of Danish Communists who had seen action in Spain during the 1930s, the group's original name was KOPA, for "Communist Partisans." Later, as non-Communist Danes joined the organization, its leaders changed its name to *Borgerlige Partisaner,* or "Middle-Class Partisans," hence BOPA. Its members, Communist and non-Communist alike, were mainly young men in their early twenties from working-class families.

Among the general public the sense of Danish nationalism grew stronger and the cold shoulder displayed toward the Germans more frigid. At the state funeral for Prime Minister Stauning, who died in May, more than twelve thousand Copenhagen residents crowded the city's largest meeting hall, the world-famous Forum, to pay public respect to the Danish statesman. Those assembled in the Forum had heard that Denmark's King Christian X was expected to attend the funeral and when a stir in the rear of the hall indicated the arrival of some important personages, the twelve thousand rose to their feet in welcome. Instead of King Christian, however, the German Minister Renthe-Fink walked down the main aisle at the head of a German delegation. Immediately the mood of the crowd changed. An observer inside the Forum reported that it was "impossible to describe with what speed the people sat down again, and as the hall is large, the movement was like a ripple and became a unique demonstration of silence." When the king finally arrived, the crowd rose to its feet again, greeting King Christian with warm applause.

Denmark's elderly king had become a symbol of unity to his countrymen. Before the war it had been his habit to ride through the streets of Copenhagen on horseback, and he continued taking these rides almost daily after the invasion. Copenhagen residents came to look upon the tall, fatherly figure of King Christian, riding without escort through the streets of the German-occupied capital, as a sign that the nation was still intact. Crowds gathered along his route, offering their hands in greeting. German sentries also snapped to attention at the king's approach, but Christian always managed not to notice the saluting Germans. His rides took on deep significance to the Danes, symbolizing the old days of peace and democracy. "He sustains us, he unites us, he guides us," the Bishop of Copenhagen remarked at the time.

By September, 1942, outside pressures began fueling the glimmers of resistance working in Denmark. The British and the Americans, with final plans for the invasion of North Africa in readiness, called openly for sabotage against transportation lines and communications facilities inside Europe, to divert Hitler's attention from North Africa and hinder Ger-

King Christian's regular horseback rides through the streets of Copenhagen provided a reminder of the peaceful past. *(Danish Ministry for Foreign Affairs)*

man troop movements when the invasion took place. In early September, the British Secretary of State for Air, Sir Archibald Sinclair, broadcasted a message to all enemy-occupied countries, Denmark included, urging them to "get ready to fight against German transport." Four days later, Christmas Moller was finally permitted to appeal over the BBC for Danish sabotage. "Action is required of us all," Moller urged. "It is our duty to have only one thing in view, that which hurts Germany most. . . . Damage and delays, bombing and resistance action—these are the means by which we will suffocate and strangle the German transport organization. Do your duty—do your work." Ronald Turnbull, the SOE agent in Stockholm, even called on the Danish Army Princes to go into action. Noting that Denmark "is the only country at present in which no organized sabotage has been carried out," Turnbull told the Danish Army underground that "London are absolutely determined to have some activity in the nearest future."

The Danish Army officers, however, refused to take action. At one point the Army's commander-in-chief, Gen. Ebbe Goertz, personally rejected a plea from newspaperman and resistance-minded reserve officer, Stig Jensen, for weapons that could be used against the Germans. To Goertz's mind, any thought of fighting the Germans was "idiotic." An active resistance movement, he insisted, would incriminate the Army officers and threaten the intelligence network they had set up.

The Germans, however, feared that the situation was growing dangerous. The constant BBC exhortations to sabotage, the Danish cold shoulder, and the stubborn attitude shown by the Danish government against German pressure that Denmark impose the death penalty and take action against the Danish Jews combined to convince Hitler that Denmark was on the brink of open resistance. Hitler decided on a change in German-Danish relations, but he needed some act to use as justification for the changes he had in mind. It came on September 26, 1942, the anniversary of King Christian's seventy-second birthday, which Hitler observed by sending a telegram of congratulations.

King Christian, adopting the country's public attitude of cool aloofness toward the Germans, sent a terse and formal telegram in reply: "My utmost thanks. Christian Rex." Hitler seized on the telegram, choosing to interpret its terseness as another sign of Denmark's growing noncooperation with the Third Reich and as a personal affront to him. He immediately ordered the recall of Minister Renthe-Fink, demanded that Denmark provide thirty thousand young men for the German armed forces, and insisted on the ouster of the Danish government and its replacement by a pro-German government represented by leading Danish Nazis.

In London, the *Daily Telegraph* headlined this story: HITLER READY TO TAKE OVER DENMARK. GESTAPO RULE THREAT TO KING CHRISTIAN. The newspaper went on to report:

> Diplomatic relations between Germany and Denmark have been to all intents and purposes ruptured by the sudden return to Berlin of the Nazi Minister in Copenhagen. Renthe-Fink's journey is explained in German circles as having been caused by King Christian's "insulting behaviour."

Nothing would now appease Hitler: neither the abject apology of the Danish government assuring Hitler that King Christian's telegram was "not intended to express an unfriendly attitude"; nor their offer to send Danish Crown Prince Frederick to Berlin so that the king's son could "express the unchangeable friendly attitude to the Greater German Reich and its head of state that the King, in pleasant recollection of former personal visits, still holds"; not even King Christian's personal expression of hope for a "close and confident" collaboration between Denmark and Germany in the coming New Europe.

Instead, Hitler assigned a new, "tough" Army officer, Lt. Gen. Hermann Hanneken, to take over the army command in Denmark, instructing Hanneken that no democratically run country could continue to exist in German-controlled Europe. And he assigned Dr. Werner W. Best, a longtime Nazi functionary, as the German plenipotentiary in Denmark. In a private conversation with Best, Hitler explained that Germany's behavior toward Denmark must become harsher and that

Denmark's status must change from that of a friendly country cooperating with Germany to an unfriendly country that would be governed as a German province. "Rule with an iron hand," Hitler told Best. Hitler, however, held back from taking over the country completely. Despite his insistence on a harsher Danish policy, he told Best that it was in Germany's interest to negotiate with a legally constituted Danish government, which while giving the appearance of independence would in reality be subservient to German wishes.

Denmark's Foreign Minister Erik Scavenius, warmly regarded in Berlin because of his pro-German views, was their choice to head this new government. After discussions in Berlin in late October with German Foreign Minister Ribbentrop and further discussions and negotiations in Copenhagen with Werner Best, Scavenius agreed to take over the top post of Danish Prime Minister and started to recruit a cabinet that would be politically acceptable to the Germans.

The London *Daily Telegraph* headlined a report from Denmark: Quisling Dane as Premier. And *The New York Times* reported: Pro-Nazi Is Named as Danish Premier. The *Times* story went on to speculate that Scavenius was "expected to find a list of collaborators suitable to the new situation, which is dominated by the fact that Nazi supervision of Denmark is now exercised by two fanatic Elite Guard officials, Major General Hermann von Hanneken, commanding the army of occupation, and Dr. Werner Best, the new Reich Plenipotentiary."

Danish Foreign Minister Erik Scavenius (left) escorts the German plenipotentiary, Werner Best, to an audience with the Danish royal family. Best and the Danes understood each other, at least for a time. *(Nordisk Pressefoto)*

Christmas Moller, broadcasting to his home country over the BBC, called Scavenius "a typical Junker" whose "point of view is not that of our people. He is without understanding of all values which the Danish people, as well as the free world, hold so dear, and for which they are fighting."

Werner Best, the new plenipotentiary, was a political activist from his teen-age years; he had joined the Nazi Party in 1930 and the party's SS stormtroopers the next year. When Hitler came to power in 1933, Best gravitated into the Himmler-Heydrich orbit, serving as chief of security services for the Stuttgart area, as director of personnel and legal departments in the Gestapo, and later as ministerial counselor in the Ministry of the Interior. With the fall of France, Best was transferred to Paris to head the military administration there, but the Paris assignment, while ostensibly a promotion, took Best away from the seat of power in Berlin, and his relations with his superiors, Heinrich Himmler and Reinhard Heydrich, soon cooled. SS Chief Heydrich, in particular, thought Best "too moderate" in his handling of French affairs, and dispatched another SS official to France with powers greater than Best's. At the end of the summer of 1942, Best had abandoned hope of advancing his career under Himmler and Heydrich and had moved to the German Foreign Service, where, under the wing of Joachim von Ribbentrop, he waited for his fortunes to change. It was from the Foreign Office that Hitler plucked him for the Danish assignment.

Despite Hitler's instructions to rule "with an iron hand," Best sought a "policy of understanding" with the Danes that would ensure the uninterrupted flow of Danish agricultural and industrial products to Germany. To safeguard this production, Denmark would be permitted a high standard of living—higher even than in Germany itself—and as much internal independence as was consistent with Germany's national interest. Above all, Best was determined not to jeopardize the Danish *Lieferungsfreude,* or "willingness to supply."

Best quickly developed a close working relationship with Danish officials who welcomed his moderation, and eventually he convinced Berlin to support his policy as well. Late in February, 1943, Berlin noted the special relationship between the two countries in an official memorandum:

> The orders of the chancellor of the Reich, Hitler, regarding the mobilization of Europe for total war do not apply to Denmark. It is emphasized that Denmark occupies a special place among the conquered countries.

In March, Best even permitted a Danish general election to take place as scheduled. German propagandists trumpeted his decision as proof that the Third Reich, despite what Allied propaganda had to say on the question, allowed internal independence for nations within the German sphere of influence. The results of the elections pleased the Germans even more. A new anticollaborationist *Dansk Samling* Party received slightly more than 2 percent of the vote, while the four major political parties, all of which were represented in the Scavenius cabinet, received close to 95 percent of the vote. Best proudly interpreted this to mean that the great majority of the Danes favored collaboration with Germany, an indication that his policy of moderation and understanding was bearing fruit.

The Western powers also pretended to see encouraging signs in the election results. The BBC applauded Danish voters for giving a "thundering 'yes' to democracy" and made much of the fact that the Danish Nazi Party (DNSAP) had won less than 3 percent of the vote, returning only three members to the Danish Parliament, the same number it had in 1939. The dismal showing of the Danish Nazis did not surprise Best, however, for he had long ago written off the party and its leader, Fritz Clausen, who, Best complained, had a "morbid fear" of being displaced by more competent men. In an official report to Berlin, Best explained that because of this fear, Clausen "has removed from the party all fit, active and independent personalities and has surrounded himself with inferior collaborators."

Whatever the interpretation of the election results, Denmark remained, in the spring of 1943, a country without an active resistance, headed by a government that viewed collaboration with Germany as the only sensible course of action.

13
August, 1943

To Werner W. Best, the German high plenipotentiary in Denmark, the internal situation in the country could not have seemed more propitious in the late spring of 1943. Danish production in all fields continued high, and Prime Minister Scavenius and other Danish governmental officials remained cooperative. Berlin considered Best's handling of the election a masterful political coup. Best basked in the admiration of his superiors. It was in a happy and contented frame of mind, therefore, that he sat down in late April to draft an official report covering his first six months in Denmark, as required by the German Foreign Office.

In his report Best reviewed the instructions he had received before leaving Berlin—to arrange for a new legal Danish government that would be compliant with Berlin's wishes, to ensure the continued flow of Danish supplies, and to uphold law and order in the country without calling for additional German personnel. Having listed the major tasks assigned him, Best went on to evaluate how well he had fulfilled his instructions.

The Scavenius government, he noted, held power legally and was friendly to the Germans; while the average Dane, in Best's view, was "sick and tired of the war" and supported a "realistic" policy of negotiations which assured the country continued "peace and order."

Incidents of sabotage were few and insignificant, Best said, and obviously instigated by enemy agents dropped by parachute. To prove his point, Best produced figures showing that Denmark's four million inhabitants were governed by eighty-five German civilian officials and an additional 130 employees, while Norway, with a population of only 2,800,000, needed a German administrative force numbering three thousand.

Under his rule, Best continued, Danish imports to Germany had increased; industrial production was up and agricultural products flowed south across the border in growing quantities, instead of declining as some

German planners had feared. Best credited his policy for these developments. "Without the good will of the farmers, which cannot be forced," he commented, "the German food situation would soon be harmed."

Everywhere that Best looked he saw encouraging signs. Communism was no longer a factor in Denmark, for most of the known Communists were in prison. The election of March, 1943, was pictured as a vote of confidence for the Scavenius government. Above all, Best viewed the Danish people as pragmatists who would do what they considered best for themselves.

Berlin accepted Best's report with enthusiasm. Within a month, the Foreign Ministry gave its full recognition and approval to Best's policy. Even Best's old boss, Heinrich Himmler, was impressed. Since arriving in Denmark, Best had taken pains to improve his relationship with Himmler, sending him copies of his official reports to Ribbentrop. When Himmler read Best's semiannual report, he praised Best warmly for his achievements and informed him in a personal letter that he had petitioned Ribbentrop to permit Best to visit him in Berlin. Himmler signed the note "Cordially yours."

Read in its entirety, Best's report pictured Denmark as a country without major problems and concluded, in the best bureaucratic fashion, that the man responsible for conditions inside Denmark had done his job exceedingly well. But Best had written his report to highlight the favorable factors in Denmark and to ignore or minimize unfavorable factors. Despite Denmark's apparent peacefulness, events were brewing under the surface that would soon alter the picture. The Army commander in Denmark, General Hanneken, recognized the signs of impending trouble and warned Berlin that sabotage was increasing and could be expected to continue to increase. But Berlin chose to ignore Hanneken's warning and to accept Best's rosy evaluations, an acceptance indicating both the relative standings of the two men in the German hierarchy and also Berlin's eagerness to believe the best and ignore the worst.

Conditions in Denmark, in fact, had started to change months before. In January, RAF bombers attacked the Burmeister and Wain shipyard in the heart of Copenhagen, damaging the main plant which manufactured diesel engines for German U-boats. Several civilian workers died in the raid and others suffered some injuries, but an unofficial inquiry afterward indicated that the majority of Copenhagen residents sympathized with the objectives of the raid and accepted the casualties as "facts of war."

Underground Danish papers drew a lesson from the raid. It was seen as offering Denmark the choice between more bombing or an increase in sabotage. If Denmark refrained from sabotage, the RAF would return to do the job, with whatever civilian casualties might result. Active Danish sabotage would eliminate the necessity for bombing but could result in German countermeasures. Slowly but perceptibly Denmark accepted sabotage as the lesser of two evils. In the first three months of 1943, acts of sabotage increased from sixteen in January, to thirty-four in February, to seventy in March. In April they jumped again, to seventy-eight individual actions. The Swedish newspaper *Varldpressen* commented that the change in Danish attitude was directly related to the RAF raid against Burmeister and Wain.

> The war is still so far away from Denmark that "official" Denmark still does not tolerate sabotage acts, but the British bombing attack on Burmeister and Wain on January 27th has brought about a considerable revision of the official frame of mind.

Several Danish resistance groups were in the field and growing in numbers. The Communist-led BOPA was still active and another major resistance organization, *Holger Danske,* named after a legendary Danish hero who supposedly rose from his sleep whenever his country was in danger, had swung into action with scattered small-scale actions concentrated in the Copenhagen area. *Holger Danske* recruited its members mainly from the middle class and professional ranks, but despite its bourgeois character, the organization was devoted to "active sabotage." By war's end it had become the largest sabotage group in Denmark, with about four hundred members.

In Jutland, the aristocratic landowner Flemming Juncker controlled several resistance groups scattered throughout the countryside. They knew the terrain well, having grown up in the gently rolling Jutland hills, and they stood ready to assist in any drop of SOE agents and weapons. A large "receiving group" worked out of the village of Hvidsten, near the city of Randers, where innkeeper Marius Fiil headed a unit made up of members of his family and several local farmers. The *Hvidsten Gruppen* (or White Stone Group) had participated in the earliest SOE drops.

By early 1943 the SOE was ready to act again, this time without relying on the Danish Army Princes for assistance. In a blunt communication the SOE informed the Princes (who also went under the name of "the League") of its decision to support civilian resistance groups:

> We want action now because we need it now, and because we think it most unlikely that the conditions for realizing the P-plan will ever exist. We hope the League will continue to furnish us with Intelligence, but we are equally determined to go ahead.

Ronald Turnbull followed up with his own explanation:

> We must emphasize again that although we understand the League's attitude, we think that it does not necessarily coincide with the United Nations' strategy, which is that the Germans must be harmed *now.*

Four SOE agents dropped in Jutland in February, 1943, and successfully reestablished radio contact with England. The first delivery of arms came down by parachute in March, quickly followed by four more SOE agents, including a new SOE leader, the suave and personable Flemming Muus. Muus, who came from a prestigious Danish family, had left the country for Liberia before the start of the war after being implicated in questionable financial activities. From Liberia he made his way to London in mid-1940, where his ease of manner and confident style appealed to the British. They gave him special training and in early 1943 sent him back to Denmark as the chief representative of the SOE. Muus landed in Jutland, where he met Flemming Juncker. Juncker knew of Muus's pre-war background and was dismayed to meet him as SOE's chief representative. The meeting between them was frigid. Muus, who had been ordered to build up an intelligence network in Jutland, quickly left Jutland and made his way to Copenhagen, where he could operate more effectively with persons who knew him only as the personable and persuasive leader of the SOE. In Copenhagen Muus consolidated his position. Within a month he met most of the active resistance leaders and, in his role as the SOE chief in Denmark, drew them together into what would eventually become a unified resistance movement.*

With the arrival of the second group of SOE agents, the BBC also stepped up its propaganda warfare. In broadcast after broadcast, the Danes were urged to revolt. Cooperation with Germany was denounced. Consistently the BBC probed Danish "wounds" hoping to provoke a break with Germany. Turnbull's warning to the Princes was echoed in a BBC warning to the country at large:

> The entire attitude taken by official Denmark may prove fatal for the future position of Denmark in postwar Europe, if the Danish nation does not in time, in an unequivocal manner, make it clear to the free world that it is wholeheartedly on the side of the united nations.

Black lists were drawn up; black-listed names announced. Listeners in Denmark, responding to the power of propaganda, could only conclude that the British were so well informed that any pro-German act would be noticed and held against its perpetrator, if Germany lost. Danes who had been convinced that Germany would win now began wondering if they had not backed the wrong horse. The BBC could, and did, point to Allied victories in North Africa and German defeats in Russia to persuade the waverers they had made the wrong decision. The crushing blow delivered by the Red Army to the forces of German Field Marshal Gen. Friedrich Paulus at Stalingrad changed the minds of many Danes. The BBC capitalized on developments; one broadcast beamed specifically to

---

* After the war, a Danish court convicted Muus of mishandling resistance funds and sentenced him to a prison term.

Denmark spoke of the "whole army which is slowly perishing with cold" in front of Stalingrad. Paulus's surrender on January 31, 1943, clinched the argument for many Danes.

The BBC encouraged saboteurs, by reporting their activities in great detail, and attacked the Scavenius government for agreeing to create a corps of Danish sabotage guards, recruited for duty in factories. The BBC argued that if Danes did not agree to guard Danish factories, German troops would have to be assigned to this duty. By permitting Danes to function in this capacity, the BBC continued, Scavenius was saving a German division from guard duty, thus providing Hitler with more men for the fighting fronts.

> If you put a Dane into a German uniform and send him to the Eastern Front to shoot Russians, then the majority agree to call him a traitor. But if you give a Dane a German revolver and give him orders to shoot his own countrymen, then he is called a sabotage guard.

The BBC campaign worked. The issue became so sensitive that Danish newspapers, under instructions from official censors, began referring to "sabotage guards" as "factory guards," and efforts were made to picture the guards as upholders of law and order. As the months passed, fewer Danes were found who were willing to take on the jobs; the climate was changing inside the country. By June the outlook of the average Danish workingman had become pronouncedly more anti-German. He had been programmed by a variety of factors to accept the concept of resistance, if not for himself, then certainly by others. German military defeats in the field, increased sabotage at home, BBC propaganda broadcasts, the heightened visibility of foreign agents inside the country—all these forces reinforced each other and carried the country, slowly but surely, toward an open break with Germany.

Acts of sabotage continued, numbering ninety-three in July and 220 in August. And Danish saboteurs were becoming more daring. The *Holger Danske* sabotage group planned a bold daylight action against the Forum exhibition hall in Frederiksberg, just northwest of Copenhagen, after the Germans had hired Danish construction workers to convert the hall into an army barracks.

On the day before the first troops were scheduled to move in, a young Danish delivery boy pedaled through the rear entrance of the Forum at lunchtime, when all Danish workmen had left the site for their midday meal. His bicycle was the type the Danes call a "Long John," with a low, underslung carriage suitable for heavy deliveries. On this particular trip, the youth carried what looked like a case of Tuborg beer but which in reality contained more than one hundred pounds of explosives. The delivery boy unloaded the case at a preselected location inside the Forum and left as he had arrived, pedaling unchallenged through the entrance. Minutes later two Danish resistance men dressed as laborers, Tom Sondergaard and Jens Lillilund, entered the building, placed the explosives in key locations, set the fuses, and made their own escape undetected. The explosion that followed pulverized the Forum's cement-block walls, broke windows for blocks around, and left only the steel skeleton of the Forum standing. The building remained unusable throughout the war. The underground press carried glowing reports of the action, gleefully noting that Danish saboteurs had blown up the Forum in the middle of a working day. For days afterward, Copenhagen residents made the journey to Frederiksberg on bicycle to gaze in awe at the naked structural skeleton of what had been Scandinavia's largest exhibition hall.

Strikes spread throughout the country. Shipyard workers in Odense walked off their jobs after the local German commander sent armed guards into the yard following a sabotage raid on the German cruiser *Lintz*, which had been undergoing repairs. Employees in other factories walked out in sympathy. From Odense the strikes spread to Esbjerg, a fishing port on the west coast of Jutland, where factory workers left their benches in protest of a German curfew, and refused to return to work until the curfew was lifted. Then strikes broke out in other Danish cities as well. Within fourteen days, factories were forced to shut down in fifteen major cities. Localized strikes turned to general strikes as months of worker dissatisfaction came to a head. Workers moved into the streets to express their anger at the German occupation forces as well as at the Danish government. Clashes broke out between Danish civilians and German troops. Several provincial cities came close to open revolt. In Odense, rioting workers attacked and severely injured a German officer who was traveling through town on his way from Norway to Germany.

Werner Best, who in May had written such a glowing report on conditions inside Denmark, grew frantic as the summer wore on. Best realized his report had been misleading, and the realization sent him into a frenzy of activity. From the beginning of August, he made repeated demands on the Danish government to take action against sabotage, but internal control was slipping from the hands of the Danish authorities into the hands of the underground. A joint appeal by the Danish Cabinet and Parliament for a return to "calm and order" was ignored and striking workers rejected a plea from their own trade-union leaders for them to return to their jobs peacefully, choosing instead to listen to the more aggressive resistance leaders, including the Communists, who had helped organize the strikes and who called on them to escalate their protests.

Best tried to ride it out, hoping the country would calm down, but by mid-August he knew that the situation was out of hand. He conferred with General Hanneken on internal unrest, a meeting that was particularly painful to Best. Almost immediately following this meeting, Best filed an official proposal with the Foreign Office suggesting that if Sca-venius and his government proved unable to reassert control, he himself should take over and run Denmark. In a personal appeal to Himmler, Best noted that "in view of developments I am taking into account the possi-bility that we must alter the way we administer Denmark."

Even as he faced proof that his policy of moderation had failed, Best hoped to maintain his position in relation to General Hanneken. In his appeal to Himmler, Best asked that if anyone in Berlin suggested impos-ing military rule in Denmark, would Himmler please support him as the man in charge. That could be accomplished, Best went on, if Himmler were to make SS and special police forces available to him. Best pleaded with Himmler to waste no time in issuing the necessary orders so that SS forces could be ready the instant they were needed. But again Best had miscalculated. General Hanneken acted more quickly than he. Before Himmler had a chance to reply, Best was summoned to the headquarters of the Army General Staff in Berlin to answer for developments in Denmark.

Best reached Berlin on August 26 and, mercifully for him, was spared a personal meeting with Hitler. Instead, Foreign Minister Rib-bentrop delivered Hitler's instructions to Best, while General Hanneken and a small group of high Wehrmacht and Foreign Office officials lis-tened in. It had been Hitler's wish, Ribbentrop explained, that Denmark, as a country of truly Nordic people, should become a cooperating

Civilians flee from a German patrol in Copenhagen during a general strike in the summer of 1943. *(Danish Ministry for Foreign Affairs)*

member of his New Order. Because of his sympathy with the Danes, Hitler had agreed to treat Denmark leniently, as Best had recommended. However, Best's policy had obviously failed and there must now be a change in policy. Military rule must come to Denmark.

Best tried vainly to explain. For more than an hour he pleaded that his policy of moderation still had a chance and that Denmark would return to normal. When he had finished, Best was brusquely told that his explanation was not accepted. Unless the Danes agreed to harsh demands, a military state of emergency would be declared and General Hanneken would take over the country.

Best returned to Copenhagen the next day, carrying with him the texts of two ultimatums. One of his closest aides, Georg F. Duckwitz, noted in his diary that the plenipotentiary "came back a broken man." Best, nevertheless, dutifully called Prime Minister Scavenius to an urgent meeting the following morning. When Scavenius arrived, promptly at nine, he found Best in a "depressed and beaten" mood. Best confessed to the Danish official that he had been roughly treated in Berlin, and considered himself "a dead man." He handed over the two German documents without further comment, except to remark that Denmark's answer was expected before the end of the working day.

The first ultimatum demanded a penalty of one million kroner from the city of Odense, imposed a city-wide curfew, closed all theaters and movie houses, and threatened the arrest of hostages if those "guilty of maltreating the German officer" were not handed over by September 5. "In case such episodes are repeated," the ultimatum warned, "even stronger measures will be taken."

The second ultimatum covered a broader scope and involved the country as a whole, demanding concessions that the Danes had hitherto resisted. It called for complete capitulation, with no promises or assurances to soften its impact—"a prohibition against any public gathering . . . a prohibition against any strike . . . a curfew . . . mandatory closing of restaurants at 7:30 P.M. . . . all guns and explosives to be turned in . . . and the establishment of Danish express courts" which would impose the death penalty for sabotage and other acts against the German Wehrmacht. The ultimatum ended curtly: "The government of the Reich expects the Danish government's acceptance of the above-mentioned demands before 4 P.M. today."

The Scavenius government, which had based its policy on accommodating the Germans, had less than seven hours to decide how to respond to the greatest accommodations yet demanded.

But Germany had pushed Denmark too far. With the lone exception of Prime Minister Scavenius, every Danish official recommended rejection of the German demands, fearing that the country would explode in violence to a state of emergency imposed by a Danish government.

Eventually even Scavenius found himself persuaded by the arguments and voted, along with all the others, to reject the German demands.

Having made this crucial decision, the Danes shrank back from provoking the Germans further. Under Scavenius' direction, a soft reply was drafted which pointed out that the Danish government's main purpose had always been to ensure "peace and order" and which noted that Denmark had expressed its willingness to take all "precautions necessary" to keep the population calm, but this was as far as Denmark would go. It could submit no more.

> Effectuation of the provisions demanded by the Germans would ruin the government's possibilities of keeping the people calm, and the government, therefore, regrets that it cannot find it right to help in carrying through these provisions.

The finished copy, presented to King Christian for approval, was hand-delivered by messenger to Best's headquarters in Dagmarhus at 3:45 P.M., fifteen minutes before the deadline set by the ultimatum. From Best's office, the news flashed to General Hanneken, who moved swiftly upon learning of the Danish response. Telephone communications with Sweden were cut within an hour, the first step to imposing a state of emergency. The early hours of August 29 were tense and filled with activity. German troops fanned quietly through the streets of Copenhagen and other cities, occupying railroad stations, powerhouses, and other key facilities, while German arrest squads swept through residential areas seizing influential university professors, editors, politicians, civil servants, and businessmen.

Promptly at 4 A.M., a German messenger awoke Scavenius to deliver General Hanneken's decree imposing a state of emergency in the country. At the same time, German troop units, following the same timetable, attacked Danish Army garrisons and depots throughout the country. But any German fears that the Danish Army might resist the take-over proved unfounded. Danish Army units had received instructions the day before from General Goertz to "surrender under protest" if the Germans attacked, and they laid down their arms with only scattered resistance. Only one artillery battery ignored orders and escaped by boat to Sweden. All other Danish units, including the Danish Royal Guard assigned to Sorgenfri Castle north of Copenhagen, where King Christian was in residence, were captured, their weapons seized and their officers and men interned.*

* Army officers on leave during the German take-over escaped immediate internment, but they were later ordered by General Goertz to turn themselves in to the nearest German headquarters, an order all but a handful faithfully observed, arriving at German command posts neatly clad in dress uniforms with their luggage brimming with the necessities of prison life. Only Danish intelligence officers who had been engaged in undercover work for the British went underground. Most of them later fled to Sweden.

The Danish Navy, on the other hand, which had suffered even deeper public humiliation than the Army after its failure to fight in April, 1940, operated under standing orders issued as early as 1941 to escape to Sweden, or scuttle its vessels, in case of a German attack. On August 28, during Danish deliberations on the possible consequences of their rejection of the German ultimatums, Rear Admiral Aage Vedel, the Navy's commander-in-chief, rejected a governmental recommendation that naval vessels "surrender under protest," as the Army units would do. Vedel believed that the Navy had been grievously hurt in the eyes of the country by the events of 1940 and that a repetition would destroy the service's credibility and honor for decades, and he convinced Danish Defense Minister Borsen to go along with the service's "escape or scuttle" instructions.

German troops attacked the main Copenhagen naval base, where most of the major vessels of the Danish Navy were berthed, a few minutes after 4 A.M. on August 29. Admiral Vedel immediately ordered the implementation of the Navy's standing instructions. His message reached all Danish ships at sea by wireless, while inside the naval base the coastal-defense artillery ship *Peder Skram* flashed the instructions by blinker light to all naval units in sight.

Minutes later the *Peder Skram* herself sank to the bottom, her hull smashed open by two giant explosions. Other explosions followed from other ships tied up at the base.

At sea the *Niels Juel*, Denmark's largest warship, received the order while lying in the narrow waters of Isefjord and immediately headed for Sweden. Before she could reach her destination, however, German Stuka dive bombers attacked, forcing the vessel aground. Her commander then ordered the systematic destruction of his ship.

The Coast Guard ship *Hvidbjornen* was also at sea in the Great Belt, the channel which separates the islands of Fyn and Zealand, when the order from Admiral Vedel was received. A German warship stopped the *Hvidbjornen* shortly afterward and sent a boarding party aboard; but while the German marines were on the ship, the Danish captain ordered a sailor to set the fuses on the charges that had been previously placed in the hold. Then he called his crew together and gave the order "Lifebelts on." Then, "Abandon ship." To the amazement of the German marines, the Danish sailors tore off their shoes and jumped into the water. As the Danish captain was about to jump himself, he informed the Germans that the ship was about to explode. The Germans panicked. Many jumped overboard with rifles and full equipment. Minutes later the charges exploded in the forepart of the ship. *Hvidbjornen* went down in one hundred feet of water.

The final toll counted twenty-nine Danish vessels sunk and many more heavily damaged. Thirteen small naval craft fell into German hands

Coastal-defense ship *Peder Skram*, scuttled by her crew to prevent seizure by the Germans. *(Danish Ministry for Foreign Affairs)*

undamaged; thirteen others escaped to Sweden. Most of the destruction took place by 5 A.M., one hour after the Germans attacked.

By the morning of August 29, when the inhabitants of Copenhagen awoke, the Danish Army and Navy had been neutralized, German soldiers were standing guard at all buildings of importance, telephones no longer rang, and mail service had been cut off. Over the radio Danes could hear announcers reading the proclamation of emergency issued by General Hanneken: "Civil servants should continue work, obeying instructions given by German authorities. . . . No gathering of more than five people . . . curfew at nightfall . . . no mail, telegraph or telephone service until further notice . . . all strikes prohibited and punishable by death. . . . All offenses to be punished at German military courts."

Martial law had come to Denmark.

The Western press seized on the events of August 29 and dramatized them beyond recognition. *The New York Times* reported "violent fighting in Copenhagen" which was "brightly illuminated" so the Germans "could see where to shoot." Danish guards at Amalienborg Castle, it was reported, "shut the iron gate and machine-gunned the Germans, several hundred of whom were wounded and some killed." A United Press dispatch reported that "thousands of German troops, with 300 tanks, were patrolling the streets of Copenhagen with machine gun nests set up to control crowds."

The next day, *Times* readers learned that "400 persons had been killed or wounded in a battle between Danes and the Germans in Svendborg" and that "scores of persons were drowned as their craft were sunk by German gunfire" during attempts to escape to Sweden. A *Times* editorial writer working from these reports called the Danes "a proud and patriotic people who had now exploded into open revolution."

Danish underground papers, being closer to the story, treated the affair more calmly. *Frit Danmark* saw August 29 as a new phase in the German struggle to gain control over Denmark. "Of course, this is a turning point," the paper commented, "but actually it only means that a condition which has developed slowly since April is now publicly confirmed."

The imposition of military rule by General Hanneken left Werner Best in a mood to blame someone. He chose Danish journalists working for established papers. On the afternoon of August 29, Best summoned a group of journalists to his office to lecture them on their shortcomings. Best's tone was more of annoyance than of anger. He began by noting his "devotion" and "patience" in seeking a course of action that would be in the interests of both countries. He had, he reminded the journalists, "seriously admonished, nay pleaded," with the press not to aggravate the situation, but the press had consistently failed to heed his warnings.

"Today I must state that to an appalling extent the press is responsible for recent developments," Best concluded. "In this ridiculous little country, the press has implanted the belief that Germany is weak. Last night you got your reward."

14

The Problem of the Jews
in Denmark

The German crackdown of August 29, 1943, altered the rules under which occupied Denmark was governed. No longer was a Danish government in existence to act as a buffer between the Danish population and the Germans, for Prime Minister Scavenius and his cabinet had handed in their resignations shortly after rejecting the German ultimatums. Now German military men ruled the country with open force, and the face of the occupying power was clear for all Danes to see. Fear spread through the civilian population, but it ran highest among Denmark's Jews, who hitherto had lived in relative safety and comfort compared to their brethren in Germany and in other occupied countries.

The previous three years had been good ones for the Danish Jews, or as good as possible for a subject people living under the threat of the swastika. From the first days of the occupation, Danish authorities and the Danish people supported the Danish Jews. The Germans in turn, hoping to gain Denmark's industrial and agricultural output by peaceful means, adopted a soft approach. Only six days after the 1940 invasion, German Minister Renthe-Fink warned the German Foreign Minister:

> The Danish authorities are apprehensive as to whether we will . . . show too much interest in the internal situation and take steps against Jews. . . . If we do anything more in this respect than is strictly necessary, this will cause paralysis of or serious disturbance in political and economic life. The importance of the problem should not be underestimated.

One year later, the chief of Danish police, Thune Jacobsen, met Heinrich Himmler at Copenhagen Airport, Himmler at the time being en route to Norway. Himmler questioned Jacobsen about the attitude of the Danish police toward the Danish Nazis; he questioned Jacobsen about the Danish Communists; and then he brought up the "Jewish problem." Jacobsen responded that "if the Reichsfuehrer SS thinks that five thousand Jews here in Denmark constitute a problem, then of course we have a problem, but the Danish population does not consider this topic a problem."

This attitude was so widespread that German publications took note of it. In the spring of 1941, the official German journal *Die Judenfrage* carried an article under the headline DENMARK—A COUNTRY WITHOUT A JEWISH PROBLEM? The author went on to complain that preoccupation with racial problems was considered "un-Danish."

In all areas of life the Jews in Denmark escaped overt persecution. They were permitted to remain in their jobs and continue their education. Jewish religious services went on uninterruptedly. So untouched were the Danish Jews that many pursued their lives as if the war did not exist. In 1942, the forty-five-year-old Marcus Melchior, Copenhagen's "second" rabbi, took stock of his career. He was the head of the Jewish School for Religious Education and the second librarian for the Jewish community, but his desire to share religious duties with Copenhagen's Chief Rabbi Friediger had been thwarted by the older man's reluctance to give up any of his power and prestige to Melchior. Rabbi Melchior considered himself completely frustrated—he was a rabbi without rabbinical office, a speaker without a rostrum. What would he be doing in five years? he asked himself. Where should he direct his stalled career? He decided to seek a new career—in law. His application to Copenhagen University was accepted, and in the fall of 1942 Rabbi Melchior began a course of study which he hoped would enable him to take his first major examination in law in January of 1944. His studies proceeded without interruption through the summer of 1943.

Even the civil rights of Danish Jews were safeguarded. The Danish criminal code, amended in 1939, provided for fines or imprisonment for anyone guilty of inciting anti-Semitism. This criminal code continued in effect after the German invasion of 1940. When Nazi officials in Berlin asked Renthe-Fink for suggestions on actions to be taken against Danish Jews, he warned that German violations of the civil rights of Danish Jews would harm relations between the two countries. If Berlin insisted upon anti-Jewish measures, Renthe-Fink proposed that Germany deprive Jewish firms in Denmark of their coal and fuel allocations from Germany. But that was as far as Renthe-Fink would go, and Berlin did not press the point.

The most virulent expressions of anti-Semitism in Denmark came not from the Germans but from the handful of homegrown Danish Nazis and could be found in the Danish Nazi paper *Kamptegnet* (Battle Emblem), which was modeled after the German Jew-baiting publication *Der Sturmer*. The newspaper repeatedly printed articles on the supposed close ties between Jews and Communists and accused Jews of running the slave-labor camps in the Soviet Union. Jews in the United States came in for particularly vicious attacks because of their alleged wealth and their "international influence." At home, *Kamptegnet* complained, young Jewish agricultural trainees working on the island of Bornholm had "besmirched" the previously "Jew-free island"; and it carried a weekly column titled "The Week's Racial Infamy" which listed the names of couples of mixed marriages. In a long series of articles on the "Jewish Problem in Denmark," *Kamptegnet* concluded that Danish Jews wielded strong (and harmful) influence in business, industry, finance, the arts, journalism, radio, medicine, and public institutions. At one time or another, the newspaper called for the "sterilization of Jews," the "solution of the Jewish problem," and the "liquidation of European Jewry." In an article published in the autumn of 1941, the paper contrasted the fate of Jews throughout Europe with their life inside Denmark: "While Jews all over Europe await their liquidation, it is interesting to see with what enormous cheek the Jews here at home continue to behave."

The anti-Semitic campaign of the Danish Nazi press, however, failed to elicit a sympathetic response from the traditionally tolerant Danes. *Kamptegnet* failed financially during its first year of operation and had to be resurrected with the help of German funds. Eventually Werner Best let the paper cease publication, so ineffectual had it become. In the middle of April, 1943, Best sent a memorandum to Berlin in which he asserted that the editors of *Kamptegnet* were responsible for the decline in its circulation from a high of fourteen thousand to only three thousand. The paper, he continued, appealed only to readers interested in pornographic stories, and its total effort did not justify the large subsidy of "8,000 kroner a month." Best went on:

> Friends of the Germans and many National Socialists among the Danes have for some time opposed the aims of the paper. They point out that this type of propaganda is not suitable to the character of the Danish people and is unlikely in any respect to win understanding of the Jewish problem among wider sections of the population.

Best, in fact, had shown little interest in pursuing the "Jewish question" during his first ten months as plenipotentiary. Despite Jewish apprehensions when he took over office, he moved slowly and cautiously on all matters relating to the Danish Jews, as had his predecessor Renthe-Fink. During November and December of 1942, his first two months in Denmark, the subject never appeared in any of his official memoranda. The first known mention of the Danish Jews in Best's files came in early January, 1943, when he visited Berlin for a series of conferences, including one with Adolf Eichmann, who proposed that the Germans set up a special camp in Denmark for the internment of prominent European Jews. Best opposed the idea. "It would," he commented, "make a bad impression on the Danes."

Later that month Best reviewed the Jewish question in an official memorandum submitted to Foreign Secretary Ribbentrop. His months in Denmark, he noted, had convinced him that an attack on the Danish Jews would be regarded by the Danes as an attack on their own independence; he cautioned against it. Best also noted that Prime Minister Scavenius had announced that he would resign if "special measures were enacted against the Jews."

Best did make some modest anti-Jewish proposals, primarily, it would seem, to satisfy the more rabid anti-Jewish officials in Berlin. If Berlin wanted action, Best suggested that Danish Jews could be removed from key positions in government and business and that a few token Jews could be arrested on political or criminal charges. When this memo reached Ribbentrop's desk, he scribbled his approval on the margin, but left its implementation to Best, who—more interested in a peaceful Denmark—failed to act on his own recommendation.

In Berlin, however, Adolf Eichmann and Heinrich Himmler both pressed for action against the Jews. So did Hitler, who became enraged whenever the question of the Danish Jews was brought to his attention. In midspring, Ribbentrop informed Best that Hitler wanted a "progress" report on the Jewish question that would include answers to some specific queries: To what extent did Jews hold key positions in Denmark? What influence did they wield? What demands could be made on Prime Minister Scavenius' government without precipitating an internal crisis in the country? Best's response, when it came, belittled the importance of the Jews, arguing that their influence was so negligible that "immediate measures against them would appear unmotivated and incomprehensible." At the same time Best assured Ribbentrop that if the time for a final solution ever arrived, he had such thorough files on the Jewish community that any roundup could be easily effected.

Throughout the summer of 1943, while Denmark teetered on the edge of rebellion, Best paid scant attention to the Danish Jews. More pressing matters occupied his mind. The events of August 29, however, were a turning point for him. From the depths of his defeat and despair, he began to fight back to regain power and prestige.

The day following the crisis, Best wrote a personal letter to Himmler: "Well, what General Hanneken has striven for from the first has happened, and what has been done cannot be undone."

Best went on to discuss his own future quite frankly. If he should be recalled from Denmark, he told Himmler, he would like to return to work under Himmler and not remain in the Foreign Office. Best still hoped this could be avoided, however. He suggested that he would be able to remain at his post in Denmark if Himmler sent a large contingent of German police to Denmark to be placed under his personal command, thus constituting a counterweight to the Army under General Hanneken.

But despite his informal approach to Himmler, Best was not ready for an open break with Ribbentrop. The day after he sent his letter to Himmler, Best filed an official telegram with Ribbentrop in which he pictured himself as the man best suited to carry out Germany's new plan for Denmark, if only he could be placed in charge of a large police contingent:

> To the Foreign Minister personally: I have received the instructions to prepare a new order in Denmark. . . . Before a government is set up and the state of emergency terminated, adequate German police forces must be set up in Denmark. Just as that policy begun in 1942, namely, to direct Denmark with the help of the country's own political factors, has hitherto been consistently carried out, so too it is now necessary to apply with the severest consistency the policy of the mailed fist and demonstrations of German might introduced on 8/29/43.

Best, however, received no answer to this telegram, and two days later he followed up with another telegram to Ribbentrop:

> I request that the commander of the security police, who will be under my orders, be sent as soon as possible in order to prepare the establishment of the new police stations and to take all other necessary steps.

Again, he received no answer.

It was a trying period for Best. The Danish government had resigned and he was dealing with the permanent undersecretaries in hopes of forming a new Danish government. In the meantime, he had to reckon with the supremacy of General Hanneken and the Army, which held ultimate control in the prevailing state of emergency. If the situation returned to normal, the pendulum of power inside Denmark might swing again, away from the Army and back to Best. If the situation did not return to normal, however, his position was weak, unless he could find some other method for winning support in Berlin.

Best pondered his predicament for close to a week. Finally he seized upon the Danish Jews as the answer to this problem. Questions of humanity were ignored; the Jews would be the pawns by which he would win back power in his continuing political struggle within the German hierarchy. On September 8, therefore, Best drafted a long telegram in which he reversed his previous position on the Jewish question and recommended a roundup of all Jews in Denmark, an action he knew would be warmly supported by Eichmann, Himmler, and, most importantly, Hitler himself.

> I hereby beg, in light of the new situation, to report on the Jewish problem in Denmark: It is my opinion that measures should now be taken. . . . The necessary steps should be taken as long as the present

state of emergency exists for afterward they will be liable to cause reaction in the country, which in turn may lead to a reimposition of a general state of emergency under conditions which will presumably be less convenient than those of today. If measures are taken during the present state of emergency, it may be that the formation of a legally constituted government will be rendered impossible and it will be necessary to set up an administrative council under my leadership. I would then have to legislate by means of decree. In order to arrest and deport some 6,000 Jews (including women and children) at one sweep it is necessary to have the police forces I requested. . . . Almost all of them should be put to work in greater Copenhagen where the majority of the local Jews live. Supplementary forces should be provided by the German military commander in Denmark. For transportation, ships must be considered a prime necessity and should be ordered in time. I beg to request a decision as to the steps I should take.

The telegram was a masterpiece of bureaucratic infighting. In it Best bowed to Berlin, made new pleas for power, and tried to undercut the Army, while at the same time placing the Army in a position to take whatever blame might result. If all went well, the credit would be Best's alone.

Berlin reacted promptly. A special representative of Heinrich Himmler, Gestapo agent Karl Heinz Hoffmann, arrived in Copenhagen on September 14, and police battalions and security officials began arriving on September 15 under the command of Dr. Rudolf Mildner, whose last post was at Katowice, Poland, where he served as SS area commander and chairman of the political committee at Auschwitz. On September 17, Best received Berlin's official reply to his telegram: Hitler had agreed to the recommended action against the Danish Jews. The following day a special group of SS Commandos arrived in Denmark under Maj. Rolf Guenther, a deputy of Adolf Eichmann. Guenther was to plan the operation.

By this time, however, the mercurial Best had had a change of attitude. What had seemed a good idea on September 8 now seemed to offer more opportunities for disaster than for advancement. One of Best's closest associates in Copenhagen, the German shipping attaché Georg F. Duckwitz, opposed the plan from the moment he learned of it. Duckwitz, a National Socialist in his youth, who had many friends among Danish business and political leaders, argued that a German roundup of the Danish Jews would irreparably harm German-Danish relations. Duckwitz saw Berlin's reply to Best's anti-Jewish proposal on September 19, two days after it had been received by Best. That night he wrote in his diary: "I know what I have to do."

Best's major rival in Denmark, General Hanneken, learned of Hitler's order the following day, September 20, and immediately cabled his reservations to the German General Staff. Hanneken was concerned that the Army would be held responsible for an action started by Best and that Army personnel would be forced to act under orders of the Gestapo:

> At Best's suggestion the deportation will be carried out during the military state of emergency. The operation will place a heavy burden on the Army which will not be able to act vigorously, particularly since it will be necessary in Copenhagen and on the Island of Fyn to use new recruits. The benefits of the deportation strike me as doubtful. No cooperation can be expected afterward from the civil administration or from the Danish police. The supply of food will be adversely affected. The "willingness to supply" of the armaments industry will be undermined. Disturbances requiring use of military police must be expected.

Hanneken's objections placed the German Army on record as opposed to the deportation, but they failed to change Berlin's mind. In due time Hanneken received a reply. The question, he was informed, had been placed before the Fuehrer again, and again Hitler had insisted upon a Jewish action, which would be *carried out during the current state of emergency.* The reply was signed by Hanneken's superior, Gen. Alfred Jodl, head of the OKW.

The German Navy in Denmark also opposed the action, for Navy officers hoped to recruit Danish sailors from among the interned Danish servicemen. A German Navy memorandum warned: "Any further political tension will lead to an indefinite postponement of the enrollment of volunteers." In Berlin, the Navy's objections were ignored, as had been the Army's. Even a cautionary note which Foreign Secretary Ribbentrop sent to Hitler on September 23, detailing some of his doubts about the action, based on second thoughts Best was having, failed to influence Hitler. He brushed aside Ribbentrop's reservations that the Jewish action could produce harmful repercussions in Denmark. The deportations, Hitler ordered, would take place as planned. On September 25, Ribbentrop passed the word to his subordinates, Best included, that the deportation would be carried out "in accordance with the Führer's orders."

The "final order" to implement the action reached Copenhagen on September 28. It instructed Best to state "when the transfer can begin." For Best, there was no turning back. Duckwitz, who was with Best that day, noticed that the plenipotentiary was extremely depressed. The situation appeared bleak to Best. The action against the Jews was imminent; Berlin had ordered the transfer of four thousand Danish soldiers to Germany for possible enlistment in the German Army; and Best had to inform the Danes that the state of emergency, imposed on August 29, would not be immediately lifted. Best concluded that the sum total of developments would lead to unrest and disturbances within the country. He warned Berlin that "the anger of the population will express itself in a way that will oblige us to use stronger German forces." Finally, there was the continued antagonism between Best and General Hanneken. The Army officer did not want the Jewish action to take place while the Army was in charge of the country. Hitler, however, had decided otherwise and Hanneken found himself in a position of being required to participate in an action he did not desire and working with a man whom he disliked. Best, with German military leaders opposed to the action, and with his own second thoughts growing stronger each hour, commented to Duckwitz that he would like to "build a bridge" so the Jews could escape to Sweden.

Officially, however, Best was still very much the competent and efficient German leader, seemingly in charge of the situation as his position demanded. Even while expressing his second thoughts to Duckwitz, Best was preparing his answer to Berlin's question—when would the action take place? Best had obviously given much thought to the time of the arrests. Rosh Hashanah, the Jewish New Year, started on Thursday, September 30, and would, he knew, be celebrated in Jewish homes on that night and on the night of Friday, October 1. He consequently informed Berlin that the roundup of the Jews should take place "during this week, probably between October 1 and October 2." Later a more definite starting time was reached—10 P.M. on Friday, when almost all Jews in the country could be expected to be at home. The arrests would continue into the morning hours of Saturday, October 2. If all went as planned, the Danish Jews would be surprised and arrested in their homes and carried off like so many bushels of potatoes.

But Best did not figure on the actions of Georg Duckwitz, who without informing his superior and despite his National Socialist background, set about warning his Danish friends of the action the Germans were planning against the Danish Jews.

15

The Rescue of the Danish Jews

By August, 1943, the Jewish community in Denmark numbered approximately eight thousand men, women, and children. The largest group, about five thousand, were considered native Danes—descendants of the Sephardic Jews who reached Denmark in the seventeenth century from Spain and Portugal, of the German Jews who arrived in the eighteenth century, and of the Russian Jews who settled in Denmark in the early 1900s after fleeing pogroms and revolutions in the east. There were, in addition, about fifteen hundred Jewish refugees who had managed to find haven in Denmark in the 1930s and another fifteen hundred who were offspring of mixed marriages and who either regarded themselves as Jews or who feared the Germans would regard them as Jews.

The Danish Jews had received various indirect warnings of the impending action against them. On August 29, Chief Rabbi Friediger and the seventy-three-year-old president of the Danish Jewish Community, the barrister Carl Bernhard Henriques, were arrested. A few days later a group of unidentified men broke into the Jewish Community's office and made off with its membership lists. Still later, a group of German police in plainclothes raided the Copenhagen synagogue and forced the librarian to hand over membership lists of all synagogue members. But these ominous signs were ignored by the majority of Danish Jews, who chose to believe other signs that indicated the Jewish community was not in danger. The release from jail of C. B. Henriques, in September, 1943, for instance, was interpreted as a sign that the original arrests of Jews had been in error. German and Danish officials, meanwhile, continued to assure the Danish Jews that they were in no danger. When members of the Jewish community complained to Danish officials following the German police raid on the Copenhagen synagogue, the officials took the complaint to Best, who assured them that the raid was *"eine recht kleine aktion"* (a very minor action) which had nothing to do with the Danish Jewish question. Nils Svenningsen, the permanent undersecretary of the Danish Foreign Office who took over most negotiations with Best following the resignation of the Scavenius government, passed on Best's assurances to the Danish Jews, most of whom eagerly accepted them. Rabbi Marcus Melchior, who had taken over as acting rabbi for the Danish community after the arrest of Chief Rabbi Friediger, consistently urged his followers to remain calm and not to heed "irresponsible" warnings. In the early weeks of September, while the German plans were taking shape, Rabbi Melchior was particularly concerned that Danish Jews resist the temptation to succumb to "hysterical fears."

The first official warning reached the Jewish community on Tuesday, September 28, and it stemmed from the decision taken by Georg Duckwitz. After leaving his meeting with Best that morning, Duckwitz telephoned the Danish politician Hans Hedtoft, a personal friend and a leading Social Democrat. Duckwitz demanded a meeting that afternoon with leaders of the Danish Social Democratic Party; he had urgent news to tell them. Hedtoft, in turn, invited Duckwitz to a private meeting that had been scheduled for that very afternoon. When the German official arrived, he found Hedtoft in conference with other Social Democrats—H. C. Hansen, Alsing Andersen, and Vilhelm Buhl, among them—and with the counselor of the Swedish legation in Copenhagen. It was a mark of the confidence the Danes had in Duckwitz that they invited him to their conference. It was a mark of the confidence Duckwitz had in his Danish friends that he proceeded to tell them of the German plan to arrest the Jews. They must, he urged, pass the warning on to the Jewish community.

Hedtoft and Hansen set out immediately to visit C. B. Henriques, who they knew would be at home in his luxurious villa in Charlottenlund. Henriques greeted them at the door and on Hedtoft's request led them into his library, where they could talk without being overheard. "Henriques," Hedtoft began, "a great disaster is brewing. The feared action against the Danish Jews is coming." Hedtoft then went on to explain how the Gestapo planned to raid all Jewish homes on the night of October 1 and October 2 and how the Jews would be transported to Germany in vessels that would be waiting in the harbor.

"You must do everything to warn every single Jew in the country," Hedtoft urged.

Henriques listened to Hedtoft without a word. When the Dane had finished, Henriques coldly replied, "You lie." He refused to accept what he had just heard. He told Hedtoft that only that morning he had visited Svenningsen and the Danish official had assured him there was no danger. And only a few hours before Hedtoft and Hansen reached his door, Henriques explained, he had received another visitor—Danish Bishop Fuglsang-Damgaard—who had come to assure the Jews that his sources, which he knew to be reliable, had assured him that no danger faced them. Against these high-level assurances, why should he believe two politicians, no matter how honorable they might be personally?

Hedtoft, who had arrived at Henriques' home in a nervous and agitated frame of mind, so pressing did he believe the danger to be, pleaded with the Jewish leader to believe the warning. Svenningsen and Bishop Fuglsang-Damgaard, no doubt, had given their assurances in good faith, but he personally believed the warning from Duckwitz and he urged Henriques to act on it before it was too late. Henriques, still doubtful about the accuracy of Hedtoft's information, let the night pass without taking action.

While Hedtoft and Hansen were trying to alert Henriques to the danger facing the Jews, the head of the Social Democratic Party, Alsing Andersen, tried to reach the Jewish community through another route. He knew that Inga Bardfeld, a young secretary in the party's publications department, was married to a Jew, Wolfgang Bardfeld, who was active in the *chaluzim* program, which trained young Jewish agricultural workers on Danish farms before they could make their way to Palestine. Andersen telephoned Inga Bardfeld at her office shortly before 5 P.M. and asked her to come to party headquarters.

The call surprised Inga Bardfeld; never before had she been summoned by so high a party official. She set out immediately to ride the six blocks to party headquarters on her bicycle. Once inside, she saw that most key members of the Social Democratic Party were present, seated around a long table. From the taut, worried looks on their faces, Mrs. Bardfeld thought the Germans were planning to arrest the party leaders. Andersen, however, explained the real reason for their concern and why he had summoned her: he wanted Mrs. Bardfeld to warn the Jewish community.

The assignment frightened Inga Bardfeld. "But what if they won't believe me?" the young woman asked. She felt that as a non-Jew, and as a relatively young woman, she was not the right person for the job.

But Andersen assured her she was. "You have close ties to the Jewish community," he said. "If necessary, you may use my name." Specifically, he instructed her to warn Rabbi Melchior, so he could alert his congregation.

Inga Bardfeld knew Rabbi Marcus Melchior only slightly, and was uncomfortable at the thought of calling him. While the rabbi had never said anything about her marriage to Wolfgang Bardfeld, he was on record as opposing mixed marriages, and she had always thought she detected a coldness in the rabbi's demeanor during their infrequent meetings. Nevertheless, Andersen had specifically instructed her to warn the rabbi and she ducked quickly into an empty telephone booth on a streetcorner to place a call to his home. She soon found herself explaining the purpose of her call to Rabbi Melchior. He questioned her closely.

What was the source of her information, he asked.

She could not tell him over the phone, but it was a highly reliable source, she assured him.

Exactly when was the action supposed to happen, he asked.

Mrs. Bardfeld didn't know exactly when, she confessed, but she had heard that it would be "soon," probably on the night of October 1.

Exactly how, Rabbi Melchior continued, would the action take place.

Again, Mrs. Bardfeld did not know the details, but she had been told that the Gestapo would make the arrests.

Her answers failed to persuade the rabbi. When he finished questioning Inga Bardfeld, he told her brusquely, "There have been too many rumormongers at work. I can't be bothered with every new rumor." He hung up abruptly, leaving Inga Bardfeld distressed and even more unsure of how to carry out her mission.

She knew she had to warn the Danish Jews, but after the rabbi's response she was certain that she would meet similar reactions from other Jews in positions of power and prestige. Her contacts were primarily with the younger Jewish refugees. Suddenly she thought of the man who coordinated the work of the *chaluzim* program, Julius Margolinsky. He had worked closely with her husband and knew her well. Margolinsky would believe her.

Quickly she rode to Margolinsky's house and explained the situation to him. He too questioned her closely about the source of the information. Face to face with Margolinsky, she felt free to confide that the news came directly from Alsing Andersen. Margolinsky immediately telephoned Rabbi Melchior, assured the rabbi that Mrs. Bardfeld's information was reliable, and insisted the rabbi act upon it. Margolinsky sent Inga Bardfeld to the rabbi's home to repeat her story in person. Only later, after she had returned to her own apartment, did Mrs. Bardfeld think of her husband, Wolfgang, who was working on the island of Fyn with members of the *chaluzim.* She wrote him that night with the frightening news.

By nightfall on the evening of September 28, three men in position to alert Denmark's Jewish community had been warned of the impending action—Rabbi Marcus Melchior, acting chief rabbi for the Danish Jews; barrister C. B. Henriques, the respected head of the Jewish Community; and Julius Margolinsky, under whose guidance more than a thousand Jewish agricultural pioneers had received training on Danish farms and had successfully made their way to other countries, all but a few to Palestine. Five hundred *chaluzim* remained on Danish farms, however, and Margolinsky immediately began organizing a messenger service to warn them to go into hiding. Margolinsky worked through the night. His greatest concern was that the Gestapo would arrive before his warnings.

C. B. Henriques waited until the next morning, when members of the executive committee of the Jewish Community met in his office, to inform them of the news that Hedtoft had given him the previous afternoon. The committee members realized that if the news proved correct they might be forced to flee the country, and they took steps to ensure that the Community's business affairs be left in good hands, authorizing an attorney to look after the Community's administrative and financial affairs during the crisis. The committee, however, did not consider the news urgent enough to organize a general warning to all Jews in the country. They were content to accept Henriques' suggestion that committee members as individuals circulate the warning to other Jews. The committee meeting broke up shortly before noon, the members going their own way, satisfied that they had handled the legal affairs of the Community in a businesslike fashion.

Rabbi Melchior also waited until September 29, a Wednesday, to spread the warning. That morning more than a hundred persons gathered in the Copenhagen temple for a special pre-Rosh Hashanah service. The service started normally, but the congregation was shocked to hear the rabbi interrupt the religious proceedings to announce that the synagogue would be closed for the New Year. He explained that the night before he had received word that the Germans planned to raid Jewish homes on Friday night and Saturday morning. Solemnly Rabbi Melchior warned all in the congregation not to be home that night and to pass on the information to friends and relatives, asking them in turn to spread the warning still further. In this way, every Jew in the country, it was hoped, would be warned in time.

Rabbi Melchior's warning to his congregation and those issued by Julius Margolinsky to the *chaluzim* were the only official warnings organized by Jewish leaders. They were sufficient, however, to start one of the most remarkable rescue operations of World War II.

Late at night on Wednesday, September 29, two German freighters sailed quietly into Copenhagen harbor and tied up at Langelinie Pier. The vessels, including the large *Wartheland,* unloaded no cargo, nor was any cargo in evidence on the pier. The ships had come on a different mission: they were scheduled to transport back to Germany the Jews who would be arrested during the evening of October 1 and the morning of October 2.

During that whole uncertain and confused Wednesday, the news of what Germany planned spread by word of mouth throughout the Jewish community: relative warned relative; friend warned friend; Jew warned Jew; non-Jewish Danes warned their Jewish acquaintances. Warning by warning, one by one, the dread news of the impending German roundup reached the Jewish population of Denmark.

A Copenhagen woman heard the news from a friend on the newspaper *Politiken*. After the war she related how she was called and asked with some urgency to stop by at the newspaper's office.

> I went up to *Politiken* and was at once received by my friend whom I had known for many years and asked "Would you like to go to Sweden?"
>
> "No, certainly not," I replied, "I too have heard certain rumors—"
>
> "They are no longer rumors but extremely grave facts," he broke in, "and in any case you must promise me not to be at home on the night of October 1."
>
> "I am not accustomed to giving promises of that sort," I replied.
>
> "Well," he said, "you will not leave here until you have promised me."
>
> Only then did I think that I understood. "But if things are like that," I continued, "then there are lots of people I must warn."
>
> "You should only think about your nearest relatives," was his reply, "since measures will be taken to have everybody informed."
>
> I promised to leave my house, and, shaken to the core, I left my acquaintance, whom I was not to meet again until May, 1945.
>
> I had only just returned to my apartment from the newspaper office when one of my colleagues, also a Jewess, who lived nearby, came to warn me. Alsing Andersen had visited her personally to inform her of the danger and had requested she also inform me; otherwise he would do it himself—but there were so many he had to go round to.

The Sompolinsky family heard the news that night at religious services organized in their home to mark the eve of the Jewish New Year. The elder Sompolinsky, owner of a secondhand clothing store in Copenhagen, conducted the services for his wife and their eight children. Theirs was a close-knit orthodox family. Toward the end of the service a young Dane entered the room unannounced and warned them to leave the apartment and go into hiding. His voice tense and hushed, the visitor urged the family to heed his warning, explaining that he had been instructed by the local branch of the Social Democrats to warn all Jews in his district. He left the apartment with tears in his eyes, begging the Jews to believe him. One of the Sompolinskys' teen-age children, David, who had just started studies in veterinary medicine, was the first to act. That evening, despite his orthodox religion's prohibition against work on holy days, a prohibition which covered use of the telephone, David Sompolinsky telephoned his Jewish friends throughout the city, warning them of the coming German raid. Those who received his call realized with what urgency David viewed the news, for they knew he would break the laws of his religion only in a very grave emergency.

Professor Richard Ege, a non-Jewish biochemist attached to the Rockefeller Institute in Copenhagen and a highly respected member of the medical faculty of the University of Copenhagen, heard the news from an associate. When he got home that evening, Ege and his wife, Vibeke, began calling their Jewish friends to invite them to a "social gathering" at their home which, they stressed, was being held for a "special reason." Those they called detected the urgency in their voices. When the Jews arrived, the Eges warned them of the German plans. Some asked where they could hide, and Professor Ege sent them to his apartment above the laboratory in the Rockefeller Institute. That could serve as a temporary haven.

Many Jews refused to heed the warnings, however. One of Professor Ege's colleagues, Dr. L. S. Fridericai, refused to go into hiding, explaining that he was scheduled to sit in on the oral examinations of some of his students who were working for advanced degrees and he would not think of disappointing them no matter how pressing the danger to himself personally. Not until Professor Ege volunteered to fill in for him during the oral examinations did Dr. Fridericai agree to go into hiding.

A Jewish judge who lived in the town of Assens, on the island of Fyñ, also refused to heed the warning. The judge was notified by a newspaper acquaintance who called from Copenhagen urging him to leave his home because "something is wrong."

"Do you know what I mean?" the caller asked.

The judge understood all too well, but still he refused to flee. "I am a Dane and I am going to stay at home where I have a right to live," he replied. When the arrests took place, the judge was among those captured.

Other Danish Jews refused to act on the warnings to flee because they did not believe the news when they were told. The Danish resistance worker Mogens Staffeldt personally visited his Jewish acquaintances and found that many scoffed at his news, "because it could not happen in Denmark." Emil Abrahamsen, a shopkeeper friend, thought Staffeldt's news was "just another silly rumor." He too refused to flee and was among those arrested in the sweep, committing suicide by poison on the German steamer carrying him to Germany.

Even Wolfgang Bardfeld, Inga's husband, had difficulty convincing the group of *chaluzim* with whom he was staying that the news in his wife's letter was urgent. "You worry too much," they told him. Only one man agreed to seek shelter with him with Danish friends. The rest stayed on the farm; all were arrested.

As zero hour approached, however, the majority of the Jews had heard the news and had fled from their houses and apartments. Rabbi

Melchior's first warning, followed by warnings from other sources, sent the Jews of Denmark scattering throughout the country seeking temporary safety with non-Jewish friends or in out-of-the-way rural cottages where they hoped the Germans would not find them.

Rabbi Melchior, his wife, and their four children fled southward to the town of Ørslev, forty miles from Copenhagen, where Melchior planned to appeal for help to the Lutheran pastor there, the Reverend Hans Kildeby. Rabbi Melchior had often stayed at the Reverend Kildeby's home, but always when he was traveling alone, and always when his visits had been planned in advance. Now as he traveled south with his family, Melchior wondered what Kildeby's reaction would be. When the two men met, Melchior explained his plight and asked Kildeby if he could help find rooms for all six in his family. The rabbi said that he understood that any family would be reluctant to provide a hiding place for six fleeing Jews, because of the danger of detection, but possibly six different households could be found which would accept single members of his family. Kildeby, who had listened quietly while Rabbi Melchior explained his plan, rejected it out of hand. "Ridiculous," he barked, "you will all stay with us." The entire Melchior family soon found themselves comfortably settled in three private rooms in the Kildeby home.

Jews without non-Jewish friends often found refuge through chance encounters. In Copenhagen, ambulance driver Jorgen Knudsen pored over telephone directories seeking addresses of families with "Jewish-sounding names." Knudsen made up long lists of "possible victims" and then, using his ambulance for transportation, systematically visited the homes to warn the occupants of the coming danger. When some Jews insisted that they had no place to go, Knudsen drove them to Bispebjerg Hospital, where, he knew, a member of the medical staff, Dr. Karl Henry Koster, was active in resistance work. (Koster's laboratory had already been used for radio transmissions to England.) Koster accepted all the Jews whom Knudsen brought to the hospital, hiding them in private quarters or dispersing them as patients in the wards. During the last days of September, as the Jews of Denmark fled their homes, Bispebjerg Hospital became a central collection point for the escapees.

Knudsen's activities on behalf of the Danish Jews, most of whom were strangers to him, were not unique. Many Jews, walking the streets of Copenhagen or riding the city's trams, were startled at the approach of strangers who offered them keys to their apartments or cottages, "where you can hide until it's safe." For Mendel Katlev, a Jewish foreman in a leather-goods factory, help came from the conductor of the suburban commuter train he usually rode to and from work. Although both men had seen each other regularly on the train, they had never spoken personally. On the afternoon of September 29, when Katlev heard the news of the impending German roundup while at work in the factory, he immediately reported to his superior that he had to leave because of an emergency. He hurried to the nearby railway station and caught an early train home. His regular conductor, surprised to see Katlev on a train during working hours, commented that Katlev was "off schedule today." Katlev told him why, remarking almost in passing that he and his family would have to find a place to hide. Without a moment's hesitation, the conductor offered Katlev, his wife, and children refuge in his own house.

So widespread was the willingness of the average Dane to help that by the evening of October 1 most Jews had found safety somewhere. One Dane wrote of his feelings: "In the midst of all the tragedy we underwent a great experience, for we saw how that same population which had hitherto said to itself, in awe of German power, 'What can we do?'—how this same population suddenly rose as one man against the Germans and rendered active help to their innocent brethren."

The German roundup began on schedule, at nine o'clock on the evening of October 1, with the shutdown of all telephone communications in the country, including flight service and "emergency lines." German troops occupied the Copenhagen offices of the official Danish news agency *Ritzau,* to ensure that teleprinter machines could not be used to warn other cities. Throughout the country, German units, using lists prepared in advance, fanned out to arrest Jewish families. The major effort took place in Copenhagen, where most of the Jews lived. At home after home, the knocks of the German soldiers went unanswered, for the majority of the Jews, having responded to the warnings, were not at home. Some still remained, however, and frightful scenes were played out that night. Whole families, caught at home, were dragged away to police vans for transport to the waiting ships. One hundred and fifty German troops surrounded the old-age home next to the synagogue on Krystalgade. By a tragic oversight, no provision had been made for the safety of the residents, who ranged in age from sixty to ninety. German troops seized them all, including an elderly woman who was paralyzed and had been bedridden for eleven years. She was bound on a stretcher and carried to the synagogue, where the other residents of the home were forcibly assembled. Gestapo agents questioned the elderly men and women about their knowledge of sabotage operations, and when they replied that they knew nothing, they were beaten and kicked. German troops looted the synagogue of valuables and, to show their contempt for their prisoners, relieved themselves inside the sanctuary.

Not all German units, however, pursued their quarry with equal vigor. Many patrols were content to knock at Jewish apartments and to leave quietly if their summons was not answered. One Jewish family slept through the night undisturbed by the knocks of the Germans who had come to arrest them. The next morning the Jewish family awoke and learned from non-Jewish neighbors that they had had visitors during the night. Even when German troops found Jewish families at home, they let many go free. In several cases they did not arrest the sick and they released those who could prove they were half-Jews. Even full Jews married to non-Jews were not arrested.

The following morning, German commanders counted the number of Jews that had actually been arrested overnight. By German standards the roundup was a dismal failure. In Copenhagen, only 202 Jews had been taken into custody, far short of the number needed to fill the transport ships. Throughout the provinces, German troops managed to arrest only another eighty-two Jews, "not enough," as one German official bitterly complained, "to justify the dispatch of a train to the concentration camp at Theresienstadt" (Terezin, Czechoslovakia), where the Danish Jews were headed. The total number arrested throughout the country totaled a mere 284 men, women, and children, and the Germans knew they had managed to seize primarily the old, the infirm, the poor, and the isolated, and that the bulk of the Jewish population in Denmark had escaped their net.

Despite the failure of the roundup, Best put a good face on the action. On the day after the raid, a German announcement asserted: "As a result of measures taken by the German authorities, the Jews have been re-moved from public life and prevented from continuing to poison the atmosphere." Best dispatched a personal report on the action to Berlin in which he stated that the action had been carried out without disturbance, adding: "As of today it will be possible to say that Denmark is free of Jews, since no Jew will be able to remain or operate here legally." Best obviously was worried what Berlin's reaction would be when they learned of the results of the raid. By his interpretation he hoped to avert the storm he feared would come.

Others too knew that the results of the raid would anger Berlin. Helmuth Moltke, one of the leaders of the resistance movement inside Germany, had arrived in Copenhagen on October 1 only hours before the raid. Through his sources Moltke had learned of the planned raid and had hastened to Copenhagen to warn the Jewish community, not know-ing that Duckwitz had already done the job. Moltke remained in the Danish capital during the weekend. On the morning following the night of the persecutions, a jubilant Moltke visited a Danish resistance worker. "I congratulate you on the wonderful result," he told his Danish friend. "Hitler wanted six thousand, and he got only a few hundred."

Hitler did in fact erupt in one of his frequent tantrums when he learned of the small number of Jews who had been arrested, but the failure of the raids particularly enraged Adolf Eichmann and his deputy, Rolf Guenther, for they had been responsible for planning the action. Years later, Eichmann bitterly recalled the Danish experience. "That small country," he complained, "caused us more difficulties than anything else."

The persecution of the Jews touched off a wave of protest in Denmark. The Freedom Council, a committee which coordinated all the resistance groups and which had come into existence only weeks before, issued a proclamation condemning "the pogroms the Germans have set in motion" and calling on all Danes "to help in every way possible those fellow citizens who have not succeeded in escaping abroad." The proclamation warned that any Dane who helped the Germans would be considered a "traitor and will be punished as such when Germany is defeated."

The underground newspaper *Frit Danmark* published an editorial on the German action which clearly linked the fate of the Jews with the fate of the country itself.

> We couldn't yield to the German threats when the Jews' well-being was at stake. Nor can we yield today, when hard punishment and the probability of being taken to Germany await us if we help our Jewish fellow countrymen. We have helped them, and we shall go on helping them by all the means at our disposal. The episodes of the past two nights have to us become a part of Denmark's fate, and if we desert the Jews in this hour of their misery, we desert our native country.

Organizations representing jurists, teachers, lawyers, engineers, government officials, the police, and social groups protested the action to the Germans. So did the Danish Supreme Court and various trade unions. The Union of Danish Youth filed a complaint, and the universities of Copenhagen and Aarhus shut down for a week in protest. Secondary schools closed their doors.

A dramatic protest came from the Danish clergy. Bishop Fuglsang-Damgaard, who on September 28 had assured the Jews they were in no danger, was so disillusioned by the German raids that he initiated a letter of protest from the Ministry of Religion to Werner Best. Copies of the protest went to all bishops in Denmark with the suggestion that pastors read it from the pulpits. The Danish clergymen complied. On Sunday, October 3, Danish churchgoers heard their pastors condemn the persecution of the Jews as contrary to Christian love and Christian religious philosophy. The protest explained that the Danish Church would never revolt needlessly against those who exercised authority, but if a choice had to be made, the church declared its "allegiance to the doctrine that bids us obey God more than man." A congregation in Copenhagen, hearing its pastor recite the words of protest, rose to its feet in spontaneous agreement at the end of the reading to join in a giant "Amen."

The German action stirred the emotions of the Danish population as a whole, from the permanent undersecretaries who were running the governmental departments, to men and women in the streets. In an official proclamation of protest, nine government undersecretaries called the German roundup "an infringement of the Danish conception of justice." Ordinary citizens responded by more direct means. One Jewish survivor gave this report:

> In train, tram or in the street, unknown Danes turned to us and offered their help or gave us money. Once someone gave me a gold ring and once in the train a man took off his coat and asked if I'd take it . . . I could not refuse. I remember one day that the tram conductor refused to accept my fare. I threw the money into his bag. When I got off he said to me in all sincerity, "I am ashamed."

For the Jews of Denmark, their mass escape during the night of the persecutions marked not the end but the beginning of a period of peril. They were still in Denmark, and the Germans were still hunting them—a German order dated October 2 instructed all Jews in the country to report to the nearest Wehrmacht headquarters and all non-Jews housing Jews to turn them over to authorities. To remain in Denmark under these conditions was no longer possible. They must think of escaping.

When the Jews looked around them, only one avenue of escape appeared open—eastward to Sweden. To the south lay Germany, the land of *Nacht und Nebel* (night and fog) and beyond Germany the rest of occupied Europe. Norway too was under German occupation and had experienced its own Jewish persecution. To the west was England, but escape by boat was impossible; German vessels patrolled the straits and major sea routes. Far to the east lay the Soviet Union, itself battered by German armies and certainly no haven, even if accessible, to the Jews of Denmark. Only Sweden was open, tantalizingly close, separated from Denmark at the closest point by only two-and-a-half miles of water—the Øresund. On a clear day the Jews of Denmark could see safety with their own eyes.

But how could the Jews reach Sweden? Every normal route of travel was closed to them. Escape from Denmark would have to be made by illegal underground routes. But the Jews of Denmark, cut off from their friends, torn from their familiar surroundings, and hunted by the Germans, were unable to arrange their own mass escape. Terrified of what the immediate future might hold, the Jews struck out on their own, without foresight or planning. Erling Kiaer, a Danish bookbinder who lived in the Swedish city of Hälsingborg, found himself in the Danish town of Helsingør on the night of October 1, when Jews from Copenhagen swarmed into town hoping to find some means of reaching Sweden. As Kiaer later recalled, the Jews "were despondent and deeply afraid and their attempts to cross the straits were panicky and unplanned. They tried to contact fishermen or sail across by themselves. By day and night they fled in all sorts of craft which they had bought, borrowed or rented."

Kiaer was so touched by the plight of the Jews that within a few days he organized an escape route of his own, transporting groups of Jews from Denmark to Sweden in a small powerboat that he purchased with his own funds. Danish police cooperated. As Kiaer later wrote:

> I was in constant touch with Denmark through a young policeman who guarded the ferry. From him I received instructions about when to anchor off the Danish shore and when to arrive. . . . I always sailed to bathing jetties. . . . We used about 50 of them, with or without the owner's permission. Some people were even kind enough to lend us their houses so we could hide people there prior to sailing.

Kiaer's associates in Denmark included a doctor, a journalist, a police official, and a lawyer, all of whom had been active in underground work before. This small group, which called itself "the Sewing Circle" and its rescue service "the Kiaer Line," found hiding places for Jews and arranged their transportation to the waterfront. By the end of October the Kiaer Line had carried hundreds of Jewish refugees to safety in Sweden.

Although the Kiaer Line was one of the first rescue routes to go into operation, others sprang up quickly, for the Jewish persecution proved a turning point for the Danish resistance. Thousands of law-abiding Danes who had previously shrunk from overt acts of resistance eagerly joined the movement. By October, Denmark's underground press was posing the question of resistance versus collaboration in terms the Danes could respond to as human beings. The question no longer was whether Denmark should resist the Germans or collaborate with them, but whether individual Danes would help the Danish Jews or stand idly by and watch them plucked into captivity and transported to Germany. To this question, Denmark answered with its heart, thereby setting into motion the greatest mass rescue operation of World War II.

How could the refugees be hidden from German arrest squads and how could they be safely transported to Sweden? Resistance leaders thought immediately of the large fleet of fishing boats that plied the waters off Denmark, sailing from scores of small ports along Denmark's eastern shore. If pressed into service, these vessels could carry the bulk of the Jews to Sweden, but the resistance leaders realized that underground organizations of some sophistication were needed to select those fishing captains who would cooperate in the rescue and to coordinate the sailings by bringing refugees to selected ports at specific times. Organizations were needed also in Copenhagen and the other major cities to handle matters before the Jews could be dispersed to the coastal areas.

In Copenhagen, where the great majority of Jewish refugees could

Two Danish fishing boats transport Jewish refugees across The Sound to Sweden. *(Nordisk Pressefoto)*

be found, the medical profession threw itself into the task of hiding the Jews during the first few days of their flight. Under the city's normal hospital-admittance procedures, all patients except emergency cases were required to report to a central classification office, *Visitationen,* located in the Kommunehospital, where medical histories were taken and preliminary evaluations made. From *Visitationen,* patients were distributed to various hospitals in the city, depending on the nature of their ailments and the beds available. When the first Jewish refugees began to seek refuge, they were adroitly slipped into this normal stream of hospital patients. On instructions from underground workers who sought out Jews in the city, refugees made their way to *Visitationen,* where they were given fictitious names and fictitious illnesses and assigned to hospital beds in various institutions, there to become lost in the general hospital population, often without their presence being known to most of the hospital staff. As the number of Jews seeking safe hiding places increased, however, this system broke down, and the Jews went directly to the hospitals, often in large groups whose identity could not be camouflaged.

At Bispebjerg Hospital a twenty-five-year-old medical student, Ole Secher, worked closely with Dr. Karl Henry Koster in harboring Jewish refugees. When Secher heard that a group of Jews was hiding in the woods outside Copenhagen, he consulted with Dr. Koster, then sought out the Jews and brought them to the hospital, where they were housed in the funeral chapel. Later these Jews, as well as those brought to the hospital by ambulance-driver Jorgen Knudsen, and those who arrived on their own initiative, moved to the nurses' quarters in a building adjacent to the hospital. After the war Dr. Koster wrote of those trying days:

> Many an elderly Miss who would usually get terribly upset if anyone put a finger on her polished mahogany table now found it completely natural that an entire family whom she didn't know occupied her flat.

Secher also arranged the departure of Jewish refugees from Bispebjerg Hospital. As a member of the Danish Students' Rowing Club, Secher had friends in many coastal towns, including the city of Nykøbing on the island of Falster, where an active resistance group had made arrangements with some friendly fishing boat captains. Secher sent the Jewish refugees to Nykøbing by train. Local underground workers picked them up and housed them in small inns and private homes until they could be placed on board boats for the voyage to Sweden. To help the Nykøbing resistance workers spot the Jews at the railroad station, Secher gave each refugee a small blue flag—the symbol of the Danish Students' Rowing Club—to wear as a means of quick identification.

The movement of Jews into and out of Bispebjerg Hospital did not escape the notice of German officials, however. One week after the abortive German roundup, troops surrounded the hospital in the evening, examined all ambulances that left and entered the hospital grounds, and set up checkpoints at entrances and exits. Dr. Stephan Lund, who was in charge of the distribution of Jews to hospitals throughout all of Denmark, described what happened next:

> Since there were two hundred refugees in the hospital that night, it cannot be said that the situation was particularly encouraging. . . . Only a higher authority had the power to order a large-scale action such as searching the hospital. We knew that the authorities in *Dagmarhus* [The Gestapo headquarters] would only come to their offices in the morning and that we had to move the people quickly, before anything happened. Thus it was that at nine o'clock in the morning a funeral cortege left the chapel. The procession consisted of twenty to thirty taxis all filled with refugees. The operation succeeded and the refugees, who knew nothing of the danger they were in, had all slept well in the nurses' apartments placed at their disposal.

Before the Jewish rescue was over, approximately eight hundred Jews had moved through Bispebjerg Hospital alone.

In the Copenhagen suburb of Lyngby, a group led by the pacifist schoolteacher Aage Bertelsen also participated in the Jewish rescue. At the time of the German invasion of Denmark in 1940, Bertelsen fully supported his country's quick surrender: he saw no reason for a "hopeless fight." Throughout the early years of the occupation, he supported the policy of collaboration that most Danes adopted toward the German occupation forces. By the summer of 1943, his views began to change and he began to understand the ideology of sabotage, even if he was not himself ready to desert his pacifist background and become active himself. The Jewish persecution changed his posture. "In the face of these open acts of atrocity, insanely meaningless, it was not a question of one's viewpoint," he wrote later. "Action was the word. . . . No honest man could possibly refrain from action after this raid, when the persecuted cried for help."

Bertelsen's home became a receiving-and-dispatching center for Jews, operating almost in the open. It was Bertelsen's policy that his home should become known as a place where anyone seeking to flee to Sweden could get aid. During the first half of October, "the house with the blue curtains," as it was described by those who passed through it, teemed with movement. The schoolmaster's wife handled the telephone and all internal arrangements, while Bertelsen did most of the outside "contact" work. They were aware of the risks they ran by operating in the open, but hoped nevertheless that they could "finish a useful piece of work" before they were closed down. By the end of October, the Lyngby group had rescued approximately five hundred persons.

The *Holger Danske* sabotage group, which had been forced to disband during the August crackdown, resumed its activities in October under the leadership of Jens Lillilund, concentrating solely on the rescue of the Danish Jews. Its central meeting point was Mogens Staffeldt's *Nordiske Boghandel* (Scandinavian Bookstore), located in a building on the Kongens Nytorv, opposite Copenhagen's best hotel, the D'Angleterre. The rear room of the *Nordiske Boghandel* became another collection point for Jewish refugees, who remained hidden inside until other hiding places could be found for them in homes near the docks—the Kongens Nytorv site being close to Copenhagen's busy port district. At the height of the rescue operation, *Holger Danske* had under its control as many as twelve fishing vessels, which by the end of October had transported approximately one thousand Jews to Sweden.

Special organizations came into existence to coordinate the activities of the field rescue groups. University students in Copenhagen created an informal *Studenternes Efferretningstjeneste* (Student Intelligence Service), which concentrated on gathering information on German activities along the escape routes; while newspapermen at *National Tidende* took over the job of maintaining contact with the various underground rescue groups. The newspapermen pooled all information, from whatever source, and made it available to those field groups in need of up-to-the-minute intelligence. The word "potatoes" came to be used as a code word for Jewish refugees. One of the newspapermen, Borge Outze, described how the calls would sound to any German who might listen in:

> Eighteen sacks of potatoes have been sold today to Mrs. Ege.... Twenty sacks were sold through the middleman at Lyngby.... It would be a good idea for the potatoes to be transferred to another place.

By these references, clearly understood by those involved, groups of Jews would be moved along their way from one rescue group to another until they boarded the escape vessels ready for sea.

For non-Jewish Danes, October, 1943, marked a rebirth of hope and dignity through action. Every boatload of Jewish refugees that sailed from Danish shores meant another victory for the underground workers who had planned the trip. With victory came confidence, and a desire for further victories. Its efforts to rescue the Danish Jews gave the Danish underground an impetus that continued until final victory.

For the Jews, however, it was a time of uncertainty and fear. By necessity they were forced to entrust their lives to strangers who they could only hope would not betray them. The results of failure were known to all: arrest, deportation, imprisonment, and possibly death. What the Danish resistance workers later remembered as the "happy Jew time" was, for the Danish Jews, a period of darkest despair. Some committed suicide before arrest. All feared what would happen to them and their families if they did not escape from Denmark. Even when the escape was successful, the experience was harrowing. One Jewish woman survivor related the story of her escape:

> We were taken by taxi to the beach near a little fishing harbor. Each of the four passengers and the organizer were then hidden under a bush by the shore. The plan was that at a certain time we were to crawl along the beach to the harbor, where there was a watchtower manned by Germans. We lay a whole day waiting for darkness. Up on the road we could hear cars drive by and we shivered with fright. . . . As far as we knew, the Germans in the watchtower had been bribed to turn a blind eye. At seven o'clock in the evening, a strange sight revealed itself. From the bushes along the beach human forms crawled out on their stomachs. We discovered that these were other passengers of whose presence we had been completely unaware. After awhile we reached the fishing boat without mishap and were herded into the hold, like herrings in a barrel. As there was not enough space down below, a few passengers were wrapped in fishing nets and in sacks on the deck. . . . Shortly after our sailing, a wind blew up and many became seasick and were forced to come up on deck and retch, as they could not bear to be in the smelly hold. Then we saw the searchlight of the

German patrol boat. The engine was immediately stopped and we were ordered to stand stiff and still around the wheelhouse, whose weak light could have given us away. Everyone thought his last hour had come and was ready to jump overboard and drown, rather than be taken by the Germans.... Tension on board was extreme.... However, the passengers calmed down after the initial danger had passed and made every effort to stay calm, although every muscle was tense for fear of discovery. The little boat had in the meantime gone off course because of the gale.... Gradually it began to grow light, but we had no idea of the boat's position.... Would we ever be saved? At seven in the morning, land was sighted, but what land? ... The boat approached the coast; we hoped that liberty was at hand. We were really in Swedish territorial waters. The Danish flag was raised and people threw their arms around one another and cried for joy. We were saved at last. The harbor we had sailed into was full of Swedish warships on whose decks sailors waved and shouted "Valkommen."

Not all transports reached their destination. One of the first large transports arranged by Aage Bertelsen's Lyngby group involved two hundred Jewish refugees who had been transported from Copenhagen and hidden in a large hayloft of a farm near the port village of Humlebaek, where they awaited news that vessels were available for them. Early in the second week of October, underground workers in Helsingør contacted Bertelsen to inform him that eleven fishing boats would be available that night in Humlebaek. Bertelsen immediately made arrangements to move

Jewish refugees come out from hiding as their vessel enters Swedish waters. *(Danish Ministry for Foreign Affairs)*

the refugees from their farm hideout to the port by truck. Later he wrote of that transfer:

> Among many pictures I remember from those days the scene at the farm near Humlebaek that night is still so vivid that it will never be obliterated. We had to load the big trucks with people as if they were cattle or sacks of produce. We lifted them up and hauled them, all of them, aged, women, and babies, across the high backboard or side-boards, and placed them crouching or flat on the bottom of the trucks, one on top of the other, so that no one was visible above the sides of the trucks. Everything took place in deepest silence, without a complaint, but the very fact that with apparent cold-bloodedness we treated human beings as if they were animals or inert matter gave this sinister scene a touch of horror. The surroundings, too, played their part: gloomy barn, the darkness of the October night, faintly dispelled by a rising moon behind rain clouds and the gleam from the lantern in the half-open stable door.

The loaded trucks, packed with refugees, set out along the coastal road to Humlebaek, where Bertelsen was scheduled to confer with two representatives of the captains of the fishing boats. The meeting took place as scheduled, but the two representatives had disappointing news for Bertelsen: instead of the eleven boats he had expected, there was only one boat available, capable of carrying only a small percentage of the refugees. Who should go and who should stay was left to Bertelsen to decide. Selection proved especially difficult, for it appeared to be a question of life and death. Bertelsen decided not to split up any family. In the end he chose to send sixteen men, women and children; each and every member of a few families rather than a member or two from all the families. As for the remaining Jews, they were led back to the trucks and returned to their hiding place on the farm, there to await new arrangements.

Every individual escape was an adventure, unpredictable and frightening. Rabbi Marcus Melchior, whose original warning had sent the Jews into flight and hiding, endured with his family a danger-packed trip from the Ørslev home of the Reverend Kildeby, where they had been hiding, to the port of Haesnaes on the island of Falster, where the six members of the Melchior family joined thirteen other refugees on a tiny fishing vessel, "fit for four or five," under the command of a young fisherman. The vessel set sail shortly after nightfall on the evening of October 8. If all had gone well, they could have expected to reach Swedish waters by morning, but their inexperienced skipper grew confused in the dark. Daybreak found the vessel sailing in large circles near the Danish port of Gedser, a terminal point for one of the main ferry lines connecting Denmark with Germany, and a particularly hazardous area because of German naval activity in the vicinity. When the fisherman realized where he was, he suggested that the boat, with its refugees, return to Haesnaes to try again another day. Alarmed at his suggestion, the refugees insisted on taking over command of the vessel and themselves set a course which successfully took them into Swedish waters. Nineteen hours after leaving Haesnaes, they finally entered the harbor entrance of the small Swedish fishing village where they were welcomed by Swedish fishermen. Rabbi Melchior later wrote of their reception by the Swedes:

> They had never before in their lives seen Jews, or refugees, not to mention Jewish refugees. But through the radio and daily press they were informed of what was going on. They put us ashore, invited us to their homes, and displayed a cordiality and kindness which did not fall short of the helpfulness with which we had been sent away from home.

Although humanitarian reasons motivated most resistance workers who helped the Jews, large sums of money did change hands in arranging the voyages to Sweden. In the tense early days of October, before underground groups regularized the traffic, individual Jews made private arrangements with individual fishing captains, and the price extracted by the captains, themselves fearful of what would happen to them if they were caught, began at 1,000 kroner (about $150) per person and ran as high as 10,000 kroner ($1,500) per person. In a few cases, greedy captains capitalized on Jewish fears to extort money from the refugees. One group of seven Jews who reached Humlebaek early in the month paid the captain of a fishing vessel 25,000 kroner ($3,750) in advance for their passage to Sweden. On the night of their scheduled departure, however, the fishing boat failed to arrive at the previously arranged rendezvous. When the Jews located the captain the next day, insisting on leaving the following night, they were told they had to pay an additional 21,000 kroner ($3,150), for a total price of 46,000 kroner ($6,900). Terrified of remaining in Denmark, the Jews had no other choice but to pay the price demanded. * Even when there was no intent to cheat, fishing-boat captains often drove hard bargains with refugee groups. On one occasion Aage Bertelsen arrived at a sailing point at night to discover a small family lost in despair on the dock. A fisherman had been there offering seats in his boat for 1,000 kroner per person. The head of the family explained that he did not have enough money to cover passage for all in his family and pleaded with the captain to take a lesser amount, but the seaman spurned his pleas and sailed off without them.

Underground groups realized that large sums of money had to be raised if the rescue was to succeed, for even the great majority of honorable and humane captains usually insisted on receiving for each voyage an amount equal to the replacement cost of their vessel. Wealthy Jews contributed handsomely to the rescue effort. C. B. Henriques gave several

* After the war the captain involved in this case was successfully brought to trial for his actions.

hundred thousand kroner and the board of trustees of the Jewish Community, which had successfully arranged its own escape to Sweden, authorized its lawyer in Copenhagen to use Community assets as collateral to obtain a loan of 750,000 kroner, which went toward the relief effort. Other money came from non-Jewish Danes—10,000 kroner from a timber merchant, a 70,000-kroner loan from a government official, 50,000 kroner from a businessman as "conscience money." Individual donations, however, no matter how large, could not finance the entire operation; a centralized "bank" was needed to receive and disburse money in the same way that information was received and transmitted by the newspapermen of *National Tidende.*

Dr. Stephan Lund of the Kommunehospital described the organization that developed:

> It was very often financial difficulties which were the most troublesome. In order to coordinate the various aspects, including the financial, the medical association embarked on broad measures of. cooperation, including contact with an unofficial committee which met a couple of times a week. This committee included representatives of various social groups—a lawyer, an industrialist, a civil servant, and so forth. In addition, contact was maintained with politicians and trade union leaders.

Although the medical association collected approximately one million kroner during the month of October, financial matters remained troublesome: bookkeeping was erratic and money was often not where it was needed, when it was needed; almost always it was in short supply. At Bispebjerg Hospital, resistance worker Ole Secher was assigned the task of "draining the Jews of money" as they passed through the institution, an assignment he considered necessary but onerous and one which the refugees, who hoped to take to Sweden as much of a cash reserve as possible, objected to strongly. Resistance leaders sold furniture and household effects from Jewish homes and apartments after their occupants had fled and constantly asked richer refugees to help pay for the passage of their poorer brethren. Heavy pressure could be applied to those who refused to cooperate. On one trip, Bjarne Sygtryggsson, a member of the Lyngby organization, guided a large group of refugees to a fishing vessel whose captain had agreed to accept 500 kroner per person for the passage. Some refugees, however, could not pay even this modest fare; and Sygtryggsson suggested that the richer refugees make up the total due. He passed his hat around for contributions, but the amount collected fell short of the amount needed. The hat went around a second time. Again contributions fell short, by several thousand kroner. At this point one refugee who had already made an extra contribution remarked that another man in the group, a wealthy Copenhagen resident, had a savings book in his possession for an account in a Copenhagen bank and demanded that the other man contribute his bankbook so the voyage could get under way. The Copenhagen man refused: he had paid 500 kroner for his passage, he did not intend to contribute more, and no amount of argument or persuasion could budge him. He broke down and gave up his bankbook only after he was offered the choice of contributing his savings or taking a refund and remaining in Denmark.

In time, the resistance groups managed to bring the average price of passage down to 500 kroner per person. For one big transport consisting of 230 refugees, Lyngby negotiators arranged a flat-sum voyage price of 100,000 kroner (approximately $15,000), or a little more than $65 for each man, woman, and child involved, one of the lowest per-person fares of the entire rescue operation. But despite the heroism of the fishermen and the gratitude of the refugees they saved, the emotions aroused by the financial transactions that took place left a bitter residue in the memories of many who were involved. Some Jews, having successfully escaped to Sweden, criticized the Danish fishermen for accepting any money at all, and among the resistance workers there was criticism of those wealthy Jews who balked at contributing a lifetime of savings so that others less fortunate could sail to safety without payment.

After the war, one underground worker wrote of those trying days: "However much we tried to make up groups of richer and poorer people, it almost always happened that in the evening we were left with a certain number of the poorest whom we had not managed to send."

Despite the difficulties involved and the uncertainties of each voyage, it became obvious by the end of the first week of October that the Danish Jews were escaping en masse to Sweden, seemingly under the eyes of German arrest squads. But no amount of prior planning or daring on the part of the Danish underground would have saved the Jews if Sweden had not opened its borders to the refugees,* if Danish authorities had not cooperated in the rescue, and finally, if German troops had not displayed, as they did, a curious lethargy in hunting down the refugee groups that, scattered throughout the country, stood out among the native population like starlings amongst a flock of bluebirds.

* Sweden opened its doors at the last minute after having been practically a closed country to Jewish refugees for a decade. Throughout the 1930s, Sweden gave entry permits sparingly and grudgingly; many Jews who made their way to Swedish shores without permits, even well-established professional men, were forcibly turned away. By the outbreak of World War II, Sweden had accepted approximately two thousand Jewish refugees. By the end of 1942 the number of foreign Jews inside Sweden had risen to slightly under three thousand, the bulk of the increase being the nine hundred Norwegian Jews who had escaped to Sweden in late 1942. As 1943 began, Sweden's borders remained tightly shut against unwanted strangers. Only in the spring of 1943, as the full impact of German defeats in Russia sank in, did Sweden's attitude begin to change. By the time of the Jewish crisis in Denmark, Sweden was ready for a dramatic shift in policy. As early as September 6, 1943, the Swedish Minister in Copenhagen, Gustaf Dardell, reported to his Foreign Office that the Jewish problem was "hovering in the air." Later that month, as news of the planned German roundup spread through Denmark, Dardell informed his government of the date and objective of the raids (his

In the final analysis, however, it was the failure of the German authorities to pursue their quarry effectively that permitted the Jews to escape. There were some arrests, of course. The family of Danish author Ralph Oppenhejm was handed over to the Germans by a Danish captain who took the Oppenhejms aboard his vessel after their boat had broken down; they were transported to the concentration camp at Theresienstadt. The Germans also seized 110 refugees (ninety of them hiding in an attic of a church) in the fishing village of Gilleleje, north of Helsingør after a Danish girl had reported to the local Gestapo chief that there was an exceptionally large concentration of Jews in town. And during the latter part of October, the Gestapo intensified its efforts and arrested many Jews from among the poorer classes who had not managed to escape. But the most common German attitude was one of acquiescence in the escape of the Jews. On almost every occasion the Germans chose to look the other way. At sea, the German naval commander of the port of Copenhagen took his coastal patrol vessels out of operation during the very period when the illegal sailings were most frequent; he reported to his superiors that his vessels were in need of repairs and unable to put to sea. On land, Jews forced to use public transportation to get out of Copenhagen faced the gravest potential danger, for the trains always carried large numbers of Germans. Non-Jewish Danes made it a practice to mingle with their Jewish countrymen, hoping thereby to make their identification that much more difficult. The stratagem was not necessary; the Germans on the trains did not want to notice the Jewish refugees. Throughout October, as German arrest squads supposedly roamed the country in search of Jews, there was not a single arrest of a Jewish refugee on any train in Denmark. One Jewish refugee who successfully escaped from Copenhagen by train described his departure from the Danish capital: "That evening there were at least as many Germans as Jews on the train, but having looked each other over, each side pretended that the other did not exist."

---

information on both counts was correct) and he reported further that leaders of Denmark's Jewish community had asked if Sweden would receive Denmark's Jews. On receipt of Dardell's communications, the Swedish Foreign Minister instructed the Swedish Minister in Berlin to inquire about the rumors and to protest any Jewish deportation. Still, Sweden refrained from assuring the Danish Jews that they would be welcome there.

The famous Danish physicist Niels Bohr helped swing Sweden's doors open. He arrived in Stockholm on September 30 and visited Sweden's Foreign Minister Guenther in the afternoon of October 2. With the outcome of the German roundup still unknown, Bohr urged Guenther to approach the Germans and request that the ships assigned to carry the Jews to Germany be diverted to Sweden instead. Guenther agreed, but he received no answer from German officials. Later in the afternoon, as the failure of the German roundup became generally known, Bohr visited Sweden's King Gustav and pleaded, in the name of humanity, that Sweden publicly announce its willingness to receive Danish Jews, if they could find their way to Swedish shores. Gustav assured Bohr that he was personally sympathetic to the plight of the Danish Jews and promised an early response. That same night, in an official announcement over Swedish radio, the government broadcasted the electrifying news that Sweden was prepared to oppose Germany and give safety and shelter to all Danish Jews for the duration of the war.

Everywhere the Germans looked the other way. German patrols who stopped cars filled with Jews accepted bribes to let the cars pass. A student active in the resistance gave this report:

> The medical association used to supply its agents with large sums of cash, so that we could use it to give bribes if we were arrested. It was usually not difficult to bribe the German soldiers, and it was also possible to come to an agreement with the Gestapo.

Some German patrols confronted with escaping Jews simply let their quarry go. Medical student Bent Petersen was stopped one night while driving to a rendezvous point with a carload of refugees, including several children. The German soldier demanded that all in the car get out to be examined. Petersen turned around and pointed at some small heads in the rear seat.

"Seien Sie doch Menschen. Wir haben ja Kinder mit [Be human. We have children with us]," he said.

The German peered into the back seat, then waved the car on. *"Weiter fahren* [Drive on]."

When the final figures were tallied, the German officials discovered that most of their quarry had escaped. Two hundred and eighty-four Jews had been captured during the raids of October 1 and 2; from then until the end of October, another 275 persons were caught, eighty-five of them half-Jews who were subsequently released. Against this figure, there was the number who managed to make their way safely to Sweden: 7,220. In saving its Jews, Denmark also embarked on a new road of resistance that would bring the country into increasingly open opposition to German occupation forces and eventually win for Denmark acceptance as a member in good standing among the Allied nations of World War II.

The rescue of the Danish Jews created a wave of excitement throughout the world. The Allied nations seized on the story as a welcome alternative to the reports of horror and atrocity coming out of war-torn Europe. But the facts themselves, heartwarming as they were, had to be embellished in the interests of the propaganda war against Germany. Propaganda experts, journalists, Jewish groups, and Allied government leaders joined forces to portray the Danish rescue of the Jews as something more dramatic than it actually was. By the middle of October, 1943, British newspapers were playing the story in large type. On October 13, 1943, the *Evening Standard* carried an emotional report on developments in Denmark, under a headline reading "Yellow Star."

> A noble voice comes out of Nazi-occupied Denmark, a voice of tolerance and defiance and of faith in humanity. "If the Germans want to introduce the Yellow Star for Jews in Denmark" announces King Christian, "I and my whole family will wear it as a sign of the highest distinction."

Actually two major versions of the legend evolved. The first alleged that when the Germans planned to introduce the Yellow Star into Denmark, King Christian declared that he would be the first to wear the star; his threat reportedly so impressed the Germans that they rescinded their order before it could be implemented. A second, more dramatic version credited King Christian with actually pinning a Star of David onto his sleeve and riding through the streets of Copenhagen to demonstrate his support for his Jewish countrymen. His action, it was said, prompted tens of thousands of non-Jewish Danes to don the star as well, thereby presenting the Germans with a unified opposition to their Jewish policies. Neither version is true. King Christian never threatened to wear the star, nor did he ever actually wear one; neither did the non-Jewish citizens of Copenhagen.

In the years after the war, however, many writers reworked the legend in articles, plays, and books of fiction and nonfiction. An article entitled "Thanks to Scandinavia" that appeared in the May, 1966, issue of the *National Jewish Monthly* reported: "King Christian deliberately wore and displayed the Yellow Badge the Jews were forced to wear; and as a result, that emblem immediately became the symbol of our courage."

There are two favorable mentions of the Danish king in Rolf Hochhuth's antipapal play, *The Deputy,* which criticized Pope Pius for allegedly failing to help the Jews. King Christian's role was offered as a model that the Catholic Pope could have followed. Probably the most widely read book that perpetuated the legend was Leon Uris's best-selling novel *Exodus.* Here is his version of events:

> From German occupation headquarters at the Hotel D'Angleterre came the decree: ALL JEWS MUST WEAR A YELLOW ARM BAND WITH A STAR OF DAVID. That night the underground radio transmitted a message to all Danes. "From Amalienborg Palace, King Christian has given the following answer to the German command that Jews must wear a Star of David. The King has said that one Dane is exactly the same as the next Dane. He himself will wear the first Star of David and he expects that every loyal Dane will do the same." The next day the Germans rescinded the order.

When the Danish-language version of *Exodus* appeared in Danish bookstores, this episode had been deleted from the book, for the publisher realized that Danish readers would know it simply was not true.

The legend lingers on in the Western world, however, passed on by word of mouth among Jewish communities and among those advocating a passive resistance to various forms of tyranny. Denmark's kindly though often ineffectual King Christian has become a symbol of his nation's heroic efforts to save its Jewish countrymen, personifying, as it were, Denmark's truly humane accomplishment in this regard. And while the details of the legend are often incompatible with the actual events, the general thrust and meaning of all the wartime and postwar stories are consistent with the facts: Denmark did manage to save the bulk of its Jewish population, the only country of occupied Europe which succeeded, for whatever mix of reasons, in accomplishing this life-saving task.

16
Toward Victory in Norway

At the start of 1943 Norway's underground military apparatus, commonly known as Milorg, was beset with problems. Many of its leaders were either under arrest or in hiding as the result of German crackdowns, its relations with the Norwegian civilian resistance were strained, and its contacts with the Norwegian government in exile in London and with the British leaders of the SOE were marked by a degree of suspicion and mistrust which no amount of diplomatic communications seemed capable of eliminating.

Milorg itself was split into warring factions. The basic debate was grounded in a question that was fated to plague Norway throughout the war: Should Milorg, regardless of reprisals, act aggressively and attempt to advance the date of final liberation, or should a "go-slow" policy, minimizing the suffering of the Norwegian people, be allowed to dominate, even at the price of a delayed liberation? Those supporting an active policy were among the younger Milorg members and the Communists, while the bulk of the older, more cautious members favored a passive posture.

An attempt to resolve the internal dispute, on paper at least, was made in January, 1943, with the drafting of a directive designed not only for circulation within Norway but also for the edification of the Norwegians in London as well as their British associates. The directive called for a heroic, "active" resistance so "that the people may find strength and self respect in the knowledge that the liberation was not only a gift from others but also a result of their own efforts." But the directive went on to warn that this "active Resistance should not commence until an Allied invasion was imminent," thereby ensuring that the Milorg organization would be preserved intact for the final campaign. Since the Allies had no intention of invading Norway at the time, nor was an invasion likely in the foreseeable future, this formulation of Milorg policy constituted victory for the more cautious elements within the organization. Those

advocating an active resistance had to content themselves with the promise that sometime in the future Milorg might take to the field against the
Germans.

But even this mild statement of resistance policy proved too aggressive for the leaders of the civilian resistance, who, under former Chief
Justice Paal Berg, had formed an "inner cabinet" known as "the Circle"
to guide Norway's overall resistance. The Circle was appalled by even
the hint of action contained in the Milorg directive. Civilian leaders
rejected any acts of violence against the Germans. They opposed the
formation of an underground army, which, they warned, would meet
disaster whenever it went into action, even if during the last days of the
war. ("It would be a 'children's crusade,' " they prophesied.) Sabotage
was also ruled out; the country, it was said, was not ready to accept the
reprisals that would certainly follow. The Circle was so fearful of any
violence that it made the incredible suggestion that SOE agents who
arrived in Norway should come unarmed, in order to reduce the possibility of German reprisals.

Political mistrust complicated relations between Milorg and the
civilian leaders. The established professional and business leaders of the
Circle regarded the relatively unknown men of Milorg with suspicion,
viewing them as potential rivals for political power after the war. The
Norwegian government in exile in London also saw in Milorg a potential
rival for power after the end of the war and, in late 1941, had placed
Milorg under the authority of the Norwegian armed forces, hoping by
this action to subordinate Milorg. But suspicions lingered on nevertheless.

This was the situation in early 1943 when an energetic and politically wise twenty-eight-year-old lawyer named Jens Christian Hauge
took over as head of Milorg and set out to reorganize the Norwegian
military resistance effort and to ease the many misunderstandings, both
with London and the civilian resistance at home.

In May, 1943, Hauge secretly journeyed to Stockholm to meet with
representatives of the Norwegian High Command, who had flown to the
Swedish capital from London. Each side came away with something it
wanted. Hauge received confirmation of Milorg's basic objective—to
establish an underground army which would be held in readiness for
future use, with sabotage held to a minimum. The Norwegian High
Command, in turn, received Milorg's assurance that it would operate
under Allied command and in accordance with Allied strategy.

Eventually an understanding was reached between Milorg and the
civilian resistance at home. In the autumn of 1943, the two groups agreed
on a joint policy that rejected an active resistance against the Germans.
"We are convinced," their joint memorandum stated, "that an active
policy will bring disasters to the people and the country which will be out
of all proportion to the military gains."

Three-and-a-half years after the German invasion, Milorg had adopted a policy which, in all important aspects, duplicated the nonviolent policy of the civilian resistance.

Despite his cautious approach, Jens Christian Hauge was an energetic and competent administrator who set about creating an organization that would avoid the mistakes of the past and recruiting an army to take over the country when liberation occurred. Milorg districts throughout the country were restructured in military fashion, with detailed tables of organization which assigned a number to every man, and every man to a specific job.

Security was stressed, for Hauge and his staff were determined to avoid the catastrophic security failures that had resulted in German roll-ups of Milorg in 1941 and 1942. To prevent any recurrence a network warning system was devised. Contact cards were prepared for each Milorg member which listed all other Milorg men the individual knew. If a Milorg member was arrested, the security officer for his unit had the responsibility of warning all contacts on the arrested man's card. Milorg realized that it was unrealistic to ask a captured member to withstand torture during interrogation, but it did ask its men to maintain silence for twenty-four hours if possible. By then, it was hoped, all those listed on his contact card would be on their way to Sweden and the Gestapo would hit into empty air when they set out to make arrests.

Morale among Milorg's rank and file, nevertheless, was low. Hauge's emphasis on paper work and organization and the prohibition against active sabotage frustrated many. "Instead of tasks, they got directives," Hauge admitted after the war. "Instead of guns, they got paper." Disillusionment set in. Throughout late 1943 and 1944, Hauge grew increasingly concerned that the frustration imposed on his men by Milorg's policy of moderation and caution would impel activist members to break away and join other smaller but more aggressive resistance groups.

In the forefront of those Norwegians calling for a policy of force against the Germans stood the Communists, most of whom had reached their position only after Hitler's attack on the Soviet Union. There had been a few Communists who advocated resistance against Germany from the earliest days of the German occupation, among them Peter Furubotn, the Communist leader in Bergen, but party leaders in Oslo ignored Furubotn; and the majority of party members could no more hear his call for resistance than could the mass of non-Communist Norwegians hear the appeals of those few non-Communist underground leaders who had supported an active resistance from the start. For the Norwegian Communists, Hitler's invasion of Russia provided a clear turning point in world affairs that overnight defined for them the correct course of action at home. Within months, the Communists adopted an active line and the slogan "Deny all weapons to the enemy." Unlike Milorg, the small but well-organized Communist apparatus sought to build a home-based resistance capable of striking out at targets of its own choosing, independently of orders from London. Through the entire occupation, the Communists held fast to their active line and never ceased to criticize Milorg's cautious policy as symptomatic of a corrupt capitalist society, more interested in protecting Norwegian industries than in defeating the Germans. Despite Norway's basic antipathy to communism (there had not been a single Communist representative elected to the pre-war Norwegian Parliament) the Communists' wartime appeal for an active resistance gained support as the war progressed.* After the war Hauge confessed that one of his most difficult problems during the last two years of the occupation was to project a militant Milorg image to hold his recruits while at the same time remaining loyal to the agreed-upon policy of a generally passive resistance obedient to orders from London.

Forces other than the Communists joined in driving Milorg to adopt, if only in theory, a more active sabotage line. In 1943, a new controversy over bombing versus sabotage split the Allies in London and pitted Norwegians of all viewpoints against British and American Air Force officers.

Allied air officers had by then become convinced that their growing armadas could bomb Germany into submission, and they determined to press the attack against all targets, regardless of location, considered vital to the German war effort. Targets in occupied countries were not exempted. To the Norwegians in London, however, the possibility of massive Allied air raids against Norwegian plants and port facilities threatened the destruction of the nation's industrial base on which the country's postwar recovery depended. Under no circumstances would the Norwegians approve an air campaign against Norwegian targets. Instead of bombing raids, they suggested an active campaign of sabotage, which they had hitherto resisted. While there might be German reprisals as the result of sabotage actions, the cost in Norwegian lives and property resulting from Allied bombing raids would be far higher. On this point all Norwegians agreed.

The Allies, nevertheless, went ahead with their bombing offensive without bothering to consult the Norwegians. Starting in early summer, 1943, Allied bombers began regular heavy raids against targets in Germany and German-occupied Europe, including Norway. In one July raid 167 Flying Fortresses dropped more than fifteen hundred 500-pound bombs on a large fertilizer factory complex at Heroy, near Oslo, causing

* The increased popularity of the Communists carried over into the postwar years, when in the first free election after liberation Norwegian voters elected eleven Communist members to Parliament out of a total membership of 150. Norway's acceptance of Communists was short-lived, however. By the early 1950s and the formalization of the Cold War between the United States and the Soviet Union, popular support for the Communists evaporated to pre-war standards.

heavy casualties among the population. The Norwegian exile government learned of the raid only after it had been carried out and filed
immediate diplomatic protests with both London and Washington. At the
very least, the Norwegians insisted, they should have been informed of
the raid before it was carried out. Before Norway received a reply to her
notes of protest, however, the American air command carried out another
major raid, again without notifying the Norwegians, this time against the
Norsk Hydro heavy-water plant at Vemork, which only a half-year
before had supposedly been put out of action by Norwegian saboteurs
operating under orders from the SOE.

The British reassessment of the Norsk Hydro sabotage raid had
begun in March, 1943, one month after the raid itself. At the time British
damage-assessment experts estimated that the facilities that produced
heavy water for Germany's atomic-bomb program had been so heavily
damaged that production would be halted for two years at least. The
British, however, had miscalculated badly. Within two months, Norwegian agents began to file disturbing reports. German engineers and Norsk
Hydro technicians had managed to get the heavy-water plant back into
production. The first heavy water was drawn off and shipped to Germany
in late June.

By August German engineers succeeded in raising production to a
level that promised to bring the plant's annual output up to three tons, far
in excess of Germany's needs. By October Gen. Leslie R. Groves, who
headed America's Manhattan Project, which was pushing toward the
creation of its own atomic bomb, had become so worried about the
increase in production at the Norsk Hydro plant that he urged Gen.
George C. Marshall to authorize a high-priority bombing attack against
the Norwegian target, despite the certainty of civilian casualties. Marshall
agreed. The assignment went to the American Eighth Air Force stationed in Britain, and on November 16, 155 Flying Fortresses from the
Third Air Division roared aloft, escorted by long-range fighters, and
headed for Vemork. In thirty-three minutes over the target, the giant
bombers dropped more than seven hundred 500-pound bombs on the
Vemork plant. Another one hundred smaller bombs rained down on the
nearby town of Rjukan. Twenty-two Norwegians died in the raid,
including one man in a forest several miles away who was killed by a
jettisoned bomb. As a high-precision raid, however, the results were
disappointing. German smoke generators effectively screened the target
area, and while there was heavy damage to surrounding facilities, the
plant itself escaped unharmed and previously produced stocks of heavy
water remained untouched.

News of the raid shocked the Norwegian government in exile,
which lodged formal protests with the British and American govern-

ments. The Norwegians complained that the damage caused by the raids was "out of all proportion to the desired effect."

> The attacks on Vemork and Rjukan were executed without the Norwegians' prior consent and without their even being informed. If the reason for the attack was the necessity of stopping . . . production of heavy water . . . specialized methods of attack would have been more suitable than bombing.

The British government took a month before it formally rejected the Norwegian note. Britain insisted upon the right to select bombing targets and insisted also that Vemork had been bombed because intelligence information indicated that another sabotage attempt would be unsuccessful. The Americans took even longer to answer. Eventually they too rejected the Norwegian protest, archly assuring the Norwegians that the raid had been thoroughly investigated beforehand, an answer that left the Norwegians in London frustrated and angry.

German reaction to the Vemork raid was prompt. On November 30, London learned of German plans to transport to Germany all the heavy-water equipment in Vemork from Einar Skinnarland, the radio operator left behind after the first sabotage raid on Vemork. In late December, Skinnarland added to his original report. He told London that the Germans also planned to ship to Germany the entire stock of heavy water at Vemork. By then it amounted to fourteen tons, and it was deemed vital to Germany's last-ditch effort to complete an atomic bomb of its own. German plans to ship the heavy water and equipment neared completion in January. The heavy water was stored in special drums marked "potash lye" and placed under the protection of a special Army unit sent from Germany to ensure the shipment's safe arrival. A senior German atomic scientist arrived at the Norsk Hydro plant to oversee personally that all precautions were taken. Negotiations began with Norwegian authorities for transportation to carry the shipment to the port of embarkation.

The rapid pace of German efforts alarmed British intelligence officers, who were remarkably well informed of German intentions by a number of Norwegian contacts. In late January British intelligence asked Skinnarland if he could determine the exact date of the shipment and if the transport could be prevented. Skinnarland replied that if London wanted action, they would have to decide quickly for the transport was scheduled to take place within a week. As for how the transport could be prevented, Skinnarland had no suggestions; he left that to his superiors in London.

Once again London faced the problem of trying to decide how to destroy Norsk Hydro's heavy water. If anything, the difficulties appeared greater than ever before. The failure of the November bombing raid ruled out a similar effort, and tightened German security around the plant ruled out another sabotage attempt. Time also pressed on the British. Whatever they decided to do would have to be done quickly, with little time for preparation and planning. The British concluded that their best chance of success lay in a series of attacks on the shipment while it was in transit from Vemork to Germany.

London's first move was to instruct one of the SOE agents in Norway, Lt. Knut Haukelid, to obtain as much information about the proposed transit route as he could. Haukelid had participated in the original Norsk Hydro raid the previous February, and since that time he had been working in the Norwegian region of Telemark building up resistance forces. On receipt of his instructions, Haukelid hurried to Rjukan for conferences with Skinnarland. He soon reported to London that the Germans planned to ship the heavy water and heavy-water equipment by rail from Vemork to Rjukan, where the shipment would be loaded onto a ferry for a long trip across Lake Tinnsjö. At the southern end of the lake the shipment was scheduled for reloading onto another train that would take the valuable cargo south to the port of embarkation. Haukelid suggested that an attack be made on the ferry, or on the train that would carry the shipment south.

London responded immediately with orders to Haukelid to go ahead with an attempt to blow up the ferry. How this could be accomplished was left to Haukelid's discretion. London, however, was not content to rely solely on Haukelid. Without informing him of their other plans, they also ordered an independent group of saboteurs to proceed with plans to blow up the train south of Lake Tinnsjö, if Haukelid failed in his efforts, and alerted the RAF bomber command to prepare to bomb the vessel that would carry the heavy water from Norway to Germany, in case both sabotage groups failed. London was taking no chances.

Haukelid had good contacts within the Vemork plant. These included a laboratory assistant, the plant's new chief engineer, and the Norwegian transport engineer, Kjell Nielsen. The Vemork men, however, were uneasy about his intentions. German reprisals for an attack on the transport would be inevitable. Beyond that, an additional danger existed for innocent Norwegian civilians. The ferry that was scheduled to carry the heavy-water shipment across Lake Tinnsjö also carried passengers, and a raid would undoubtedly claim civilian lives. Haukelid queried London if the mission was absolutely necessary. London replied:

> Matter has been considered. It is thought very important that the heavy water shall be destroyed. Hope it can be done without too disastrous results. Send our best wishes for success in the work. Greeting.

Haukelid proceeded in systematic fashion. Before deciding on the exact time and method of attack, he took a reconnaissance trip on the ferry, clad as an ordinary workman. The trip provided much valuable information. He learned that it took twenty minutes for the ferry to reach the deepest part of the lake and that it then traveled over deep water for at least an hour. He also realized that he had to sink the ferry quickly, once it was over deep water. A slow sinking could conceivably enable the ferryboat captain to race for shore and beach the vessel before it sank. Haukelid had barely completed his preliminary reconnaissance before he heard from Transport Engineer Nielsen that the heavy-water shipment was ready to move. Nielsen had purposely arranged the transport so that it would make the early sailing of the Lake Tinnsjö ferry on Sunday morning, February 20, when civilian passengers could be expected to be at a minimum.

The heavy-water shipment left Vemork by rail late Saturday afternoon and arrived in Rjukan a few hours later. Heavy German patrols, operating under orders to stay with the shipment until it was loaded onto the ferry, guarded the railroad station throughout the night. While the Germans posted themselves around the railroad station, Haukelid made his move shortly after midnight on the twentieth, creeping onto the ferry *Hydro* where it was tied up for the night. Haukelid later reported to SOE headquarters what happened to him and two underground associates on board the ferry:

> Almost the entire ship's crew was gathered together below around a long table, playing poker rather noisily. Only the engineer and stoker were working in the engine room, so there was no question of going in there. We therefore went down to the passenger cabin, but were discovered by a Norwegian guard. Thank God he was a good Norwegian. We told him that we were on the run from the Gestapo and he let us stay.

Once safely on board, Haukelid and an associate, Rolf Sorlie, placed nineteen pounds of high explosives against the forward hull, choosing the location with care. They wanted to place their explosives as far foward as possible so that when the explosion took place, the vessel would sink bow first, raising the stern and propeller out of the water and preventing the ferry from making any headway toward shore.

Twelve inches of water had seeped into the bilge and the saboteurs were glad to see it. The explosives were positioned beneath the waterline, thus concealing the charges from any chance discovery. Two alarm clocks, serving as double backups, were connected to electric detonators to trigger the explosive mechanism. Haukelid securely set both clocks on a rib of the vessel.

The wiring of the time mechanism required closer calculation and some guesswork. The ferry loaded with the heavy water was scheduled to depart at ten o'clock the following morning. If it sailed exactly on schedule, the vessel would reach deep water at 10:20 A.M., but local people knew, and so did Haukelid, that the ferry seldom sailed on time. Haukelid therefore estimated the departure time at 10:10 A.M. and then, allowing himself an even greater margin of error, set the explosive charges to go off at 10:45. He knew that at that time the ferry would still be over the deepest portion of the lake.

With the explosive charges set, the sabotage party hurried off the ferry, shaking hands with the unsuspecting Norwegian watchman as they left. Once on solid ground, the party split up. Haukelid headed for Sweden and Sorlie returned to link up with Einar Skinnarland, who had been ordered to report on the success of the mission. Transport Engineer Nielsen, who had arranged for the heavy water to make the Sunday sailing, was rushed to the local hospital for an emergency appendectomy. Haukelid knew that Nielsen would come under suspicion and insisted that the engineer have a cover story to account for his whereabouts on the morning of the sailing. Cooperative surgeons at the hospital performed the operation without inquiring too deeply. They understood that it was an emergency even if not in the usual medical sense of the word.

By ten o'clock that morning, the train carrying the heavy-water shipment had been shunted onto the ferry and all cars were secured. Fifty-three persons, including civilian passengers, crew, and some German soldiers, climbed aboard. At the wheel was *Hydro*'s skipper, Captain Sorensen. The ferry sailed, as Haukelid had estimated, a few minutes after 10 A.M., and chugged resolutely down the lake, drawing into deeper water with each passing minute. The charges blew at 10:45 A.M. Captain Sorensen, who survived the disaster, thought *Hydro* had been torpedoed. Almost immediately the ferry began to settle by her bows. As the angle of descent grew more pronounced the freight cars carrying the heavy water wrenched free from their deck anchors and plunged into thirteen hundred feet of water. Passengers and crew abandoned ship frantically. Within minutes the *Hydro*, along with twenty-six passengers and crew, plunged after the sinking freight cars. Twenty-seven others aboard the ferry, including Captain Sorensen and four German servicemen, were rescued. All the heavy-water equipment, however, and most of the tanks of heavy water were irretrievably lost. Whatever hopes the Germans had of using Norsk Hydro's heavy water in their atomic reactor research sank with the demolished equipment to the bottom of Lake Tinnsjö.

The operation's mastermind, Knut Haukelid, did not learn of the outcome for some time. All Sunday he traveled without knowing if his efforts had succeeded. Only the next day in Oslo did he discover his success. An evening Norwegian newspaper carried the headline: "Railway Ferry *Hydro* Sunk in the Tinnsjö." His feat did not pass unrecognized, however. A grateful Britain later awarded him the Distinguished Service Order.

The mission to destroy the heavy-water ferry was not the only major sabotage operation of 1944. Despite Milorg's reluctance to become involved in sabotage, pressures for action were mounting: England demanded the destruction of specific targets; the Norwegian government in exile also came out in support of selective sabotage, preferring sabotage to a continuation of Allied bombing raids; while at home hundreds of men and women joined the resistance with the determination to do something to harm the enemy.

Successful operations were carried out by Milorg units against pyrite mines which provided the Germans with important supplies of sulfur, and against silicon carbide works near Arendal, an operation which effectively halted production for several months. In the winter and spring, a group of saboteurs under the command of Gunnar Sonsteby began operations in and around Oslo and soon became known as the "Oslo Gang." Working on orders from England, the Oslo Gang effectively disrupted the production of the Korsvold airplane plant, the acid factory at Lysaker, the Norse Vacuum Oil Plant at Loenga, the oil reserves at Svensend's Street, the locomotive works at Kragerø, and the munitions factory at Kongsberg. Another successful sabotage action came in the late summer of 1944 when Milorg saboteurs destroyed the Holmestrand Aluminum Works, which produced ninety tons of Duralumin plates for the German aircraft industry each month.

The work of military sabotage groups was indirectly aided by a loosely knit "Factory Organization" which received orders from the Milorg leadership. Its membership extended to most of the major plants, rail depots, repair shops, and shipyards of the country and while its primary mission was to prepare to safeguard vital industrial equipment during the closing phases of the war, its members were called upon at times to delay production of certain key items or to turn out faulty equipment urgently needed by the German war machine. At those plants where Communist influence among the workers was strong, the Factory Organization sought to go beyond these objectives and to initiate deliberate sabotage. At the Akers Shipyard in Oslo, where absenteeism sometimes ran as high as 33 percent of the work force, Communist leaders insisted on going ahead with plans to blow up the shipyard despite Milorg leader Hauge's objection to the plan because it had not been approved by London. Hauge refused to provide any explosives for the action. Although discouraged, the leadership of the Akers Factory Organization decided among themselves to act independently, using what limited amounts of explosives they could gather together on their own. The attack was successful. Much of the yard was put out of action. Two days later, Hauge, to his chagrin, heard the BBC describe the action as a "fine piece of sabotage."

The distrust between Milorg and the Communist underground in Norway continued to the end of the war. At no time would Milorg provide arms for Communist groups. As the war neared its end, Milorg's reluctance to cooperate with the Communists grew even more adamant. Milorg's fear of a Communist coup after the occupation proved a consistent theme throughout the war. Nor could the Communists hope to obtain arms directly from England, for in return for Milorg's promise to accept London's authority, London recognized Milorg as the sole representative of the Norwegian military resistance. All arms went to Milorg, which consistently withheld them from those who were determined to use them. Morale among the underground forces in Norway sunk to a new low. Much of their energy was devoted not to the struggle against the Germans but to internal disputes that would, they were sure, carry over into the postwar period.

Morale among the Norwegians in England was even lower. Most were highly motivated men who had escaped from occupied Norway and who had made their way to England over dangerous routes. Once in England, however, most of these Norwegian refugees faced years of frustration. Although the Norwegian Air Force and Navy acquitted themselves admirably in action under British operational control, Norwegian Army units in Britain, which absorbed the bulk of the young Norwegian refugees, were fated to sit out the war. Headquarters for the Norwegian army command, located at 83 Pall Mall, became known as the "house full of officers" whose duties consisted of supervision of units that were in a perpetual state of training. Commanding officers of Norwegian Army units stationed in Britain reported a high incidence of disobedience, mental illness, and suicide among both officers and men as the years of inactivity progressed. Young line officers who graduated from the Norwegian Military Academy established in England in 1942 found themselves assigned to a Training Group for Officers *(Trenings Gruppe for Befal)* at St. Andrews, Scotland, after earning their commission. Instead of seeing combat, the Norwegian officers were put through months of further training, until they began to call their unit the Tired Old Officers *(Tratt Gammeli Befal)*, the initials *TGB* being the same. In the late spring of 1944 several officers at St. Andrews threatened to resign their commissions because of their forced inactivity. Thirty were given extended leaves with pay and permitted to join the Norwegian Navy as able-bodied seamen, to see service with motor torpedo boats assigned to guard the flanks of the Normandy invasion fleet.

The long-awaited Allied invasion of France under Gen. Dwight D. Eisenhower in June of 1944, which marked a new phase in the war against Nazi Germany for the Allies, provided no similar change for Norwegian ground forces stationed in Britain or for Milorg's efforts at home. Senior Norwegian Army officers in London resisted appeals from Norwegian line officers and soldiers to fight in France. The Norwegian

High Command was determined not to squander Norwegian blood on the Continent and to have an army in being for a triumphant homecoming. In Norway news of the invasion created a flurry of excitement within Milorg in the belief that the invasion would bring with it a call for direct action. No such call was forthcoming. Instead, SHAEF (Supreme Headquarters, Allied Expeditionary Force) sent Jens Christian Hauge a lengthy directive which specifically prohibited action on the part of resistance forces. The Allied Supreme Command had one overriding concern at that moment—Operation Overlord, the invasion of the Continent; all other goals were subordinate to Overlord. National uprisings in particular were unwelcome, for they would only serve to arouse the Germans at a time when the Allies could provide no assistance. The Allies feared that any uprising would be quickly crushed by the Germans, thereby eliminating the underground organization as an effective force before it was actually needed. SHAEF warned Milorg:

> No Allied military offensive operations are planned for your theatre, therefore no steps must be taken to encourage the Resistance Movement as such to overt action, since no outside support can be forthcoming.

The SHAEF memorandum went on to assure Hauge that specific sabotage actions were permitted "on a limited scale," provided they were undertaken "in such a way as not to commit the Movement as a whole, whose primary role is *protective.*"

By this directive SHAEF confirmed once again the basic thrust of Milorg. The organization was destined to see limited action while preparing itself for the day of Norway's liberation. Only then could it at last advance into the light of day as the armed representative of the Norwegian resistance.

By September, three months after the invasion of France, SHAEF was still determined to hold Milorg to an inactive line. Of the German troops then in transport from Norway to the mainland of Europe, Hauge was told: "Let them come. We shall beat them in Germany."

Hauge himself, fully in accord with the SHAEF directives, issued a statement of his own to Milorg districts in September. It stressed the theme that only London could order Milorg into action. As the last autumn of the war neared its end, however, and the defeat of Germany appeared more certain, Hauge's attitude changed. He now feared that too passive a role might reflect unfavorably on Milorg in the days after liberation. Obedience to SHAEF was one thing, but the appearance of having participated in the fight against Germany was also important. For political as well as morale reasons some escalation of Milorg's role was essential. With this in mind, Hauge traveled to London in November, 1944, to participate in a series of high-level talks with senior officials on

General Eisenhower's staff. Still SHAEF hesitated; the time was not right for action. Milorg could count on SHAEF's support for its task of building an underground army, but SHAEF officials, though personally sympathetic, remained unyielding: the Germans were not to be provoked. Unrestricted sabotage was forbidden.

Developments on the battlefield changed the situation overnight. On · the day before Hauge was due to leave London, Gen. Karl von Rundstedt threw massive German forces against the Allied lines in the Ardennes Forest punching gaping holes in the defenses and threatening to split the Allied forces in two. Germany's last, desperate counterattack caught the Allied commanders by surprise. The strength of the German attack was greater than they had deemed possible. With such an army opposing them in the field, the Allies decided that everything must be done to prevent reinforcements from Norway reaching Rundstedt's attacking divisions. Hauge's orders were immediately changed. Milorg was now commanded to attack transportation lines in Norway at once. Norwegian resistance groups were to risk all to halt German troops. Hauge returned immediately to Norway to implement his new orders, but the signal for action had come too late. After years of inactivity, Milorg was incapable of action. Throughout the crucial months of December, 1944, and January, 1945, Milorg mounted less than thirty individual sabotage attacks against German transport, many of them so minor that traffic was interrupted for only a few hours.

The most successful attack took place to the north of Trondheim, where a railroad bridge on the only north–south rail line in the area was blown up, blocking traffic for two weeks. Unfortunately for Milorg's reputation, the demolition of the bridge was accomplished not by a Milorg unit but by a special SOE action group sent in from England specifically for the mission. By the time Milorg was geared for action, the crisis in the Ardennes had passed. Milorg had missed its one opportunity to provide significant service to the Allied cause.

17
The Threat of the *Tirpitz*

One German battleship among all others haunted the British home fleet throughout the war. Her name was the *Tirpitz* and she was, when ready for sea in January, 1942, the largest and most powerful battleship afloat. For most of the next three years her very existence posed a major naval threat to the Allied navies.

Construction of the *Tirpitz* started in 1936. Although naval treaties in effect at the time supposedly limited her size to a displacement of 35,000 tons, the vessel actually was designed and built with a displacement of 42,500 tons. And German naval designers went all out in her armament and protective armor. Her main turrets mounted eight fifteen-inch guns, while fifteen inches of armor made of the best German steel protected her hull. To help defend the vessel against aerial attack, the Germans covered her main deck with plating eight inches thick, strong enough to withstand any bomb then in existence. During her construction period the *Tirpitz* outclassed anything the British or American navies had afloat or under construction, including the new fourteen-inch-gun battleships of the *King George V* class that British shipyard workers were building.

The German battleship—still officially unnamed as was the German custom—was launched on April 1, 1939, in Wilhelmshaven. Adolf Hitler attended the launching ceremonies, an occasion which he used to make a bellicose speech. Among the applauding listeners was Admiral Erich Raeder, the chief of the German Navy and the man responsible for building up the German fleet after World War I. The honor of christening the vessel went to Frau von Hassell, the wife of the German Ambassador to Rome and the daughter of the late Admiral Alfred von Tirpitz, who had been responsible for building Germany's fleet before World War I. As the bottle of wine smashed against the battleship's hull, workmen lowered two great signs into place over the bows. On them, in heavy Gothic letters, the name of the battleship could be read: *Tirpitz*.

The ship began her sea trials in the Baltic in mid-1941. They proceeded smoothly and by year's end Hitler and his admirals faced the question of how they could best use the giant ship. Serious problems faced the Germans. Although German armies were still scoring impressive victories on land, German surface warships had not proved themselves at sea. Their poor past performance made the German Navy, and Hitler, reluctant to throw the new *Tirpitz* against the British Navy. In May, 1941, British warships had tracked down and sunk her sister ship, the *Bismarck*, then the pride of the German Navy. Hitler wanted no repetition of the *Bismarck* disaster for the *Tirpitz*. Even if Hitler and his naval chieftains had wanted to use their new warship aggressively, however, fuel oil had become so critically short by early 1942 that extended operations in the North Atlantic were practically ruled out. Only when the prize was very tempting and the danger to German units at a minimum would the German naval command consider sending a vessel like the *Tirpitz* onto the high seas. Until that time, the *Tirpitz* would be used as a threat in being, stationed in waters that would offer offensive opportunities and at the same time enable the powerful warship to play a role in the defense of German-occupied Europe. Hitler's eyes turned northward. In early 1942 he still lived in fear of a British landing in Norway. If the *Tirpitz* was stationed there, he reasoned, she would be available to counter any British thrust; she could, if opportunity presented itself, lash out at any unprotected merchant convoy sailing the northern route to Russia; and at the very least, her mere presence in Norwegian waters would pose extremely difficult problems for the British. On January 12, therefore, Hitler ordered *Tirpitz* to sail for Trondheim. "Every ship," he declared, "which is not stationed in Norway is in the wrong place."

Before she sailed, Admiral Raeder explained the strategic role of the battleship in a formal memorandum to his command. The *Tirpitz*, he wrote, would "protect our position in the Norwegian and Arctic areas by threatening the flank of enemy operations against the Northern Norwegian areas, and by attacking White Sea convoys." The *Tirpitz* would also "tie down heavy enemy forces in the Atlantic so they cannot operate in the Mediterranean, the Indian Ocean, or the Pacific."

Britain was fully alert to the *Tirpitz* threat. British naval chiefs had begun pondering how the Germans would use their new battleship and how the British Navy could contain her long before the *Tirpitz* was ready for sea. In the autumn of 1941, Sir Dudley Pound, First Sea Lord of the British Admiralty, reached the conclusion that he had to maintain three vessels of the *King George V* class available at all times to be sure of superiority over the single German battleship, two on active status and one in reserve. "If the *Tirpitz* did manage to break out," Pound explained, "she would paralyse our North Atlantic trade to such an extent that it would be essential to bring her to action at the earliest possible moment."

Thus the stage was set for a naval chess match to be played out in the cold waters off the Norwegian coast for the highest of stakes.

Tirpitz sailed for Trondheim from Wilhelmshaven on the night of January 14, 1942. Four destroyers escorted her northward. All vessels arrived safely, and undetected, in the Norwegian port on January 16. The following day British reconnaissance aircraft reported to the British Admiralty that the *Tirpitz* was no longer in German waters. A widespread search was immediately launched to locate her. Every operating branch of the British Admiralty was placed on full alert. Though British naval intelligence did not believe that the *Tirpitz* was attempting to break out into the Atlantic, the mere possibility that this was her mission was enough to force the British to alter their naval operations. Main units of the British home fleet sailed for Icelandic waters to guard against the *Tirpitz* slipping into the Atlantic from the north. The Admiralty also canceled the sailing of a merchant-ship convoy headed for the Russian arctic ports of Murmansk and Archangel with badly needed war supplies. Not until January 23 could the British naval staff relax. On that day the *Tirpitz* was finally located in a fjord fifteen miles east of Trondheim. The German battleship was camouflaged, heavily protected by antisubmarine nets, and in position where she could strike out on a major sortie at any time, but for the moment, at least, the *Tirpitz* was not an immediate threat at sea.

In London, Winston Churchill followed the *Tirpitz* affair with his customary interest in naval matters. He realized all the implications of the move by the *Tirpitz* into Norwegian waters. On January 25, he explained his views in a message to the Chief of Staff's committee:

> The presence of *Tirpitz* at Trondheim has now been known for three days. The destruction or even the crippling of this ship is the greatest event at sea at the present time. No other target is comparable to it.

Churchill ordered the naval command to press forward with plans to attack the *Tirpitz* with midget submarines; he ordered the Royal Air Force to bomb the ship by air (sixteen land-based bombers attacked within a week but failed to score any hits); and he authorized a Commando raid on the giant French naval dock at St. Nazaire, which, though far removed from the scene of action, could conceivably play a role in the British effort to neutralize the *Tirpitz*. After the war Churchill commented on the importance of St. Nazaire:

> St. Nazaire was the only place along all the Atlantic coast where the *Tirpitz* could be docked for repair if she were damaged. If the dock, one of the largest in the world, could be destroyed, a sortie of the

Tirpitz from Trondheim into the Atlantic would become far more dangerous and might not be deemed worth the making.*

Before the St. Nazaire raid took place, the *Tirpitz* made what the British Admiralty feared most—her first sortie into the Atlantic. On March 5 German reconnaissance aircraft operating from bases in northern Norway sighted an Allied convoy of fifteen ships north of Iceland in the vicinity of Jan Mayen Island. Because of the direction in which the convoy was headed, the Germans knew that the ships hoped to reach one of the two major Russian arctic ports, either Murmansk or Archangel. The Germans also knew that the convoy, which was defended by only light escort vessels, would have to pass through the relatively constricted waters between Bear Island (Björnöya) and the northern tip of Norway, a passage constricted even further by the southern limits of the polar ice cap. It was here that German U-boats concentrated to pick off Allied merchantmen; it was here that German bombers based in northern Norway could most easily attack their prey; and it was here that a German surface raider with the speed and firepower of the *Tirpitz* could find rich pluckings amid a weakly defended convoy. *Tirpitz* received orders to sail late on March 5. She left her berth in Trondheimfjord early on the sixth and raced northward. As she sailed, the Germans learned that still another convoy, the second one a westward-bound convoy returning with empty holds after delivering supplies to Russia, would be in the vicinity of Bear Island at the same time as the heavily laden eastward-bound convoy. *Tirpitz*, therefore, could hope to pounce on two convoys, each weakly defended.

Tirpitz's departure from Trondheimfjord, however, was observed by a British submarine stationed outside the fjord and although the German battleship's speed prevented the submarine from attacking, the sub's commanding officer flashed a warning to the British Admiralty: *Tirpitz was at sea.* Alarm bells rang throughout the Admiralty. Every British naval command in the Atlantic went on instant alert and the British home fleet, correctly assuming that the *Tirpitz* was hoping to attack the Russian convoys, immediately headed for the area south of Bear Island, where the British hoped to bring the *Tirpitz* to action. While the *Tirpitz* and her escort vessels hunted the two Allied convoys, the British home fleet hunted the *Tirpitz*. But in the darkness and heavy seas, both hunter groups failed to find their quarry. The *Tirpitz* failed to make contact with the Allied merchantmen, and the British home fleet failed to close with

---

* The raid against the St. Nazaire dock took place late in March, 1942. Eighteen assault vessels carried 630 Commandos to the target. British casualties were heavy. Four hundred and three men were either killed or captured and ten of the eighteen assault boats were sunk. Four other vessels were so badly damaged that they failed to return to their home base. Despite the heavy British losses, the mission was considered a success: the St. Nazaire dock was knocked out of action for the duration of the war.

the *Tirpitz*. A disappointed German naval command ordered the *Tirpitz* to return to a safe Norwegian port, while the British home fleet continued its search for the *Tirpitz* on sea and in the air. Twelve Albacore torpedo bombers from the aircraft carrier *Victorious* sighted the *Tirpitz* as she headed for Narvik and attacked, without success, losing three planes to German anti-aircraft gunners. *Tirpitz* reached safety in Narvik. A few days later *Tirpitz* slipped back to Trondheim. The results of her first sortie were disappointing to German naval leaders: the *Tirpitz* had sunk no enemy ships and had herself been caught undefended by British aircraft from the *Victorious*. Admiral Raeder vented his concern in a secret evaluation for Hitler:

> This operation reveals the weakness of our naval forces in the northern area. The enemy responds to every German sortie by sending out strong task forces, particularly aircraft carriers, which are a menace to our heavy ships. The extreme weakness of our defenses is evident from the fact that the enemy dares to advance in the coastal waters of the northern area without being smashed by the German air force.

British naval experts, however, viewed the sortie from a different perspective. *Tirpitz*'s failure to reach the convoy was viewed as a piece of luck. What most impressed the British was not that the *Tirpitz* had failed to score, but that she had sailed in the first place; and what she had done once, she could do again, with luck riding with her next time. British naval leaders lived in fear of the *Tirpitz*'s making another sortie. This fear soon resulted in one of the greatest convoy disasters of the war.

On June 27, 1942, almost four months after the first unsuccessful sortie by the *Tirpitz*, an exceptionally large Allied convoy sailed from Iceland for the Soviet arctic port of Archangel. Designated as Convoy PQ 17, it consisted of thirty-four merchant ships, an oiler, and three additional merchant vessels which were designated as rescue ships for the entire force. PQ 17 sailed under especially hazardous conditions. Not only did its great size render defense difficult, but by the end of June almost continuous daylight had arrived in the arctic zone, making the task of German hunters that much easier. Churchill, however, had insisted the PQ 17 sail for Russia, which was then reeling under the second summer German offensive. Anything would be risked to ensure that Soviet armies remain in the field against the Wehrmacht.

Admiral Sir John Tovey, commander-in-chief of the British home fleet, had only three destroyers and four cruisers—two British and two American—to assign as close cover for the convoy. His distant covering force included the British battleship *Duke of York,* the American battleship *Washington* (sailing for the first time under British command), the carrier *Victorious,* two cruisers, and fourteen destroyers. Tovey assigned this heavy force to positions northeast of Jan Mayen Island, far enough away from the convoy to escape German air attack but in position to move quickly to the scene of action should major German vessels take to the high seas.

Against these forces, the Germans had the *Tirpitz* and *Hipper* with four destroyers in Trondheim, and the pocket battleships *Scheer* and *Luetzow* with six destroyers in Narvik. Tovey anticipated that if the German capital ships were to sail, the results might well be catastrophic. "The strategic situation," Tovey wrote, "was wholly favorable to the enemy."

Tovey's final instructions called on the British close escort of four cruisers and three destroyers to be responsible for the convoy west of Bear Island; submarines were to protect the convoy east of the island. Tovey specifically prohibited the cruisers from sailing east of Bear Island into the Barents Sea, unless the threat to the convoy consisted of surface vessels which the cruisers could successfully fight. In effect, this instruction meant that the cruisers could not pass east of Bear Island if there was a chance that they would run into the *Tirpitz*.

German U-boats and reconnaissance aircraft sighted the convoy on July 1, four days after it had sailed from Iceland, and informed attack controllers in Norway of the convoy's size, speed, and direction. German torpedo bombers attacked the following day but scored no hits. As late as the morning of July 4, the convoy was still intact, thanks to heavy fog which prevented German aircraft from pressing their assault. On the fourth, American vessels in the convoy broke out new Stars and Stripes in honor of Independence Day, but German planes were aloft, and hunting, waiting for a break in the fog. Their first victim was an American merchantman, "hit through a hole in the fog." She sank immediately. Two other merchant ships were sent to the bottom within the next hour.

The remaining thirty-four merchant ships and the oiler with their escorting vessels reached the cruisers' turn-back line at noon on the fourth, but at this critical point the Admiralty in London countered the cruisers' previous instructions and gave the vessels permission to continue on to the east of Bear Island, "should the situation demand it." With the convoy expected to come under renewed German attack, London obviously had decided that PQ 17 needed more protection as it passed through the area of greatest danger.

The Admiralty's new and unexpected order worried Admiral Tovey, who was aboard the *Duke of York* with the distant covering force. He had only recently lost two other cruisers east of Bear Island and he feared that the Admiralty's authorization for the PQ 17 cruisers to sail east of Bear Island would result in further losses. He was, however, reluctant directly to countermand his superiors in London. Tovey, therefore, drafted another message to the cruisers which, while not specifically countermanding the Admiralty, gave the cruiser commander leeway to ignore the signal just received from London: "Once the convoy is east of 25 degrees East or earlier at your discretion, you are to leave the Barents Sea unless assured by Admiralty that *Tirpitz* cannot be met."

Since longitude 25 degrees east is approximately the longitude of Bear Island, Tovey's message was interpreted by the cruisers as a signal for them to obey their original instructions and turn back at the earliest possible opportunity. The commander of the cruiser force acted promptly on this assumption. At six in the evening of July 4 he informed Admiral Tovey that the cruisers would turn back in four hours. Before the cruisers actually turned back, however, the Admiralty flashed still another signal to the ships at sea: "Further information may be available shortly. Remain with convoy pending further instructions."

By 7:30 P.M. of the fourth, therefore, the four cruisers and three destroyer escorts were still with Convoy PQ 17, which despite the loss of three ships was still a functioning convoy whose captains, as they later testified, believed that if their "ammunition lasted, PQ 17 could get anywhere."

The German naval staff, meanwhile, had followed the progress of PQ 17 closely. The convoy with its rich prize of merchantmen appeared ripe for the taking; all conditions seemed perfect for the *Tirpitz* to sail. German naval commanders, eager for a victory at sea, decided to send their great battleship into action along with the three other major vessels in Norwegian waters, the pocket battleships *Scheer* and *Luetzow* and the heavy cruiser *Hipper.* The German plan called for the *Tirpitz* and the *Hipper* to attack the convoy's cruiser and destroyer escort while the *Luetzow* and *Scheer* made mincemeat of the merchant ships. The entire operation was supposed to be carried out before the heavy British covering force built around the *Duke of York* could reach the scene of action.

It was a workable plan. If resolutely carried out, it could have provided Germany with the victory at sea it sorely needed. But Hitler hesitated. He refused to permit the *Tirpitz* to sail until the whereabouts of the British aircraft carrier *Victorious* could be ascertained. Hitler's fears threatened the entire operation. Admiral Raeder realized that any delay in *Tirpitz*'s sailing could place the battleship out of striking range of the convoy. Without notifying Hitler, therefore, Raeder ordered the *Tirpitz* and the *Hipper* to sail from Trondheim to join the pocket battleships *Scheer* and *Luetzow* at Altenfjord (Altafjord), a port near the northernmost tip of Norway. There they were still in position to strike at the convoy when and if Hitler gave permission to sail. By the evening of July 4, that permission still had not been given.

The British, however, did not know of Hitler's hesitation to risk his major ships. British intelligence had received word that the four German raiders were in Altenfjord, within a few hours' sailing time of the convoy, and were convinced that a major surface raid was in the making. If the

German warships sailed on the evening of July 4, they could reach the convoy as early as two o'clock on the morning of July 5. And if the *Tirpitz, Hipper, Scheer,* and *Luetzow* sailed, the four cruisers, three destroyers, and all the ships in convoy PQ 17 would be in extreme danger. It seemed inconceivable to the officer of the British Admiralty that the Germans, with such a rich target so close at hand, would not act decisively. So while Hitler hesitated, the Admiralty acted.

At 9 P.M. a signal flashed from the Admiralty to the commander of the cruiser force: "Most immediate. Cruiser force withdraw to westward at high speed."

This signal seemed to deliver the "further information" promised in the Admiralty's 7:30 P.M. message and the four cruisers immediately turned back, leaving PQ 17 unprotected except by three destroyers.

At 9:23 P.M., another message flashed from the Admiralty, this one addressed to the convoy itself: "Immediate. Owing to the threat of surface ships, convoy is to disperse and proceed to Russian ports." This message could only be read as a warning of extreme urgency, requiring drastic action on the part of the convoy commanders. At sea, the ships broke formation, while maintaining the general course that would, if all went well, eventually bring them to a Russian port.

But thirteen minutes later, a third signal reached the ships of the convoy: "Most Immediate. My 9:23 of the 4th. Convoy is to scatter." The order to scatter, with a wartime priority of "Most Immediate," could only be read to mean that London was in possession of information indicating that powerful German forces were close at hand. Each ship was now on its own. No longer were the ships obligated to try to reach a Russian port.

The orders to disperse and scatter had not been given lightly by the Admiralty. Convoy experience had shown that ships in formation present a more difficult target than individual vessels sailing alone. Officers in the Admiralty realized that German aircraft and U-boats would find the pickings much easier with the ships dispersed rather than sailing in formation, but the threat of a sortie by the *Tirpitz* and the other German raiders was deemed an even greater danger. The British Admiralty, therefore, gave its order to scatter in anticipation of what the Germans might do, preferring what it thought was the lesser, known risk of dispersal to the greater, potential risk of having the German warships catch the convoy in close formation and with no defense. For the ships at sea, the danger seemed imminent indeed. They expected German masts to appear above the horizon at any moment.

At the time the scatter order reached the convoy, *Tirpitz* and the other German warships were still in Altenfjord, waiting for orders to sail. Hitler still hesitated. He did not give permission for the *Tirpitz* to sail until late in the morning of the next day, July 5. By then the convoy was too far away for effective action. Nor was there any need for the *Tirpitz;* by ordering PQ 17 to scatter, the Admiralty had placed the individual vessels at the mercy of German aircraft and U-boats. They picked the ships off almost at will, turning the waters of the Barents Sea into a shooting gallery the likes of which had not been seen in the war before. German U-boats and bombers sank twenty-three ships in the convoy. The loss in matériel was especially heavy: of 4,246 military vehicles carried by the convoy, 3,350 were lost; of 594 tanks urgently needed by the Red Army, 430 went down to the bottom; of 297 airplanes, 210 were destroyed. When the *Tirpitz* finally did sail, she was quickly recalled by Admiral Raeder after he learned that German submarines and aircraft were doing such an effective job. Not a single U-boat was sunk. The Luftwaffe lost only five of 202 aircraft thrown against the convoy.

The *Tirpitz* had scored her first major victory even though it had not been her giant guns that had earned the credit. The mere threat that the *Tirpitz* might sail had been sufficient to panic the British Admiralty into making a decision that enabled the Germans to wipe most of the ships of Convoy PQ 17 off the surface of the northern seas.

The PQ 17 disaster and the continued threat posed by the *Tirpitz* increased British determination to sink the German battleship. The next serious effort came in the autumn of 1942, when the British Navy put into action a daring plan to attack the *Tirpitz* as she lay at anchor in Trondheimfjord, using two-man human submarines called Chariots, which the British had perfected that summer. To get the Chariots into Trondheimfjord within striking distance of the *Tirpitz,* the British needed an inconspicuous vessel that would not arouse the suspicion of German naval patrols. They finally settled on the *Arthur,* a nondescript cutter of a type common to the waters around Trondheim. *Arthur's* skipper, a Norwegian resistance leader named Leif Larsen, also appeared admirably suited to the task at hand. He had successfully completed several voyages between the Shetland Islands and the Trondheim area, and he was willing to pilot his vessel deep into Trondheimfjord, past the German patrols that he knew guarded the entrance to the fjord.

The *Arthur* under Larsen's command sailed from the Shetlands late in October, with two Chariots lashed and camouflaged on deck and six British seamen hidden belowdecks, four for the actual attack and two as a backup crew. Larsen carried with him forged papers, including a German notice informing Norwegian sailors that contact with England was punishable by death, and a manifest that accurately described his cargo as peat, a substance in wide demand in fuel-hungry wartime Norway. Once inside sheltered Norwegian waters, Larsen ordered the two Chariots lowered overboard, for towing underwater up the fjord.

Halfway toward their target a German patrol boat signaled the

Arthur to halt. A young German naval lieutenant jumped aboard to inspect the vessel's papers. Although he inspected the vessel fore to aft he failed to locate the six British sailors hidden in a secret compartment built belowdecks, nor did he observe the two Chariots riding silently behind the *Arthur* at the end of their towlines. Satisfied that the *Arthur* was what she appeared to be, the German signed the necessary papers authorizing *Arthur* to proceed further upfjord and returned to his own vessel. Within minutes, the *Arthur* chugged out of sight, the two Chariots still safely in tow. Larsen knew that nothing stood between him and the *Tirpitz* except fifty miles of water. Excitement grew as *Arthur* made her way upfjord. The British crewmen emerged from their hiding place, anticipating the action ahead. The sea was calm, the weather fine, and *Arthur* sailed in the lee of towering mountains, untouched by the stiff wind that blew on the other side; the Chariots followed easily behind.

Shortly below where the *Tirpitz* was anchored, however, there was a bend in the fjord which would bring the *Arthur* into exposed waters. Larsen anticipated a rough passage. He knew that once around the bend he faced a stiff head wind and choppy seas. The change in sea conditions hit the *Arthur* shortly after dark. The vessel began pitching violently and the men on board felt the tug of the towing wires as the *Arthur* rose to ride the crests. Suddenly there was a particularly strong tug and immediately afterward *Arthur* began meeting the seas with a new, lighter motion. Larsen was dismayed. He knew that the change in the manner in which his vessel was meeting the seas could mean only one thing: the Chariots had broken free. For the men on *Arthur* it was the bitterest of blows. They had successfully made the long and dangerous voyage from the Shetlands to within five miles of the *Tirpitz*, but the Chariots with their explosive charges had sunk beyond chance of retrieval, and they had no other weapons with which to attack the *Tirpitz*, lying open before them.

Although disheartened at the turn of events, Larsen still had the men under him to worry about. They landed at a secluded spot along the shore, scuttled the *Arthur*, and set off overland for Sweden. All but one reached Sweden safely and eventually made it back to England. Their mission, however, had been a total failure. *Tirpitz* had escaped untouched and still rode at anchor in Trondheimfjord, still a major threat to the British Navy.

While Britain worried what the *Tirpitz* would do next, Hitler was growing increasingly disillusioned with his surface fleet. The giant warships required enormous amounts of Germany's dwindling supply of fuel oil whenever they went to sea, and in Hitler's opinion they seldom produced results worth the cost. The Navy's lack of victories at sea also irked the Fuehrer. One engagement, on New Year's Eve, 1942, pitted the *Luetzow, Hipper,* and six German destroyers against a weak British force escorting a convoy to Russia. Although the German vessels should have easily overpowered the British force, the British ships fought them off, sinking one German destroyer and severely damaging the *Hipper* in the action. The British losses totaled two ships sunk—a destroyer and a minesweeper. Because of communications difficulties with German headquarters in northern Norway, Hitler first learned the results of the engagement from a BBC broadcast, a factor which increased his anger and feeling of humiliation. Three days later Hitler summoned Admiral Raeder to his Wolf's Den headquarters at Rastenburg in East Prussia (now Ketrzyn, Poland). He received Raeder with cold formality, addressed his faithful naval chief sarcastically as "Herr Grossadmiral," and then ripped apart the courage and performance of the German Navy in a bitter ninety-minute diatribe. He called the recent action by *Hipper* "typical of German ships" and described the German fighting character at sea as "just the opposite of the British who, true to their tradition, fought to the bitter end." Hitler said he had come to the end of his patience with the surface raiders. He proposed to scrap the large ships because they had not contributed their share to the nation's war effort, while requiring a heavy outlay of men and resources. He compared the largest ships at sea with the cavalry on land: both were outdated. He ended the conference by demanding that Admiral Raeder, who had built up the fleet, prepare plans to scrap his most important vessels—including the *Tirpitz*. Raeder left the conference a shaken man. By the end of the month (January, 1943) he resigned the post he had held since 1928. Hitler promptly appointed Admiral Karl Doenitz, who had commanded all German U-boats, as the new commander-in-chief of the German Navy.

Despite his background as a submarine commander and his unfamiliarity with surface warfare, Doenitz disapproved of Hitler's plans to scrap Germany's surface raiders. As the Navy's new commander-in-chief, Doenitz adopted the view of his predecessor that even an inactive German "fleet in being" was a powerful weapon that required the British to maintain strong naval forces in the Atlantic at all times, thus depriving them of the use of these vessels in other theaters of war. Hitler, surprisingly, accepted these views from Doenitz, the submarine expert, although he had previously rejected them when advanced by Raeder. He rescinded his order to dismantle the fleet. In March, Doenitz won Hitler's grudging permission for the surface raiders to sortie forth again against Allied convoys "when suitable targets presented themselves." Hitler even gave Doenitz permission to transfer the battleship *Scharnhorst* to northern Norway, to join the *Tirpitz* and *Luetzow* at Altenfjord, where they had moved to be closer to the convoy routes and farther away from British air power.

British naval intelligence located the three major warships in Altenfjord and the Admiralty, frustrated in its previous attempts to sink the *Tirpitz*, decided on another attack, this time using recently developed midget submarine minelayers known as X-craft. Winston Churchill gave the mission his enthusiastic backing; he had pushed development of the experimental vessels specifically with an eye toward their use against the *Tirpitz.*

Six regular British submarines, each with a forty-eight-foot X-craft in tow, sailed from northern Scotland on September 11, 1943, and headed for Altenfjord, more than a thousand miles away. Each X-craft carried a crew of four and two 4,000-pound explosive charges, one on each side of its hull. The plan formulated by the Admiralty called for three of the X-craft to place their explosive charges under the *Tirpitz,* two to attack the *Scharnhorst,* and one to go after the *Luetzow.* The vessels were so constructed that crewmen dressed in frogmen's outfits could leave the vessels while submerged in order to cut through any antisubmarine nets protecting their quarry and then make a safe return to their mother ship.

The mission began badly. Two of the X-craft were lost at sea while en route to Altenfjord, one broke down just outside Altenfjord, and one disappeared without a trace as the vessels approached the nets protecting the German anchorage. The two remaining X-craft, designated as X-6 and X-7, surveyed the anchorage through their periscopes and discovered that only the *Tirpitz* was in harbor—*Scharnhorst* and *Luetzow* had sailed unexpectedly a few days before. But at least their major target was at hand, riding comfortably at anchor a few hundred yards away. The X-craft pressed their attack.

Crewmen from both X-craft cut holes in the outer nets protecting the *Tirpitz* and then, as if by magic, found an opening in the inner net. There was now nothing between them and their target, which was still unaware of their presence. With the target close by, however, X-6 ran aground and was forced to surface. German sailors immediately opened fire with small arms (X-6 by now was so close that the battleship's larger guns could not be depressed enough to fire) and an alert German officer piloted one of the battleship's launches to the X-craft, threw a line around its tower, and attempted to pull it away from the *Tirpitz.* But the X-6's engines were more powerful. Slowly it gained headway, dragging the German launch with it. As X-6 came alongside the *Tirpitz,* however, she began to sink from the damage inflicted by German fire. Her four crewmen scrambled out at the last minute and were taken aboard the German launch for transfer to the *Tirpitz* for questioning. The X-7, meanwhile, made good her approach to the *Tirpitz,* placed her two charges undetected, and then turned to make good her escape. But the nets that had been so easily traversed on the inward voyage snagged the vessel going out. X-7 was forced to surface and immediately drew fire from alert *Tirpitz* gunners. X-7 sank in Altenfjord, carrying two of her crew to their death. The other two crewmen survived and were taken prisoner. By now all six of the original X-craft attack force had been sunk or lost at sea, but eight tons of amatol explosive had been placed under the hull of the *Tirpitz*. The charges went off with a giant shudder a few minutes after the X-7 sank. On board the *Tirpitz*, shock waves rippled through the vessel, which vibrated "strongly in a vertical direction." All electrical power failed, throwing the ship into complete darkness.

German damage engineers, assigned to assess the damage after the shock waves had subsided, returned with depressing news: one of the ship's turbines had been shaken from its bed, one of its main turrets was jammed, all range finders and fire-control equipment was inoperable, and the basic framework of the ship had also been damaged, which meant that she would no longer be able to steam at full speed. Some damage could be repaired in Altenfjord, but much of the structural damage could not be repaired without a visit to a dockyard in Germany.

When the full extent of the damage inflicted on the *Tirpitz* by the X-craft became known to Hitler and Admiral Doenitz, they decided against bringing the battleship back to Germany. Instead, they decreed that the *Tirpitz* should be made as seaworthy as possible in Norway, that her fire-control equipment be repaired, and that she should remain in Norway for use as a floating battery. *Tirpitz*'s days as an operating vessel capable of carrying the naval war home to the British and American navies were over. Two months after the X-craft attack, the German northern-naval-group commander advised German naval headquarters that "as a result of the successful midget submarine attack, the *Tirpitz* has been out of action for months." The British, however, did not know how seriously *Tirpitz* had been damaged. As all the X-craft had failed to return, the British did not know how many, if any, explosive charges had successfully been placed. All the British Admiralty knew, and this from reconnaissance flights over Altenfjord, was that the *Tirpitz* was still afloat. Even though the *Tirpitz* would never again sail against British shipping, the British believed she was still a threat and that attempts to sink her must continue.

Having failed to sink the *Tirpitz* by sneak underwater attacks, the British decided to destroy her by bombing. The *Tirpitz* had survived five bombing raids by planes from the RAF and the aircraft carrier *Victorious* in 1943, but British air commanders believed that the ship must fall victim to a prolonged bombing campaign. The onset of winter darkness delayed the start of a concerted bombing effort, and then the first raid of 1944 was carried out not by the British but by fifteen Russian bombers, each armed with a two-thousand-pound bomb, which set out for Altenfjord on February 10, 1944, from an airfield in the Soviet arctic zone.

Eleven Russian bombers lost their bearings over the foggy northern terrain and failed to reach Altenfjord. The four bombers that managed to get there failed to hit the *Tirpitz*, even though there was a full moon shining and only light anti-aircraft fire to divert them.

With the failure of the Russians, the British gave the job to the Royal Navy's Fleet Air Arm. The Navy moved quickly. One hundred and twenty-one Barracudas, Corsairs, Hellcats, and Wildcats flying from six carriers—*Victorious, Searcher, Emperor, Furious, Striker,* and *Pursuer*—surprised the *Tirpitz* on April 3 as she prepared for sea trials in an arm of the Altenfjord. Fifteen bombs struck home, including four 1,600-pounders, killing three hundred men aboard the *Tirpitz* and piercing the battleship's armored upper deck. The ship's main eight-inch armored deck, however, withstood the impact and *Tirpitz*, though heavily damaged, remained afloat.

Admiral Doenitz was determined to have *Tirpitz* repaired. In a report to Hitler he wrote:

> This ship is to be repaired and to remain stationed in northern Norway. This course will be followed even if further damage is sustained. Regardless of how much work and manpower may be involved, the repairs must be made. After all, the presence of the *Tirpitz* ties up enemy forces.

The results of the April raid, however, encouraged the Fleet Air Arm, which mounted a series of attacks in the following months in an attempt to sink the *Tirpitz*. All met with frustration and failure. An attack on May 15 had to be abandoned because of low cloud cover which hid the target; an attack on May 28 was canceled because of bad weather; an attack by forty-four Barracudas on July 17 failed to achieve surprise and the aircraft dropped their bombs blind, failing to score any hits; two attacks on August 22 cost the British three aircraft and failed to damage the *Tirpitz;* and an attack on August 24, by thirty-three Barracudas and twenty-four Corsairs, some of them armed with one-thousand-pound bombs, failed to accomplish its mission because of a heavy smoke screen thrown up by the Germans, which again forced the bombers to attack "blind." And even though a lucky hit sent a one-thousand-pound armor-piercing bomb crashing through eight decks of the *Tirpitz*, to lodge in the ship's vitals, the bomb failed to explode and the battleship escaped damage. The failure of the August 24 raid, coming as it did after several previous failures, raised doubts that the Fleet Air Arm could accomplish its task. Before calling off the Navy's efforts, the British decided to give its naval fliers one more chance. The final raid was launched on August 29, when aircraft from the carriers *Indefatigable* and *Formidable* roared aloft and headed for the *Tirpitz*. Weather and visibility were good, but the German warning system was equal to the challenge. The Navy bombers found a thick smoke screen and heavy anti-aircraft fire protecting the *Tirpitz* when they arrived over the target. Again they attacked blind, failed to score any hits, and retreated after losing two planes to German anti-aircraft fire.

It had been as disappointing a series of attacks as could be imagined by the Navy's Fleet Air Arm. From April, 1944, through August, 1944, the Naval Air Arm had planned nine attacks against the *Tirpitz*. Six attacks had actually been carried out and although the bombers had scored seventeen hits on the German vessel, at a cost of seventeen planes, the *Tirpitz* still remained afloat. Late in August, as the realization sank in that carrier-based planes could not inflict fatal damage to the *Tirpitz*, the joint planning staff in London discussed other methods of sinking the *Tirpitz*. By that time, giant twelve-thousand-pound "Dam Buster" bombs had been developed and used to good effect against German dams, U-boat pens, power stations, canals, and factories. It was now proposed to drop the Dam Busters on the *Tirpitz*, using RAF Lancasters flying from bases in northern Scotland to deliver the bombs against the target in Altenfjord.

Because of the distances involved, however, the Lancasters would not be able to return to Scotland after the attack but would have to continue on to bases in northern Russia. General Eisenhower, commander-in-chief of all Allied forces in Europe, gave his personal approval to the attack, and Russian authorities promised to cooperate. But before the first flight took place, the weather deteriorated sharply and the commander in charge of the Lancaster force decided that he would prefer to start his attack from airfields in Russia rather than Scotland.

Thirty-four Lancasters took off from Scotland on September 11 and landed on rough Russian airfields in the Soviet arctic zone the next day. Six Lancasters suffered irreparable damage on landing, but the remaining twenty-eight, after refueling, took off for Altenfjord on September 15, after a scout Mosquito plane reported clear skies over the target. As the Lancasters neared Altenfjord, however, they saw a curtain of smoke rising over the fjord. The pilots knew they were too late for surprise. Silent puffs of anti-aircraft shells rose to meet them as they made their bombing run against the *Tirpitz*, aiming where they hoped the battleship lay. Although the Lancasters were forced to bomb blind they scored one direct hit and two near-misses, causing additional serious damage to the *Tirpitz*. Still, *Tirpitz* remained afloat.

Shortly after the September 15 raid, the Germans moved the damaged *Tirpitz* to the arctic port of Tromsø, where she was positioned as a floating coastal-defense battery. British reconnaissance planes located the *Tirpitz* in her new anchorage; by October 18 the British had established her exact position: three miles west of the center of town. Since the move from Altenfjord to Tromsø had brought the *Tirpitz* within range of Scottish-based bombers, there was no longer any need to utilize Russian airfields for aerial attacks. The next attack, therefore, was planned on the assumption that the Lancasters could depart from and return to Scottish bases. The raid took place on October 29. Thirty-eight Lancasters armed with twelve-thousand-pound "Tall Boy" bombs, their hardened steel noses capable of ripping through sixteen feet of concrete, roared aloft and headed for Tromsø. The attack, like so many before it, ended in failure —heavy cloud cover obscured the target and the only additional damage suffered by the *Tirpitz* was inflicted by a near-miss which hit near the aft section of the vessel.

Bad weather set in shortly afterward, delaying the next attack. Not until November 12 did the weather clear enough to enable thirty-two Lancasters to fly another raid. The bombers left Lossiemouth, Scotland, at 3 A.M. on the twelfth, cruised at an economical speed over the North Sea, crossed the Norwegian coast north of the Arctic Circle, and then maneuvered to attack the *Tirpitz* from landward, hoping thereby to catch their quarry by surprise. As the bombers approached the *Tirpitz*, they realized that they had in fact achieved surprise. There was no smoke to hide the target, and German fighter planes had not appeared in the skies to harass their bombing run.

The first planes dropped their bombs from fourteen thousand feet. There was a long wait before the flashes below started to show. Then the pilots saw one bomb explode on shore close to the *Tirpitz*. Two more bombs exploded on the ship itself. Then a fourth bomb also hit the ship. A column of smoke rose into the sky as one of *Tirpitz*'s magazines exploded. Long before the attack was over, the RAF pilots knew they had severely damaged the *Tirpitz*. There was still better news to come. As the last plane left the scene of action, its crew could see the *Tirpitz* begin to turn over slowly. The German battleship, racked by three direct hits with twelve-thousand-pound bombs and two near-misses, was sinking. Fourteen hundred of her crew were trapped inside and drowned as the ship sank; only 397 were saved.

The raid ended the *Tirpitz* threat: no longer would the British have to worry about the world's most powerful battleship. But the destruction of the *Tirpitz* had come very late in the war. By the time Churchill learned of the sinking, he had already visited liberated Paris with Charles de Gaulle. The sinking of the *Tirpitz*, which had loomed so large in the minds of British naval officers for so long, was now almost a sidebar to even greater and more glorious victories in store for the Allies.

18
War in the North

The summer of 1944 saw the once proud German armies in retreat on both the Western and Eastern fronts. In the west, Allied troops had broken out of their Normandy beachhead and were driving for the Rhine. In the east, Russian armies were pushing the Germans back toward their homeland, striking out in force all along the front. By the middle of August, the Red Army had penetrated to the border of East Prussia and had practically wiped out the German Army Group Center in its advance toward Warsaw. North of Leningrad, Red Army troops were attacking units of the German Army Group North and had driven Finnish troops reeling back across the Northern Dvina River. And while the fighting in Finland was still far from Norwegian territory, the direction and threat of combat along the Finnish front promised that the liberation of Norway could begin sometime late in 1944, if the Russians continued to press their advance against the faltering German-Finnish defense.

By August Finland was on the brink of collapse—her resources depleted, her manpower decimated in the summer fighting. Sixty thousand Finnish soldiers were listed as dead, missing, or wounded in two months of fighting alone. Despite German promises that the Third Reich would provide more men and matériel for the Finnish defense, the Finns sued for peace, as they had done after the Winter War of 1939, when the Allies had promised to come to Finland's aid. Negotiations with the Russians started in late August and were concluded in September, when Finnish representatives initialed a final armistice in Moscow.

The armistice, however, did not end Finland's problems, for Russia demanded that Finland turn on her former ally and take all steps necessary to ensure that German troops evacuate Finnish territory. In the event that Germany refused to withdraw, the Finns faced the prospect of sending their weary army into action against the Wehrmacht. Gen. Lothar Rendulic, commanding general of the German Twentieth Mountain Army, called on Finland's Field Marshal Mannerheim, who had assumed the office of president early in August, to warn against such a development. Armed conflict between German and Finnish forces, Rendulic maintained, would mean losses for both sides that could run as high as 90 percent, since the "best soldiers of Europe" would be fighting each other. Rendulic's heavy-handed argument was not lost on Manner-heim. Despite the exaggerated rhetoric and the praise for the Finnish soldier's fighting qualities, Rendulic was warning Mannerheim that German forces would strike back hard if the Finns turned on them.

Decisions reached in Germany solved the problem for the Finns. By early September the German High Command had become convinced that the Finnish front could not be held and ordered the 200,000 men of Rendulic's Twentieth Mountain Army to retreat from southern and central Finland into the northernmost section of the country, there to protect Finnish nickel mines whose output was still considered vital to Germany's war effort. The German lines in northern Finland extended into the Soviet arctic and had been stable since 1941. The OKW had no doubt that the Twentieth Army could successfully hold the area, re-gardless of any Soviet offensive and regardless of what the Finns might do.

The Twentieth Army advanced northward as if moving through enemy territory. German commanders took precautions to protect its flanks and rear elements against Russian attacks and the possibility of Finnish attacks as well, for Rendulic could never be sure when Russian pressure would force his former allies to attack. It was not an easy retreat. Temperatures fell below zero in late September; and fresh Red Army troops from Siberia, using armor for the first time, pursued the outnum-bered Germans. The appearance of Russian T-34 tanks on the battlefield surprised German commanders, who for three years had accepted the doctrine that tanks could not operate in arctic terrain. As for the German infantry, they broke and ran on several occasions when the Russian tanks lumbered into view.

Rendulic, however, made good his withdrawal. His troops dug in along a broken front on both sides of the Russian-Norwegian border. Major German units manned positions near the Russian port of Pechenga and near the Norwegian port of Kirkenes, a few miles to the west. Still other German units maintained defensive positions in northern Finland, just below the border. For a few days in early October, a period of quiet descended on this frozen northern front as the opposing sides prepared for the next round of fighting.

Russian troops of the IC Assault Corps launched their expected offensive on the morning of October 7, hitting the German lines at their weakest point, between the Second and Sixth mountain divisions. The Russian attack, massing an estimated four divisions backed by artillery, air, and armor support, quickly swept over German strongpoints. Again, the Russian use of tanks surprised the Germans, who still stubbornly held to the doctrine that arctic terrain ruled out tank operations. Russian engineers, however, had thrown crude wooden roadways over impassable sections of the front and brought the T-34s up to the line under cover of darkness. Within two days, the Second Division's defensive lines were crumbling and Russian troops broke through the gap, threatening to encircle the Sixth Division holding positions to the south. Both divisions were forced to retreat. Within a week, the Russians brought about the collapse of a front the Germans had worked on for three years.

The rout of German forces near Pechenga opened the door to Norway. On October 14 Russian troops swept across the border into Norway's northernmost province of Finnmark, a bleak, forbidding land of treeless tundra where fifty thousand inhabitants, many of them no-madic Lapps, lived widely scattered existences over 48,000 square miles of territory. The long-awaited liberation of Norway had begun. Kir-kenes, the first important port on the Norwegian side, fell to the Russians a few days later after a bitter battle which left the town almost completely destroyed.

Russian troops pressed their offensive and in three weeks reached the Tana River, approximately sixty-five miles beyond Kirkenes in a north-westerly direction. There, with winter hard upon them, and with their supply problems increasing, the Russian troops halted and dug in for the winter. The Red Army had accomplished its primary mission—it had driven all German troops out of Russia's northernmost territories. A further advance into Norway was ruled out, not only because of the difficulties of a winter campaign but also because Russian commanders considered the northern front of minor importance to the total war effort against Germany.

Germany, however, could not gauge Russia's intentions and feared for the Twentieth Mountain Army. Its situation was not promising. In a review of the entire strategic position in Scandinavia and Finland, the operations staff of the OKW tried to list all foreseeable possibilities. The most obvious danger seemed to come from the Russians. Continued pressure by Red Army troops could wear down the Army in a series of costly battles and bring about its destruction. Trouble could also be anticipated from Finland, which declared war on Germany early in October. Finnish patrols immediately began operating along the German Army's southern flank and the OKW concluded that a strong Finnish thrust from the south could cut off General Rendulic's line of retreat. There was even the possibility that the Russians would mount an even more powerful offensive toward Narvik in an effort to cut off the entire Army.

Events occurring in Europe also affected the Scandinavian picture. The loss of submarine bases in France convinced the OKW that British air and naval forces which had previously been thrown against the French bases would now be transferred north, to be committed against submarine bases in Norway. This warning, in turn, ignited Hitler's old fear that the British would land along the Norwegian coast. When all considerations were presented to Hitler in the form of a balance sheet, the Fuehrer reluctantly agreed to consider Operation *Nordlicht,* a plan drafted by the OKW for the withdrawal of Rendulic's Twentieth Mountain Army through Finnmark to Narvik, there to make a final last stand. The clinching argument came from Dr. Albert Speer, the Third Reich's war-production chief, who reported to Hitler that Germany held an adequate stockpile of nickel for her war needs. With the basic reason for defending northern Finland thus eliminated, Hitler gave the order for *Nordlicht* to begin. Hitler, however, still intent on preventing the Russians from expanding their hold on Norwegian territory, ordered Rendulic to evacuate all civilians from Finnmark and to scorch the frozen earth behind him as he retreated. Any Russian pursuers, Hitler insisted, must find a land empty of all people, shelter, and supplies. Hitler expected cooperation from Norwegian Quisling authorities in evacuating the civilian population, but he placed direct responsibility on General Rendulic. In a message dated October 28, Hitler warned:

> The commander in North Finland is responsible to see that the Fuehrer's order is carried out ruthlessly. Only in this way can German troops avoid the danger of a Russian advance.

Rendulic moved promptly to comply. He ordered every building, house, and hut in Finnmark destroyed. All stores of food and equipment and all livestock were to be either moved or destroyed. The entire population was ordered deported en masse. "Anyone who stays behind," Rendulic warned, "will perish in the arctic winter."

Joseph Terboven, the German Reichskommissar in Norway, issued his own decree:

> The evacuation necessitates the removal of the civilian population, as the enemy has proved that in those territories occupied by him he ruthlessly and brutally forces the civilian population to give him active assistance in achieving his aims. This means that no other means of existence of any kind can be left to the Bolshevik enemy in the fighting zone. All such installations, such as housing accommodations, transport facilities and foodstuffs, must be destroyed or removed. The population in these districts will therefore be deprived of the bases for their existence, so that in order to be able to survive they must evacuate to those Norwegian territories which are still protected by the German Wehrmacht. He who does not comply with these unequivocal instructions exposes himself and his family to possible death in the Arctic without house or food.

Norway's Quisling police chief Jonas Lie rushed to Finnmark to support the German efforts by a series of decrees issued in the name of the Norwegian government. If Norwegians fell into Russian hands, Lie predicted ominously, "it would mean murder, plunder, terror, rape, atheism and moral degradation. And when winter comes," Lie continued, "where will you get bread, butter and sugar?"

By the first of November the German Twentieth Mountain Army was in full retreat and the destruction of Finnmark had begun in earnest. Special Army demolition squads, assisted by units of the Norwegian Nazi *Hird* organization, trailed behind the main troop units, burning and leveling in their wake. Town after town fell victim to Hitler's scorched-earth policy. At Hammerfest, the razing began on November 3 when *Hird* troops set fire to houses on the outskirts of town. The next day torches were applied to houses closer to the center of town. Animals were killed and left lying on the ground. They soon disappeared under a layer of arctic snow. Within two days Hammerfest was a dead city.

The burning torches flared throughout all of Finnmark and the sounds of explosions rumbled through the silent arctic air. Bewildered and frightened civilians watched their homes go up in flames and then allowed themselves to be forced onto small fishing craft for voyages southward along the coast. Hundreds more straggled along with the retreating German Army over the single road—Reichsstrasse 50—that led to the south.

Some small communities were hit twice by German demolition parties. Inhabitants who had escaped the first deportation were rounded up and the pitiful huts they had built from the wreckage of their original community put to the torch again. Any household animals that had escaped the first slaughter were methodically killed. By the end of the year more than 43,000 Norwegians living in Finnmark had been forced from their homes and evacuated from their familiar surroundings. In late December, General Rendulic proudly reported to his headquarters that only two hundred inhabitants had escaped evacuation. He promised to hunt them down until not a single Norwegian remained alive in Finnmark. By the end of January only a handful of stragglers remained in the area east of Lyngenfjord, struggling to survive amid the wreckage of their deserted towns.

But by that time representatives of the Norwegian government in exile had themselves begun to trickle back into Finnmark, with the consent and cooperation of the Russians, and had begun to reassert Norwegian sovereignty in the region.

The Norwegian exile government and Allied military chiefs in London had closely followed developments on the northern sector of the Eastern Front since the early winter of 1943, when it became apparent that Soviet units might be the first to reach Norwegian soil. The Norwegian Army in exile assigned one of its respected regular officers, Col. Arne Dahl, to draft contingency plans in the event of a Russian advance into Finnmark. Dahl, convinced that warfare would bring extreme danger to Finnmark's population, urged that a strong effort be made to send in civilian administration teams. He also proposed a strong Norwegian military presence, to "show the flag" in liberated Finnmark.

By the spring of 1944 the Allied nations were ready to consider the political consequences of a Russian advance into Norway. At a meeting in London on May 17, 1944—Norway's National Day—Norwegian, British, American, and Russian negotiators agreed that the Norwegian government would have full responsibility for the civilian administration of liberated territories and would resume legal constitutional authority as soon as military conditions permitted. While the agreement did not specifically mention what would happen after the war, it seemed to imply that all Allied troops would withdraw from Norway after the cessation of hostilities.

It was not until after Russian troops had actually entered Norwegian territory, however, that Soviet Foreign Minister Vyacheslav Molotov informed the Norwegian Ambassador to Moscow that the Soviet government was willing to receive a Norwegian delegation. Discussions proceeded smoothly and the Soviet Union soon agreed to the dispatch of a Norwegian military mission to Norway.

Colonel Dahl, who had worked on the contingency plans, was placed in command of the Norwegian expedition. To his dismay, he found that the "strong force" he had suggested had dwindled to token size: The Norwegian presence in northern Norway consisted of 250 men of the Independent Mountain Company No. 2, who sailed without transport, artillery, or field communications.

The Norwegian company embarked on the British cruiser *Berwick* in late October and joined a convoy to Russia on October 30, reaching Murmansk on the evening of November 7. The Norwegians debarked to a friendly but nonchalant welcome from the Russians. Soviet Army drivers transported the Norwegians to a brick barracks, itself a sign of hospitality in the housing-short arctic, but no high-ranking Soviet officials were on hand to greet them nor was there any indication that the Russians considered their arrival anything more than a minor diplomatic sideshow. Colonel Dahl thought the Russian officers whom he eventually met seemed bemused by the problem of how to deal with a Norwegian colonel who was offering the Red Army the services and assistance of a company of 250 untested Norwegian infantrymen.

On a personal level, however, the Norwegians found the Russians open and friendly. One member of the Norwegian company described his first trip into town:

I was inside a truck sitting next to the fur-clad driver and trying to make conversation in Russian. My knowledge of Russian was limited to three words: "friend," "enemy," and "house." So I kept saying, "Russia, America, England, Norway—friends. Germany—enemy." The Russian laughed heartily.

On another occasion, Lt. Tonne Huitfeld, the company's intelligence officer, received an invitation from a Russian liaison officer to attend an informal celebration in the officer's home to mark the anniversary of the November Revolution. Huitfeld found the Russian officer living in one room with his wife and child. Wife and child retired shyly behind a partition when the Norwegian entered and remained there while the two officers spent a happy evening toasting each other with vodka and feasting on dried fish.

A shortage of available transport delayed the Norwegians in Murmansk for several days. The contingent didn't arrive in Kirkenes until November 11, a full week after the Soviet fall offensive had ground to a halt. Several more days passed before the Russian corps commander summoned Dahl to his field headquarters, located in a hut in the Finnish woods just south of the Finnish-Norwegian border, and assigned the Norwegian Independent Mountain Company No. 2 to reconnaissance duty along the Tana River. The Russian general was obviously disappointed at the size of Dahl's force, but he treated Dahl with all the respect due the representative of a friendly sovereign power, and he gave Dahl and the group of administrators who had accompanied him to Norway full authority to deal with civilian matters in Finnmark. Dahl was also urged to build up his Norwegian force as quickly as possible, by whatever means possible, and thus take over necessary recon-and-patrol duties during the winter.

By late November the Norwegians were in position along the Tana River. They began to probe westward, following in the wake of the retreating Germans. Lack of transportation, poor communications, and an almost total absence of intelligence information on German whereabouts hampered their actions. Dahl knew little of what was happening in large areas of the no-man's-land while long coastal stretches and much of the interior remained out of the reach of his patrols. Nevertheless, he urged his company on, hoping to learn more about the condition of the countryside and the intentions of the Germans. He also took steps to build up his force. Two companies of Norwegian police troops which had undergone training in Sweden flew into Kirkenes from Stockholm in American warplanes. Other Norwegian troops in Sweden, hearing of the existence of Dahl's unit, crossed Finnish territory on their own initiative to join his force. Dahl also mobilized an infantry battalion from among inhabitants of eastern Finnmark, which had been overrun by Russian troops before the German evacuation order could be implemented. By early 1945 Dahl's force numbered three thousand men.

As the Norwegian unit increased its size, Dahl sent out more frequent and farther ranging patrols. Teams of Army officers and civilian administrators, traveling by sled and reindeer into interior regions and by small fishing craft along the coast, brought the Norwegian presence back to previously unvisited areas. A civilian administrator who accompanied one of the sea patrols reported what they had found:

> It was a dilapidated old craft we got hold of. The engine and the steering gear were practically worn out and we had no sails. She was only fit for sheltered waters, and in peacetime it would have been considered sheer madness to take her out into the Arctic Ocean. The first place we came to was Vadso. Here, 80 per cent of the buildings had been destroyed. The next port of call was Havningberget. Here we had a pleasant surprise. The village was intact. The Norwegians had cut off the telephone lines, and the Germans, thinking they had been cut off, had fled. So we sailed westwards, plunging our way through the heavy seas beneath the bleak rocks. The Germans had had more time further west and things were gradually getting worse. At Berlevag, a fishing port of some 1,600 inhabitants, there was not a single house left. Those who had not been carried off by the Germans had hid in the mountains. Only 76 people remained. We found them searching amongst the ruins for a tin of food or a piece of timber. They were living in the basements of the burnt-down houses, with the icy wind whistling through the holes. Dead horses lay scattered among the ruins. At Gamvik, only ten miles south of the North Cape, not a house, shack or fishing lodge was standing. The inhabitants—some 500 people—had fled into the hills and the Germans had caught only ten of them. Diphtheria had broken out and was threatening the whole community, crowded together in caves and mud huts. Twenty-seven people were living in a mud hut ten feet long with a piece of canvas for a door. Only those who were ill or infirm returned with us. The others refused to leave their homesteads. They were born and bred on that barren soil and they would pull through somehow.

Through the winter, Norwegian patrols pushed farther west into Finnmark, often striking out on long-range reconnaissance patrols behind German lines. A forward headquarters was eventually established near Skoganvarre, where the German Luftwaffe had had one of its major arctic airfields. By the time the Norwegians arrived the field was undefended, although German engineers had mined it heavily and had planted booby traps throughout the area as a reminder of their former presence. Before the end of the war, Norwegian sappers removed eighty thousand mines from Finnmark.

As Norwegian patrols fanned out over the undefended areas of Finnmark, a clearer picture emerged of the consequences of the German scorched-earth policy, which Allied propagandists were depicting as the "rape of Finnmark." * Destruction was indeed widespread and the civilian population had suffered in the forced evacuation, but the feared loss of life among the civilian population had not occurred. Despite Hitler's instructions to Rendulic to apply the policy ruthlessly, the Germans had made transportation available to the Norwegian civilians and German military units refrained from executing stragglers. And those who escaped evacuation managed to survive the winter, accustomed as they were to life under arctic conditions. To Dahl's surprise, he discovered there was little loss of life in Finnmark, although there was widespread destruction of property and livestock.

By April Norwegian units reached Alta, where they clashed with German troops who had been left behind to guard the airport outside town. By the first week of May, the Norwegians concluded their occupation of the province of Finnmark, but the German Twentieth Mountain Army had made good its withdrawal. German units were still in fighting shape, with their equipment intact and their troops under tight discipline. Strong units of the German force were dug in along the Lyngenfjord for their final stand. The small Norwegian contingent under Colonel Dahl could make no headway against them.

The war ended with the undefeated German Army manning positions below Lyngenfjord, with the Norwegian troops under Dahl incapable of farther advance, and with Russian troops in eastern Finnmark, their mission completed, preparing to pull back. Within a short time of the last German capitulation, Red Army troops withdrew from all Norwegian territory, much to the surprise of many Norwegians.

---

* A Russian journalist who visited the Russian-controlled portion of Norway wrote an article that received wide circulation in which he accused the Germans of "depriving thousands of men, women and children of shelter and cold-bloodedly condemning them to privation, cold and hunger." The Norwegian Crown Prince Olav in London complained at a press conference that the German action "might well mean that part of Norway will be uninhabitable for a great number of years."

19
Toward Victory in Denmark

As far back as 1941 Danish Army intelligence officers were beginning to feed significant amounts of military intelligence to England by
way of Stockholm. The intelligence section of the Danish General Staff
operated very much in the open at the time. Offices were regularly
manned and top intelligence officers were listed on the Danish Army's
organizational roster, their names public and known to the Germans: Lt.
Col. Einar Nordentoft commanded the military-intelligence organization; Lt. Comdr. Poul Morch was his deputy in charge of naval affairs. An
energetic and capable staff served under them. The open existence of the
Danish intelligence staff was an anomaly in occupied Europe, but no more
so than the special situation Denmark experienced during the first years of
occupation. Ostensibly Denmark was self-governing, and to comply with
the fiction of Danish independence, Germany permitted the Danish
Army to remain intact, including its intelligence division.

But the possibility existed—and it was recognized as a possibility in
1941—that the Germans would eventually learn of the close ties between
the Danish and British intelligence organizations and crack down on the
Danish operations. In that event, a new undercover intelligence apparatus
would be needed, staffed by agents unknown to the Germans and ready
to take over where the open organization left off. After consultations with
his senior officers, Colonel Nordentoft appointed a young reserve lieutenant, Svend Truelsen, as backup officer for intelligence operations.
Truelsen had been attached to the General Staff as an intelligence officer
before the war but had gone on inactive duty after the occupation. In
1941, he was serving as the executive secretary to Arne Hogsbro Holm,
the civilian director of the Agricultural Council, a governmental body
responsible for maintaining statistics on Denmark's farm output. Nordentoft ordered Truelsen to remain inactive, and inconspicuous, until his
services were needed.

In August, 1943, the Germans imposed emergency military rule in Denmark and arrested the bulk of the Danish Army. With the exception of Maj. Hans Lunding, who was seized while on duty at Army head-quarters, all top officers in the intelligence section escaped arrest and immediately went underground. In the days after the crackdown, Truelsen met with them daily. At one of their regular secret meetings, held early in September in the botanical gardens at Charlottenlund, Truelsen received disquieting news from Maj. Volle Gyth, one of Nordentoft's closest advisors. Gyth told him the situation was so precarious that the entire intelligence staff was preparing to escape to Sweden and that Truelsen should make plans to take over field operations in Denmark. Truelsen's instructions were of a broad nature: he was required to rebuild an intelligence network in Denmark that would acquire information on German military activities in the country and feed that information to a new Danish intelligence headquarters the escaping staff planned to es-tablish in Stockholm. From Stockholm the information would be passed on to London. Gyth told Truelsen that as long as Denmark could provide solid information to the Allies, the British would not interfere directly in the country, and internal intelligence would remain in Danish hands. Time, therefore, was a crucial factor; Truelsen would have to rebuild in a hurry.

Truelsen first thought of recruiting regular Army officers who had been on leave when Germany imposed martial law and who had not yet heeded General Goertz's order to turn themselves in. He met secretly with fifteen officers of all ranks, and using Colonel Nordentoft's name as authority, urged them to join him in rebuilding an intelligence network. He stressed the need for "trained eyes to do military intelligence" and appealed to their patriotism to help him in his task. To a man, the officers refused to join, telling Truelsen they planned to obey their com-mander-in-chief and voluntarily undergo internment rather than partici-pate in undercover activities.

Frustrated and disappointed in his fellow officers, Truelsen turned next to a group of police officials whom he had known from his days on the General Staff. The police were strategically located, they normally handled a large volume of information, and they were for the most part anti-German. As executive secretary of the Agricultural Council, Truelsen could visit them without question. His recruitment among the police went smoothly. He selected only those with whose politics he was familiar from pre-war days, and most of the police officials he approached were willing to cooperate. Truelsen made only one concession to facili-tate their participation. He avoided using the word "intelligence," for in wartime Europe intelligence meant "spying," an activity which fright-ened most nonprofessionals. Instead, he recruited the police for "resistance work," which by the autumn of 1943 had gained respectability among the Danes.

Late in October, the Germans released all Danish Army and Navy officers who had been interned in August, and Truelsen began recruiting agents from among the released officers. This time he had the entire officer corps to draw upon and he successfully recruited eighty young officers to work as field agents or headquarters personnel. He placed the majority of the officers as "clerks" in the Agricultural Council. Truelsen's superior in the Council, Arne Hogsbro Holm, although not directly involved in resistance work, was aware of Truelsen's activities and made no objections to the sudden influx of new workers into his department. Truelsen also established a more secret intelligence headquarters in a series of apartments in a new residential building on Dronningsvaregade. In a report to his superiors Truelsen described the Dronningsvaregade headquarters:

> The five apartments which were used as offices for everyday work and as residences for some of the staff were in a new block, in which it was possible to secure adjacent flats. They covered all means of ascent in the building and had adjacent balconies and common end walls. The back panels of cupboards were loose and by cutting a hole in the walls between the flats, it was possible to pass from one to the other. The apartment used as an office had a microphone fitted into the letter box, connected with a loudspeaker in the office, which made it possible to hear what was happening on the staircase, and to know, for example, if a Gestapo raid were taking place.

To gather information in the field, Truelsen used his new officer recruits and selected civilians. One of the first civilians to join, Ole Lippmann, worked for the hospital-supply firm of Simonsen and Weels and had close contacts with Danish medical men. Truelsen gave Lippmann the job of "demilitarizing" the military officers and training them as "salesmen" for his firm. Under Lippmann, the firm of Simonsen and Weels built up a sales force far larger than the firm's volume of business would justify. Its new salesmen spent much time making contact with police officials throughout the country and checking the location of German military units and fortifications. Much of the information they gathered was sent back to the clerks in the Agricultural Council, on meat-production forms that were specially marked to indicate to the clerks that the report contained coded information of a nonagricultural nature.

To gather naval information, Truelsen recruited lighthouse keepers, pilots, harbor masters, ferryboat skippers, railway personnel, former naval officers, and members of sailing and rowing clubs. All naval intelligence funneled through Truelsen's Copenhagen headquarters before being passed on to the Danish intelligence headquarters in Stockholm for evaluation by Nordentoft and Morch. Truelsen later described how the information reached Stockholm:

> A number of routes were used by the Intelligence Service for forwarding material across the Sound. The boat used had secret spaces for mail in the water and petrol tanks and a secret space for passengers. As the organization progressed, a number of routes were gradually established from the east coast of Zealand to several destinations on the Swedish coast. If reports were to be sent by courier, they were carried in special containers placed in the rectum or vagina.

By November, after two months of strenuous organizing, Truelsen's operations consisted of agents in the field, a receiving organization admirably placed in the Agricultural Council, intelligence headquarters established in the flats on Dronningsvaregade, and a reliable means of communication with Stockholm. Truelsen had even revived the intelligence system operating in northern Germany. Truck drivers who regularly traveled into Germany with loads of fish became his primary agents.

Truelsen had organized quickly in accordance with instructions, but in pushing forward so rapidly he ran risks of exposure. These he accepted in the interest of speed. His network went "active" in mid-November and information immediately began flowing to Colonel Nordentoft's headquarters in Stockholm. As a loyal Army officer and a former aide-de-camp to General Goertz, Truelsen also wanted to involve the Army in his work, despite the Army's reluctance to cooperate. Truelsen therefore made copies of all reports available to General Goertz, who had been released from internment on October 20 along with the rest of the Danish officer corps. A courier from General Goertz picked up each day's packet of secret information. Within less than a week after his network had gone active, the courier informed Truelsen to report to Copenhagen's central police station at Halmtorvet.

Awaiting him there Truelsen found two of General Goertz's chief aides, Captains Viggo Hjalf and Schiotz-Eriksen. Both officers were among the most conservative of Denmark's officer corps and were reputedly pro-German. (Schiotz-Eriksen had joined the Danish Nazi Party in the days following the German invasion of 1940, considering it the wave of the future, but had dropped his membership soon afterward when the country as a whole failed to move toward militant Nazi politics.) By the fall of 1943, although no longer openly pro-German, they still mistrusted the resistance, which they viewed as Communist-inspired, and they had backed General Goertz in his decision to build up an underground army which would be held as a "force in waiting" until the end of the war, to assure that Communists did not usurp power in the country. Until then the Army would not participate in the resistance, nor would it take any action against the Germans. From the coldness of their greeting, Truelsen knew that he was in for a difficult meeting.

The two officers began by sharply criticizing Truelsen's intelligence work. The police commissioner had heard, Captain Schiotz-Eriksen observed, that Truelsen's network in Jutland had "gone active." This indicated a "serious lack of security," and Schiotz-Eriksen suggested that Truelsen curtail his activities immediately in the interests of safety. Truelsen objected. The fact that the police commissioner had learned of his network was not in itself surprising. Many of his agents in Jutland were policemen and he had always assumed that their superiors would become aware of their activities. "There is no breach of security," Truelsen commented, "because we are all involved together."

Schiotz-Eriksen persisted, next raising a political consideration. Speaking for General Goertz, he demanded that Truelsen put an end to all intelligence work for the Allied cause. Henceforth Truelsen's network (which admittedly "was very cleverly put together") should concentrate on gathering information about resistance groups inside Denmark, passing on this information only to General Goertz's "little General Staff" of which he and Captain Hjalf were members. Truelsen angrily refused. He pointed out that the Army itself should become active in all forms of resistance work so it would be counted on the Allied side when Germany was eventually defeated. Under no circumstances would he agree to turn his intelligence apparatus against Danish resistance forces.

"Are you refusing a direct order from General Goertz?" Schiotz-Eriksen demanded.

"Yes," Truelsen replied, "and I demand a personal meeting with the general to explain the reasons why."

The meeting broke up soon afterward. Schiotz-Eriksen hurried to inform General Goertz of Truelsen's reaction while Truelsen reported the substance of the meeting to Colonel Nordentoft in Stockholm and to members of the Danish Freedom Council in Copenhagen. Days later a compromise was hammered out. Under pressure from the Freedom Council and his own officers in Stockholm, General Goertz finally agreed that Truelsen's intelligence network could continue in operation against the Germans, but he insisted that only reserve officers could participate. If questioned, General Goertz could then claim that no regularly commissioned officers of the Danish Army were involved. Truelsen thus had won reluctant permission from General Goertz to continue his work for the Allied cause.*

* In the spring of 1944, Truelsen drafted a secret report for the SOE on "Danish Military and Naval Intelligence Service in Denmark following 29 August, 1943." In it he dealt diplomatically with General Goertz's aversion to action against the Germans. "In the beginning," he wrote, "the Army did not wish to be involved in the project. Later the General gave his authorization for the work to begin, but he did not wish that line officers should be used at first, since a possible exposure might entail a new internment of Army officers who were particularly conspicuous after their release." Truelsen, however, was always plagued by conflicting loyalties. He criticized the Army's lack of aggressiveness in private while protecting its image in public. Other resistance leaders were less

Concurrently with the negotiations concerning the fate of Truel-sen's intelligence network, other negotiations were under way between the Freedom Council and Army officers on the broader questions of sabotage and resistance. The Freedom Council argued for stronger ac-tion. The Army continued to insist that its primary aim should be to prepare for the days after Germany capitulated. These differences were ironed out in a series of meetings and agreement was reached on how the resistance would be organized. Under the terms of the agreement, the military chiefs acknowledged the Freedom Council as the central au-thority in the country's fight against the Germans, until such time as the king could freely choose a new government. The military chiefs also acknowledged that the primary aim of the resistance should be active opposition to the German occupying forces. Toward this end they agreed to minimize their anti-Communist propaganda, in the interests of soli-darity at home. As a final sign of their willingness to cooperate, the military also agreed to assign a permanent representative to the new Command Committee, organized by the Freedom Council to coordinate all resistance activity. This committee was initially composed of Mogens Fog, a college professor sympathetic to the Communists; Frode Jakobsen, one of the founders of the resistance organization known as "the Ring"; and Flemming Muus, the suave and personable SOE representative in Denmark. The Army, however, had changed only its official line. Char-acteristically, the man selected by General Goertz to represent the ser-vice on the Command Committee was none other than Capt. Viggo Hjalf, a member of the "little General Staff," who only a few weeks earlier had tried to persuade Svend Truelsen to turn his intelligence network against the Danish resistance.

The Freedom Council's success in establishing some control over the resistance in Denmark began to bear fruit in 1944. The country was divided into six resistance regions, each independent of the others, but each supposedly under the ultimate control of the Command Committee. The peninsula of Jutland, site of the heaviest German fortifications in the country, comprised three of the nation's six regions—northern Jutland, central Jutland, and southern Jutland. The island of Fyn, with its indus-trial city of Odense and its key ports of Nyborg, Middelfart, Svendborg, and Faaborg, constituted a fourth resistance district. A fifth region took in all of the principal island of Zealand with the exception of Copenhagen, which was a region in itself. Under instructions from the Command Committee, underground army groups formed in each region. Recruits were given instruction in the use of weapons and in military tactics, in

---

concerned with protecting the Army's reputation. Ole Lippmann's standard comment was that regular Army officers found it "biologically impossible" to join the resistance, preferring the pomp and routine of barracks life to "gunsmoke and unauthorized actions."

preparation for when they might be called into action. As in Norway, the Danish underground army, led by Danish Army officers, looked ahead to the day of Germany's defeat, when their services would be needed to protect the country's industries and transportation and communications facilities. Unlike Danish sabotage and guerrilla organizations, the Danish underground army did not contemplate action against the Germans; and since underground army units formed in areas that had already seen the growth of sabotage groups, friction erupted in the field, almost as a natural by-product of the suspicion that existed between irregular leaders and military officers. Until the end of the war, internal animosities plagued the resistance effort, despite all efforts by the Command Committee to improve cooperation among resistance groups.

In Jutland, Anton Jensen, who had started a resistance group in the winter of 1940, composed of former Danish Boy Scouts, and who had since then become one of the more aggressive guerrilla leaders, famous throughout the country under the codename Jens Toldstrup, found it impossible to work effectively with the regular Army officer, Colonel Bennike, who was assigned to his region in the spring of 1944 to train underground soldiers in the use of explosives. By summer the two men no longer were on speaking terms. Colonel Bennike refused to answer messages from Toldstrup and complained to the Command Committee of his "irresponsibility," while Toldstrup in turn appealed to the SOE leader in Denmark, Flemming Muus, hoping to have Bennike recalled for "timidity."

On Zealand, newspaperman Stig Jensen, who had become responsible for all arms drops on the island, ran into problems with Captain Schiotz-Eriksen after the Army officer volunteered men to help Jensen distribute arms received by air from England. Jensen, always pressed for manpower, accepted thankfully. Later he learned that all the arms entrusted to Schiotz-Eriksen had been delivered to underground army units led by Army officers, the so-called O groups, rather than to old-line resistance organizations who had been active for some time and who needed arms for missions against the Germans. Although the Command Committee decreed that all arms received in Denmark should be distributed equally among all resistance groups, the more conservative O groups, committed to a policy that minimized risks and danger, continued to receive the bulk of the arms. In the late spring of 1944, for instance, five hundred machine guns were purchased in Sweden and transported to Denmark by underground routes. All five hundred weapons wound up in the hands of officer-led groups. In the following few months another 2,500 machine guns arrived in Denmark. These too were delivered to the O groups, with only a handful reaching the sabotage organizations. As for BOPA, the Communist organization, it received not a single weapon from the Swedish shipments.

Those arms that filtered down to the active resistance groups came primarily from weapon drops arranged by the SOE and its American counterpart, the Special Operations branch of the Office of Strategic Services (OSS), which started a Danish section in January, 1944. The staid O groups inside Denmark could not control the distribution of these weapons because, shunning the risks involved in receiving illegal arms, they left that hazardous job to the more daring sabotage groups. Men from these groups made sure that their own units were adequately armed. Nor did the Allies hold back on weapon deliveries. From January, 1944, until the end of the war, the combined SOE-OSS headquarters delivered to Denmark 16,605 U. S. carbines, more than six million rounds of .30-caliber ammunition, 600 bazookas and 7,000 rounds of bazooka ammunition, close to 74,000 pounds of Composition "C" plastic explosives, and 264,500 feet of detonating cord, as well as an assortment of pistols, revolvers, firearm-cleaning kits, and other equipment. At least 2,500 additional carbines reached Denmark by sea, carried by fishing vessels and motor torpedo boats. By the summer of 1944 sufficient arms had reached the active resistance groups, including BOPA, to make widespread sabotage possible, and the Danes, spurred by German defeats in the field, pulled off a series of major actions that stung the German occupying force.

Of all the resistance groups, BOPA scored the hardest hits, starting with the giant Globus factory in the Copenhagen suburb of Glostrup.

Danish metal workers produced hundreds of submachine guns and pistols for use in sabotage raids. *(Danish Ministry for Foreign Affairs)*

There, under heavy guard, skilled Danish workers manufactured replacement parts for German warplanes and heavy weapons. BOPA
leaders had eyed the Globus plant as early as the summer of 1943, but had
decided then that the plant was too heavily guarded for a sneak attack to
succeed, and a lack of weapons had precluded a frontal attack. When
weapons became available in 1944, BOPA took a second look at the
Globus facility. But the plant's defenses had been strengthened in the
intervening year and an attack now appeared even more difficult: German engineers had built bunkers at strategic points and additional armed
guards, most of them Danish Nazi veterans of the pro-German *Frikorps
Danmark* which had fought on the Russian front, patrolled the plant's
perimeter twenty-four hours a day.

But BOPA was determined to press an assault on the Globus.
Eventually it decided on a bold frontal attack to be carried out during the
day, when an attack would be least expected. BOPA hoped that surprise
and heavy firepower would enable the attacking force to overwhelm the
guards and carry out the plant's destruction. Speed was essential, however. German units billeted close by could reach the plant within minutes
after an alert. To guard against this eventuality, BOPA leaders also
assigned machine-gun units to cover key intersections near the plant,
with orders to fight off German reinforcements which might arrive while
the attacking force was still inside the plant. One of the BOPA fighters,
Knud Raaschou-Nielsen, assigned to a machine-gun post on Roskildevej,
the largest avenue leading to the Globus plant, described his unit's mission
in an account written after the war:

> Erik was to be the gunner. Lars who had also been a soldier would
> help, and I was to load the magazines, because we did not have many of
> them. All traffic was to be stopped, and German soldiers shot without
> warning.

The attack began at 7 P.M. on June 6, the day of the Allied landings
in Normandy. An early-summer sun still hung over the horizon as the
covering parties took up their posts. The attack started with split-second
precision. Raaschou-Nielsen wrote:

> The moment we stopped, the fight began. First a couple of crackling
> machine pistol salvoes, then ordinary shooting that sounded as if it
> came from many places. Then came a few thundering crashes and I
> could not believe that the attacking force could have started blowing
> up the plant so quickly. But one of my colleagues, in an expert way,
> explained, "hand grenades."

At the main plant itself, the attack caught the guards by surprise.
Heavy fire laid down by the BOPA saboteurs overwhelmed any opposition before it could form. Firing steadily, the assault force moved through

The Kino-Palaeet, a major Copenhagen cinema and showcase for Nazi films, was blown up by saboteurs in March, 1944. *(Nordisk Pressefoto)*

the plant, placing explosives in selected spots. Outside, the men manning the covering positions could hear the "shooting continue undiminished."

> The landscape looked just as peaceful, and we lay there keeping an eye on the road as if the whole thing did not concern us. It could have been a game of robbers by a bunch of boys, or autumn maneuvers, if it had not been for a woman in one of the villas screaming hysterically every time a hand grenade was thrown. People began streaming out. Some of them even brought their children, and twice I had to run and get curious people in cover behind some rose bushes. In the summer of 1944 people were so unused to events of war that they exposed themselves and their children to danger out of curiosity.

Within fifteen minutes the firing stopped, and the trucks that had carried the attack force to the factory raced back toward Copenhagen, "heavily laden with saboteurs, most of whom wore steel helmets with Danish flags painted on the sides." Curious onlookers lined the roads near the plant, cheering the trucks as they passed.

The covering force left last. As the three-man machine-gun crew that had been stationed on Roskildevej jumped into their car, expecting German troops to appear at any moment, they discovered that their fuel gauge read EMPTY. A stray bullet had pierced the tank. Quickly they transferred to an abandoned bus whose passengers and driver had taken shelter when the firing started. Other BOPA men were already inside. Dr. Erik Hagens, a physician who had been assigned to the operation, took the wheel and headed for Copenhagen. As the bus passed a German control point closer to town, bullets ripped into the vehicle. Raaschou-Nielsen described what happened:

> Several panes were smashed and I dived down instinctively. The vehicle swayed and almost stopped. Several of us cried, "Go on," but when I looked at Hagens he had fallen back in the driver's seat with blood gushing out from the back of his head.

Another BOPA member climbed over Hagens' body and continued driving. At a safe spot on the outskirts of Copenhagen, the bus pulled to a halt and the men piled out, carrying their weapons with them.

> We created some attention, both because of the weapons and because two in the group had been badly splashed with blood. From some of the houses people called after us, "God be with you boys." Then we ran over fields and past garden plots until we finally reached a summer house that our leader knew of. Here we hid the weapons under a porch.

The two men with blood-stained clothes sought help from strangers in the neighborhood. The civilians quickly grasped the seriousness of the situation. Without asking a single question they provided clean clothes for the two men and promised to wash the blood-splattered clothes by the next day, in case the saboteurs wanted to return for them.

The group parted at a streetcar terminus. Raaschou-Nielsen commented: "A couple of us took Number 8 into town. It was strange to sit in the street car and hear people talking about the bacon allotment and the percentage of synthetic wool in woolen cloth. I was home again around 9 P.M.."

The attack had been successful beyond all expectations. The attacking force had knocked the Globus plant out of operation without the loss of a single man. The lone fatality was Dr. Hagens, the member of the support unit who had been mortally wounded on the ride back to town. Within days General Eisenhower's Supreme Headquarters radioed a message of congratulations to the Danish underground.

Two weeks later BOPA squads struck again, this time against the *Dansk Riffelsyndikat* in Copenhagen's Frihavn (Free Port) district, Denmark's only factory manufacturing small arms, antitank guns, and artillery equipment for the Germans. An attack force of thirty men, hidden inside vehicles that carried signs reading EMERGENCY FIRE and AMBULANCE, slipped successfully past guards at the main gate. Once inside, they surprised the guards, herded all workers into an open space within the factory grounds, set their explosives, and warned everyone to flee when the plant's sirens sounded, for that would signal the detonation of the explosives. As at the Globus, covering parties waited anxiously outside, but unlike the Globus operation, the action against the *Riffelsyndikat* proceeded without a shot being fired. Knud Raaschou-Nielsen again was posted with a covering party, and he described his group's state of mind while waiting to learn the outcome of the action:

> We chatted as well as we could, but we were very tense and the talk was slow. We got a little nervous when some German marines headed for us. "Feuer, bitte," they said. (Matches, please.) Relieved, we checked our pockets for matches and were even polite enough to light their cigarettes for them.

Finally, the men noticed the "EMERGENCY" trucks leaving the compound. One driver had a "canny grin" on his face. Raaschou-Nielsen wrote:

> We knew that everything was OK, and we almost shouted aloud with delight. At the same moment the siren of the factory sounded and the workers began streaming through the gate—evidently scared and nervous. Heavy explosions followed, and I could see a large cloud of smoke billowing up from the free port.

Five giant explosions racked the *Riffelsyndikat* plant, leaving the building a flaming shell. When Danish firemen arrived on the scene they found only the walls standing. The interior of the plant had turned into a glowing mass of fire. Thousands of Copenhagen residents streamed to Frihavn that afternoon to get a better look at the ruins. Others rode the suburban trains that passed by Frihavn, commenting with approval on what they saw. The following day, *Information* reported the results of the action and warned Danes not to be too enthusiastic in public:

> In connection with sabotage events, there may be reason to warn people against being too frank in the crowds that form. Informers work with great results in crowds. He who makes himself interesting or tells about things that he has seen exposes not only himself but also the men he praises and admires to serious risks. Keep quiet.

The month of June also saw an escalation of small-scale actions against German-controlled transportation and communications facilities. In that single month, saboteurs from various resistance groups carried out nineteen separate attacks on Danish railroads, three times the average for the five preceding months. As sabotage increased, Denmark braced for German reprisals. They were not long in coming. The primary reprisal instrument was the Danish Schalburg Corps, organized in April of 1943 and manned by demobilized veterans of the Danish *Frikorps*. Staunchly pro-Nazi in outlook, and under the day-to-day control of German officers, the Schalburg Corps became a retaliatory sabotage-and-terror organization, hitting out at targets dear to the hearts of Danes whenever

A postwar caption with this official Danish photograph reads: "Danish people rounded up at gunpoint by collaborator." *(Danish Ministry for Foreign Affairs)*

A street in a working-class district of Copenhagen after a German "murder patrol" had passed. German authorities ordered reprisals for acts of sabotage and for the murder of pro-Nazi collaborators, which resistance leaders liked to call "executions." *(Nordisk Pressefoto)*

Members of the Hipo Corps, a pro-Nazi auxiliary police force manned by Danes, at gun practice on a country estate. *(Nordisk Pressefoto)*

Danish resistance fighters destroyed facilities important to the Germans. By the summer of 1944 the Danish resistance realized that whenever they struck at the Germans, the Schalburg Corps would strike back, in what became known as *Schalburtage.*

One day after the attack on the *Riffelsyndikat, Information* reported that the "Copenhagen police were on the alert as Schalburtage must be expected as a reprisal." Within two days the Schalburg Corps struck. Schalburg terrorists set fire to the Royal Danish porcelain factory and placed incendiary bombs in Copenhagen's famous Tivoli Gardens. Other Schalburg operatives bombed Copenhagen's community center and wrecked the student union at the University of Copenhagen. *Information* provided detailed coverage:

> At one o'clock in the night, about 50 Schalburg men forced their way into Tivoli. The men wore uniforms and were thus untouchable by Danish police. At 1:45 the first explosion was heard, which destroyed the Glass Hall. In quick succession the other buildings were destroyed . . . the Concert Hall . . . the Gambling Hall . . . Mirror Hall . . . Heering's Pavillion and Divan III Restaurants. At daybreak Tivoli looked as if the Germans had been there, which indeed they had, indirectly. Last night the world-known Danish Porcelain Factory suffered . . . hundreds of thousands of kroners' worth of porcelain crushed. The work of the terrorists is completely useless. Tivoli and the Porcelain Factory count little against the Rifle Syndicate. As an act

The pro-German Schalburg Corps engaged in counter-sabotage against firms run by officials whose attitude toward Germany was "not correct." This was the main office of the East Asiatic Company in Copenhagen. *(Danish Ministry for Foreign Affairs)*

of muddling, their work is no good either; Copenhageners know very well who did what. The actions must be considered a war of nerves carried out according to direct German order. Dr. Best must be called the actual leader. A worthy task for the plenipotentiary, the emissary of the Führer.

By the middle of June Berlin had become deeply concerned by the unrest in Denmark. Heinrich Himmler sent special orders to Dr. Werner Best on June 15 to stamp down on sabotage. Ten days later, Best proclaimed a state of emergency throughout the country, setting a curfew between the hours of 8 P.M. and 5 A.M. All meetings and public gatherings were prohibited.

The Danes replied by laying down their tools. The next day, twelve hundred workers at the Burmeister and Wain shipyard in Copenhagen left work early, telling shipyard officials that they "had to tend their gardens." They were not on strike, they assured their superiors; they were merely leaving work early to care for their vegetable gardens. With a curfew in effect, they explained, they would not be able to travel to their garden plots to put in the necessary time, and consequently they planned to leave their regular jobs before quitting time so they could get to their gardens and back home during hours when they were legally permitted on the streets. All workers used the same excuse, even those without gardens.

There was little garden tending that evening, however. Thousands of Danes turned out into the streets after curfew, demonstrating against the Germans. German patrols opened fire. *Information* reported:

> Copenhageners stood in groups of hundreds on street corners so they could escape down the bystreets when the German patrols came. To the Danish police they said, "Don't interfere with this"; and the police didn't. When a patrol approached a crowd, it fired and people fled. In many places, however, the Copenhageners set fires in the middle of the streets. Old papers, mattresses and garbage were burned. People closed the streets with barricades of paving stones, vans, bicycles, and threw things at the Germans, who fired around in wild fury. At one place the inhabitants raised a red standard and sang the "Internationale" when the Germans came. The Germans formed a regular rifle line.

When the city finally quieted down, six Danes had been killed and dozens more wounded.

The following day thousands of workers from other industries joined the strike, threatening the city with a curtailment of essential services. At this tense stage, the Germans executed nine men of the Hvidsten sabotage group who had been arrested months before. Among those killed were innkeeper Marius Fiil, one of his sons, a son-in-law, and six male neighbors. Two of Fiil's daughters were sent to concentration camps in Germany. When the news of the executions became known, the mood of the country turned even uglier. Workers in the Vesterbro section of Copenhagen turned out en masse, overturning busses and trams, stopping the suburban trains and setting fires and barricades in the streets. *Information* commented: "Last night the demonstrations had a range and intensity like never before."

A furious Werner Best summoned the Danish undersecretary for foreign affairs, Nils Svenningsen, to his office and threatened even more violent German countermeasures unless the strikes were halted. Svenningsen in turn summoned other undersecretaries and trade-union leaders to an emergency meeting. Even while they met, they heard news that more barricades were being erected all over Copenhagen. As cautious Danes, the undersecretaries still harbored the spirit of compromise. After long deliberation, they drafted an appeal to the citizens of Copenhagen to call off their strike and return to work, hoping thereby to forestall further German reprisals.

> The strike in Copenhagen has brought the population of the capital to a disastrous situation. The supplies of food and other necessities are already failing. The danger of measures with irreparable consequences is impending. Restorat on of the city's normal life is a necessary condition to avoid threatening activities. Everybody is therefore earnestly requested to resume their daily work.

As Danish politicians, however, the undersecretaries also realized that the temper of the country was not what it had been during the first years of the occupation. Copenhagen roiled with anger. The undersecretaries therefore included in their declaration a short passage critical of the Germans. It blamed "the occupation power for regrettably bringing about various measures." This muted criticism failed to influence the strikers, but it did infuriate Werner Best. When he read the wording of the proclamation later that afternoon, he summoned Svenningsen to another meeting. The proclamation, he informed Svenningsen, was unacceptable: Denmark should brace itself for stern measures. Within hours Best made good his threat. German troops, acting on his direct orders, cut off all water, gas, and electricity to the city. He announced an even more stringent military curfew. Best was prepared to deny the city all necessary services until the population ceased their demonstrations.

Late in the evening of June 30, the Freedom Council held an emergency meeting of its own to consider what its reaction should be. To help its members reach a decision, the council invited the country's former Prime Minister, Vilhelm Buhl, for consultations. Buhl had served as Prime Minister in 1942 and was heir apparent for the position in the first postwar government. Above and beyond these considerations, the council considered him sound, sensible, and solid, a man they could work with and trust. To their surprise, Buhl sided with the undersecretaries. He supported their proclamation and expressed the belief that the city would soon calm down. He pointed out that a weekend was approaching and observed that many workers would be expected to leave the city then, some to work on their garden plots, where the potatoes were growing and the strawberries ripening, others for picnics and excursions into the countryside. By the following Monday, he predicted, they would be ready to return to work.

The Freedom Council was unconvinced. Buhl and his fellow politicians, they felt, were out of touch with the mood of the people. The strike had erupted spontaneously, unlike the directed and planned strikes of the previous summer. Instead of asking the workers to back down, the council felt that pressure should be applied to the Germans. When the meeting broke up, Aage Schoch, a former Conservative newspaperman, walked home to his flat in Frederiksberg. Again the people were in the streets. Bonfires flamed at street intersections and barricades had been thrown up on the main avenues. As he walked, Schoch mentally composed the text of the message he would draft in the name of the Freedom Council. It was ready the following morning:

> This is the greatest national demonstration ever to have taken place in Denmark. The repeated attacks of the Schalburg Corps on lives and property and the systematic breaking down of law and civil rights by the German occupying forces have exhausted the patience of the people. The Freedom Council supports the continuation of the strike until the Schalburg Corps is removed and State of Emergency restrictions are lifted.

Street fighting intensified the next day. Resistance fighters and workers ripped up cobblestones to hurl at German patrols. Trenches were dug. More barricades were erected and shooting erupted in various quarters of the city. For peaceful Denmark, the toll was awesome: twenty-three Danes killed and another 203 wounded. The city was a battlefield. Still the strike continued. "Several barricades the Germans have dared not to cross," *Information* reported, "and there are streets that they do not enter at all."

The next day, the Freedom Council issued another proclamation:

> During the past twenty-four hours German methods have grown in brutality. They have blocked all roads out of the city. They have stopped all supplies into the city. The population in the streets is brutally shot at by motorised patrols.

German artillery moved into position around the densely populated Vesterbro area, the center of the workers' resistance, cutting off all

June, 1944. Copenhagen. Striking workers set fires and build barricades in the Vesterbro section.
(Nordisk Pressefoto)

avenues of escape. Inside Vesterbro, the Danes prepared for battle.

At this critical point, the willingness to compromise that marked relations between the Danes and the Germans came into play again, through the mediation of H. H. Koch, the permanent undersecretary of the Ministry of Social Welfare. Koch had entree to Best's office and to the secret headquarters of the Freedom Council. Moving between the two sides, Koch managed to win concessions from both. On his part, Best agreed to withdraw the hated Schalburg Corps from the city and assured Koch that Wehrmacht patrols would refrain from shooting at citizens. He also promised that he would consider lifting the state of emergency after the strike ended. With these assurances, the Freedom Council issued still another proclamation. For propaganda purposes it underlined the German concessions and proclaimed a "Victory for the people." For practical reasons, however, the council called on the strikers to return to work. Within forty-eight hours, the strike was over.

For the Germans, the people's strike brought home several lessons: The climate in Denmark had drastically changed; the Freedom Council had consolidated its position with the population; old-line civilian politicians carried little influence; even the Danish police were suspect, for they had refrained from acting against the strikers and had taken steps to halt looting only under the most extreme German pressure.

Clearly the barometer for the Germans was falling in Denmark. Strong protective measures would have to be taken to prepare for the storm to come. And Germany still had the strength and the will to crack down hard. By late summer Germany was determined to wipe out every group that could take to the field against them. Although never officially mentioned in any internal memorandums, Germany was preparing for the final throes of war.

The first blow fell in September against the one organized Danish force that could be used against Germany—the country's nine thousand police. To German minds, the Danish police had become unreliable—they had failed to act aggressively during the people's strike, and they consistently shut their eyes to sabotage. Werner Best, who had initiated the action against the Danish Jews, now ordered SS and German police troops to disband the Danish police force, take over all police duties in the country, and deport to German concentration camps those policemen considered most likely to join the resistance.

The raids took place on September 19 under cover of false air-raid warnings which sounded in the major cities of Copenhagen, Aarhus, Aalborg, and Odense shortly before noon. While the sirens wailed, German troop units in trucks pulled up outside police headquarters and substations. The soldiers dismounted quickly and surprised the Danish police inside. In Copenhagen, the Army troops received assistance from

SS men in civilian dress who had infiltrated the main police headquarters earlier that morning. They were holding pistols to the heads of top police officials when the troops arrived. Policemen on patrol at the time of the raids were picked up individually throughout the rest of the day. Arrests went as smoothly in smaller towns and villages and along the Danish-German border in southern Jutland, where Danish border gendarmerie still walked their posts. By the end of the day close to ten thousand policemen and border guards had been arrested or, in the case of rural police, disarmed and sent home.

Deportations began that same night. Two thousand men from the Copenhagen force were selected for imprisonment in Germany. Vans carried them in long silent convoys to Copenhagen's Free Port, where the police were herded aboard the steamer *La Plata*. The ship sailed that night with its cargo of prisoners, many of them in shock at the sudden and ominous turn of events in their lives. Of the remaining police and border guards, several hundred were imprisoned in Denmark, while the bulk of the force, mostly those over fifty-five and those who served rural communities, were allowed to remain at liberty with the understanding that they would not bear arms and would not engage in organized activity against the occupying powers. The arrests, deportations, and warnings served their purpose. Until the end of the war, those policemen still at liberty proved too demoralized to take effective joint action, and from September 20 onward, the only Danish police seen in uniform in the country were those whom Werner Best permitted to stand guard outside King Christian's residence at Amalienborg. Their function, however, was strictly decorative.

With the disbanding of the Danish police, lawlessness spread through Denmark and a sense of unease settled upon the country, heightened by the realization that the final agonies of war were to come. The fabric of Danish life, maintained with such effort during four years of war, seemed to be ripping apart. Black marketeers openly set up stalls on major thoroughfares of the cities and could be heard hawking ration coupons, cigarettes, and other items in short supply. The crime rate increased sharply; saboteurs operated with abandon. By October, 1944, enough arms for five thousand men had been dropped in Denmark. (Within the next few months, arms for an additional twenty thousand men reached the resistance groups.) Railroad sabotage in Jutland hit such a peak that German transportation officers ordered units moving down from Norway to reinforce the Western Front to travel by ship to Aarhus, in central Jutland, and thus bypass the northernmost port of Frederikshavn and the perilous rail passage through northern Jutland, where Danish saboteurs were especially active. Fear and uncertainty gripped both sides. German officers realized that their days were numbered; the Danes in turn feared the last frantic lashing out of the Germans. But the thrust toward victory superseded the Danish fear of German retaliation. Danish resistance escalated, and it brought with it the anticipated German counterterror. Gestapo squads moved against resistance groups whenever and wherever they could be found. The entire German counterespionage apparatus threw itself into the struggle. They scored their greatest success in Jutland, where the Danish underground was most active and most open. Numerous arrests took place in Jutland; resistance records were seized; and captured underground fighters were subjected to interrogation and torture to force them to reveal further details of the resistance movement. Panic gripped the Jutland underground. Its leaders reported to London that they were in imminent danger of being "rolled up."

While the Germans moved against the resistance in Denmark, the Danish section of the combined SOE-OSS headquarters in London concerned itself with problems of its own choosing. By the fall of 1944 the Allies were looking ahead to the eventual defeat of Nazi Germany. In October, combined headquarters drew up a broad plan, code-named Socrates, that spelled out procedures to seize all Gestapo records when the Germans were forced to retreat from the country. At that time, they knew, the Allies would be concerned with the accurate identification and arrest of top Gestapo agents, not only to ensure that the anticipated capitulation went smoothly, but also to pinpoint those Germans and Danes who would be regarded as "unfriendly" in the postwar world. Copies of the Socrates plan were sent to resistance leaders in Denmark, who were expected to play leading roles in the seizure of Gestapo archives.

Among those leaders was Fritz Tillisch, chief organizer of the Danish resistance in central Jutland. Tillisch read the plans for Socrates with incredulity. He knew that all Gestapo records were housed in Gestapo headquarters that had been set up in buildings of Aarhus University. He also knew that those records were being scrutinized at that very moment for clues that could lead to the immediate arrest of other agents operating under his command. While London concerned itself with intelligence matters of a long-range institutional nature, he and his organization were facing immediate problems of life and death. On October 15, therefore, Tillisch drafted an urgent message to London, pleading for a special operation far from the thoughts of his London superiors:

> Underground in Jutland about to be torn up by Gestapo. It is more important to destroy archives and save our people than to save archives and have our people destroyed. I beg forcibly that colleges four and five be destroyed by air attack. They are the two most westerly buildings in the university block. Urgent.

Tillisch's message was forwarded to the Danish intelligence section of the SOE, which was now headed by Maj. Svend Truelsen, the officer who had revived the military intelligence network in Denmark in the autumn of 1943. Truelsen had fled Denmark in midsummer of 1944 after Gestapo agents learned his identity. When he had reached London, via Stockholm, he had been placed in charge of all Danish intelligence in the combined SOE-OSS headquarters. Truelsen knew Tillisch as a responsible and unemotional agent; he had, in fact, recruited Tillisch for operations in central Jutland only the year before. If Tillisch described the situation as "urgent," Truelsen knew it must be very grave indeed. London's answer to Tillisch's message was transmitted the very next day: "Give soonest all flak positions within a radius of one kilometer from colleges four and five Aarhus University. Give exact information position of the colleges."

It took Tillisch's organization three days to obtain information on German anti-aircraft positions, but the information finally in hand was encouraging. "No AA within radius of one kilometer from the colleges," he reported.

London reacted more rapidly. Within forty-eight hours of London's receipt of Tillisch's second message, orders were cut for an aerial bombardment of Gestapo headquarters in Aarhus which, if successful, would destroy all records in Gestapo hands as well as any Gestapo chieftains in the building at the time. The assignment for the attack went to the daring Mosquito pilots of the RAF's Second Tactical Air Force, No. 2 Group. The Mark IV Mosquitos flown by the No. 2 Group were specifically designed for attack. Built of light wood by the British aircraft firm of De Havilland and each powered by two Merlin 21 engines, the Mosquito bombers carried no guns for their own defense, relying instead on speed, maneuverability, and the element of surprise to press home their attack. Mosquitos proved particularly effective in low-level hit-and-run bombing attacks that brought them over targets like streaks of lightning and sent them zooming out of sight before the thunder of their bombs faded away. Because they had no defense against anti-aircraft fire or bullets from German fighters, Mosquito pilots maintained a policy of never making a bombing run twice. But to make good on the first run required detailed advance planning, pinpoint navigation at low altitude, and a precise and aggressive bombing run. After the war, Air Vice Marshal Basil Embry, who commanded the Second Tactical Air Force, described the planning that preceded attacks against specific targets in built-up areas such as the Aarhus University buildings:

> When called upon to destroy that kind of target, we constructed a model of it and also of the town. We then placed the town model on a table and examined it at eye level, obtaining exactly the same oblique view, in miniature, as if we were flying over the town at a height of

fifty feet. On the town models we marked the known positions of all light flak guns and took these into account when selecting the approach route. We used the target model to help the crews to recognize their objective and to decide aiming points.

Before being called upon to raid Gestapo headquarters in Aarhus, the Second Tactical Air Force had conducted a successful low-level attack against Gestapo headquarters in Amiens, as well as against the central population registry in the Hague, where the Gestapo maintained its archives on the Dutch resistance. Civilian casualties resulted from these raids, but they were accepted as the price of war. Civilian casualties were also expected in the Aarhus raid, for the Danish resistance knew that captured underground workers were interrogated daily inside Gestapo headquarters, though the exact identity and number of prisoners undergoing interrogation on any particular day could not be known in advance.

Responsibility for scheduling the raid fell on Major Svend Truelsen, who worked in cooperation with operations and intelligence officers of the Second Tactical Air Force. The air officers worried primarily about availability of equipment and the weather over target. While Truelsen realized the importance of logistics and meteorological factors, he also impressed upon the airmen the importance of timing the raid when it would do the most damage. He suggested the time period between 11 A.M. and noon on any suitable working day. As he pointed out to the British officers, Gestapo men were punctual about beginning work in the morning, showing up promptly at their offices at nine and departing, just as promptly, for lunch at noon. The raid therefore would have to take place during the morning hours. An intelligence officer asked if an afternoon attack would be considered acceptable, say, at 2:30 P.M., after the Gestapo returned from lunch, but Truelsen explained that while Gestapo workers were punctual in leaving their offices for lunch, they often were not punctual about their return. He also ruled out a weekend attack, which even if successful could not be expected to catch any Gestapo officials in their offices. So it was decided: the raid would take place on the first weekday morning when weather conditions offered hope for success. As it turned out, that date was October 31, 1944.

Three squadrons of Mosquitos, each consisting of six planes, roared aloft from an airfield in northern Scotland, skimmed across the North Sea at an altitude of approximately fifty feet, climbed slightly as the coast of Jutland rose ahead of them, and then leveled off to continue their tree-trimming flight toward Aarhus. Low clouds hung over Aarhus that day, but the planes came in beneath the cloud cover and achieved complete surprise. Not a shot was fired as the first wave made its bombing run.

Two resistance workers undergoing interrogation inside the building heard the roar of the mosquito engines seconds before the first bombs burst. Ruth Philipsen, a twenty-seven-year-old courier for Fritz Tillisch, dived under a washstand while the two Gestapo agents who had been questioning her hid beneath a desk. Bombs from the first wave exploded just outside the door, but the interrogation room itself escaped undamaged. There was a momentary lull, then the second wave of Mosquitos roared overhead. Philipsen and her interrogators ducked again. This time a single bomb hit the room, which exploded in a cloud of dust and flying debris. When the dust had settled, Philipsen crawled out from under the washstand. She was cut and bruised but otherwise uninjured. Surveying the scene, however, she saw that her two interrogators had not been as lucky. One lay dead, sprawled under the table. The other had disappeared from sight. Philipsen assumed he was also dead, buried beneath the rubble. She scrambled from the room, made her way to the grounds surrounding the building, and fled, bleeding and shaking, to a nearby house. No one stopped her as she ran. The Danish homeowner at whose door she appeared gave her shelter for two weeks, until Tillisch's organization arranged for her safe transfer to Sweden. The other underground worker, Pastor Harald Sandbaek, was buried in debris for five hours before German rescue workers dug him out. But they did not realize he was a prisoner and delivered him to the main Aarhus Hospital along with all the others injured in the raid. Sandbaek also eventually reached Sweden.*

London waited anxiously to learn the results of the raid. Then the news came, in a jubilant message from Tillisch: "Bombing of Gestapo Aarhus OK. Gestapo HQ completely destroyed. Only one bomb failed. Congratulations to all concerned."

Four hours later, Tillisch sent another message: "Ambulances were carrying Germans for several hours. We cannot yet give number of killed. In one of the buildings 15 Gestapos had their offices. It is supposed that all of them were killed. We hope so." The next day, Tillisch provided further details: "Killed Germans supposed to be about one hundred and fifty or one hundred and sixty-five. Killed Danes twenty or thirty. Most of them informers. All card indexes burned. We are very thankful to you."

The combined SOE-OSS headquarters in London was equally jubilant. One item, however, puzzled Truelsen. Photos taken by the last

* Danish newspapers, believing that Sandbaek had been killed, reported his death. He had been an outspoken anti-Nazi clergyman before he joined the resistance as a member in good standing of an arms receiving unit and of an execution squad assigned the task of liquidating informers. The Germans accepted the reports of Sandbaek's death and failed to press a search for him while he was recovering in Aarhus Hospital. As for Ruth Philipsen, the Germans believed that she also had perished in the raid and dutifully informed Philipsen's mother of her "unfortunate" death as a result of the Allied bombing raid. What the raid actually had done for Philipsen was to end twenty-five days of imprisonment during which she was beaten repeatedly, tortured with thumbscrews, and interrogated almost daily (one time for thirty-six continuous hours).

Mosquito over target showed that a large fleet of private cars had been parked in the courtyard outside Gestapo headquarters, far more cars than should normally have been there. Truelsen could not explain it and queried Tillisch about the matter. His answer, a few days later, gave a gratifying finishing touch to the whole operation. Tillisch reported that on the day of the raid Gestapo officials from various parts of Jutland had gathered in Aarhus for a high-level policy conference. They had arrived in their private cars and had parked them outside the Gestapo head-quarters. These were the cars that had puzzled Truelsen. The Gestapo officials from all over Jutland, Tillisch added triumphantly, had been inside headquarters when the Mosquitos attacked.

Within two weeks of the attack on Gestapo headquarters in Aarhus, Kai Winkelhorn, an American officer who headed the Danish section of the OSS, conferred with senior intelligence officers of the Second Tactical Air Force about the possibility of conducting another low-level Mosquito attack, this time against Gestapo headquarters in Copenhagen. This raid would pose even more difficult problems than the operation against Aarhus, for Gestapo headquarters in Copenhagen was located in Shellhus (Shell House), a relatively new building in the very heart of the city. To further complicate the attack, the Germans had imprisoned several important resistance leaders in cells built on the top floor of Shellhus, among them two members of the Freedom Council, Aage Schoch and Mogens Fog, who had been arrested in a German sweep only a few weeks before. The Germans trusted that Danish resistance forces still in operation would learn the names and location of the imprisoned leaders (which they did) and would pass on this information to London (again the German assumption was correct). London would then realize that to bomb Shellhus would mean almost certain death for some of the most important Danish resistance leaders.

Despite the hostages, Danish resistance leaders who remained at large urged an immediate attack. Germany had threatened to "fight terror with terror" and the Gestapo was making almost daily arrests. The Danish resistance leaders feared that if the Gestapo was allowed to continue its crackdown unimpeded, every underground organizer active in Denmark would be caught and executed before the end of the war. The danger was deemed so great that those resistance leaders still in operation were willing to sacrifice their comrades in captivity at Shellhus in order to save the lives of those who were still at large.

In London plans were drawn up for the attack, but the decision to implement the plans was delayed. Not only did the political question raised by the hostages trouble the British, but there were technical and logistics problems as well: identification of Shellhus would be more difficult than identification of the Aarhus University buildings, Copenhagen was heavily defended by anti-aircraft batteries, and planes were scarce.

Every available Mosquito was being thrown at targets along the Western Front, where Allied troops were pushing the Germans back into the territory of the Third Reich. Any questionable operation, which the Shellhus raid appeared to be, must of necessity receive a low priority.

For three-and-a-half long months, while Denmark continued to plead for a raid, Basil Embry, the commander of the Second Tactical Air Force, refused to authorize the necessary orders until someone in a "responsible" position "in the field" determined that the need was indeed as great as the Danish resistance said it was. There was a catch to Embry's apparently reasonable stipulation, however, for at the time he was demanding that a responsible field determination be made, there was no "responsible" Allied official in Denmark to make this determination. Flemming Muus, the fast-talking SOE leader, had just been recalled to London to answer allegations of misuse of resistance funds. Before a determination could be made, therefore, a replacement for Muus had to be found. That replacement had to be briefed and then successfully dropped into Denmark, and once in Denmark he would have to gain his bearings in order to make a reasoned evaluation of the situation. All of this would take time, which suited Embry's purposes beautifully.

The task of finding a replacement for Muus fell to Svend Truelsen, as always sympathetic to the plight of the Danish resistance. He acted quickly, choosing as Muus's replacement Ole Lippmann, who like Truelsen had been forced to flee Denmark in the summer of 1944 to escape arrest by the Germans. After his arrival in Britain, Lippmann had gone through parachute training, so he was ready to move as soon as he got the assignment. He dropped into Denmark in February, 1945, with orders to take over Muus's activities as chief SOE representative in the country and to answer, with a clear-cut yes or no, whether an air raid should be mounted against Gestapo headquarters in Copenhagen's Shellhus. Once he reached Copenhagen, Lippmann renewed his contacts with resistance members. As the new SOE chief in Denmark, he automatically became a member of the Freedom Council's Command Committee. He also attended full sessions of the Freedom Council as an observer. In all his meetings with resistance leaders, Lippmann sought to determine if there was a need to destroy Shellhus and if that need was great enough to justify the expected losses. The need for secrecy complicated Lippmann's task, for in seeking the considered opinions of others, Lippmann himself could not openly discuss the planned raid.

Within days of his arrival in Copenhagen, a series of particularly effective German raids provided the answer that Lippmann sought. In three coordinated forays, Gestapo personnel in Copenhagen captured the most important contact man for many resistance groups, the leader of the underground army in the Copenhagen area, and a resistance worker who played a key liaison role between the military resistance and the underground press. The arrest of the three men, who between them knew most of the leading figures still active in the resistance, threatened the complete destruction of the underground organization. Lippmann concluded that the planned operation against Shellhus, which had been code-named Carthage, should be implemented at the earliest possible moment. He informed London in a report dated March 4: "It is definitely felt that Carthage would provide a pause, and pause is needed."

Lippmann's message gave Embry the "field determination" he required and the plans to bomb Shellhus, which had been in the drafting stage, were brought out for closer scrutiny. Svend Truelsen was again relieved of most of his duties in order to work closely with intelligence Officers of the Second Tactical Air Force in preparing detailed plans for the attack. Truelsen's intelligence organization produced a wealth of information, including details on Gestapo use of the Shellhus office space and German anti-aircraft defenses in the area, as well as a full description of the target and its surrounding neighborhood. The Germans, it was learned, had taken pains to camouflage Shellhus in battle tones of green and brown, but this attempt to make the building more difficult to detect from the air actually served the opposite purpose, for the Germans failed to camouflage the surrounding buildings and Shellhus consequently stood out in sharp contrast to all other structures nearby. RAF planners considered the German camouflage attempt an advantage for the attackers, not for the defenders.

Eighteen Mosquitos were assigned to carry out the raid. As in the attack against Gestapo headquarters in Aarhus, they would make their bombing runs in waves of six planes each. And again as in the Aarhus raid, the planes were scheduled to make their attack on a weekday morning between eleven and twelve. The RAF thereby hoped to duplicate the success it had scored in its pre-lunch raid at Aarhus.

The Mosquitos, with Mustang fighter escorts, reached Fersfield Airfield in Norfolk for preflight briefings on March 19. RAF briefing officers instructed the pilots to aim their bombs at the base of Shellhus and to avoid bombing the upper floor where the prisoners were lodged. Little hope was held out that the hostages could survive the raid, however. Although the Mosquitos were famous for their bombing accuracy, it did not seem possible that eighteen planes could deliver their bombloads with such pinpoint precision that the upper floors would escape damage while the base of the building was being smashed to dust. Svend Truelsen, who spoke at the briefing, tried to reassure the pilots about the plight of the prisoners. He pointed out that the resistance leaders faced the risk of execution after interrogation. It was, he said, a question of dying under an RAF attack or dying at the hands of a German execution squad.

Weather conditions on the morning of March 21, although not perfect, were good enough for the mission to proceed. The bombers took off first, closely followed by their Mustang escorts, and set course across the North Sea for a section of the Jutland coastline where intelligence reports had indicated German anti-aircraft defenses were the weakest. Visibility was poorer than expected and the flight across the North Sea was rough and bumpy. Salt spray coated the windshields, reducing the pilots' ability to see still further. Despite the poor visibility, the planes made good their approach to the coast of Jutland and, once over land, kept closely to their flight plan, crossing over the island of Zealand south of Kalundborg shortly before 11 A.M., exactly on schedule. With Zealand beneath them, the bombers headed for a large lake south of Copenhagen where the three waves were supposed to separate. The first wave of six planes had orders to continue straight on with its bombing run; the second wave was supposed to circle the lake once, and then go in for the attack; the third wave was to circle the lake twice before following the other planes toward the target. By these maneuvers, the three waves would reach Shellhus separated by one-minute intervals, a necessary precaution even in an attack that hinged on surprise for its success. Distance and time had to separate the attacking waves. Otherwise there was a danger that the planes in the second and third waves would run into explosions from bombs dropped by planes preceding them.

Everything went as scheduled south of Copenhagen. The second and third waves began their circling maneuvers while the first wave streaked for the center of town. The lead plane reached the target at 11:14 A.M. Its bombs smashed precisely into the bottom floor of Shellhus. The second plane of the first wave, piloted by Air Vice Marshal Basil Embry and navigated by Peter Clapham, came in a split second later. After the war Embry described the bombing run:

> Peter said, "That's the target. Straight ahead of us over those small lakes." We were now tensed for the moment of bomb release. Suddenly a bridge appeared ahead of us and I saw some poles, possibly light standards, sticking up. I eased the aeroplane up a little and then down again a few feet. By this time Peter had the bomb doors open, and the target seemed to be approaching us very fast. I pressed the bomb release and pulled up just over the top of Shell House, and then down again almost to street level.

The third plane of the first wave, following close behind Embry's, also made a successful run on the target, but the fourth plane, some seconds behind, struck a tall light pole and crashed onto Frederiksberg Alle, near the Jeanne d'Arc Catholic School for Children. Within seconds a pillar of smoke and flames rose above Frederiksberg Alle directly in the target approach path that would be flown by the planes of the second and third waves.

The impact of the crash sent a giant shudder through the Jeanne d'Arc School where 482 children between the ages of seven and seventeen were busy at their studies. Their teachers, all Catholic nuns, immediately ordered the students to proceed toward shelter areas in the basement of the building. The students responded as they had been trained to respond, calmly and without undue haste. As they made their way toward the shelter areas, each student clasping the hand of a desig-nated partner, the deadly Mosquitos in the second and third attack waves were speeding toward the school at nearly three hundred miles per hour, their pilots confused by the twin columns of smoke rising ahead of them, one from Frederiksberg Alle in the immediate vicinity of Jeanne d'Arc Catholic School and the other, some distance away, from Shellhus.

The first two planes of the second wave realized in time that the smoke rising from Frederiksberg Alle did not mark the target area. They pulled away without dropping their bombs. But pilots coming in behind them mistook the school for Shellhus and bombed the school directly. Within less than three minutes, at least eight of the twelve planes in the second and third attack waves had dropped high-explosive and incendiary bombs on the school, scoring many direct hits. Those pilots who realized that a ghastly error was taking place went on to carry out their assigned mission, attacking Shellhus with outstanding accuracy, but it was the Catholic school filled with children and not the Gestapo headquarters that bore the brunt of the attack that day.

Casualties in the school were tragically high. When Danish firemen finally got the blaze under control late that afternoon and began sifting through the wreckage, they found the bodies of eighty-six dead children, including forty-two who had been huddled together in a cellar shelter area, and seventeen adults.

Casualties at Shellhus were far lighter. Although the building had been rocked by high explosives and set afire by incendiaries, the death toll numbered only thirty-five. Among the dead were nine Danish prisoners housed in cells on the top floor and twenty-six Gestapo employees who had been caught on lower floors by the Mosquitos.

Despite the tragic bombing of the Jeanne d'Arc School, the Freedom Council reacted joyfully to the raid. Even while fires still burned in Shellhus and the school, the council sent a message to London via Ole Lippmann: "City wild with excitement about Shellhus bombing. Reliable sources maintain 30 Danish patriot hostages were liberated, among them two leaders. Warmest congratulations." The council's early figures were only slightly inaccurate. When a later count was made it was discovered that twenty-seven, not thirty, resistance leaders had actually made their escape, but these twenty-seven included the two Freedom Council members, Mogens Fog and Aage Schoch.

Four days later Ole Lippmann transmitted another message to

RAF Mosquitos bombed the lower floors of Copenhagen's Shellhus with pinpoint precision, hoping to destroy Gestapo files stored down below while saving the lives of Danish resistance leaders imprisoned on the top floor. *(Danish Ministry for Foreign Affairs)*

London that evaluated the results of the raid less enthusiastically. In the intervening period Lippmann had learned that those Gestapo personnel killed during the raid were office workers or minor functionaries. All the top German leaders whom the Allies had hoped to kill had escaped, including Gen. Gunther Pancke of the SS, Danish Gestapo chief Karl Heinz Hoffmann, and his chief aide, Otto Bovensiepen. They were all unexpectedly away from their offices that day, attending the funeral of a fellow Gestapo agent who had died of natural causes. Lippmann complained: "Whether *Carthage* has proved the great relief expected it is impossible to say. The damned funeral is responsible for a lot."

The raid, however, did give the Danish resistance some relief from Gestapo pressure. Most German files concerning resistance activity were destroyed in the fire that blackened Shellhus, and even though the Gestapo immediately set about trying to rebuild their secret files and dossiers, time was no longer on Germany's side. Within less than two months, German forces had laid down their arms in Denmark and Norway, ending for all time the threat against the Scandinavian underground forces.

20
In the Camps

Call the roll of the concentration camps and Scandinavian prisoners were there: Auschwitz in Poland, the largest killing center the world has ever known; Bergen-Belsen near Hannover, originally a "model camp" run by the Wehrmacht for prisoners of war, which was allowed to deteriorate until prisoners too weak to move shared bunks with rotting corpses; Ravensbrück, the women's camp fifty miles north of Berlin where German surgeons removed bones from the limbs of Polish women prisoners in the interest of science; Dachau, where salt water was forcibly pumped into the stomachs of military prisoners to test survival techniques at sea; Sobibor, Lublin, Treblinka, the awesome death camps in the east; Buchenwald, where Ilse Koch created lampshades out of human skin; Neuengamme, on the outskirts of Hamburg, a center for a string of satellite camps; and, finally, Theresienstadt, an old fortress town on the Eger River near Prague, Czechoslovakia, which the Nazis turned into a ghetto for the Jews of Europe.

In these camps, and in all the others scattered throughout Europe, Scandinavian prisoners could be found. As a large nationality grouping within the total concentration-camp population, however, Scandinavian prisoners suffered less than the prisoners of other nations. When the final tally was made after the war, it was discovered that the great majority of Scandinavians had survived the concentration camps. Most returned home even before the war ended, and they returned home in better physical and psychological condition than most of the other inmates—thanks in part to their own governments, which consistently tried to improve the conditions under which Scandinavians were imprisoned, and in part to the Germans themselves, who insisted on viewing the Scandinavians as fellow Aryans, deserving of better treatment than the Jews, gypsies, and Eastern Europeans who filled the camps. With the exception of the Norwegian Jews, Scandinavians received preferential treatment no matter where they were imprisoned. In Stutthof, Danish Communist prisoners fared better than non-Communist Poles. In Schildberg (Ostrzeszow, Poland), Norwegian officers interned in a private school in the suburbs lived a life only minimally less comfortable than they would have lived at home. One Norwegian naval officer commented after the war on the fact that not one Norwegian officer-prisoner tried to escape throughout the long period of imprisonment. "Why should we have tried to escape?" he said. "We lived too well in Schildberg."

Naturally, there were differences in the camp experiences of the various Scandinavian prisoner groups. The Germans treated Norwegian military-officer prisoners and Danish policemen prisoners more leniently than they did those Scandinavians arrested for political resistance work; and the Jews from both countries, like all Jews arrested throughout Europe, were set apart from the bulk of the prisoner population.

The Norwegian Jews arrived in Auschwitz in late 1942 at a time when that killing center, which was to represent the epitome of mass-execution methodology and technology, was still in its early stages of operation. For Jewish prisoners every aspect of life at Auschwitz was a preliminary to death: they faced hunger and exposure, overwork and unsanitary conditions, sadism and torture. Even if spared outright execution, the longer a person lived under concentration-camp conditions, the slimmer were his chances for survival. And time was not on the side of the Norwegian Jews. The women and children and the men who were too old or too weak to work went straight to the gas chambers. Able-bodied Norwegian Jews were put to hard labor. Most of them died of maltreatment, hunger, or disease before the end of 1943.

Odd Nansen (the architect son of the Norwegian polar explorer Fridtjof Nansen), himself imprisoned in Sachsenhausen for resistance work, heard of the plight of the Norwegian Jews in Auschwitz from a fellow inmate at Sachsenhausen. Nansen, who kept a diary of his years of imprisonment, described what he learned of the fate of the Norwegian Jews in Auschwitz:

> Yesterday I was talking to a Jew. There actually are a few of them alive in the camp. This one is named Keil, is a watchmaker, and has been in Norway. He came here from Auschwitz in Poland. An extermination camp of the worst type. What he told me about that camp was so horrible, so incomprehensible in ghastliness, that it defied all description. He told me that of the Norwegian Jews who were sent there . . . only a very few were still alive: about 25 was his estimate. Most of them were gassed. Whole transports went straight into the gas chamber and thence into the crematory. Men, women, and children of

all ages. . . . I asked about Dr. Becker and his brothers. They had all died in the gas chamber. The Kaplan family? Only one, the youngest boy, was still alive. He had been spared for some reason, probably because he was in a squad where they needed him. The whole Sherman family had been killed. And all, all the others! Keil himself had been spared because he was a watchmaker. They needed watchmakers to repair all the hundreds of thousands of watches they were stealing from the dead. I asked him about Rabbi Samuel. Oh, he died on the steps of a hut. He was returning from work, was done for, just collapsed and was dead. Klein, the Klein family; oh, they all died in the gas chamber. Muller, Bernstein and all, all the rest of them, dead all dead. Starved to death, beaten to death, worked to death, or sent to the gas chamber.

Of 760 Norwegian Jews deported to Auschwitz, only twenty-four survived the war, a survival rate of 3 percent. And most of those who did survive originally arrived in Auschwitz as healthy, active teen-agers whose strength was useful to German work-squad commanders and whose adaptability and resourcefulness were such that they could successfully lose themselves amid the general prison population.

In contrast to the Norwegian Jews, the Norwegian Army and Navy officers interned in 1942 received preferential treatment that enabled all but a few to survive the experience. The officers had been permitted to remain at liberty following Norway's capitulation in 1940, but early in 1942 German authorities, fearing that the officers could pose problems in the future, took steps to arrest all officers then at liberty. The arrests were conducted with all due consideration for military courtesy. Norwegian officers, ordered to report to Grini Prison outside Oslo, were given time to prepare for their internment. Lt. Col. R. Roscher Nielsen, a member of the Norwegian General Staff, was personally visited by a solicitous civilian German official who informed him that while he was being placed under arrest as a prisoner of war, he could take all the time he needed to pack his belongings for his internment. Nielsen spent the better part of the day packing what he thought he would need in prison, and then set off with the German for Gestapo headquarters in Victoria Terrasse; from there he was taken to Grini along with other members of the Norwegian General Staff.

The Norwegian officers were transported by train to Kristiansand, where they boarded a ship for Hamburg. Once in Germany, the officers boarded another train for a long trip through Germany to Schokken, Poland, the site of a POW camp for officers. As Nielsen remembered the trip, "everybody was very polite to us along the way." At Schokken, the Norwegian officers received food parcels from the Danish government which their camp commandant, "a very religious former German Air

Force officer," permitted them to keep unopened. (In all other camps, food parcels had to be opened immediately to prevent the food being stored for escape attempts.)

The Norwegians were later transferred from Schokken to Schildberg, where their treatment was even better. Food packages followed them to their new quarters as a matter of course. The Germans permitted excursions into town under loose escort and assigned Italian prisoners in the camp to cook for the Norwegians. At Schildberg the Norwegians lived a relatively normal life. One Norwegian officer, Lt. Rolf Scheen of the Navy, spent his time interviewing other naval officers on their experiences during the 1940 fighting; his manuscript on the Norwegian naval war was ready for publication in 1946.

Only near the end of the war did the Norwegian officers experience what they considered a "bad time." With Russian armies advancing from the east, the Germans ordered the Norwegians to march westward to escape the Russians. Although the conditions of their transfer were harsher than their life at Schildberg, the Norwegian officers still fared relatively well. Food they had in plenty, from parcels sent by the Danes, and when they tired of walking, they "bought their way onto the top of wagons" traveling west, using American cigarettes, which had been included in the food parcels, as hard currency. The Norwegians eventually reached Luckenwalde, south of Berlin, where they remained until liberation, listening to the progress of the war over small radio receivers which German authorities permitted them to keep. One day the Norwegians awoke to find that the German guards had fled. Minutes later combat-tested Russian troops of the Red Army entered Luckenwalde. Although the arrival of the Russian troops meant that their liberation was at hand, there were some among the Norwegians who looked upon the Red Army troops as descendants of Attila the Hun and who expressed gratification that it was not Russian troops, but German Wehrmacht soldiers, who had marched down Karl Johans Gate in Oslo in April of 1940.

Another group of Scandinavian prisoners who fared equally as well as the Norwegian officers was the Danish policemen arrested in the fall of 1944. Of all Danish prisoners, the policemen suffered the lowest fatality rate in the camps. Of 1,981 Danish police imprisoned in Germany, eighty-two died during the war or in the immediate postwar months, a fatality rate of 4 percent; many among them had been sick before their arrest. For their part, the Germans sought to soften the blow of imprisonment for the Danish police. Within three months of their arrest, several of the more seriously ill were permitted to leave the camps and return home, a concession granted to no other nationality group.

The Norwegian officers and the Danish police were not typical inmates of the Third Reich's concentration-camp system, however. The Norwegian officer POWs had not been captured in combat but had voluntarily turned themselves in when ordered to do so by German authorities; the Danish police, while arrested for political reasons, were always a group apart—in their eyes as well as in the eyes of the Germans—and never suffered the full weight of oppression that fell upon most other prisoners. Other imprisoned Scandinavians were more typical of the general population of the camps, yet even these groups received preferential treatment in comparison to non-Scandinavian prisoners. Most were interned at Sachsenhausen, one of the "better-class" camps. Sachsenhausen was not a death camp, nor was it designed to hold prisoners especially repugnant to the Third Reich. In its early days of operation there was even some talk of "rehabilitation" for its inmates. By the 1940s, however, few Germans bothered to express any thought of rehabilitation, but those Norwegians and Danes who found themselves at Sachsenhausen in the 1940s benefited to some degree from the more relaxed approach the Nazis had had in the 1930s, when the camp was first opened. But no matter what camp they found themselves in, most Scandinavian prisoners received preferential treatment. Norwegian students imprisoned in Buchenwald lived together in separate barracks, where they could maintain a sense of group solidarity that improved their chances for survival—other prisoner groups were thrown into barracks without regard to nationality. Camp authorities permitted Norwegians to wear long hair (an important consideration in winter) and civilian clothes (an important psychological factor) unlike other prisoners, whose heads were shaved and who usually lost their personal clothing upon arrival in camp. Samuel Steinman, a young Norwegian Jew who survived imprisonment in the east, reached Buchenwald in January of 1945. He described the Norwegian students as "living in quite another world from the rest of the prisoners." In all camps many Scandinavians found themselves working in German offices where they mingled with German workers and made influential contacts that could be used to improve life further for their fellow prisoners.*

Packages from home helped the Scandinavian prisoners survive. Starting as early as 1942, they received packages of food, clothing, and luxuries sent to them by their governments, the International Red Cross, and individual Scandinavian clergymen. For many Scandinavian

---

* For most non-Jewish Danish and Norwegian prisoners, the period between their arrest and their arrival at a concentration camp was often more traumatic, both physically and psychologically, than the actual camp experience. Prisoners suspected of resistance work were subjected to solitary confinement, interrogation, and torture. Threats and beatings were common; more extreme forms of torture were used whenever the Germans thought the situation required it. By the time their interrogation was over, many were already so battered that death or permanent impairment followed, even if they were subjected to no further hardships in camp.

prisoners, the packages meant the difference between survival and death. Mons Haukeland, a Norwegian Army officer imprisoned for resistance activity, and thus lodged with other political prisoners instead of regular Army officers, lost thirty-three pounds in the first three weeks of his confinement. Once he began to receive food parcels, however, his weight stabilized at a life-supporting level and remained at that level until the end of the war. By peacetime standards, all concentration-camp inmates were seriously underweight, but most Scandinavian prisoners managed to escape turning into *Musselmen,* as the walking skeletons who haunted the concentration camps were known.

At times the parcels from home provided the Scandinavians with embarrassing amounts of food and clothing. Odd Nansen described the arrival of packages for him in November, 1943:

> Yesterday I'm blessed if I didn't get three parcels, and the day before my sleeping bag plus a double blanket. Talk of grandeur. The sleeping bag is made to pull over one's head, and with that and a double blanket I'm all right for the winter. Inside the sleeping bag Kari had smuggled two kilos of glorious dairy butter. Also a big bag of Norwegian tobacco, and a good many cigarettes and a whole heap of plug. Tobacco, butter, crispbread and other good things, also a whole bottle of oil and a big jar of real honey. Now we can begin to share.

Lisa Borsum, a Norwegian woman of high social standing imprisoned for harboring resistance workers, recalled the receipt of packages in Ravensbrück:

> One day clothes awaited us. We received the following: a woolen frock, an apron, two pairs of stockings, a pair of shoes, two sets of underclothing and a pair of gloves. It was peculiar to see the change in us. Not only did we feel better, but the others treated us differently. The law of the snobs existed in Ravensbrück too. Everywhere we were treated with more respect. We became the elite. There was no question of being pushed in the lavatories any more. Someone even opened the door for me. Even the SS were interested. The food parcels poured in and we became popular among the other prisoners.

Other prisoners offered to wash the clothing of Norwegian women and to mend their stockings and dresses, in return for food. The Norwegians, Borsum reported, fell "for the temptation" and "became capitalists," permitting their clothes to be "washed in warm water by prisoners who knew how to 'organize' such things," at the cost of "only a little food." On another occasion, when eight barrels of herrings arrived in Ravensbrück for the Norwegian women, the camp commandant called the Norwegians together. Lisa Borsum described what happened next:

> We could take as much as we could eat, but we had to take it all at

once. They could not store the barrels. We could give away what we did not want ourselves, but not to people from the east, even though they were the ones who needed it most. We decided to give what was left over to the women in the block. Seldom has the block had such a feast. Everyone got something. Those hungry women loved the salt, fat herrings.

Danish prisoners also received life-supporting packages of food and clothing from their government, which refused to abandon them after their imprisonment in German concentration camps.

Even Danish Jews lived a relatively charmed life in the camps, in comparison to their Norwegian brothers and sisters. Unlike the Norwegian Jews, Danish Jews were not sent to one of the death camps in the east but to Theresienstadt, which was not a concentration camp as such but a whole community turned into a ghetto, officially described as a place where Jews could live a life of their own. In wartime Germany its name did not imply horror; in fact, many considered it a special favor for Jews to be permitted to live there. Wounded German Jewish veterans from the First World War, Jewish ex-servicemen who had earned the Iron Cross First Class or a higher decoration, descendants of mixed marriages, old people over sixty-five, and people who had made an outstanding contribution to German life—these were the favored classes officially permitted into Theresienstadt. Arrivals underwent preliminary searches by German SS officers and Czech police, but then they were left alone— Jews among Jews. Jewish officials of the Self-Administration of the Ghetto recorded all vital statistics of the new arrivals. Jewish doctors vaccinated those passing through its gates. While Theresienstadt did have an overall SS command, the town otherwise was a complete *Judensiedlung,* or Jewish settlement, populated by Jews and administered by Jews. The German attempt to depict Theresienstadt as a "model town" was surprisingly successful. Some Jews, seeking a privileged ghetto in which to pass the troubled war years, bought their way into Theresienstadt by purchasing life annuities in the ghetto from the Gestapo. Many even purchased their own train fares to reach the town.

Once inside Theresienstadt, however, these ghetto volunteers faced conditions only minimally better than in the typical concentration camp. Death from disease cut down many new arrivals; transports to the east eliminated many more. The figures for the first year proved especially frightening. Jewish workers started transforming the toylike fortress town into a ghetto prison in November, 1941. Between that time and the end of 1942, close to 110,000 Jews were admitted and duly registered on the arrival books. By the end of 1942, however, just under 50,000 of those admitted were still living there. Of the remaining 60,000, 16,000 had died in the ghetto while 44,000 more had been shipped to camps in the east.

For most Jewish arrivals in Theresienstadt, the ghetto proved more an assembly point on the road leading to the east than a privileged haven. By the end of the war close to 140,000 Jews had reached Theresienstadt, many with high hopes. Of this number, close to 87,000 were transported to the east, about 33,000 died in camp, 2,000 slipped away on their own initiative, and only 17,320 were still living in Theresienstadt when American troops liberated the town. Even in the Third Reich's "model ghetto," the odds for survival were no better than one in eight. The lucky ones included privileged "Old Reich" Jews, those Jews who had special connections or special friends, and the Danish Jews who arrived in Theresienstadt in the autumn of 1943.

The first handful of prominent Danish Jews arrested during the German crackdown of August 29, 1943, were sent immediately to Theresienstadt. Among them were Rabbi Friediger, the spiritual leader of the Jewish community, and Professor Erik Warburg, the king's physician, who continued his medical practice in the ghetto and soon became a popular doctor even with the Germans assigned to the town. The first sizable contingent of Danish Jews to reach Theresienstadt numbered 284 men, women, and children who had been arrested on the night of October 1 and 2; they arrived a few days after their arrest. One hundred and ninety additional Danish Jews reached town in two later transports, one in the middle of October and the second near the end of November.

Special ceremonies greeted the first mass arrival of the Danish Jews. The camp commander and senior SS officials presided at an "official reception" for the Danish Jews. Dr. Paul Epstein, Theresienstadt's Jewish elder and head of the town's "independent Jewish administration," welcomed the Danes in a fulsome speech. When Dr. Epstein had concluded, Rabbi Friediger, acting as spokesman for the Danish Jews, moved to have the new arrivals indicate their appreciation by a vote of thanks. This was duly carried out while German camp officials looked on with approval. Only after this carefully arranged ceremony had been concluded were the Danish Jews "processed" into Theresienstadt.

Danish officials began making inquiries on behalf of the Danish Jews even before the last group of 190 arrived in the ghetto. On October 22, the German Foreign Ministry's political department reported to Foreign Minister Ribbentrop that the Danish chargé d'affaires in Berlin had requested permission to send parcels to the Danish Jews and to visit Theresienstadt. Within less than a month, this intervention bore fruit. The Germans agreed to permit the Danish Red Cross to send parcels containing the deportees' own clothes to the ghetto and personal letters were also permitted; but for the time being the Germans refused to allow the Danes to send food or medicine or to visit the Jewish prisoners.

Danish government officials and civilian volunteers—among them many underground workers who had helped rescue the Jews—rushed to prepare the clothing parcels in the hope that if the Germans became accustomed to distributing clothing to the Danish Jews, they could eventually be persuaded to deliver parcels of food and medicines as well. Clerks in the Ministry of Social Welfare, working under the direction of the Ministry's permanent undersecretary, H. H. Koch, compiled lists of names and addresses of deported Jews, which they delivered to Professor Richard Ege and his wife, who had arranged shelter for hundreds of Jewish refugees during the month of October, 1943. The Eges, working in the open—for the project had been authorized by the Germans—recruited a small group of volunteers and sent them into the houses and apartments of the deported Jews to collect and pack their personal clothing. These parcels were sent off to Theresienstadt. Although Ege at times hid small packages of medicine among the clothes, he held back from sending a great quantity of medicine for fear of German reprisals. Nor did he dare send any food, which because of its bulk and weight could scarcely be hidden. But he continued to worry about the health of the deported Jews and soon came up with a novel way to circumvent the German ban on medicine and food. Ege took the German prohibition at face value: the Germans had proscribed the dispatch of either food or medicine and he would not send food or medicine. But Ege reasoned that the ban did not include vitamins, which were neither medicine nor food but which could give vital nutritional support. Once his plan had shaped in his mind, Ege persuaded Danish drug firms to turn out special multivitamin pills in large quantities. These he casually included among the parcels of clothing that German authorities had agreed to distribute, secure in the knowledge that if his deception were discovered, he could always argue that he had followed German instructions to the letter and had sent neither food nor medicine. The Germans, however, never learned of the vitamins packed amid the clothes; and within a few months, Ege and his associates had succeeded in sending enough vitamin pills to the Danish Jews in Theresienstadt to supply five hundred persons with all necessary vitamins for a full year. The Danish Jews had vitamins to spare.

Having outwitted the Germans once, Ege next sought to circumvent the German ban on food. Again he found a solution within the ground rules set up by the Germans themselves. Ege knew that the agreement reached between Danish and German authorities in November, 1943, permitted Danish Jews to receive personal mail. The following month, Ege learned to his amazement that personal mail reached the prisoners in Theresienstadt even if originally sent to their old addresses in Denmark: conscientious German postal workers handled this mail as they would other personal mail, tracing the whereabouts of the Jews and eventually delivering the letters to the recipients in the camp.

This discovery raised an intriguing question. If the German postal system operated so efficiently handling even prisoner mail as it would regular civilian mail, could it not be used to deliver food parcels as well? The Danes decided to test this hypothesis. In January, Ege recruited forty Danish clergymen, gave each the names of ten Jewish prisoners, and instructed them to send food parcels of varying sizes and shapes to individual prisoners on an irregular basis. The plan worked. The first illegal parcels of food reached the Theresienstadt Jews in February of 1944. Before long the clergymen in Denmark, with the help of underground assistants, were sending off as many as seven hundred food parcels a month, which German railway and postal authorities dutifully delivered to Theresienstadt. Even inside the ghetto, German postal authorities fulfilled their responsibilities and delivered the illegal food parcels to the Danish Jews. The German postal system proved so efficient that it even provided proof that the parcels were getting through to the recipients. The clergymen made a habit of requesting return receipts for each parcel sent. Some receipts arrived in the hands of the original senders within nine days of mailing.

Negotiations, meanwhile, continued between Danish and German officials to legitimize the dispatch of food and by June, 1944, the Germans finally officially agreed to permit what had been going on unofficially since February. From then to the war's end, Danish Jews in Theresienstadt regularly received packages of food that meant the difference between death and survival for many. During the five months before the first food packages arrived, twenty-four Danish Jews died in Theresienstadt. After the food started to arrive, the mortality rate dropped by more than 50 percent: the fourteen-month period between February, 1944, and April, 1945, when the Danish Jews were liberated, saw the death of twenty-seven more Danish Jews. For the Danish Jews, the parcels from home provided a psychological dividend as well as a nutritional aid. After the war Rabbi Friediger commented:

> All the psychic well-being that accompanied the better food was just as important as the physical, and the mind was fortified by the wonderful realization that at home they were thinking of us and working for us. For—so we thought—when those at home take care that we shall not starve to death, then they will also find ways and means of delivering us from this hell.

Negotiations continued on the Danish request to visit Theresienstadt to see at first hand how all the deported Jews were faring. The matter came up for decision before Adolf Eichmann, the *Obersturmbannführer* in charge of Section IV B4 (Evacuations & Jews) of the Gestapo, operating under the overall control of the Reich Security Main

Office (RSHA). Eichmann seemingly proved sympathetic. He visited Copenhagen in the winter of 1943 to discuss the Danish request with Werner Best and while there agreed that no Danish Jew in Theresienstadt would be transferred to one of the killing centers in the east. Eichmann also agreed that representatives of the Danish Red Cross and the Danish government could visit the camp, but he postponed setting a definite date for the visit. Eichmann filed a confirming telegram with Best after his return to Berlin:

THE RSHA AGREES IN PRINCIPLE TO THE PROPOSED VISIT, BUT THIS SHOULD NOT TAKE PLACE BEFORE THE SPRING OF 1944.

An internal Gestapo memorandum explained the reason for the delay: "The RSHA considered that for visual reasons the visit would be possible only after the 'trees in leaf' had made the landscape more beautiful." ·

Eichmann hoped to pull off a gigantic deception. Even though he headed the largest cold-blooded killing operation the world had ever known, he was still concerned with Germany's public image. He saw in the proposed Danish visit a means not only of calming the fears of the Danes about their Jewish prisoners, but the fear of the world at large about the fate of all imprisoned Jews. To accomplish his purposes, therefore, Eichmann determined to turn Theresienstadt into a "model ghetto," but for this, he needed time; there was much to do at Theresienstadt. Hence the delay until the trees could come to leaf. But the Germans were not content to leave everything to nature. They embarked on a massive face-lifting program inside Theresienstadt to make the ghetto appear as an attractive and pleasant place in which to live. Work began in early May. Able-bodied Jewish prisoners, taking orders from German foremen, applied fresh coats of paint to the run-down houses; gardeners planted shrubs along the major thoroughfares and swept and scrubbed the streets until they sparkled. Flower beds bursting with spring blossoms appeared as if by magic at key intersections. Construction workers built a new playroom for the children of the ghetto, and gaily decorated signposts sprang up at crossroads, directing the wondering residents to such places as the "CHILDREN'S PLAYGROUND," the "POST OFFICE," and other points of interest within Theresienstadt. By June the ghetto had been transformed into a sinister parody of a *gemütlich* Bavarian town. .

One problem remained, however. Despite the cosmetic work that had been done on Theresienstadt, the ghetto was still vastly overcrowded. More than 34,000 Jews were jammed into the ghetto and evidence of the crowded conditions appeared everywhere. No visiting team could fail to note the evidence, no matter how carefully they were guided on their tour. The Germans solved their problem with one slashing stroke. Three thousand recent arrivals, about half of them Dutch Jews, were shipped to Auschwitz, where most were put to death in the gas chambers. With the population density of Theresienstadt thus somewhat eased, the Germans proceeded to apply the finishing touches in preparation for the Danish visit. Danish prisoners moved into more luxurious living quarters, newly furnished and decorated with potted plants and gay prints. Only then did Eichmann agree to set a date for the Danish visit: his model ghetto would be open for outside inspection on June 23, 1944.

Dr. Paul Epstein, head of the ghetto's Jewish administration, summoned all Danish inhabitants to an emergency assembly on the night before the scheduled visit. Epstein came to the assembly directly from a meeting with the SS commandant, and acting on German orders, he proceeded to instruct the Danes on how they should conduct themselves the following day. Under no circumstances were they to voice any criticism of the town or its administration. If asked about the death of a relative, the Danes would on no account mention either malnutrition or an infectious disease. If asked how long they had been living in their quarters, the Danes were to reply "for some time." If these instructions were not heeded, Epstein warned, the Germans were prepared to stop all food parcels and to deport the transgressors to the east.

Final preparations for the visit went into effect on the morning of June 23. Sick and shabbily dressed inhabitants were ordered to remain out of sight through the entire day; tubercular patients were locked up in special "holding rooms"; Czechoslovakian police were relieved of duty for the day and SS troops ordered to don civilian clothing. Finally, in the new homes of the Danish prisoners, some members of each household were ordered to hide themselves in upstairs quarters so that the feeling of spaciousness in the downstairs rooms would have greater impact. Everything was thus in readiness for the three-man inspection team.

Two were Danes: Frantz Hvass of the Danish Foreign Ministry and Dr. Juel Henningsen of the Danish Ministry of Health. The third member, a Swiss doctor named Rossel, represented the International Red Cross. They arrived in midmorning and found a welcoming committee headed by Dr. Paul Epstein on hand to greet them. Epstein began by briefing the visitors on the structure and administration of the ghetto, which he euphemistically called "the Jewish settlement area." Then the inspection team set out for its tour, carefully guided by Dr. Epstein and German officials over a preselected path—past the park ablaze with flowering plants . . . past the Children's Pavilion, where nurses wheeled infants in baby carriages . . . into the "home for the aged" that had been carefully weeded of all tubercular and debilitated patients . . . and finally into the living quarters of the Danes.

Rabbi Friediger, acting as spokesman for the Danish Jews, welcomed the inspection team. The Danish members passed on to the rabbi the official greetings from King Christian X and from Bishop Fuglsang-Damgaard, Denmark's ranking churchman. The visitors were obviously pleased with what they saw, commenting among themselves on the spaciousness of the apartments visited. At no time, however, did they try to see the upper floors nor did they try to depart from their carefully conducted tour to strike out on their own to explore other sections of the ghetto. For their part, the Danish Jews complied perfectly with their instructions. They uttered not a word of complaint in the presence of the visitors nor did they hint, by word or gesture, that they were all actors in a giant farce produced by the Germans for an audience of three.

From the German point of view the inspection was an outstanding success. The three-man team left Theresienstadt that same day, apparently satisfied with the results of their visit. All three subsequently submitted written reports, and these pleased the Germans even more. Although there were minor variations in the tone of the reports, all three investigators reported that they found the town clean, the housing adequate, the people healthy, their clothes tidy, and the sanitary and health arrangements excellent.

Dr. Rossel, who wrote the most glowing report, personally thanked the German Foreign Ministry for the visit. Frantz Hvass expressed Denmark's appreciation. Even Dr. Henningsen, whose report was the most skeptical, gave Theresienstadt good marks. So pleased were the Germans with the fruits of their labors at Theresienstadt that they gave wide publicity to the reports and even produced a documentary film on the ghetto to disprove the "lies" being spread throughout the world about Germany's treatment of the Jews.

The Jewish inmates of Theresienstadt reacted with mixed emotions to the visit. Rabbi Leo Beeck complained of the investigators:

> They appeared to be completely taken in by the false front put up for their benefit. Many of the houses were so overcrowded that a tour through one of them would quickly have revealed the real state of things. The commission never bothered to climb one flight of stairs. Perhaps they knew the real conditions—but it looked as if they did not want to know the truth. The effect on our morale was devastating.

To others the mere arrival of an official inspection team brought hope. One prisoner wrote of his feelings, after the war:

> The optimism, exaggerated and mistaken though it may have been, prevented frustration, stimulated the spirit of resistance, and strengthened the will to live—and thanks to this the people held out. The nimbus surrounding the SS was dispelled and faith in the final collapse of the Germans grew.

Throughout Theresienstadt, in fact, news of the inspection raised hopes among prisoners of all nationalities. These hopes crumbled in the autumn of 1944 as massive new transports carried thousands eastward from Theresienstadt to their death in the killing camps.

There were seven separate transports during the month of October, 1944, alone. The last reached Auschwitz on October 30, bringing to more than eighteen thousand the number of Theresienstadt Jews transported to the east after the Danish–Red Cross visit in June.

For Danish Jews, however, the visit produced lasting improvements. Eichmann had permitted the visit to take place because he was confident the Danish Jews would make a good impression. Having fulfilled their part of the bargain, the Danish Jews were rewarded with even better living conditions: food rations increased and those Danes who had moved into showcase quarters for the visit were permitted to remain in them. There was one final reward. The Germans exempted all Danish Jews from the evacuation trains that rolled toward the east during the last hectic months before Russian armies overran the killing centers.

21
The White Busses

As early as 1942, when the first Scandinavian prisoners began arriving in German concentration camps in sizable numbers, a small group of men and women operating in the Scandinavian capitals as well as in Berlin itself secretly began to plan for the eventual release, or rescue, of the prisoners. Although the individuals involved belonged to no formal organization—consisting as they did of a mixed assortment of clergymen, educators, diplomats, journalists, and underground workers—they shared a common fear for the safety of the prisoners and the common belief that some organization should be developed to rescue the Scandinavians from the German camps when an opportune time presented itself.

A young Norwegian journalist, Odd Medboe, who had good connections in Germany, drew the first strings of the organization together in the summer of 1942, when he traveled through Germany and Denmark, ostensibly for journalistic purposes. Medboe had been selected by a group of influential Norwegians, including Oslo's chief medical officer, Andreas Diesen, to see what could be done to help the Norwegian political prisoners who were being sent to German camps in growing numbers.

Medboe stopped first in Berlin, where he conferred with Professor Didrik Seip, a Norwegian expert in ancient Scandinavian history. Seip had himself been arrested in 1940 because of his opposition to German occupying authorities, but he had been freed shortly afterward on the personal initiative of Heinrich Himmler, the German security chief, who was an avid reader of Scandinavian history and an admirer of Seip's work. Upon his release from prison, Seip was persuaded to continue his academic work in Berlin, where his personal safety could be assured by Himmler's protective interest and where he could not, even if he were so inclined, become active in resistance work.

At a luncheon meeting with Seip and several of his academic colleagues, Medboe outlined Norway's concern about the Scandinavian prisoners and asked if Seip knew of any way they could be helped. In Seip's opinion it was far too early to begin to seek the release of the prisoners through negotiations, but he and his colleagues promised to start recording the names and prison addresses of all Scandinavians against the day when detailed lists would be needed.

Medboe traveled next to Hamburg for talks with the Reverend Conrad Vogt-Svendsen, a Norwegian clergyman attached to the Norwegian Seamen's Mission. The mission had been established in the 1890s to care for the spiritual needs of Norwegian sailors in Germany. With the outbreak of World War II, the Germans continued to honor the original agreement under which the mission had been established and the mission remained fully staffed and operational throughout the war. Its clergymen, responding to wartime priorities, soon shifted their primary concern to the Scandinavians in German prisons. By the time Medboe talked with Vogt-Svendsen, the clergyman had already begun keeping detailed lists of the whereabouts of all Scandinavian prisoners that came to his attention. He readily agreed to continue with his work and to cooperate in any other way possible.

From Hamburg, Medboe moved on to Copenhagen, where he met the Danish resistance worker Rear Admiral Carl Hammerich, who quickly understood the need for a rescue organization to prepare for future developments. Hammerich suggested that the fish trucks that regularly ran between Denmark and Germany constituted a ready-made transportation system for use whenever needed. He too promised his fullest cooperation.

With Berlin, Hamburg, and Copenhagen "in hand" so far as preliminary planning was concerned, Medboe traveled to Stockholm, where he reported to Niels Christian Ditleff, the Norwegian Minister who had been assigned the task of looking after the affairs of Norwegian prisoners.

Throughout the rest of 1942 and through all of 1943, this informal network continued to build against the day when action would be required. Professor Seip in Berlin acquired twenty large trucks which were held in readiness, with extra gasoline for ten days of operation. In Copenhagen, the Danish Ministry of Social Welfare, on Hammerich's initiative, made large stores of food available to the Danish legation in Berlin, also for storage against the day of need. Hammerich also made good on his original suggestion for transportation and organized a large fleet of trucks, busses, private cars, and ambulances—the so-called Jutland Corps—that was ready to move on short notice. By the summer of 1944 the network was in place and ready to respond to whatever calls on its service developed.

The first call came on December 1, 1944, when German authorities notified Denmark that two hundred Danish policemen who had fallen ill in Buchenwald could be picked up and transported back to Denmark, at the Danes' convenience. The Jutland Corps had its first assignment, and it carried out its mission with smooth precision. Ten vehicles, including four busses and four ambulances, set out from Copenhagen on December 5 with several doctors and nurses aboard and enough food and medicine to care for the prisoners for one week. The convoy also carried enough schnapps to bribe any number of Germans along the way. By December 11 the convoy had made the round trip to Buchenwald and back and had safely delivered 198 Danish policemen to the Danish camp at Frøslev, where they received emergency medical care. Only one policeman had died en route. H. H. Koch, the permanent undersecretary of the Ministry of Social Welfare, greeted the first arrival of Danish prisoners with warm satisfaction. He had been deeply involved in negotiations leading to the transfer and he hoped that the first mission of the Jutland Corps would be the forerunner of other similar missions in the near future. As for Admiral Hammerich, the Dane most responsible for creating the Jutland Corps, he heard about its successful trip in a prison cell on the sixth floor of Gestapo headquarters in Copenhagen's Shellhus, where he was imprisoned with other Danish resistance leaders. Three months later he perished in the British bombing raid that destroyed the building.

Despite the groundwork that had been laid to rescue the Scandinavian prisoners, the year 1945 started with all but a handful of Scandinavians still in the concentration camps. The first mission of the Jutland Corps had not been followed by other transfers, and negotiations between the Scandinavian countries and Germany had bogged down. Germany, in its death throes, had no energy left to deal with the question of the release of prisoners, -no matter how sympathetic the individual German might be. And those Scandinavians trying to win release of prisoners had neither the personal prestige nor the political power to pry open the concentration-camp doors.

In February, 1945, a new figure entered the negotiations who did have the personal authority to ensure that his arguments would at least be heard. He was Count Folke Bernadotte, a high-ranking Swedish Army officer and an influential member of the Swedish nobility. Bernadotte was in charge of the Swedish organization that handled the internment of American and British airmen who had made forced landings in Sweden, and because of his work on behalf of the Allied airmen, he was warmly regarded by Allied authorities. Gen. Dwight Eisenhower invited Bernadotte to meet with him in liberated Paris. Eisenhower greeted Bernadotte with "unaffected friendliness," thanked him for what he had been able to do for Allied airmen in Sweden, and went on to discuss the general war situation and what neutral nations such as Sweden could do to help in the problems that would arise with the termination of hostilities.

While in Paris, Bernadotte also met with the Swedish consul general, Raoul Nordling, and his conversation with Nordling turned his thinking about impending problems toward more specific channels. Bernadotte knew that Nordling had been instrumental in negotiating the release of hundreds of French prisoners from German prisons in Paris, before the Germans surrendered the French capital. Until Nordling had intervened, the Germans had planned to deport large numbers of French men and women held in Paris prisons to prisons inside Germany. Nordling had convinced the Germans to leave the prisoners behind, for humanitarian reasons. Bernadotte's conversation with Nordling sparked a thought in Bernadotte's mind—couldn't he "do something similar for those who were languishing in German concentration camps"? Bernadotte's concern was heightened by rumors that German authorities meant to liquidate all prisoners in the concentration camps as Germany neared collapse.

On his return to Stockholm, Bernadotte conferred with the Norwegian Minister, Ditleff, who urged him to use his influence and prestige to persuade Nazi authorities to free Scandinavian prisoners from the camps before the end of the war. Bernadotte agreed to make the attempt. However, he knew that for any such effort to succeed he had to negotiate with a German official of the highest rank, one who was capable of acting independently: no one lower than the head of the SS, Reichsfuehrer Heinrich Himmler, would suffice. Himmler had the authority and the position to act independently, and Bernadotte knew that on many occasions Himmler had expressed a liking for the Scandinavian countries and their peoples. Bernadotte believed that if he could meet personally with Himmler, he might win concessions.

Bernadotte traveled to Berlin in February, 1945, ostensibly to discuss the repatriation of Swedish-born women who had married Germans, but actually to contact Himmler.

Himmler, however, was unavailable; as commander of the German armies on the Oder front, he was away from the capital for long stretches of time. Bernadotte could get to see only Himmler's second-in-command, Ernst Kaltenbrunner, the chief of the security police. Kaltenbrunner received Bernadotte politely. He offered the Swedish diplomat cigarettes and wine (Bernadotte noted that the cigarettes were Chesterfields and the wine Dubonnet) and then asked the reason for his visit. Bernadotte, who was not ready to reveal the real reason, replied that relations between Sweden and Germany were "extremely bad" and suggested that Himmler occupied a position "that would make it possible for him to adopt measures calculated to improve Swedish-German relations." Bernadotte's response intrigued Kaltenbrunner. What exactly did Bernadotte have in mind? he asked. Bernadotte refused to elaborate, contenting himself merely to repeat that a meeting with Himmler could improve Swedish-German relations. Kaltenbrunner, impressed with Bernadotte's reputation and presence, agreed to pass Bernadotte's request for a personal meeting with Himmler on to Himmler and to use whatever influence he had to arrange the interview.

Kaltenbrunner was as good as his word. Within a few days, a meeting was arranged between Bernadotte and Himmler. It took place on February 12 in a large hospital at Hohen-Luchen, seventy-five miles north of Berlin. Himmler greeted Bernadotte wearing a green military uniform, without decorations, horn-rimmed spectacles perched on his nose. Bernadotte thought he looked like a "typical unimportant official." In the conversation that followed, Himmler proved affable and open, with a sense of humor the Swede thought tended "rather to the macabre."

Bernadotte opened the discussion by bringing up the "hostile feelings" Sweden felt toward Germany and suggesting that steps could be taken to improve relations. Himmler refused to concede that Germany was at fault and produced "a number of arguments to illustrate the innocence and humaneness of Germany's policy." The talks continued in an animated fashion, touching on several related topics. Finally, Himmler asked if Bernadotte had any concrete proposals to improve relations between the two countries. Bernadotte hesitated—then proposed that Germany release Scandinavian prisoners from concentration camps in Germany for transport and internment in Sweden. Himmler reacted as if he had been struck. "If I were to agree to your proposals," he stated, "the Swedish papers would announce that the war criminal Himmler, in terror of punishment for his crimes, is trying to buy his freedom."

Only on one condition would Himmler consider Bernadotte's request: Sweden and the Allies would have to give some concession in return for the release of the prisoners, possibly an assurance that sabotage would cease in Norway. Bernadotte replied that the concession requested by Himmler was "quite unthinkable." Himmler replied that without a concession he could not release the Scandinavian prisoners.

Despite his refusal, Himmler was not ready to see Bernadotte go away empty-handed. On Bernadotte's request he agreed to collect all Norwegian and Danish prisoners into two camps where the Swedish Red Cross could care for them, and he also agreed that aged and sick prisoners, as well as women prisoners with children, would be allowed to return to Norway and Denmark after having been assembled in the camps. The outcome of the first negotiating session with Himmler pleased Bernadotte. While he had not won Himmler's agreement to the release of all

Scandinavian prisoners, he had won agreements that would bring some Scandinavians home and gather others together into selected camps so they could be more easily cared for and helped. To show his appreciation for the interview, Bernadotte, knowing Himmler had a deep interest in Scandinavian runic inscriptions, presented the head of the SS with a seventeenth-century Swedish work on the subject, a gesture that "noticeably affected" Himmler, who expressed his gratefulness that Bernadotte should have thought of giving him this particular gift, considering conditions as they then stood.

Himmler quickly made good his promises. A few days after the meeting, Bernadotte called on the German Minister of Foreign Affairs, Joachim von Ribbentrop, to report on his visit with Himmler, and found that Ribbentrop knew all about the agreement; a memorandum from Himmler had informed him of all major subjects discussed. Ribbentrop hastened to assure Bernadotte that he would not oppose the promises Himmler had made: Scandinavian prisoners would be assembled at two camps and selected Scandinavian prisoners would be freed. But Ribbentrop brought up one practical difficulty that had previously gone unmentioned: since all German vehicles were required for the war effort, Sweden would have to provide the busses and trucks for the transport of prisoners. It was, Ribbentrop assured Bernadotte, a minor logistics problem, but one which the German Foreign Minister thought it wise to mention.

Before leaving Berlin, Bernadotte received additional confirmation that Himmler's promises had been made in good faith. During a conversation with Brigadefuehrer Schellenberg, one of Himmler's key aides, Schellenberg commented that Himmler had authorized him to inform Bernadotte that all Norwegian and Danish prisoners would be assembled not in two camps, but in the Neuengamme concentration camp near Hamburg, and that Bernadotte should make plans to have a Red Cross column of trucks ready to move in the near future. Schellenberg also told Bernadotte that Himmler had mentioned their meeting with pleasure, especially noting Bernadotte's kindness in presenting him with the gift volume on runic inscriptions.

Bernadotte immediately returned to Stockholm, where he reported the outcome of his meetings in Berlin to his government and to Gen. Helge Jung, the commander-in-chief of the Swedish Army. Jung drafted orders for a detachment of thirty-six busses, twelve trucks, and various support vehicles, including kitchens, motorized workshops, and ambulances, to assemble at the earliest possible time in Sweden's southernmost province of Skåne. Regular Swedish Army personnel manned the Swedish vehicles, which were painted white for the mission and bore giant red crosses on their sides and roofs. The Swedish soldiers took note of the humanitarian purpose of their assignment and replaced their military insignia with the insignia of the International Red Cross.

The White Busses, as the Swedish detachment soon became known, sailed by boat for Denmark on March 11 and reached Odense that same day. The following day, the detachment traveled to Jutland, where vehicles of the Danish Jutland Corps joined the convoy. Later that afternoon, the entire convoy, now numbering eighty-seven vehicles, crossed the Danish-German frontier and made its way through the bombed-out German cities of Flensburg, Kiel, and Lübeck before reaching Schloss Friedrichsruh, where the Swedes established their headquarters in the castle of Prince Otto von Bismarck and his wife. From Schloss Friedrichsruh, the Danish vehicles moved off independently—one small convoy headed for Buchenwald to pick up seventy-five Danish policemen and another to Mühlberg to pick up sixty-five more Danish police. The main convoy headed for Neuengamme, where the Scandinavian prisoners were being assembled.

In the camps themselves, Scandinavian prisoners heard the rumors of their impending release with hope, tinged with disbelief. Yet the war obviously was nearing an end and the rumors about the White Busses persisted. Odd Nansen heard the rumors in Sachsenhausen on February 25, two weeks after Bernadotte's first meeting with Himmler.

> When we got back from work there was big news. The Swedish Red Cross has been negotiating with Germany, in fact direct with Himmler, and the negotiations have led to a favorable result. We're to leave he‹ . . . to Neuengamme which is to be an assembly camp for all Norwegians. Neuengamme by the way is known to be a bad camp.

The next day Nansen recorded this comment on the day's developments:

> The rumors are spinning on, and the fairest and most joyful prospects are being unrolled. We're to leave here in sunshine buses and to be waited on and tended by Swedish Lottas. . . . But otherwise things are just the same. We marched out to work today as usual.

In Ravensbrück, Lisa Borsum first heard about the White Busses from a fellow prisoner known for her rumormongering and discounted the news. But the rumors built on each other; each day more people added more details. One prisoner finally found the courage to enter the commandant's office and ask if the rumors were true. The reply was affirmative. All Scandinavian prisoners were to be freed, including the *Nacht und Nebel* prisoners.

By mid-March the White Busses had begun transporting Scandinavian prisoners from various camps to Neuengamme. By April 1 several thousand Scandinavian prisoners had been assembled in the camp—2,200 Danes and Norwegians from Sachsenhausen, 600 Scandinavians from

Dachau, 1,600 Danish policemen from Buchenwald, smaller contingents from other camps. Their transfer triggered strong emotions, both among those who were directly involved and those prisoners who were forced to stand by and watch. Odd Nansen, one of the first to reach Neuengamme from Sachsenhausen, was appalled to learn that German authorities had assigned the Scandinavians to buildings already occupied by prisoners of other nationalities. As the Scandinavians arrived, the former inmates were being bodily thrown from the buildings. "The misery passed all bounds and baffled all conception," Nansen wrote. "In every bed there were three or four, indeed sometimes five or six men." Many of those evicted had disintegrated into *Mussulmen,* walking skeletons barely able to move under their own power. Yet they too were thrown out of their bunks. Nansen continued:

> Here come thousand after thousand of "well fed" Norwegians and Danes and to make room for us, many times that number of other prisoners—Russians, Poles, Ukrainians, Dutchmen, Frenchmen and others—have to clear out of their blocks and squeeze together in rooms that were overcrowded already. Now every Norwegian and every Dane is to have his bunk: one man in each bunk! Of course it causes bad feeling. To other prisoners, we, who were to blame, must appear in the most unfavorable light.

To make room for the incoming Scandinavians, the Germans occasionally requisitioned the White Busses to remove prisoners from Neuengamme to camps nearby. Nansen witnessed one such transport of *Mussulmen:*

> All the *Mussulmen*—most of them already doomed—lit up with ineffable joy and hope when they saw the white Red Cross busses and grasped that they were to leave in them. It was a pitiful sight. Most of the *Mussulmen* had too little strength left to hoist themselves onto the running boards by their arms. They had to be lifted in. Then off they went . . . to Braunschweig, and there they were marched into a new hell. Again the barbed wire closed round them.

Although the Scandinavians reacted to the plight of the other prisoners with horror and pity, the inhuman conditions of the camps had dehumanized them as well; the law of survival operated with full power. One Swedish driver, after transporting a group of *Mussulmen* to another camp where they were almost certain to die, commented coldly to Nansen: "Charity begins at home." Scandinavian women imprisoned in Ravensbrück eagerly seized their daily issue of bread as they left camp to board the White Busses, even though they knew that they could expect to be fed soon and that many of their former comrades were starving to death. "One never knew what lay in store," explained Lisa Borsum. "We were entitled to our day's ration and we were determined to take it." A male prisoner who had been imprisoned in Buchenwald with the Danish policemen bitterly recalled their departure:

> When they were fetched by the Bernadotte buses, they put all the bread and food they could carry in their bags to take it along from the camp. Before the eyes of starving, dying half-naked prisoners they carried food, clothes and blankets with them.

Another Buchenwald prisoner complained about the Danish policemen:

> Among all the prisoners there was solidarity, but the Danish policemen were outside it. The others in the camp starved. The policemen had plenty of Red Cross parcels. It never occurred to them to give anything away.

The arrival of the Danish police in Neuengamme also produced bitterness among other Danish prisoners. Frederik Olsen, a Dane who had been arrested for "Communist activity" in his hometown of Aalborg, reached Neuengamme in late March, 1945, shortly before a group of Danish police arrived. Olsen was questioned about his experiences after the war:

> QUESTION: Were there Danish policemen when you arrived?
>
> OLSEN: The policemen weren't there when we arrived, but during the last days of March the first arrived. About a hundred. I think they came from Buchenwald. They were to be collected for the repatriation. They were warmly and well dressed. They drove on the place for roll call. There they unloaded their luggage.
>
> QUESTION: Luggage?
>
> OLSEN: They had lots of luggage. Big bags. Suitcases. The bags were solid English goods.
>
> QUESTION: How . . .
>
> OLSEN: Well, later on we were told that they had bartered the food that they had not been able to stuff themselves with. They had parcels from home and from Sweden too. They had plenty of bread and other good things too.
>
> QUESTION: And you stood there looking?
>
> OLSEN: That was what we did. Shortly after the arrival of the policemen, two of them opened the door of the barracks where we lived. A detective from Aalborg and a police commissioner. They looked around. The leader of our barracks was called Jacob. He walked up to the two policemen. "We need a couple of men," snarled the police commissioner.

"Need a couple of men, what do you mean?"

"To carry the luggage into the barrack where we are going to live."

I can see them standing there. They wanted us Danish prisoners to carry their stuff in.

Not all Scandinavian prisoners arrived in Neuengamme in such good shape. Norwegian prisoners from Natzweiler arrived in particularly weak condition. They had lived under especially harsh conditions at Natzweiler and had been transferred to a camp south of Stuttgart in March where they received even smaller food rations. Nansen commented on their arrival:

> Everyone was starving. The camp [near Stuttgart] was so tucked away that the Swedes would scarcely have found it if the Norwegian seamen's pastor in Hamburg hadn't been so indefatigable in tracing the Norwegians who were hidden away there.

Scandinavians in Bergen-Belsen suffered fiercely from disease, as did all inmates imprisoned there. Ten Norwegians and one Dane arrived in Neuengamme from Bergen-Belsen on April 8. All suffered from typhus. They brought news of thirteen other Scandinavians who had died of typhus on the day of their departure. Three days later more Scandinavians arrived in Neuengamme from Bergen-Belsen. Nansen noted in his diary: "A transport of Danes came in today. Two hundred from one of the outlying squads. Most of them were skeletons. A number couldn't stand."

But daily during the last weeks of March, 1945, and the first weeks of April, the Scandinavian contingent in Neuengamme grew steadily in numbers, the hopes of the inmates rising with the prospect of early release. By April 1, however, the order for their release still had not been given. Another negotiating session was needed. Count Folke Bernadotte again journeyed to Hohen-Luchen for another meeting with Himmler. This time he found Himmler "somber" and "nervous." Bernadotte informed Himmler that the transportation of prisoners to Neuengamme was proceeding but that conditions inside the camp were "vile." He urged Himmler to permit the release of all prisoners immediately. Again Himmler hesitated. He was still apprehensive of Hitler's reaction and he feared the repercussions that would come if he permitted the freeing of all Scandinavian prisoners without gaining concessions in return. "If all were to be sent at the same time," Himmler commented, "it would attract too much attention."

Bernadotte understood what Himmler was suggesting. He quickly proposed a staggered-release program which would permit the early release of those prisoners considered least offensive in the eyes of the Germans while providing for the eventual release of all Scandinavian prisoners. Bernadotte suggested that the first prisoners to be released should be the Danish policemen who had been imprisoned only since the autumn of 1944. German authorities viewed the Danish police as a sympathetic group who had been imprisoned only because of the exigencies of war. The second group, Bernadotte suggested, should be made up of invalids, who would be taken to Sweden for medical care. Next a small number of Norwegian students should be freed, with their actual number being determined by German authorities. Finally, Bernadotte suggested, a certain number of Scandinavian civilians should be freed, with the approval of the camp commander.

Himmler agreed to this proposal. The staggered-release system would provide him with the protection he needed while providing Bernadotte with the assurance that, once the transfers were started, they would continue until all Scandinavian prisoners had been freed. But first the release of those prisoners considered least repugnant to German eyes—the Danish policemen.

Four hundred and fifty Danish policemen left Neuengamme in the White Busses on April 3. They were closely followed by 594 more policemen on April 5. The first "sick transport," consisting of seventy-four Norwegian, twenty-four Danish, and two French women, left Neuengamme on April 8 and crossed into Denmark, where they were received by Danish Red Cross workers. The women went on to Sweden the following day.

By mid-April, the White Busses were making trips almost daily, delivering their overjoyed passengers into the welcoming hands of Danish relief workers. On April 10, another 473 policemen reached Denmark; on April 11, a second "sick transport," consisting of forty-nine men and eighteen women, crossed the border; on April 12, 101 men were freed; on April 14, 246 more men arrived in Denmark; on April 16, 258 men; and on April 18, 137 men were released from Neuengamme while 420 Danish Jews boarded Swedish busses in Theresienstadt for the long and perilous trip through Germany to Denmark.

The next day, April 19, Himmler agreed to free all Scandinavian prisoners, regardless of classification. The situation by then was approaching chaos: American troops under Gen. George S. Patton had thrust into Czechoslovakia; Russian troops were penetrating Berlin; northern Holland had been liberated; and resistance in the Hamburg area was crumbling. Inside the concentration camps all controls practically disappeared.

The Danish Jutland Corps responded quickly to Himmler's order. Practically overnight a fleet of ninety-four busses with accompanying ambulances, motorcycles, and trucks sped into Germany. During the two days of April 20 and 21, the Jutland Corps transported 4,255 Danes and

Norwegians out of Neuengamme to the Frøslev camp in Denmark. In Frøslev, prisoners were still under the ultimate jurisdiction of Gestapo guards, but conditions there were much better—Danish doctors treated the ill; Danish relief workers provided food and clothing. Bernadotte visited the Frøslev camp in late April and reported to his government that the spirits of the Danish and Norwegian prisoners were high. "The mere fact of having left Germany behind them made their hearts lighter," he commented.

As the end of April approached and German resistance crumbled everywhere, some concentration-camp commandants loaded prisoners onto freight trains that took off for unknown destinations. Bernadotte noted that at Neuengamme "the non-Scandinavians were pushed into freight trains whose destination no one knew. Questioned about it, the German commandant shrugged his shoulders: *'Keine Ahnung* [I have no idea].' The freight trains, like others of those ghostly trains that had so often steamed eastward in German-occupied countries in the years just past, disappeared in the distance with their human cargo."

Some of these ghost trains headed for Denmark. One train of fifty-six cars reached the Danish city of Padborg on April 30 with four thousand Ravensbrück women inside. All the women were non-Scandinavian. H. H. Koch of the Danish Ministry of Social Welfare was on hand when the train arrived:

> It was a strange and sad sight. They tried to keep the women in the cars, better to be able to control them, but it was hopeless. As soon as the doors were opened, they jumped out and started to cook potatoes, in small pans which they had with them. They cooked by small fires along the railroad track.

Danish officials thought the April 30 transport was the last and the worst. They were mistaken. On May 2, they heard that another train, this one consisting of sixty cars carrying 2,800 non-Scandinavian women, was on its way. The women were described as half-naked and crying with hunger. H. H. Koch described their arrival in Padborg: "They leaped out of the cars and attacked everything that might be eaten, including potato peels and grass. The people threw some bread to them and they fought like wild animals over the bread."

For Scandinavian women, the experience was happier. Ravensbrück prisoner Lisa Borsum rode to freedom on Swedish busses which looked to her like a "garland of white hope." On the trip to Denmark, Borsum and her fellow prisoners "danced in the aisles while moving from seat to seat to exchange happy impressions with other women." Each bus carried one Swedish attendant who was responsible for providing assistance as needed and a Gestapo guard who was responsible for maintaining order on the bus. But the attitude of the Gestapo men had changed as well. Many joined in the festivities, smiling at the happy women and sharing the food provided by the Swedes.

Once the women were inside Denmark, welcoming committees provided food and friendly smiles. Hot chocolate flowed in seemingly endless quantities and Danish women kept outdoor picnic tables laden with enormous mounds of bread, pots of rich butter, and cheeses of all varieties. But what impressed the Ravensbrück women most poignantly and what convinced them that their concentration-camp ordeal was over was not the food the Danes set before them but the fact that Danish women had placed fine white tablecloths on each table and had taken the extra time to decorate the tables with small bouquets of spring flowers.

Nine thousand Norwegians were imprisoned in Germany for various lengths of time during the war years. The great majority survived the ordeal although the death rate varied widely among different prisoner groups. Practically all Norwegian Jews—736 out of 760—were killed. Practically all Norwegian officers survived—1,169 returned out of a total number of 1,175. Among 624 imprisoned Norwegian students, there were seventeen deaths; among 271 Norwegian policeman, there were thirteen deaths; among two hundred Norwegian women sent to Ravensbrück, there were five deaths. The largest Norwegian group imprisoned in Germany consisted of men and women arrested for resistance work or political activity, or because they were "common criminals." *
This group numbered 5,970; the deaths among them numbered 753.

The final death toll for all Norwegians imprisoned in German concentration camps showed that 1,530 Norwegians had perished while in German custody, a death rate of approximately 17 percent. If the Norwegian Jews had not been practically eliminated, the Norwegian death rate would have been 9 percent.

Variations in the death rate among Danish prisoner groups were less than among Norwegian groups. There were eighty-two deaths from among 1,981 imprisoned Danish policemen; thirty-nine deaths from among 137 frontier gendarmes; fifty-eight deaths from among 474 Danish Jews; 124 deaths from among four hundred Danes imprisoned as "common criminals"; and 259 deaths from among 2,983 political prisoners. Overall Danish figures show that from a total of 5,975 Danes imprisoned in Germany, there were 562 deaths, a death rate of just over 9 percent.

---

* In Norway, as well as in other countries occupied by the Germans during World War II, the classification "common criminal" did not carry the same definition as it does during periods of peace. The Germans stretched the definition of common criminal to include many whose "crimes" had strong political overtones.

The combined totals for Scandinavian prisoners show that 14,975 men and women from Denmark and Norway were imprisoned in Germany. Deaths from this number totaled 2,092, for a combined Scandinavian death rate of under 15 percent, far lower than the death rate for other nationality groups. The support given to Scandinavian prisoners by their governments helped keep the death rate low. So did the German attitude toward Scandinavian prisoners. Near the end of the war, when the Swedish White Busses and the Danish Jutland Corps vehicles were shuttling Scandinavian prisoners to safety each day, the Reverend Conrad Vogt-Svendsen, one of the Hamburg-based Norwegian clergymen, asked a Nazi official why Germany was willing to save the Scandinavian prisoners. The German official did not have to ponder his answer. "It is now time," he assured the Norwegian churchman, "to save the best of the remaining people of Western Europe."

22
Liberation

German forces in Denmark during the last days of the war in Europe numbered 136,000 Army troops, 19,000 naval personnel, and an additional 17,000 Luftwaffe airmen under the overall command of Gen. Georg Lindemann, a choleric and impulsive officer who had served with no special distinction on the Eastern Front. His ground troops were equally undistinguished. About 10 percent of the Army was non-German—Hungarians mostly, with smaller numbers of Russian and Polish volunteers. As for the German troops themselves, they were either elderly soldiers, poorly trained recruits, or Wehrmacht men convalescing from wounds received in other theaters of war. Men of this low fighting caliber were deemed sufficient for the occupation and defense of Denmark. No elite unit ever served on Danish soil.

German forces in Norway presented a different picture. Troop strength there never dropped below 300,000 and reached a peak of between 400,000 and 420,000 at Christmastime, 1944, when General Rendulic's Twentieth Mountain Army began arriving in the country en masse from Finland. Unlike the German troops stationed in Denmark, the German forces in Norway were always among the best in the German Army, for Hitler insisted that only well-trained and well-equipped units could defend the country against the British invasion he was convinced would come.

But Hitler's fears of a British invasion never materialized, and for the average German soldier duty in Norway came as close to peacetime service as was possible in war. Drill followed drill and the dull routine of garrison life was seldom interrupted by action. Only in the far north did German troops see combat, against weak Norwegian and Finnish patrols that occasionally made forays against German positions in the closing weeks of the war. Throughout the rest of the country, German units regularly observed Sunday as a day of rest and relaxation even as the Third Reich was going down in flames, a fact which infuriated Lt. Gen. Franz Boehme, who took over the armed-forces command in Norway in January, 1945, after General Falkenhorst returned to Germany for a new assignment. Boehme considered the Sunday holidays his soldiers were enjoying a "regrettable failure to appreciate our total situation." Boehme was hard put, however, to suggest how Sundays should be spent. His best recommendation was that they should be devoted to pursuing "courses in National Socialist leadership."

Starting in the autumn of 1944, SOE-trained Norwegian agents began arriving back in Norway to prepare for the day of liberation. The agents came with orders to help organize Milorg units to take over Norwegian industries, power plants, and transportation lines when the Germans surrendered. They were not, however, to engage German troops in combat or to initiate sabotage actions without specific prior approval from London.

When the SOE agents arrived they found that the Milorg organization existed primarily on paper. One of the agents, Ragnar Ulstein, who had escaped to England by boat in 1942, returned to the "silent district" of Sogn og Fjordane, south of Ålesund, in October, 1944, and quickly discovered why it was so silent. Not one man was active in the military resistance. Ulstein had to start recruiting from the ground up. By Christmas he had recruited two hundred men, but they were without arms, uniforms, or training. And to Ulstein's dismay, he found that many former Norwegian Army officers who had escaped imprisonment in Germany were unwilling to help him in his mission. On one occasion, when Ulstein tried to recruit a Norwegian major who had served in the pre-war Norwegian Army, the officer demanded assurances of absolute safety for his family, which Ulstein could not provide, and then stipulated that under no circumstances would he go underground. At that point Ulstein requested that the former major forget the whole conversation. Only after the German surrender did the major offer his services to command Milorg troops during the first days of the liberation, and Ulstein, although bitterly disappointed in the officer's earlier response, "gladly accepted" his offer, for the shortage of officers was still critical.

Another SOE agent, Arne Kjelstrup, who had participated in the successful sabotage operation against the Norsk Hydro heavy-water plant in 1943, parachuted back into Norway in October, 1944, this time on a mission to organize Milorg units to guard the Nore area. He also had to build an underground military unit from scratch. He found recruitment difficult. Only in the spring of 1945, with the end of the war clearly in sight, did recruiting become somewhat easier. By May, 1945, he had sixty men on active duty, housed in tents in the countryside, plus another nine hundred men on reserve. They were, however, under strict orders to avoid fire fights with the Germans. Kjelstrup's unit, like all other Milorg units in Norway, could shoot at the Germans only if they themselves were directly attacked.

Norwegian SOE agent Alv Johnsen parachuted into Norway in February, 1945, to work with Milorg units in District 11, in the Østfold area near Sweden. His first meetings with Milorg leaders dealt a "stunning blow" to Johnsen's expectations. District 11, he found, had only a few active and competent men. The field reports on which London had based its evaluations had been misleading. The number of men, their state of training, and the number of weapons were all exaggerated. Johnsen was astonished to learn that only a small percentage of the men listed as members of the Milorg companies actually knew they were on the rolls as Milorg men. Even the "active" men were poorly trained and unarmed.

Johnsen was also surprised by living conditions among the civilians. Allied and Norwegian-exile authorities in London had promulgated the view that the German occupation of Norway was excessively harsh and that starvation among the civilian population was common. To Johnsen's surprise, he found that the civilians in District 11 had sufficient food and that they could lead a normal life under the German occupation provided they refrained from active resistance work. Johnsen's return to Norway thus provided a double shock. Not only had the intensity of the Norwegian resistance been exaggerated in London but also the harshness of life under the German occupation. Johnsen faced the difficult task of organizing an active resistance force to work against an occupying power that the population as a whole had come to accept as a comparatively benign presence. Johnsen did succeed in signing up six hundred men by war's end, but even then he considered that only fifty of them were sufficiently trained or motivated for military action if the call for action ever came.

Despite the difficulties under which they worked, SOE agents such as Ulstein, Kjelstrup, Johnsen, and others who dropped back into Norway during the last months of 1944 and the first months of 1945 eventually did establish a series of military bases in the mountains of Norway where arms and equipment could be received and stored. The first base, "Elg," was established in south-central Norway. Elg was followed by "Bjorn West," north of Bergen, and by "Varg," in the mountains north of Kristiansand. The SOE and the Norwegian High Command in London shared joint responsibility for the bases, while field command responsibility was entrusted to Norwegian nationals who had been trained by the SOE in Britain. All bases, however, operated under orders to refrain from combat unless attacked, an order which earned for the officers and men of the mountain detachments the sobriquet of "blueberry pickers."

Milorg leaders in Norway welcomed London's instructions to avoid combat, believing, as they did, that Norway had everything to lose in an open fight that pitted Milorg's untrained battalions against Germany's 400,000 first-line troops. On those rare occasions when aggressive SOE leaders, itching for combat before the end of the war, led Milorg troops into action, top Milorg officials made their displeasure known immediately. In April, 1945, SOE agent Peter Holst, commander of an Elg sub-base in the Eggedal, permitted his force of about ninety Norwegian soldiers to maintain their positions in the face of a sweep by approximately 150 German troops. The Norwegians, well dug in, repulsed the attack easily but lost seven men in the fighting. Despite the losses, Holst was pleased with the outcome of the engagement. His Milorg force had performed well under fire: they had stood their ground and wounded or killed at least fifty Germans. Local Milorg leaders, however, were furious that he had not retired from his positions before the Germans arrived and complained to Holst's superior at Elg, charging Holst had ignored orders by going into action "against a superior force" and that Holst personally bore a "great responsibility" to the dependents of the men killed in action. Other Milorg officials joined in denouncing Holst's initiative. The controversy was smoothed over (Holst's father moved in influential circles among the Norwegians in London) but bitterness over the affair lingered on into the postwar period. In an attempt to defuse the passions aroused by the fight, Jens Christian Hauge, the commander-in-chief of all Milorg forces in Norway, put out the explanation that Holst's force had been surprised by the Germans and had been forced to defend itself, but local Milorg leaders in the Eggedal never accepted the necessity for the loss of seven lives.

The Eggedal action, however, was an anomaly in occupied Norway. Until the very end of the war, Norwegian military resistance forces avoided combat whenever possible and eagerly complied with instructions from London to maintain discipline, refrain from provoking the Germans, and wait for the day of liberation.

Hitler's Third Reich crumbled to death in the last days of April and the first days of May. On April 30, Hitler presided over his last noon situation conference in his underground bunker fortress. Russian troops were only blocks away. After final farewells to a few intimate associates, Hitler retired to his room, where he shot himself in the mouth with a revolver. On May 4, the German High Command surrendered all German forces in northwest Germany, Denmark, and Holland to Britain's Field Marshal Bernard L. Montgomery. The BBC Danish broadcast delivered the news to Denmark at eight-thirty-five that evening. The Danes reacted with a mixture of outward joy and inner confusion. Everything was suddenly completely different, yet nothing had changed, at least not to the eye. Germans still patrolled the streets and buildings—the word hadn't reached them yet. Life went on as before. But there was a feeling that something had to be done.

At the frontier station at Krusaa in Jutland, a sign reading "WEL-COME TO DENMARK" appeared on the side of a border-crossing hut, in anticipation of the arrival of the first Allied troops. In southern Jutland, Danes began moving to the border to greet the liberating troops, although when they would come, or who they would be, was unknown. Throughout the whole country, Danish families reacted to the news of the German surrender by placing candles on their windowsills, each household following the lead of its neighbor. From the houses and apartments in Danish towns and villages and from the windows of countless farmhouses the candles broke the night with their soft yellow glow, signaling the end of a period of occupation and the start of what the Danes hoped would be a happier future.

With the announcement of the surrender, four Danish journalists stationed at Krusaa decided to move south into Germany to find the British. They drove an ambulance bedecked with an assortment of flags and signs. German guards at the border saluted their passage.

The Danish journalists made their way to Rendsburg and then to Kiel without running into the British. Turning back toward home, they finally found the British at Neumünster and presented themselves at 6 A.M. on the fifth of May to a sleepy young British lieutenant who received them in a plush four-poster bed. When he was convinced that they were actually Danish journalists who had passed, unchallenged, through sixty-five miles of German-held territory, the lieutenant graciously uncorked a bottle of whisky in welcome.

From Neumünster the Danish journalists were escorted to the British division staff at Bad Segeberg for an interview with a division officer. By the time the Danes had obtained their story and returned to Krusaa that afternoon, they found the small frontier station radically changed. Danish gendarmes, only recently released from German prisons, once again patrolled the border. Members of the underground resistance groups marched with them. Banners reading "WELCOME TO DENMARK" and "THANK YOU FOR YOUR DEED" stretched across the road. Danish, British, American, and Russian flags fluttered everywhere. And thousands upon thousands of Danes had gathered to welcome the British troops.

Actually the first British troops to enter Denmark were a company of the Thirteenth British Airborne Battalion that came to Copenhagen by plane, escorting Maj. Gen. R. H. Dewing of the British Army, head of the SHAEF mission to Denmark. They arrived on the afternoon of May 5.

General Dewing reviewed a company of Danish Life Guards who stood at attention at the airport, greeted representatives of the Danish resistance, and then drove off with his staff for Copenhagen in a hastily assembled convoy of trucks and automobiles. Cheering residents lined Amager Landevej as the convoy headed for the center of town. Danes of the resistance rode on the hoods of vehicles, carrying machine guns in their arms. Parents lifted young children onto their shoulders to see the British troops. "Like two living walls the population of Amager stood pressed so tightly against each other that the cars had difficulty getting through," *Politiken* reported.

The reception was the same in southern Jutland, where the first British troops crossed into Danish territory a little after 6 P.M. on May 5.

Major elements of the British Army began arriving in Denmark on May 7, when the main air party of the SHAEF mission landed in Copenhagen while strong armored units of the Royal Dragoons crossed the border from Germany into Denmark. The next day, May 8, headquarters personnel and troops of the British First Parachute Brigade arrived and took command of all British forces in the country as well as of all German forces. German troops, as eager to see the end of the war as were the Danes, laid down their arms without incident. No violations of the surrender agreement were reported.

British Field Marshal Montgomery taking Copenhagen's salute on May 12, 1945. *(Danish Ministry for Foreign Affairs)*

Only on the Danish island of Bornholm did German forces reject the terms of the capitulation and offer resistance to Allied forces. But Bornholm was a special case. Its position in the western mouth of the Baltic Sea, fifty-seven miles from Denmark and twenty-two miles from Sweden, gave it special military importance as a naval base. Throughout the war, the German maritime command with headquarters in Kiel was responsible for the defense and occupation of Bornholm. What determined German actions on Bornholm during the last days of the war, however, was not its geographic location, nor details of the German command structure, but the fact that the first Allies to demand surrender of the island were not British or American officers but commanders of Russia's northern European army.

In April, 1945, Commander Kamptz, the senior German officer on Bornholm, set out to build up the defenses against a possible Russian attack. The chief Danish administrative officer on Bornholm, Peter Stemann, visited Kamptz during the month and "remarked in a noncommittal and joking way that for the sake of Bornholm and its inhabitants" Kamptz need not go to any great trouble to defend the island against attack. The German commander sternly informed the Dane that he intended to pursue a vigorous defense of the island against Russian troops.

By May 6, two days after the German capitulation in Denmark, Kamptz was still busy fortifying Bornholm. German troops numbered more than twenty thousand combat personnel, including a full division that had managed to reach Bornholm from Poland with much of its equipment intact. German anti-aircraft gunners fired on Russian planes flying reconnaissance missions over the island. Kamptz's belligerence was supported by the German High Command. After its May 4 surrender, the German general headquarters issued a clarifying memorandum:

> When we lay down our arms in North Germany, Denmark and Holland, it is because the fight against the Western powers has lost sense. In the East, however, the fight goes on, to save as many people as possible from Bolshevism and slavery.

Early on the morning of May 7, Kamptz met with Stemann and a handful of other influential Danes. The Danes urged the German to surrender; it was, they told him, "time to stop." Kamptz, however, refused to surrender to the Russians. He told the Danes he would surrender only to the British; even a lone British officer landing on Bornholm would suffice. Stemann left the meeting with this impression:

> I might have made him capitulate even to me, since there were no Englishmen available. But to the Russians, no. For that would be against the conditions of capitulation. Russia was the enemy and he was set to defend Bornholm against her.

As a result of his meeting with Kamptz, Stemann conceived the idea of providing him with a Danish military unit to which he could surrender. Stemann had heard of the arrival in Denmark of the Danish Brigade, consisting of Danes who had received military training in Sweden. Stemann phoned Copenhagen to request that a company from the Danish Brigade be dispatched to Bornholm to negotiate a German surrender. His request was ignored. Bornholm, he was informed, fell within the Russian zone. Neither British military officials nor Danish leaders were willing to intrude into what was understood to be a Russian operation.

Events moved rapidly to a climax on Bornholm. Russian aircraft bombed the town of Neksø on the eastern shore and Bornholm's capital of Rønne in midmorning, killing nine civilians. In midafternoon, the official German radio broadcasted news of the final German capitulation, which was scheduled to go into effect at one minute past midnight on the morning of May 9. Kamptz still refused to surrender to the Russians. Until the deadline arrived, Kamptz considered his old orders still valid and those orders called for him to defend the island against the Russians. Kamptz was determined to do his duty as a good soldier until the end. Russian bombers appeared over Rønne for the second time shortly before dusk, attacking the town again and dropping leaflets addressed, "To the Garrison Commander, the Island of Bornholm."

> To avoid unnecessary sacrifices, we propose that you capitulate. For negotiations on conditions of surrender of the island and garrison, please send negotiators to the harbor of Kolberg at 10 A.M. on May 8. We guarantee that there will be no danger to those undertaking the voyage. Signed: Air Commander, Slepenskov.

Upon reading a copy of the Russian ultimatum, Stemann contacted Kamptz to urge acceptance. Kamptz refused, telling Stemann that he had "orders to let only the English land on Bornholm." Nor did he intend to send a negotiating team to the Baltic port of Kolberg (Kolobrzeg, Poland) the next day. Again Stemann called Copenhagen, urgently requesting that a British delegation be dispatched to accept Kamptz's surrender. Again his request was refused.

When German negotiators failed to make an appearance in Kolberg the next morning, the Russian air commander sent fifty bombers over Bornholm. They dropped approximately fifteen hundred 200-pound bombs on Rønne, Neksø, and other targets. Civilian casualties were light, for Stemann had ordered both towns evacuated, but property damage was estimated in the millions of kroner. On the very last day of the war, the tail end of the bitter conflict which Denmark had largely escaped lashed out to touch the island with its fire and destruction. Bornholm felt forgotten as well as battered. Mainland Denmark, living through the first heady days of liberation, ignored the island's plight. Radio Copenhagen, busy reporting details of the establishment of a new government under former Prime Minister Vilhelm Buhl and of the expected arrival in Copenhagen of Field Marshal Montgomery, gave scant attention to the raids on Bornholm.

Kamptz followed his orders to the letter. At one minute after midnight on May 9, he ordered German troops on the island to step down from their stations. The first Russian troops arrived in six motor torpedo boats in Rønne harbor later that day, landed without opposition, and transported Kamptz and the senior Army officer on the island to Kolberg, where their surrender was quickly accepted. In the days that followed, five thousand Russian troops swarmed into Bornholm. They cut all communications between the island and mainland Denmark, prohibited the sailing of any vessel, and created fear among the Danes that the Russians planned to stay on Bornholm permanently. Within one week the Russians transported more than twenty thousand German combat personnel to the mainland; the last contingent left on May 16. The following day, the Russians permitted the resumption of communications between the island and the mainland and on May 22 the colonel commanding the Russian troops on Bornholm met with Danish officials to deliver a memorandum of reassurance concerning the presence of Russian troops on the island:

Red Army troops had already consolidated their control over Bornholm by the time this Russian military delegation arrived in Copenhagen. *(Nordisk Pressefoto)*

On May 9, 1945, units of the Red Army landed on the island of Bornholm, which they cleansed of German troops because it lies behind our German zone of occupation. The island will be occupied temporarily, by troops of the Red Army, until questions in Germany in connection with the war have been solved. The Red Army on Bornholm will refrain from disturbing the normal life of the inhabitants or interfering in matters of Danish administration.

The Russian message, published in Bornholm newspapers as well as in other Danish and foreign publications, allayed Danish fears. Eleven months later, in April of 1946, the Russians made good their promise by pulling all Red Army troops out of Bornholm and returning the island to Danish control.

Even while the Germans were laying down their arms in mainland Denmark, German intentions in Norway provided an element of lingering concern to the Allied Supreme Command. General Boehme, the German commander-in-chief in Norway, had under his command an undefeated army entrenched in easily defended positions. On May 5, Boehme reported that his Twentieth Mountain Army and other Wehrmacht elements were prepared to handle any assignment "within the limits of their strength." The war may have been burning itself out in mainland Europe, but General Boehme was determined to maintain an active defense in Norway in case German leaders decided to make a last ditch stand in *Festung Norwegen* (Fortress Norway).

Allied military commanders made unsuccessful attempts to reach General Boehme by wireless throughout May 6 and May 7. Even after the unconditional German surrender at General Eisenhower's headquarters at Rheims on May 7, Boehme could not be reached directly. He had, however, received the news, for at 10:15 P.M. on Monday, May 7, Boehme told his troops over Radio Oslo that all military operations were to cease. In an emotional address he appealed to their sense of duty:

This capitulation hits us very hard, because we are unbeaten and in full possession of our strength in Norway, and no enemy has dared to attack us. In spite of all that, in the interest of all that is German, we also shall have to obey the dictates of our enemy. Clench your teeth and keep discipline and order. Obey your superiors. Remain what you have been up to now—decent German soldiers who love their people and homeland more than anything else in the world.

Boehme's speech was the signal for Milorg forces to come out into the open and begin occupying important plants and military installations. They met no German resistance. The Germans, in fact, proved more than willing to cooperate in a peaceful transition of power.

Arne Kjelstrup, the SOE agent in charge of Milorg forces in the Nore-Kongsberg area, approached the local German commandant to inform him that Milorg men would begin arresting Norwegian Nazis the next day. Kjelstrup sought an "understanding" with the German officer: Milorg would not attack the Germans if the Germans would not attack Milorg. The German officer understood immediately.

In the port town of Ålesund, the local Milorg leader called on the German commandant to tell him the home-front forces planned to take over the next morning.

"Will they be in uniform?" the German officer asked.

"Yes," replied the Norwegian.

"Will they be armed?" the German continued.

Again the answer was affirmative.

"In that case," the German said, "I will instruct my troops to avoid any fights."

On the night of May 7–8, top-level home-front leaders informed German headquarters at Lillehammer of the nationwide role Milorg planned to play. The home front also sought an "understanding" with the German command. Would the appearance of a "civilian army" the next day pose any dangers to a peaceful capitulation? The Germans delayed their answer while senior military officials conferred among themselves, but finally they told home-front negotiators that the Germans would look upon the appearance of Milorg men as a guarantee of law and order, and would not begin hostilities.

The next morning, Milorg men—many of them recruits of only a few days' standing—appeared on the streets of Norwegian cities. Most were dressed in civilian clothes; only the white armbands they wore indicated that they were members of the Norwegian underground army. The Norwegian home front issued a special message to its forces:

> The enemy has now surrendered and we will soon be sovereign in our own land. But remember: capitulation is not the same as peace. The enemy still has weapons. Let us, in the midst of rejoicing, observe order and discipline. Do not offend the fallen enemy, or take the law into your own hands.

The official SHAEF mission, headed by a British brigadier, reached Oslo on that afternoon of May 8 and made its way to Lillehammer, eighty miles north of the capital, where General Boehme was headquartered. Until the last, Boehme hoped that the existence of an undefeated German Army in Norway could be used to win concessions, but the SHAEF negotiators insisted on complete capitulation. All Wehrmacht forces were ordered to withdraw from their fortifications and to assemble at key points for demobilization. Boehme signed reluctantly. Two days later, he complained to the German Armed Forces High Command that the capitulation terms were "unbearably severe." What particularly galled Boehme was the sight of Wehrmacht soldiers being reduced to an "immobile, defenseless mass of humanity" while Russian prisoners of war in Norway were being treated with "incomprehensible esteem." "Woe to the vanquished" were the last words of his message.

The Allied buildup of troops in Norway proceeded slowly. Small advance parties of British and Norwegian troops reached Norway on May 9 and larger contingents from the First Airborne Division—the Red Devils of Arnhem—and the Norwegian Parachute Company arrived the following day. The bulk of the First Airborne Division flew in on May 11.

On May 12, three British cruisers arrived in Oslo carrying more troops and Norway's Crown Prince Olav, who held the title of Commander in Chief of the Norwegian Forces. Wave after wave of cheering greeted the Crown Prince when he stepped ashore. With him were three Norwegian ministers representing the Norwegian government in exile. They were less warmly received. The suspicion that had existed throughout the war years between those Norwegians who had escaped to London and those who had stayed behind had not been dispelled by peace. But the presence of the crown prince on Norwegian soil symbolized the end of the occupation and the return of the official Norwegian government. On May 14, the home front responded by issuing a proclamation to the nation declaring that their duties had come to an end.

Norway's King Haakon delayed his return until early June in order to make a symbolic homecoming. Haakon had fled the country aboard the British cruiser *Devonshire* on June 7, 1940. For his return to Norway, Haakon chose to travel on another British cruiser, the *Norfolk*, and to time his arrival so that he could set foot in Oslo on June 7, 1945, exactly five years to the day after he had been forced to flee. Oslo gave him a "tremendous ovation."

The end of the war meant freedom for approximately 72,000 Russian POW slave laborers in Norway who had been assigned to road construction projects between Trondheim and Bodø. Bernt Balchen, an American officer of Norwegian birth who arrived in Bodø in mid-May, found the Russians close to starvation and living in work camps where as many as fifteen thousand of them were crowded into quarters that normally would have held less than half that number.

Allied authorities found Soviet authorities strangely uninterested in the fate of the men. "It was almost as if they had written them off and didn't know what to do with them," one Allied officer commented.

Norwegians who returned to Finnmark in the spring of 1945 found these ground huts where the Germans kept their Russian prisoners of war. *(Norsk Telegrambyra)*

Although repatriation started slowly it picked up speed in June, and by early July some forty thousand Russians had been repatriated. By the end of October, when the SHAEF mission to Norway wound up its work, all the Russians had been repatriated with the exception of those whose nationality was in doubt.

In addition to the Russian POWs, Norway harbored another ten thousand civilian slave laborers scattered in camps near the major cities —Oslo, Trondheim, and Tromsø. About half were Poles and the other half were Dutch, Czech, and French nationals. Although these slave laborers lived under somewhat better conditions than did the Russians, Allied authorities found that they too were undernourished and "grievously short of clothes" at the time of liberation. By midsummer most of the ten thousand had been returned to their homelands.

Non-Germans found within the ranks of the German armed forces presented special problems. As the German military units pulled out of Norway, the number of non-Germans who insisted on staying behind increased sharply. By mid-July Allied civil-affairs officers listed more than thirty thousand men in this category, almost 10 percent of the German armed forces in Norway. Poles (fourteen thousand) and Czechs (twelve thousand) accounted for the bulk of this non-German force. They were separated from their units, housed in special camps under Allied military

A young German soldier awaits repatriation from Denmark.
(Nordisk Pressefoto)

control, and placed on waiting lists for transport back to their native countries.

Norwegian and SHAEF civil-affairs officers also had to handle the return of some 35,000 Norwegians who had escaped to Sweden during the war. These Norwegians were collected in Swedish assembly areas, divided into destination groups, and then repatriated by rail to Oslo, Trondheim, and Narvik. Local arrangements were made in these cities for dispersing the returnees to their homes. All 35,000 were home by the middle of July.

The repatriation of the German armed forces, however, presented SHAEF authorities with their biggest problem, for even after the end of hostilities the Norwegian theater received low priorities in manpower and transportation. Nevertheless, both the Allies and the Norwegians wanted the Germans out of Norway as quickly as possible; only with the Wehrmacht gone could Norway feel that the occupation had truly ended.

German discipline remained high. German combat units, ordered to disarm, complied promptly. In remote areas without Milorg or Allied representation, German officers assigned elite German units to guard the rest of the Wehrmacht soldiers until the Allies could produce the necessary supervisory personnel. Even when no British or Norwegian forces were at hand, German commanders proceeded to disarm their own troops—the first time in history that a superior military force disarmed itself without having suffered a military defeat. Discipline was maintained on the trip home. Units stuck together, officers and men continued to observe the chain of command, and the German forces returned to Germany with a feeling that while their country had been defeated, they and their units were still unbowed. Not until their return to Germany would the utter devastation and total ruin that had befallen their mother country sink home.

The German withdrawal from Denmark was equally orderly, although Wehrmacht troops leaving Denmark presented more the typical picture of a defeated army. Many soldiers were recuperating from wounds suffered on other fronts; few returned to Germany with any illusions left.

A mixed force of English troops, Danish resistance workers, and members of the regular Danish border guard sealed the border between Jutland and Germany and mounted checkpoints along the two major roads leading from Jutland into Germany. In the first days after the German capitulation, German units were permitted to take their personal weapons and equipment with them into Germany, where they were subsequently disarmed. By the middle of May, however, border control was tightened. German troops filing down from the north in long, depressed columns were stripped of their weapons and whatever Danish

German troops returning home were stripped of all arms and possessions before leaving Denmark. *(Nordisk Pressefoto and U.S. Office of War Information)*

currency and valuables they carried with them. By the end of June, more than 215 million kroner had been recovered from German units, including pocket money taken from German soldiers. The typical German soldier was permitted to take home only the clothes on his back and whatever food he could cram into his knapsack. As the German units neared the border, English combat troops vented their feelings, and those of the Danes, on the defeated enemy. SS troopers were forced to run into Germany—kicked across the border by English soldiers. Wehrmacht soldiers were allowed to walk into Germany unmolested.

The arrival of peace unleashed violent passions that had been held in check during the years of occupation. In both Denmark and Norway, resistance workers moved against suspected informers and collaborators with as much hatred and disregard for personal civil liberties as the collaborators had moved against resistance workers during the war. Danish intelligence agents posted on the Jutland-German border plucked hundreds of collaborators, suspected traitors, German Gestapo agents, and SS officials from the columns of retreating Germans. Within the first six weeks after liberation, more than eleven hundred arrests had been made at the border, while the number of those arrested throughout Denmark totaled more than twenty thousand, among them several hundred Danish "field mattresses," young women whose only crime had been consorting with German soldiers during the occupation. It was a common sight in the major Danish cities to see groups of suspected collaborators transported through the streets in open trucks, their hands raised aloft in abject surrender. Secret illegal reprisals were so common that the Danish branch of the War Resisters International Council, a pacifist organization, complained to the new Danish government that "members of the resistance movement have killed or maltreated persons and are trying to force the judges to sentence all arrested by the movement." The council called on the government to disarm and disband all resistance units "before their merits under the occupation are overshadowed by encroachments after liberation."

Official Denmark, however, also moved with vengeance against those who had chosen the wrong side during the war. On June 1, 1945, Denmark passed a new criminal code which authorized prison terms for those who had reaped economic rewards from working for the Germans or who had lent assistance, by word or deed, to the occupation power. The code also authorized prison terms for those Danes who had enlisted in German military or police units, and it gave judges the right to impose the death penalty on those who "exercised police-like activity through

In the postwar period the Danes arrested more than twenty thousand of their countrymen who were suspected of collaboration. Young women who had befriended German
servicemen were also arrested and shamed before their neighbors. *(Nordisk Pressefoto)*

service" in one of the Danish Nazi terror organizations.* Under the new criminal code, even Danish contractors and workers who with Danish governmental approval had helped build fortifications on the western coast of Jutland were in danger of conviction. In practice, however, only those contractors judged "too eager or cooperative" and only those workers who had served as armed sabotage guards were brought to trial. The average prison sentence for those convicted of fortification work was two years and three months.

Special laws covered public servants. Mere membership in the DNSAP, the Danish Nazi Party, was a punishable offense for government officials, though membership in the DNSAP without other evidence of collaboration was in itself not sufficient cause for criminal proceedings against ordinary men and women.

Despite the bitterness against collaborators that erupted immediately after liberation, most prison terms, when they were finally handed down, were fairly short: for service in *Frikorps Danmark,* which fought on the Eastern Front—two-and-a-half years; for service as factory guards—two years and eight months; for service in the SS—two years and nine months; for service as armed marine ·guards—three years and four months; and for service in the Danish Nazi *Hipo* Corps, a terrorist paramilitary organization—four years.

Of the twenty thousand arrested in Denmark in the postwar period, 12,877 men and 631 women received prison sentences. Sixty percent of the men were sentenced to prison terms of less than two years; only 15 percent received sentences of more than four years. Among the women, only 6 percent were sentenced to terms longer than four years. Prison terms of between ten and twenty years were handed out to 246 men and eight women who were convicted of more serious crimes. Life sentences were imposed on sixty-six men. And the death penalty was ordered for seventy-six men and two women. Neither woman was executed, however, and thirty of the men received reprieves.

Ironically, those guilty of the least serious crimes received relatively harsher treatment than those convicted of more serious crimes. The minor war criminals, because of the simplicity of their cases, came to trial quickly, when the passions of hatred and revenge were still high. Those convicted of more serious violations, because of the complexity of their cases, did not come before a judge until some months had passed and time

* The death penalty was a sign of the bitterness with which even sensible Denmark greeted the immediate postwar period. Danish law in effect at the time of the German surrender prohibited the death penalty, and Denmark had effectively resisted German demands for the death penalty throughout the occupation years. But in the first month of peace, Denmark not only authorized the death penalty but made it retroactive to the years of the occupation.

had had a chance to cool the passions that liberation had unleashed.

By the summer of 1946 a new spirit of accommodation arose in Denmark. The criminal code covering war crimes was revised, permitting prisoners to be released on parole. And these parole provisions were liberally implemented. When the postwar decade had run its course, it was discovered that most of those sentenced to terms of more than eight years had served less than half of their full sentences; those sentenced to terms of three to eight years had served half of their time; those sentenced to terms of one to two years generally had to serve their full sentence. Despite Denmark's liberal parole policy, the implementation of the policy discriminated, again, against those who had been charged with relatively minor crimes. Not only did those accused of minor crimes receive comparatively harsher sentences in relation to their crimes than did those convicted of more serious offenses, but they also served proportionately more of their sentences than did the more important war criminals. Time victimized the minor war criminals sentenced during a period when national hostility to collaborators was at its peak; they found themselves completing their prison terms before the period of legal forgiveness set in.

Public feeling in Norway also ran high against collaborators and German officials. Although the home front officially warned against a "night of the long knives," many who held positions of power in Norway

Allied intelligence officers in Norway, with the assistance of a secret informer, screen German troops in search of Gestapo agents hiding in the ranks of the regular German Army. *(Office of War Information)*

during the occupation feared that the long knives would flash nonetheless. As the war neared its end, Reichskommissar Joseph Terboven and General Riedess of the SS blew themselves up in a bunker located in the residence of the crown prince, which Terboven had taken over for his own use during the occupation. Jonas Lie, the Norwegian minister of police and head of the Norwegian SS, shot himself to death in a schoolhouse in western Oslo after being surrounded by Milorg men. Other Quisling officials took their own lives as their day of reckoning approached. One *Nasjonal Samling* prison director killed his two children, his wife, and himself in fear of what awaited him and his family. When the prison director's elderly father heard what had happened, he and his wife took their own lives as well.

The German capitulation brought mass arrests. Thousands of members of the *Nasjonal Samling* Party were seized, some whose only "crime" had been party membership. By July 1 Norwegian prisons and concentration camps were filled to overflowing with fourteen thousand new inmates. By the end of the year more than ninety thousand persons were arrested, investigated, or interrogated for wartime activities. More than half this number—46,000—eventually were convicted of wartime offenses.

The Grini concentration camp outside Oslo, the site of imprisonment for anti-Nazi Norwegians during the war, housed the greatest number of collaborators. Prisoners at Grini, renamed Ilebu, suffered from overcrowding, poor food, and unsanitary conditions as well as maltreatment from guards, some of whom ordered inmates to perform exhausting physical exercises, beat or whipped prisoners without cause, and made sport among themselves by firing over the heads of inmates to frighten and intimidate them.

Norway's greatest living author, eighty-one-year-old Knut Hamsun, was among those arrested and placed in prison for pro-Nazi views. His age and worldwide reputation did little to soften his treatment. When Soviet Foreign Minister Vyacheslav Molotov commented to a group of Norwegian diplomats that Norway was treating its great writer with harshness, Terje Wold, Norway's Minister of Justice in London, responded disapprovingly to the Russian: "Don't be soft." Ordinary men and women suspected of collaboration could expect little mercy or understanding from their captors. Norwegian women who had kept company with German soldiers were denounced as "German tarts," had their heads forcibly shaved, were paraded through the streets in various stages of undress. Though guilty of no violation of law, more than a thousand so-called German tarts were placed in prison under what authorities called "preventive detention."

As the war-crimes trials got under way, newspapers reflected the anger and frustration of the public. Bitter letters appeared denouncing the "appalling leniency" in the treatment of arrested collaborators. Civic groups bombarded the government with petitions demanding "firmer" handling of war criminals. Defense attorneys were sharply criticized for providing legal counsel to accused collaborators, and in public forums and in the daily press, those who urged moderation were denounced for their "silky" or "velvety" attitudes toward the "striped" or "streaky" collaborators. In contrast, those who advocated an "iron hand" against collaborators proudly placed themselves on the "ice front." A few of the most active resistance fighters noted, to their dismay, that many of those who were the most unrelenting in their condemnation of collaborators had been inactive in the resistance until the last few weeks of the occupation.

Norway, unlike Denmark, prosecuted members of the *Nasjonal Samling* Party even in the absence of any other evidence of collaboration. The Norwegian Supreme Court, in a split decision, ruled that membership alone was grounds for prosecution. Norway, however, again unlike Denmark, did not prosecute workers who had labored diligently to help Germany build fortifications for the defense of Norway. The country's chief prosecutor went after only those workers who had left regular and well-paid jobs to perform work of direct military importance to the Germans. As a result, tens of thousands of Norwegians escaped prosecution even though they had willingly worked on German construction projects; while thousands of other Norwegians were imprisoned, fined, or deprived of their civil rights merely for having joined the *Nasjonal Samling* Party. In postwar Norway, the injustice that sent an otherwise inactive N.S. member to jail while permitting a willing worker for the Germans to remain at large was easily ignored.

Of 46,000 Norwegians found guilty of war crimes, 18,000 received prison sentences and 28,000 were fined or were deprived of their civil rights. Despite public demands for "firm" handling, the majority of those sentenced to prison received comparatively short terms: approximately 14,000 of those sentenced to prison were given terms of less than three years; 3,500 received sentences of more than three years; six hundred were sentenced to more than eight years; and eighty were sentenced to life imprisonment. Thirty Norwegian collaborators and fifteen Germans were sentenced to death for wartime treason or atrocities.

Within two years Norway was ready to forgive the bulk of its war criminals. By the summer of 1948 parole was granted to all war criminals who had served half their sentences. In the next few years, the provisions of parole became even more lenient. Prisoners who had been sentenced to twenty years or more walked out of prison after serving an average term of six-and-a-half years, while those sentenced to life imprisonment won release after serving an average term of eight years and three months. Among those sentenced to death, however, twelve Germans and twenty-five Norwegians were actually executed, among them Quisling's minister of church and education, Ragnar Skancke, and Henry Oliver Rinnan and seven members of his notorious "Rinnan gang," which had been responsible for the arrest of more than one thousand Norwegian underground members, many of whom lost their lives by execution and maltreatment in German concentration camps. Rinnan himself was convicted of thirteen murders.

But Norway's most important capital trial, one which produced headlines throughout the world, brought Vidkun Quisling, the country's Minister President, before the bar of justice to answer a string of charges involving theft, murder, and treason. To the last days of the war, Quisling had clung stubbornly to his position as Minister President of Norway and to his hopes of eventually ruling over an independent country. After a meeting with Hitler in January, 1945 (a meeting held with the Red Army only 110 miles from Berlin), the joint communiqué issued by Hitler and Quisling took no account of Germany's desperate situation, optimistically stating that "Germany will restore the complete liberty and independence of Norway after victory." There is some evidence that Quisling allowed himself to believe Hitler's assurances.

At his trial Quisling was questioned about the meeting. He testified:

> When I talked with Hitler for the last time, at the end of January, I asked him precisely what the situation was and he replied that Germany would get by. I believe the Germans based their expectation on "over valuation" of the German offensive on the West Front at Christmas, and partly on secret weapons that were not ready.

A few weeks later, after Quisling's return to Norway and after the war news had turned even more foreboding for Germany, Quisling seems to have given thought to turning Norway into a bastion which would be defended by both Norwegian and German troops. Quisling's confidential secretary, Harald Franklin Knudsen, whose father had been British consul to Norway in the 1920s, reported after the war that Quisling hoped a last-ditch stand in Norway would provide a way out for him as well as for what remained of the Wehrmacht and the Third Reich.

> Having smashed Germany, the Western Powers would face two alternatives—to sacrifice much blood and money in overpowering strongly entrenched positions, at the same time destroying Norway, or to negotiate a Norwegian peace that allowed the Germans to remain and to form the backbone of a Nordic defense in any future East-West war. Scandinavia would then be able to muster two million men and the Northern flank against Russia would be definitely secured.

The news of the German surrender in Denmark on May 4 found Quisling still out of touch with the realities of the war. On hearing the news, Quisling immediately called on Reichskommissar Terboven and General Boehme to discuss what they could do on their own to avert catastrophe. Terboven cut off Quisling's discussion. In Terboven's view, Quisling's only realistic course of action was to flee the country. He offered to make a Luftwaffe airplane available to fly Quisling to Spain or a long-range U-boat to take him to South America. Quisling rejected both offers. He told Terboven that he could justify his actions in Norway during the war and that he would be vindicated by his countrymen. Quisling returned to Gimle, his villa in Bygdo, to await the German capitulation he now realized was coming. Members of his Norwegian *Hird* organization stood guard outside to prevent attempts to kidnap or assassinate him.

Quisling holed up at Gimle with six ministers and an assortment of minor subordinates. Before Germany's final capitulation, he received Bjorn Foss, a member of Milorg District 13's action group, who offered Quisling and his wife safe conduct to a villa in the Oslo suburb of Holmenkollen and the protection of home-front forces "until your case comes up." Quisling refused to place himself in Milorg's custody; he told Foss he wanted to negotiate further. Foss left with Quisling still insisting on the title of Minister President and still refusing to surrender to Milorg forces.

Developing events quickly overtook Quisling. The German capitulation that went into effect on May 8 forced Quisling to send his minister of social welfare, Johan Lippestad, to police headquarters at Møllergaten 19 to discuss his own surrender with acting police chief Heinrich Meyer and L'Abbe-Lund, chief of the criminal division of the home front. Norwegian authorities told Lippestad that Quisling was expected to turn himself in at Møllergaten 19 the following morning at seven o'clock. If he did not surrender voluntarily, he would be taken by force.

Quisling could not believe Lippestad's report. The Minister President of Norway was being ordered to turn himself in to police headquarters "like an ordinary criminal." Annoyed with Lippestad, Quisling himself picked up the phone to make a series of calls to Milorg leaders: he objected to his arrest; he threatened to call up 200,000 to 300,000 men to come to his defense; he objected to the timing of the ultimatum. To L'Abbe-Lund he complained: "Such a short warning is unheard of."

L'Abbe-Lund replied coldly: "Police are not accustomed to give warning of intended arrests. I advise you to do as you are instructed."

Quisling hung up, only to attempt another telephone call ten minutes later. This time he wanted to speak to Crown Prince Olav in London to arrange to transfer authority in an orderly way. The telephone operator refused to put through his call. Quisling made one final call to

General Boehme, but the German officer could no longer be bothered with the Norwegian Minister President. Quisling retired to spend a troubled last night of freedom.

Shortly after six-fifteen the next morning, Milorg sentries outside Gimle noted a procession of vehicles leaving the mansion and taking the road for Møllergaten 19. The motorcade arrived at Møllergaten 19 a half-hour later and Quisling, wearing a greatcoat and a soft felt hat, stepped out of his Mercedes-Benz limousine (it had been a gift from Hitler) and entered police headquarters, there to undergo initial questioning:

"What is your name?"

"Vidkun Quisling."

"When were you born?"

"July 18, 1887."

"What was your occupation?"

"I am the former Minister President of Norway."

When his preliminary questioning was over, Quisling was locked into a bleak cell furnished with a lone chair, a small table, a wooden plank bed, a washbowl, and a toilet bucket. A small window, ribbed by iron bars, cut into the gray-stone exterior wall and permitted the light of the northern summer to filter in. Quisling was held incommunicado while formal charges were prepared against him. Even his wife, Maria, who had been taken into custody although not charged, could not visit him. On one occasion Quisling was removed from his cell to visit a site where hostages had been executed and buried in a mass grave. A police commissioner at the scene asked Quisling if he knew anything of the events. He is reported to have replied: "No, I never expected this." The Oslo newspaper *Aftenposten* described Quisling as "visibly shaken as he was led past the openly hostile crowd that had gathered to see the traitor."

Quisling's trial began on August 20, 1945, in the large assembly hall of Oslo's main Freemason's Lodge, which was turned into a provisional courtroom for the event. The largest number of foreign correspondents ever assembled in Norway showed up to cover the trial, presided over by Judge Erik Solem, thin-faced and bushy-eyebrowed, with a voice that could be cutting and sarcastic. Public attention focused on Quisling's appearance and behavior in court. *Aftenposten* wrote: "He has grown thinner. The dark suit hangs loosely about him. His face has furrows it did not have previously."

If there were any doubt in his mind, Quisling quickly learned that he faced a hostile court. On the first day of the trial he complained to Judge Solem that he had lost thirty-five pounds while in jail. Judge Solem cut off his complaint. "That is nothing to what some of our people lost when you put them in concentration camps."

Vidkun Quisling was taken from his jail cell to visit a site where Norwegian hostages had been executed. An Oslo paper reported that "the traitor Quisling was visibly shaken." *(Wide World Photo)*

Quisling on trial in Oslo. The minor charges stung him to fury. *(Norsk Telegrambyra)*

The specifics of the crimes charged against Quisling ranged from such minor offenses as the theft of silverware and works of art from the royal palace to murder, complicity in the deportation and death of Norwegian Jews, and treason against Norway, both before and after Germany's invasion. The treason charge read:

> For assisting the enemy and disgracing Norway and Norway's war allies. Seeking to bring Norwegian soldiers and allied troops into the hands of the enemy. Seeking to betray Norway or its allies by encouraging mutiny or other faithlessness. Seeking to cooperate with a potential enemy to bring the country under foreign control.

Quisling pleaded "Not guilty" to all charges.

Once on the stand, Quisling proved an erratic witness in his own behalf. When allowed to speak in general terms about his political philosophy and his concern for Norwegian interests, he often presented persuasive arguments. One foreign correspondent wrote: "Quisling made a profound impression." The Swedish magazine *Vi* commented: "Quisling's defense was many-sided. It had its effect on us foreigners . . . in his own way he was impressive."

However, he was not impressive in handling details. In answer to charges that he had conferred with a certain German official before the invasion of Norway, Quisling repeatedly denied knowing the name of the official in question. Later, when evidence was introduced showing that the German had been an intermediary in arranging Quisling's first meeting with Rosenberg, Quisling merely shrugged his shoulders and remained silent. In answer to charges that he had accepted German financial support, Quisling denied the charge only to change his testimony when the editor of the *Nasjonal Samling* newspaper *Fritt Folk* testified that Quisling personally had given him 70,000 kroner which he said had come from the Germans. Quisling suddenly "remembered" that he had in fact received money from German sources but he insisted it was an inconsequential point. In answer to charges of theft, drunkenness, and debauchery, Quisling lost his composure and replied in emotional terms, often approaching tears in his denunciation of the charges. The American-Norwegian magazine *The Norseman,* covering the trial, observed that these minor charges "were what stung him to fury. What the prosecution was trying to do was to remove any trace of dignity from the puppet."

Quisling's trial was interrupted at midpoint to permit a medical and psychiatric examination. By all accounts, Quisling was subjected to a vigorous physical and psychological examination that included electrical explorations of the brain. Even those unsympathetic to Quisling's cause described his examination as "severe." Supporters decried the "wires pushed into his cranium." The examining physicians concluded that Quisling was sane and the trial continued toward its conclusion. In his closing arguments for the defense, Quisling's counsel conceded that legal medicine had judged Quisling sane, but he insisted that Quisling was no ordinary man and that his was not an ordinary case. The law of sanity had not been designed, he argued, to deal with a borderline case such as Quisling nor were medical authorities competent to judge the question of Quisling's sanity. Their tools of measurement were too imprecise.

The final argument for the defense came from the former Minister President himself. Given the opportunity to speak without interruption, Quisling collected himself for one last effort. He spoke for eight hours without once referring to his notes. His appeal described his childhood, his humanitarian work in Russia after World War I, and his subsequent Army career. He covered in detail his political philosophy as it evolved during the 1930s and he ended by describing his efforts—for motives which he described as patriotic and unselfish—to protect Norwegian interests during the occupation. Time and again in his final defense Quisling repeated his conviction that he had been right to sacrifice the lives of a few Norwegians so that the majority could live a softer, safer life. He insisted that history would clear his name. He suggested that those who opposed his policies should be on trial, not he, and he assured the court that given the chance to do it all again, he would do it exactly the same.

As Quisling's long and rambling speech continued, observers in the courtroom were reminded of his defense counsel's argument that the legal definition of sanity might not suffice for Quisling. There was about the man, and his speech, disturbing elements of unreality. "Those of us sitting in the courtroom," the correspondent for *The Norseman* wrote, "listening to Quisling, couldn't help feel that there was something in what his counsel said." Quisling concluded his speech on a disorganized pathetic note that revealed a man out of touch with the world in which he operated:

> To me, politics is not a matter of party interests, professional job seeking, or personal ambition and lust for power. It is a matter of self sacrifice and practical action in the service of the historical develop-ment for the benefit of one's own country and to promote the reali-zation of God's Kingdom on earth which Christ came to establish. If my activities have been treasonable, as they have been said to be, then I would pray to God that for the sake of Norway a large number of Norway's sons will become such traitors as I, but that they will not be thrown into jail.

The criminal court was ready to hand down its verdict on Sep-tember 10. While ten Norwegian soldiers stood guard over Quisling,

Judge Solem slowly read each paragraph of the judgment, which ran for thirty-five typewritten pages. Its reading took more than an hour and a quarter.

As the first specific charges were read, Quisling reacted by lifting his chin slightly, a mannerism he had adopted during his years in office as a gesture of superiority and aggressiveness, but as the reading of the judgment droned on, Quisling's defiance drained away. He leaned forward heavily, supporting his head first on one hand and then on the other. A reporter who covered the trial wrote: "It steadily became a more ghastly face after the reading of each misdeed. Here were enough charges to send a whole company to death, if they could be distributed."

The verdict, when it came, surprised no one in the courtroom. Quisling won acquittal on some of the minor charges—those that had stung him to fury—but he was found guilty on all major charges, including murder and treason. His sentence: death.

The Norwegian Supreme Court, headed by Justice Paal Berg, the elderly jurist who had led the home front during the war, made quick work of Quisling's appeals. On October 13, the Court upheld the original verdict. A few days later, the Court rejected a petition of reprieve submitted by Quisling's wife.

At 2 A.M. on October 24, police guards took Quisling from his cell in Møllergaten 19, whisked him into a car for a quick trip to Akershus Castle, and there, in a courtyard, stood him up against a wall before a ten-man military execution squad. Quisling was dead within a half-hour of leaving his cell.

Other trials of key figures involved in the Norwegian drama followed on the heels of Quisling's. Colonel Sundlo, the elderly Norwegian officer who had surrendered Narvik to German forces, was tried for treason by a military court martial but was found not guilty of that charge. His fellow officers preferred to believe his actions the result of military incompetence rather than treason. Sundlo was convicted only of collaborating with Quisling during the German occupation; on this charge he was sentenced to hard labor for life and stripped of his commission. Gen. Nikolaus Falkenhorst, who had led the German invasion of Norway and Denmark in 1940 and who had served as military commander of German forces in Norway through most of the war, was sentenced to death by a British military court in 1946, but his sentence was later commuted to twenty years in prison. Falkenhorst served only seven years of his sentence. Allied authorities released him in 1953 because of a heart condition.

Erich Raeder, former commander-in-chief of the German Navy and a key figure in planning the invasion of Norway, went on trial in Nuremberg as one of the twenty-four defendants accused of major war crimes. The judgment against him charged:

> The conception of the invasion of Norway first arose in the mind of Raeder and not that of Hitler. On October 10, 1939, Raeder discussed the matter with Hitler; his War Diary entry for that day says Hitler intended to give the matter consideration. . . . It is clear from this evidence that Raeder participated in the planning and waging of aggressive war.

Raeder was found guilty on three major counts and sentenced to life imprisonment.

Alfred Rosenberg, Hitler's "ideologist" who headed the Nazi Party's office of foreign affairs, was convicted of four charges, including "crimes against peace." The final judgment linked Rosenberg closely to Hitler's invasion of Norway.

> Rosenberg played an important role in the preparation and planning of the attack on Norway. Rosenberg, together with Raeder, was one of the originators of the plan for attacking Norway. Rosenberg had become interested in Norway as early as June, 1939, when he conferred with Quisling. As a result, Rosenberg arranged for Quisling to collaborate closely with the National Socialists and to receive political assistance from the Nazis. When the war broke out . . . Quisling began to express fear of British intervention in Norway. Rosenberg supported this view, and transmitted to Raeder a plan to use Quisling for a coup in Norway.

Rosenberg was sentenced to death for his war crimes and he was hanged at Nuremberg on October 16, 1946.

Denmark also brought high German and Danish Nazis to trial. Dr. Fritz Clausen, who had hoped to be Denmark's counterpart to Quisling, was arrested and placed on trial, but died of a heart attack during a police interrogation before the case against him could be concluded.

The German plenipotentiary in Denmark, Werner Best, was brought to trial along with Maj. Gen. Hermann Hanneken, Gen. Gunther Pancke of the SS, and Otto Bovensiepen, the Gestapo chief in Denmark. They were charged with 380 acts of terrorism and with the responsibility for the deaths of 136 Danish Jews and Danish policemen. The sentences were handed down in September, 1948: General Hanneken was sentenced to eight years in prison; General Pancke to twenty years; and the court imposed the death penalty on both Gestapo Chief Bovensiepen and Plenipotentiary Best. The following summer, however, a Danish appeals court, while affirming Pancke's twenty-year term, reversed General Hanneken's conviction and set him free. The court also commuted Bovensiepen's death sentence to life imprisonment and commuted the death penalty against Werner Best to five years in prison. In his appeal Best successfully argued that German officials in Berlin had initiated the action against the Jews and that he, therefore, could not be held personally responsible for their fate.

While the war-crimes trials were winding toward their conclusion in Denmark and Norway, both countries moved forward to erase the psychological and physical scars of the occupation. Both countries had survived the war in remarkably good shape. Only in Finnmark did the Germans leave widespread destruction behind. Throughout the rest of Norway, the country's industrial base and transportation network survived almost untouched. Public utilities were generally undamaged. Industrial plants still operated. The railway system, though less efficient than in pre-war years, was in good enough repair to meet the country's needs. All ports remained open for shipping.

Denmark was even more fortunate. Civil-affairs officers for the British military government reported that physical conditions in Denmark were "far better than in any other liberated country." Allied authorities found to their joy that the tiny country not only could feed itself but had surplus food on hand to export to starving nations of Europe. In the first four months after liberation, Denmark produced a surplus of 36,960 tons of butter, 4,480 tons of eggs, 5,600 tons of beef, 17,640 tons of pork, 784 tons of cheese, 22,400 tons of potatoes, and 89,600 tons of fish. Allied authorities insisted that Denmark make this food available to the starving countries of Europe and strongly hinted that the amount of assistance the victorious Allies would provide to Denmark would be influenced by Denmark's cooperation in meeting the food needs of other countries. Denmark understood what was expected of her. The first food ship left Copenhagen for Great Britain in early June, carrying 1,500 tons of butter for the Britishers. Within a month more than 15,000 tons of food had been shipped to the United Kingdom alone, and the Danish government found itself forced to reduce food consumption at home to comply with Allied demands. Public opinion turned sharply critical. Throughout the war the Danes had suffered no food shortages, even during Germany's most critical periods. Now liberation brought with it unexpected shortages of key food staples. Before the end of June Danes were complaining that while "Germany put her heel on Denmark, the Allies sit on her."

Liberation brought other pressures on the internal fabric of the nation. When the Danish Jews who had escaped to Sweden in 1943 returned home in the summer of 1945, they found that the country which had once united to ensure their safety was now caught in the grip of a bitter wave of anti-Semitism.

Anti-Semitism against Danish Jews had in fact begun earlier, in

Dr. Fritz Clausen, the Danish Nazi leader, in Frøslev Prison Camp after the war where, it was said, he was put to hard labor. Photograph was obviously posed for propaganda purposes. Note the empty wheelbarrow and Clausen's banker-like clothing. (*Danish Ministry for Foreign Affairs*)

Sweden where friction developed between Jewish and non-Jewish Danish refugees. The Jews, arriving in 1943, were settled primarily in Swedish cities, almost as a matter of course. They had been city dwellers in Denmark and they came to Sweden in family groups, a factor which made Swedish officials reluctant to assign Jewish men to physical-labor projects in the rural districts. By 1944, however, the character of the typical Danish refugee had changed. He was now usually an able-bodied young man from the country, without means or family, who had been forced to flee Denmark because of involvement in underground work. Swedish authorities routinely sent these refugees to the northern forests, where they performed "pioneer work." The discrepancy between the comparatively easy life of the Jewish families who lived in Swedish cities and the harsh life experienced by young, non-Jewish Danes who toiled in the northern lumber forests was not lost on the non-Jews.

Not all Jewish refugees experienced a cold reception on their return to Denmark. For many, the homecoming proved a joyous occasion. Many found that friends and neighbors had taken the trouble to prepare their old apartments for their return. Familiar pieces of furniture stood in accustomed spots; personal belongings were neatly laid out in bureaus or hung in wardrobes; pantries bulged with food. And in many cases, the refugees found it possible quickly to resume their old jobs or again claim businesses they had left in the care of non-Jewish Danes. But there were other, darker homecomings as well. Some Jews found that their furniture had been sold to help finance the Jewish rescue of October, 1943, and that their apartments were now occupied by new tenants, who refused to move. In September, 1945, at least thirteen hundred Jewish refugees were living in temporary government quarters. Even more serious were the problems connected with employment. Jobs once held by Jews had been taken over by non-Jews and the returning refugees were forced to go job-hunting in a country struggling to regain its economic stability. Bitter disappointment also awaited many Jewish businessmen who had signed over their companies to acquaintances or friends on the understanding that ownership would be transferred back to them upon their return. In many cases, the new "owners" insisted on the legality of the wartime transfer and refused to admit that special arrangements had been made. Some Jews lost their businesses completely; others regained control only after long legal struggles.

In the strange atmosphere of the post-liberation period, when questions of patriotism and collaboration were daily topics, when economic disruption heightened tension and bitterness, when fatigue and a sense of anticlimax were almost tangible, the seeds of anti-Semitism sown by the Nazis during the occupation finally germinated.

Throughout Copenhagen, Danes began to use the word "Jew" as a term of abuse. Jewish families met unconcealed discrimination when they sought to rent apartments. Jewish workers were hired only if no non-Jewish workers were available. The Danes complained that the Jewish refugees were not grateful enough for what had been done for them in October, 1943. They should have been coming home with love in their hearts and expressions of thanks on their lips, not with complaints about maltreatment or appeals for sympathy.

Jewish and non-Jewish leaders in Denmark maintained silence on the disturbing development for months, as if silence would make the problem disappear. The Communist writer Paul Henningsen brought the issue out into the open for the first time in an article, "Anti-Semitism After the War," which appeared in *Land og Folk* in early January, 1946:

> Between man and man, when no Jews are present, the problem is vigorously debated, but in public it is considered tactless to mention it. Such a situation is intolerable, and I take the liberty of raising the issue although I know that many of Jewish origin consider silence more suitable. The character of the Danish people is the concern of us all. . . . When millions have died in recent years, it would be naive to ignore the existence of the problem.

Rabbi Marcus Melchior quickly followed with an article of his own, "Anti-Semitism in Denmark—Despite Everything."

If one happens to tread on someone's toes in a bus, one is a "damned Jew." On Stroget the cry "Jew" is heard more than one cares to think, not only toward Jews who are disliked but toward anyone with whom there is a score to settle. Many Jewish children suffer from this situation in the public schools, where it is no longer a question of anti-Semitism in its more "delicate" form but a transition to something far more serious and dangerous.

Denmark's flirtation with anti-Semitism lasted until the turmoil of liberation had passed and the country had returned to quieter ways of life. In subsequent years, an effort was made to gloss over this period and to present Denmark as a country untroubled by the ugly passions which afflict so much of mankind. By the 1960s Rabbi Melchior had forgotten, at least in public, the anti-Semitism of the late 1940s. "What was remarkable," he often remarked, "was not that the Danes helped us to escape, but that they welcomed us back with such open arms after the war." Non-Jewish Danes also chose to forget, for both Jew and non-Jew alike preferred to present to the world, and to themselves, the picture of Denmark as a country "without a Jewish problem."

Norway also reacted with discrimination against those who had spent the war years out of the country or who had suffered psychological as distinct from physical injuries as a result of wartime experiences. For the physically disabled, Norway provided pensions, preferential job treatment, understanding, and respect; but those who had been psychologically wounded, among them thousands of merchant-marine sailors and concentration-camp survivors, received less sympathy and no material benefits.

The treatment of the merchant-marine sailors proved particularly unenlightened. Many had been young men in their teens when the outbreak of war caught them at sea aboard Norwegian merchant ships. Many thousands of these young men remained at sea for the next five years, seeing ships and companions blown out of the water, waiting for the torpedoes to strike.* At sea "for the duration," they seized what recreation and escape they could during the short periods of shore leave by frequenting waterfront bars and brothels in port cities around the world. By the time the war was over, many had developed neurotic or psychotic symptoms while others had become confirmed alcoholics—alcoholism itself being a symptom of psychological stress. These men returned home after the war to an unsympathetic society which classified

---

* The Norwegian merchant navy represented the country's major war effort in the Allied cause. At the start of the war, Norway's merchant fleet consisted of approximately 1,000 ships, with a total tonnage of 4.7 million tons. These ships, manned by approximately 38,000 officers and seamen, played a major role in the Battle of the Atlantic. By the end of the war, roughly 50 percent of the Norwegian merchant fleet had been sunk and 4,000 Norwegian sailors drowned.

them as "asocials." Friends and acquaintances showed little understanding when they tried to describe how it had been at sea under constant threat of U-boat attack. Families turned on them, complaining that "they had changed." The authorities blamed their alcoholism on "moral weakness" and rejected the possibility that the high incidence of neuroses and alcoholism found among the heroic merchant mariners of World War II had its roots in the war. The sailors, consequently, were not entitled to invalid pensions, no matter how incapacitated they proved to be.

Concentration-camp survivors faced an equally insensitive public once the initial shock of the extermination-camp story had been absorbed by the Norwegian public. Psychological symptoms often took years to develop, but the horrors of the camps had by then faded from public consciousness and the country as a whole would not accept the idea that the symptoms were connected with the concentration-camp experience. In the absence of a specific injury connected to the time spent in a concentration camp, no war pension could or would be granted. It was almost as if the country, for deep pyschological reasons of its own, had closed its eyes to the plight of those survivors who had suffered the worst psychological blows. There must have been, in this reaction, an unconscious unwillingness to understand. After the war, those who had remained in Norway took pleasure in describing the occupation they had lived through as the ultimate war experience. Those persons who could claim, as could the concentration-camp survivors, that they had experienced worse conditions than the conditions at home faced resentment and rejection.

The inequity of Norway's treatment of its merchant-marine invalids and its concentration-camp survivors troubled a small group of physicians who, in the 1950s, formed the Association of War Invalids, which hoped to convince the public and the Norwegian government that there were signs of invalidism other than the loss of an eye, a hand, an arm, or a leg. It took many years before the group could convince the country of the connection between the hardships at sea and in the camps and the symptoms subsequently shown by the victims.

The efforts of the association made slow headway. Not until 1968 did Norway change its law relating to war-invalid pensions. When finally enacted, the new legislation approved pensions for petitioners who had experienced "extremely stressful" conditions for six months or more during the war and who subsequently had suffered psychological or medical disabilities. More than a quarter of a century after the end of the war, Norway finally accepted the idea that those whom the rigors of war had torn apart internally were as much entitled to public support as those more visibly injured. For many, however, the new law came too late.

Thousands of those who had been among the most grievously afflicted had already died of their invisible wounds.

There was another, unexpected, by-product of the work of the Association of War Invalids which proved particularly upsetting to Norwegians. In the mid-1960s, when the association began its efforts to persuade Norway's national assembly to change its war-pension law, Norwegian authorities asked the association for an estimate of the number of Norwegians who could qualify for pensions if the "six months under extreme stress" criterion were officially adopted.

Medical men on the association's board began by classifying those groups that could possibly contribute new pension applicants and discovered that they were working with a base population of close to a quarter-million people divided into six distinct categories:

Norwegian servicemen on active duty in 1940	50,000
Merchant-marine sailors	38,000
Norwegians serving in armed forces outside Norway	28,000
Political prisoners and concentration-camp inmates	40,000
Members of the home-front civilian resistance	50,000
Members of Milorg, the military resistance	40,000
Total	246,000

The investigators next confronted the question of how many from this base population had been under extreme stress for at least six months. The answers, when they became known, did much to ensure the passage of the new legislation, for it was found that those who qualified under the new six-months-stress criterion were far fewer than had been anticipated.

None of the military forces on active duty when the Germans invaded Norway in April, 1940, could qualify under the six-months standard. All fighting in Norway had ended within two months.

On the other hand, all of Norway's 38,000 merchant-marine sailors qualified under the new criterion; most of them had been at sea for years. The evaluating panel considered their heavy losses and concluded that wartime service at sea was psychologically stressful even if the enemy had never actually been sighted.

No more than 5,000 of the 28,000 men who had served in military units outside Norway were judged to have been under extreme stress for at least six months, and approximately 4,000 of these were merchant-marine gunners who, although sailing on merchant ships, were registered as serving with the Royal Norwegian Navy.

The estimates that rocked the nation and that met stubborn opposition, however, were related to the resistance forces. These estimates provided a blow to the image of the heroic Norwegian resistance that had been created during and after the war. Of the 50,000 who supposedly were members of the civilian resistance, only 800 men and women qualified under the six-months criteria. Of the 40,000 members of the military resistance, only 1,000 qualified. (More recent statistics indicate that even these numbers were inflated.) Given the Norwegian population of slightly less than three million at the start of the war, the percentage of resistance members who survived the war and who were judged to have been under stress for at least six months during the occupation approximated five ten-thousandths (.0005) of 1 percent.

Other statistics support the conclusion that the Norwegian resistance played an inactive role in the fight against the German occupying power. Throughout five years of war and occupation, the Norwegian resistance lost less than fifteen hundred men and women. Most of those who died perished in prison or in flight to England, or were executed as hostages. Only 162 died as the result of direct clashes with the Germans during guerrilla raids or sabotage actions. If the intensity of a country's fight against an occupying power is measured by those who fall in open struggle, the statistics of the war years indicate that the Norwegian resistance, despite individual heroic actions, was not a significant force against the Germans. Ironically, the five thousand Norwegian men who fought with the Norwegian Legion on the Eastern Front alongside German troops suffered greater hardships and losses than the army of the resistance. Six hundred and eighty-nine Legionnaires were killed on the Eastern Front.

Years after the end of World War II, Dr. Odd Øyen, who saw active service with Milorg and who participated in the work of the Association of War Invalids, commented critically: "If all the Allied countries had done as much to fight Germany as had Norway, Hitler and his associates would still be ruling Europe today."

Military commentators hailed the German conquest of Norway when it occurred as a masterful exercise of German military efficiency and gave the campaign a special place in the annals of the Second World War as the first successful combined operation of land, sea, and air forces. The occupation of Norway delivered to Hitler several advantages: the flow of Swedish iron ore and Finnish nickel was assured; German warships could use Norwegian naval bases either to break out into the Atlantic or lash out against convoys to Russia; on land, German forces could move through northern Finland against the Russian arctic ports of Murmansk and Archangel to interdict whatever military supplies managed to reach these by sea. Above and beyond these advantages, the conquest secured Germany's northern flank against a British attack that Hitler always feared would come.

These advantages, however, look better on paper than they did in reality, for once Norway had been occupied, the promise that Norway held out to German military leaders never came to fruition. The German Navy, inhibited by fear of committing her major units and restricted by fuel shortages, failed to use Norwegian bases effectively. Even against convoys to Russia, Germany failed to utilize Norwegian naval and air bases to the fullest extent. In 1941, when the first convoys sailed, over-confident German leaders did not recognize their importance. By the time this miscalculation had been corrected, the balance of naval power had shifted and the Allies were able to keep open the vital northern sea route to Russia. Nor did the Germans mount a campaign on land to cut the railroads leading south from Murmansk and Archangel. Throughout the most crucial period of fighting on the Eastern Front, Russia thus continued to receive war supplies over the arctic route, supplies which a more farsighted and aggressive Germany could have stopped.

To Hitler's mind, however, the most important advantage gained from the occupation was the protection it gave to Germany's northern flank. And the occupation did protect his northern flank, but in the long run this protection proved to be costly indeed in men and matériel. Germany, which had conquered Norway with what amounted to a reinforced corps, found itself obliged to defend the country with an army of at least 300,000 men committed to a static defense. When General Falkenhorst testified after the war before a Norwegian commission of inquiry, he described the Norwegian campaign, which he had planned, as "absolutely unnecessary." It meant, he complained, "a dispersal of forces." Gen. Alfred Jodl, head of Hitler's operational staff, also criticized the Norwegian campaign. "The Norwegian coast gave us strategically no advantage against Britain," Jodl commented, while the occupation "tied down 300,000 men in order to protect our conquests, and these remained useless for the remainder of the war."

In evaluating the military wisdom of Germany's invasion and oc-cupation of Norway, unanswerable questions present themselves for consideration. Norway certainly posed a threat to Hitler's northern flank, but how serious was the threat? Was it in fact a matter of life and death? Once the occupation was a *fait accompli,* did Germany need to commit as large a force as it did to assure continued control of the country or would a token force have sufficed? And if Germany had committed a smaller force, who is to say the British would not have come (for Churchill shared Hitler's fascination with action in the north)? The final, overriding questions concern German diversion of strength to Norway when weighed against the demands of total war. Was Norway necessary? Was

Norway justified? To these questions there are no conclusive answers.

In a postwar study of the northern theater of operations, the American military historian Earl Ziemke wrote that when all factors are considered and "a balance is cast, they lead only to the conclusion that the Northern Theater was both essential to Germany's conduct of the war and a stone around its neck."

For five long years, the presence of German occupation forces posed complex and subtle questions of resistance and collaboration for the citizens of Norway and Denmark. How any individual responded involved a mix of many factors—his political orientation, his perception of the war as the war progressed, the degree of direct pressure applied against him, and, finally, the essence of his total personality as expressed during times of crisis, a quality difficult if not impossible to measure beforehand and equally difficult to satisfactorily explain afterward.

The official Norwegian and Danish view of the occupation concentrated on the opposition to German rule and on the individual Scandinavian's abhorrence of the Nazi philosophy. Enough evidence exists to make a credible case. Both nations could point with justification to many acts of heroism in the field, from the Norwegian SOE attack on the Norsk Hydro heavy-water plant to Denmark's intelligence operations during most of the war, a service General Eisenhower described as "second to none." Both nations could cite, with honor, civilian resistance against the Germans, from Denmark's rescue of its Jews to the struggle of Norwegian teachers against Nazi thought-control. Sabotage there was in both countries, and men and women willing to die in the fight against the Germans, and enough acts of resistance to earn for both countries status as allies of the Western powers.

But if Germany had won the war, Denmark and Norway could have presented an alternate case for favorable consideration by the Third Reich. On the governmental level, both Denmark and Norway, it could have been argued, willingly accommodated the Germans. For more than three years, the Danish government followed a policy of peaceful negotiation. Even after the government resigned in August, 1943, a *modus vivendi* came into play permitting cooperation and communication between German officials and Danish civil servants. In Norway, Germany had the service and support of the Quisling regime. Volunteers from both countries, it could have been pointed out, fought on the Eastern Front in the common struggle against the Bolshevik enemy, and the resistance movement in both countries, despite individual acts of sabotage instigated by agents sent in from abroad, was weak and ineffective. Scandinavian workers eagerly toiled for German wages, and Danish agriculture provided increasing amounts of food for Germany throughout the war. Finally, if Germany had won the war, both Norway and Denmark could have argued that a body of public opinion existed within both countries that looked with respect and admiration on Germanic culture. At no time, even when the tide of battle turned sharply against Germany, did the majority of the Danes or Norwegians come out in active opposition to the Germans.

Neither view of the Scandinavian reaction to World War II accurately reflects reality. Even taken together, the opposing viewpoints express different aspects of the total picture, touching on those specific highlights, events, and occurrences that can be recorded, fixed, or observed, and leaving out the unspoken thoughts, the hidden acts, and the unconscious motivations of those involved.

To understand Denmark and Norway under the German occupation is to attempt to comprehend the human response to crisis, for both countries responded to their ordeal in human terms: torn by conflicting demands, involved with the needs of their bodies as well as their honor, changing with events, and always, always, seeking to survive.

Acknowledgments

Particular problems face any researcher attempting to investigate a period of history that still has the power to affect the emotions of those old enough to remember, especially if the period under study was fraught with bitterness and controversy, as were the years of World War II in Scandinavia.

The normal resources of the historian are insufficient to provide him with all the necessary tools and information. Much contemporary documentation and original source material is simply not available, for personal reasons as well as for reasons of state. The researcher is therefore forced to work with something less than the full record.

New complications arise when the researcher turns to previously published works on the period under review. It soon becomes apparent that many of the books and articles already in print were written during the war or shortly thereafter and are, as a result, highly colored by wartime politics and passions.

Nor can the normal techniques of the journalist be relied upon to develop the story fully or accurately. Interviews with participants and eyewitnesses, notoriously suspect at all times, are especially unreliable when the events under examination occurred thirty or so years in the past. Time plays havoc with memory. Wartime emotions distort postwar recollections. Psychological forces that operate on those interviewed without their awareness can distort the story.

Under these conditions, the researcher is forced to base his account of what happened, and why, on whatever primary source material is available and on those secondary interpretations and evaluations of events which seem to him consistent with other explanations and with his own understanding of how people react under pressure and danger. In the final analysis, therefore, he falls back on his own judgment of the material in hand.

During the five years of research that went into *The Bitter Years,* I consistently applied certain standards to the material that came my way. In respect to the printed material, whether found in government archives or in the libraries of Scandinavia and the United States, I asked when and by whom any item was written and from what vantage point. Those wartime pamphlets and books designed for propaganda purposes or to plead a special position have been evaluated as such.

In interviewing those directly involved in events, I tended to discount all stories that portrayed the participant or his friends in a heroic light, unless those stories could be substantiated by other credible sources. The practical result of this approach was to view with cautious skepticism those stories that provided a derring-do view of the war years and to accept as more probably true those interpretations that emphasized the ambivalence and complexity of the events and personalities involved. No doubt this approach in itself could have produced some misplaced emphasis in the manuscript, for there certainly were many heroes and many gallant actions during the war, but I can only explain to the reader my attitude toward research so that he or she can respond to the events portrayed with some understanding of my outlook and perspective.

No writer can duplicate reality; the best any writer can do is to approach reality to the extent that the information at hand and his understanding of it permit. In this task he must depend in large measure on the fairness and sensitivity of many others who have been there before him.

In the preparation of the volume I have indeed been indebted to many who have been there before me—to authors and historians who have previously dealt with parts of the panoramic story; and to those impressive participants in wartime events who were detached enough (and strong enough emotionally) to offer me access to their contemporary files and records, and access, too, to their conclusions and thoughts about the German invasion and occupation of Denmark and Norway, even when those conclusions were critical of themselves and of beloved fellow countrymen.

For those readers who might want to go over in greater detail some of the printed material that I have pursued and to explore more fully the developments covered in this volume, certain guidelines can be offered.

For contemporary views of the activities of the German Fifth Column and for fuller popular explanations of the defeat of Norway and Denmark, the reader has an almost unlimited reservoir available of newspaper and magazine articles on the northern campaign in the Western publications of that period. Almost without exception, these articles—and the propaganda pamphlets that were printed concurrently—confirmed the view of Norway and Denmark defeated by treason, trickery, and surprise. Excerpts from only a few could be included in the text and those sources that were used were specifically named.

Likewise, the material on the occupation of Denmark and Norway that was printed during the war—most of it distorted in the interests of propaganda or policy—comprises an almost endless stream of newspaper and magazine articles, pamphlets, radio scripts, books, reports, and personal testimonies, each a part of a gigantic mosaic of wartime image-making, each containing elements of truth along with inaccuracies, each reflecting the pressures operating at the time of publication. Again, only a few representative examples have been included in this text, and they have been named.

The postwar years brought another flood of books and articles that built on the distorted reportage and propaganda of the war years to confirm, in the public's mind, the myths and inaccuracies of the past. These books, some of which are mentioned in the text, are the natural literary spin-off of any emotional climactic experience such as a world war. Those mentioned in this text are representative of a particular genre, no better than others, and no worse.

To differentiate from those works mentioned in the text as examples of the mythmaking process in print, I would recommend two serious works that contain much information useful in understanding the period. The first, *The German Fifth Column in the Second World War* by Louis DeJong, is an excellent treatment of the German Fifth Column—the fears it engendered in countries opposed to Hitler and the realities of its existence. Two chapters are devoted to Norway and Denmark. The second, *The Rescue of the Danish Jewry* by Leni Yahil, covers the experience of the Danish Jews and includes the most extensive exploration of the myths involving King Christian and the Yellow Star.

Two official British histories provide extensive material on British military and diplomatic thinking in regard to Scandinavia during the autumn and winter of 1939–40. They are J. R. M. Butler's *Grand Strategy*, Volume II, and Sir Llewellyn Woodward's *British Foreign Policy in the Second World War*. Winston Churchill's *The Gathering Storm* also provides material covering this period. Douglas Clark's *Three Days to Catastrophe* and Max Jacobsen's *The Diplomacy of the Winter War* detail the convolutions of Allied policy concerning Finland, while Earl F. Ziemke's *The German Northern Theater of Operations* provides information on the German plans for Scandinavia.

By far the most comprehensive review of the *Altmark* affair in all its naval and diplomatic ramifications can be found in the Norwegian publication *Altmark Saken, 1940*, written by Reidar Omang. It contains the texts of notes that passed between the British and Norwegian governments and a lengthy summary, in English, of the chronology of the events. *The War at Sea 1939-1945*, Volume I, by Capt. S. W. Roskill is the official British history of the naval war and includes a short section on the *Altmark* incident. *The Gathering Storm** also contains information about the *Altmark* from the British perspective, as well as the text of some Admiralty orders. For personal accounts by participants, see Philip Vian's *Action This Day*, Patrick Dove's *I Was Graf Spee's Prisoner*, and Thomas Foley's *I Was An Altmark Prisoner*.

The most thorough treatment of the military planning for Operation *Weseruebung* can be found in *The German Northern Theater of Operations*. The full texts of many German memorandums and orders relating to *Weseruebung* that are reproduced in this volume were taken from *Brassey's Naval Annual, 1948*, edited by Rear Admiral H. G. Thursfield. *Hitler and His Admirals* by Anthony Martienssen covers much of the same ground as *Brassey's*. For a more general treatment of the Scandinavian theater of war in 1940, see William Shirer's *The Rise and Fall of the Third Reich*. *Norway, Neutral and Divided* by Halvdan Koht gives the Norwegian view of some events but should be read with some reservations, as it was written while the war was still on by one of the participants. *Germany's Underground* by Allen W. Dulles covers the activities of C. J. Sas in informing the Scandinavians of the impending invasion. The attitude of the Danes and Norwegians during the period immediately preceding the invasion was drawn from contemporary newspaper accounts and from an article on the Danish king during World War II by Lieutenant Colonel Thaulow that can be found in Borge Outze's *Denmark During the German Occupation*.

There are many books that cover the fighting in Norway in great detail and, to a lesser extent, the fighting in Denmark. The account that appears in these chapters was drawn from various sources. *The German Northern Theater of Operations* utilizes German sources to present the campaign as it was seen from Berlin and the headquarters of General Falkenhorst. *The Campaign in Norway* by T. K. Derry is the official British account of the operation. For an official British history concentrating on the naval engagements, see *The War at Sea, 1939-1945*, Volume I. Another good general account of the Norwegian fighting can be found in J. L. Moulton's *A Study of Warfare in Three Dimensions*. Bernard Ash, primarily an author of fiction, covers the same general grounds in *Norway, 1940*. Volume II of *British Foreign Policy* is also useful. Laurence Thompson's *1940* is a popular history that includes sections on Scandinavia. *Denmark: Hitler's "Model Protectorate"* by the Danish author Sten Gudme provides useful detail on the invasion of

* Subsequent citations of books previously cited by title and author are henceforth cited by title alone.

Denmark. An article on "The Danish Army on April 9, 1940," by Col. R. Mikkelsen can be found in *Denmark During the Occupation.*

General accounts of the growth of the resistance movement can be found in the following publications: *Norway, 1940–1945; The Resistance Movement* by Olav Riste and Berit Nokleby; *Norway and the Second World War* by Amanda Johnson; *The German Invasion and Occupation of Norway* by Paul C. Vigness; *A Brief History of Norway* by John Midgaard; *A Short History of Norway* by T. K. Derry; *A People Who Loved Peace, the Norwegian Struggle Against Nazism* by Roy Walker; and *Nazis in Norway* by Ake Fen. *Journey to London* by Dik Lehmkuhl covers the story of the Norwegian government at war.

The account of Quisling's role in the Norwegian drama can be found in the general accounts and in two pro-Quisling works: *Quisling, Prophet Without Honor* by Ralph Hewins and *I Was Quisling's Secretary* by H. Franklin Knudsen.

Accounts of the struggle of Norwegian schoolteachers can be found in *Norway's Schools in the Battle for Freedom* published by the Royal Norwegian Government Information Office, and in *Tyranny Could Not Quell Them* by Gene Sharp, a Peace News Pamphlet. *The Fight of the Norwegian Church Against Nazism* by Bjarne Hoye and Trygve Ager covers the opposition of the churchmen to the Nazi occupation.

For information on Norwegian Jews during World War II see Raul Hilberg's *The Destruction of the European Jews* and Gerald Reitlinger's *The Final Solution.* An article by S. Ralph Cohen, "Scandinavia's Jewish Communities," published in the *American Scandinavian Review,* summer, 1968, provides a short history of the Jews of Norway.

The growth and activity of the Norwegian resistance movement and of SOE (Special Operations Executive) operations inside Norway are covered, in part, by many books and articles, although there is no single work in English covering the entire field. A short general review can be found in *Norway, 1940–1945. European Resistance Movements, 1939–45, Proceedings of the Second International Conference on the History of the Resistance Movements,* has a chapter on "The Resistance Movement in Norway and the Allies (1940–45)" by Sverre Kjestadli, which concentrates on the relationship between Milorg, SOE, and the Norwegian government in exile. Some useful material on the general topic can also be found in *Norway and the Second World War; Norway, Her Invasion and Occupation;* and *The German Occupation of Norway.*

For background information on the raids on the Lofotens, see *Norway, the Commandos. Dieppe* by Christopher Buckley; *The Epic of Lofoten* by H. George Mikes; and *Secret German Documents* seized during the raid on the Lofoten Islands on the fourth of March, 1941. Other accounts of the Lofoten raids can be found in the general military histories.

Material in this text on the sailings by fishing vessels between the Shetlands and Norway was drawn primarily from *The Shetland Bus* by David Howarth. The material on interrogation techniques was drawn from the *Preliminary Report on Germany's Crimes Against Norway* by Finn Palmstrom and Rolf Normann Torgersen, an official Norwegian government document, and *The Gestapo at Work in Norway* by the royal Norwegian government in London.

An excellent account of the SOE sabotage operation against the Norsk Hydro plant is contained in David Irving's *The German Atomic Bomb*. A more personalized account of the raid, by one of the men who was involved in it, can be found in *Skis Against the Atom* by Knut Haukelid. My own account of the events was written on the basis of information provided in these books and from interviews with Joachim Ronneberg and Arne Kjelstrup, both members of the SOE attack team. Ronneberg provided copies of operational reports he wrote on the mission, and Kjelstrup made available a monograph on the subject, *The Heavy Water Operations in Norway, 1942-1944,* which had been compiled by Colonel J. S. (Jack) Wilson, who headed the SOE's Norwegian section. Other printed sources which mention the Norsk Hydro raid include *Now It Can Be Told* by Leslie R. Groves and *By Air to Battle—The Official Account of the British Airborne Divisions.*

There is no single volume in English that covers all aspects of Denmark's social, political, and military history during the years from 1940 to 1943. Two articles by the Danish historian Jorgen Haestrup, whose writings reflect the official viewpoint of postwar Danish governments, provide a broad summation of Danish-German negotiations during this period and of the growth of the Danish resistance. They are: "Exposé," published in *European Resistance Movements, 1939; First International Conference on the History of the Resistance Movements;* and "Denmark's Connection with the Allied Powers During the Occupation," published in *European Resistance Movements, 1939–45: Proceedings of the Second International Conference on the History of the Resistance Movements.* Another brief review of Denmark during the war can be found in Haestrup's *Panorama Denmark, From Occupied to Ally.*

The British propaganda effort in relation to Denmark is covered in authoritative and scholarly fashion by Jeremy Bennett in *British Broadcasting and the Danish Resistance Movement.* Bennett's book, while concentrating on the role of the BBC, provides a perceptive analysis of events inside Denmark as well as how those events influenced, and were influenced by, British wartime policy. All excerpts from BBC broadcasts printed in this text are from Bennett's book.

The war and immediate postwar years produced a plethora of books and pamphlets on Denmark. Most are marred for today's reader by their wartime rhetoric. All must be read with caution. Nevertheless, three books from that period do provide understanding of life in Denmark under the Germans: *Denmark: Hitler's "Model Protectorate"*; Paul Palmer's *Denmark in Nazi Chains*; and *Denmark During the German Occupation.*

A wartime publication of a different caliber is the British Ministry of Economic Warfare's "confidential" study titled *Denmark Basic Handbook.* The Ministry was the parent organization under which the SOE operated, and its *Handbook,* dated October, 1943, was designed to provide background information for all those with missions or interests in wartime Denmark. The *Handbook* contains verbatim translations of many German and Danish documents and speeches. Its tone is factual and analytical, taking due notice of German successes when applicable and often crediting German officials for their deft handling of the negotiations with the Danes, specifically in regard to the elections of March, 1943.

The basic work available in English on the rescue of the Danish Jews is Yahil's scholarly *The Rescue of Danish Jewry.* It contains a wealth of information and was the prime source for most of the first-person accounts printed in this book, as well as for the text of most of the telegrams sent by and to German officials. For eyewitness accounts by participants in the rescue see *October, '43* by Aage Bertelsen and *A Rabbi Remembers* by Dr. Marcus Melchior. Bertelsen's book covers the events through the eyes of a Danish resistance worker; Melchior's book covers the rabbi's entire career and includes a description of his escape from Denmark. Two other more general works on the European Jews which mention the events in Denmark are *The Final Solution* and *The Destruction of the European Jews.*

The dramatic British effort to sink the *Tirpitz* is covered in depth in several books, two of which concentrate entirely on the German battleship and British attempts to destroy her. They are: *The Tirpitz* by David Woodward, and *Sink the Tirpitz!* by Leonce Peillard. The story of the *Tirpitz* is also covered in Volumes I, II, and III of *The War at Sea,* the official British history of the Second World War. *The Shetland Bus* is strong on detail of the attempt to sink the *Tirpitz* using two-man human torpedoes.

Material on the German retreat through Finnmark can be found in *Journey to London; The German Occupation of Norway; Look to Norway* by William Warbey; and *The German Northern Theater of Operations.*

The story of the Danish resistance in the latter years of the war is covered by several books printed in English. Robin Reilly's *The Sixth Floor* concentrates on events leading up to the RAF raid on Shellhus. Sir Basil Embry's *Mission Completed* provides another perspective on the RAF raids. *British Broadcasting and the Danish Resistance Movement* reports on developments as seen from BBC offices in England. *Panorama Denmark* provides a factual outline. Both *Denmark During the German*

Occupation and *Civilian Resistance as a National Defense* include chapters on the latter years of the Danish occupation.

The material on German concentration camps was drawn primarily from three encyclopedic works: *Destruction of the European Jews, The Final Solution,* and Nora Levin's *The Holocaust.* While these volumes primarily relate to the concentration-camp phenomenon as it affected the Jews of Europe, they contain extensive information on the operation, character, and personnel of the camps and on the treatment accorded various nationality groups. *The Rescue of the Danish Jewry* covers the experience of the Danish Jews in Theresienstadt. For the experiences of Norwegian prisoners, see Leo Eitinger's *Concentration Camp Survivors.* Odd Nansen's *From Day to Day* provides a Norwegian prisoner's diary of his years of imprisonment. For a brief and personalized comment on the negotiations with Heinrich Himmler that led to the rescue of the Scandinavian prisoners in the spring of 1945, see Count Folke Bernadotte's *The Curtain Falls.*

Material on the German capitulation in Norway and Denmark and the immediate post-liberation period can be found in the following volumes: *The German Northern Theater of Operations; The German Occupation of Norway; Norway and the Second World War; Look to Norway; Journey to London; The Rise and Fall of the Third Reich; History of the Kingdom of Denmark* by Palle Lauring; and *Civil Affairs and Military Government, Northwest Europe, 1944–1946* by F. S. V. Donnison.

For further information on Quisling's trial, see "Quisling on Trial" by Anthony Wigan, an article in the November–December, 1945, issue of *The Norseman.* For the effects of concentration-camp life on surviving inmates, see *Concentration Camp Survivors.* For the postwar period of anti-Semitism in Denmark, see *The Rescue of Danish Jewry.*

Information on the charges and sentences of German military leaders can be found in *The Trial of the Major War Criminals, Proceedings of the International Military Tribunal.* Volume VI of *War Crimes Trials Series,* edited by E. H. Stevens, covers the trial of General Falkenhorst.

The list of those individuals who gave freely of their personal reminiscences and private files numbers well over two hundred Danes, Norwegians, Germans, and Americans. To each and every one of them I am deeply indebted. It is possible that this book may have been written without their assistance, but it is doubtful if it could have reflected the spirit of the times, to the degree it does, without their cooperation.

Most of the information involving the popularly accepted view of the invasion and occupation was derived from a lengthy series of interviews I conducted with Danes and Norwegians who participated in the events. Their reminiscences of the war years faithfully reflect what appeared in print, often with subtle though not contradictory variations. In dealing with memories such as these, it is pointless to try to determine if what a person remembers thirty years after an event is the event itself or what he subsequently read of the event, for in the construction of popular myths the elements are all intertwined: rumors, facts, fears, hopes, anecdotes heard, reports read, all combine to form one unified whole, and it is that total picture which concerns us here.

For the various chapters involved with the actual German invasion and occupation of Denmark and Norway, I have received invaluable help from scores of individuals. Many private citizens in Norway and Denmark granted interviews to discuss the atmosphere in the two countries during the time of the invasion and during the fighting that followed. Among them were Dr. Odd Øyen, in 1940 a Norwegian Army lieutenant who saw action at Elverum; Gen. Mons Haukeland, in 1940 a captain with the Norwegian Fourth Brigade, which saw action at Valdres and Bagn; Gen. R. Roscher Nielsen, in 1940 a member of General Ruge's staff; and scores of junior officers and enlisted men who provided a picture of the demoralization and disorder which generally characterized the Danish and Norwegian armed forces in action.

Many Norwegians who were active in the resistance, either with Milorg or with SOE, were kind enough to discuss the climate of the years after the invasion and provided supplementary material which was incorporated in the text of this book. Some of those interviewed were Dr. Ole Jacob Malm, a Norwegian underground worker; Knut Moyen, a Milorg leader from 1941 to 1942; Jens Christian Hauge, who succeeded Moyen in 1942 and headed Milorg until the end of the war; Arne Okkenhaug, a leader of the Norwegian teachers' resistance; and Ragnar Ulstein, who participated in the second Lofoten raid. Norwegian historians Berit Nokleby, Olav Riste, and Magne Skodvin also granted some of their time to review the broader trends of the occupation, although my naming them here does not imply that they are responsible for any inaccuracies in this account.

Information obtained from personal interviews with Norwegians who were active during the war helped fill out this account of the period under review. Those to whom I spoke included saboteurs Oluf Reed Olsen and Gunnar Sonsteby; Norwegian Army officers Peter Holst and Alv Johnsen; Communist underground worker Ornulf Egge; the Reverend Conrad Vogt-Svendsen, a Norwegian clergyman who was based in Hamburg during the war years; and Odd Medboe, a young Norwegian journalist in the 1940s who helped organize the rescue apparatus that eventually brought Scandinavian prisoners out of Germany before the end of the war.

For the story of Norwegian and Danish prisoners in German concentration camps, I am indebted to various Scandinavians, including R. Roscher Nielsen and Rolf Scheen, two Norwegian officers imprisoned in Germany with the bulk of the Norwegian military men; Samuel Steinman, one of the few Norwegian Jews to survive the concentration camps; Lisa Borsum and Helmer Bonnevie, Norwegian prisoners who spent years in German camps; and scores of other prisoners whose names do not appear in this text but who provided further details on the experiences of Scandinavian prisoners in the concentration camps. Lisa Borsum also made available the unpublished manuscript of her prison diary, *Fange i Ravensbrück* (Prisoner in Ravensbrück). The Danish historian Jorgen Barfod provided statistics on Danish deaths in the concentration camps. Dr. Odd Øyen, the Norwegian resistance fighter who as a medical man was closely involved with postwar survivors of the concentration camps, provided statistics on Norwegian deaths in the camps.

Material on the fighting in Finnmark was obtained from personal interviews with Gen. Arne Dahl, the Norwegian commanding officer of the Norwegian forces in Finnmark; Col. Tonne Huitfeldt, the Norwegian unit's intelligence officer; Gen. Joseph Remold, commanding officer of the Sixth German Mountain Division; and Bernt Balchen, a former U. S. Air Force officer who participated in transporting Norwegian troops into Kirkenes by air.

I also interviewed close to one hundred Danish men and women who were involved in the events of the war and who represented varying points of view at the time. They included Foreign Ministry official Nils Svenningsen; BOPA leader Borge Ting; the pro-German lawyer Carl Popp-Madsen; SOE agent Ole Lippmann; Danish Army officers Hans Lunding and Niels Bjarke Schou; and resistance fighters Anton Jensen (code-named Jens Toldstrup), Flemming Muus, Flemming Juncker, Stig Jensen, Flemming Larsen, Jens Lillilund, and Mogens Staffeldt. Many professional journalists including Svenn Sehusen, Kate Fleron, Ebbe Munck, Borge Outze, and BBC announcer Terkel M. Terkelsen also contributed to this account. All gave freely of their time and information, often making available otherwise unpublished letters and diaries. Interviews with them provided specific information of value. Even more important, they provided explanations of the complexities of the Danish experience during the occupation years and provided a realistic framework against which the printed records could be evaluated.

Other Danes who gave of their time and information included Freedom Council members Mogens Fog, Erling Foss, and Aage Schoch; Danish intelligence officers Poul Morch and Svend Truelsen; and resistance workers Ruth Philipsen and Harald Sandbaek, both of whom survived the RAF bombing of Gestapo headquarters in Aårhus, as Schoch and Fog survived the RAF bombing of Gestapo headquarters in Copenhagen. Those who provided specific and detailed information about the rescue of the Danish Jews included Inga and Wolfgang Bardfeld, Professor Richard Ege, Hanna Kaufmann, Jens Lillilund, Julius Margolinsky, the late Rabbi Marcus Melchior, Borge Outze, Dr. Ole Secher, Mogens

Staffeldt, Nils Svenningsen, and Svend Truelsen. Hans Henrik Koch, the Danish undersecretary of the Ministry of Social Welfare during the latter war years, provided information about the return of Scandinavian prisoners to Denmark before the end of the war. Kai Winkelhorn, a Danish-born U. S. citizen who served with the OSS during the war, made available previously unpublished contemporary reports that included the texts of military messages transmitted during the war as well as OSS judgments and evaluations made at the time.

Still other Danes who provided valuable background information on the occupation included Pastor Poul Borchsenius, who was active in the resistance in Jutland; Mrs. Gudrun Fiil, who lost her husband and many other members of her immediate family to the Germans because of their resistance work; Danish Army officer Erik Jorgen Fournaise; historian Jorgen Haestrup; Arne Hogsbro Holm, the wartime secretary-general of the Danish Agricultural Council who permitted Svend Truelsen to operate an intelligence-gathering organization from the offices of the council; Stefan Hurwitz, who headed the Danish Refugee Administration in Sweden in 1943 and 1944; Dr. Erik Husfeldt, a member of the Freedom Council; Frantz Hvass, a member of the Danish Foreign Ministry during World War II and one of the three-man investigating team which visited Theresienstadt in 1944; Nils Koster, a Danish Communist imprisoned by the Germans during the occupation; Aksel Larsen, the chairman of the Danish Communist Party in the 1940s and a member of the Danish Parliament; and Erik Nyegaard, a member of the *Holger Danske* sabotage group.

In addition to those who provided information about the war years, I am also deeply indebted to many individuals and organizations for logistic and professional support. Without their assistance this book could never have been completed. A grant from the George C. Marshall Memorial Fund of the Danmark-Amerika Fondet in Copenhagen helped finance my research mission in Denmark. Fund Chairman J. V. Thygesen, Miss K. M. Ahlmann-Ohlsen, and Miss Sonja Bundgaard-Nielsen were especially helpful in arranging research assistance. I am particularly grateful to the investigative and translating help offered by Miss Lykke Rasmussen, who, under the auspices of the Danmark-Amerika Fondet, worked with me on parts of the story of the Danish occupation.

Officials representing the governments of Denmark, Norway, and Germany were also helpful in my efforts to pull together the varied elements of the story. Those officials who provided direct and sympathetic assistance included Preben Hansen, Erik Hogsbro Holm and Soren Dyssegaard of the Danish Ministry of Foreign Affairs; Tim Greve of the Norwegian Foreign Ministry; Jon Embretsen, former director of the Norwegian Information Office in New York; and Rudolf Tegtmeier and

Winfred Bonse of the German Information Center in New York, who helped arrange a research trip through Germany.

Three representatives of the Scandinavian Airlines System—S. Ralph Cohen in New York, Soren Bertelsen in Copenhagen, and Odd Medboe in Oslo were also helpful, not only in arranging transportation but in providing introductions in Scandinavia.

The bulk of the library research for this volume was conducted in the Frederick Lewis Allen Room of the New York Public Library at Forty-second Street and Fifth Avenue in Manhattan. I am thankful to library officials for the many months they permitted me to take up residence in the Allen Room, where authors can work in leisure, in comfort, and in the company of others similarly engaged in serious projects. And to the many authors in the Allen Room—Irene Mahoney, Susan Brownmiller, Robert Caro, Ferdinand Lundberg, and Ruth Gross among them—whose interest in my project helped support me in my efforts, I offer my special thanks and my wishes for a productive day.

I also offer my special thanks to my mother, Marian Petrow, a professional librarian, who checked the bibliographic references for accuracy and helped in the editing and typing of this manuscript in its various stages; to Howard Cady, my editor at William Morrow and Company whose kindness and understanding helped bring this volume to completion; to my wife, Margot, who responded at all times with honesty and perception to the manuscript in progress; and to our children, Julie, Jay, and Steven, who understood and, I hope, accepted what I was engaged in during the past five years of our lives.

Finally, I thank all those unnamed Danes and Norwegians who spoke to me from their hearts about the war years, even when their hearts were still filled with pain and sorrow.

Forest Hills, New York
January, 1974

Bibliography

Books

Adamson, Hans Christian, and Per Klem, *Blood on the Midnight Sun.* New York: W. W. Norton and Company, 1964.

Ash, Bernard, *Norway, 1940.* London: Cassell & Company Ltd., 1964.

Astrup, Helen, and B. L. Jacot, *Night Has a Thousand Eyes.* London: Macdonald and Company, 1953.

Balchen, Bernt, *Come North With Me.* New York: E. P. Dutton and Company, 1958.

Bennett, Jeremy, *British Broadcasting and the Danish Resistance Movement.* Cambridge: Cambridge University Press, 1966.

Bernadotte, Count Folke, *The Curtain Falls.* New York: Knopf, 1945.

Bertelsen, Aage, *October, 1943.* New York: G. P. Putnam's Sons, 1954.

Brandt, Willy, *In Exile.* London: Oswald Wolff Ltd., 1971.

British Airborne Divisions, *By Air to Battle.* London: His Majesty's Stationery Office, 1945.

Brock, Theodore, *The Mountains Wait.* London: Michael Joseph, 1943.

Buckley, Christopher, *Norway, the Commandos. Dieppe.* London: His Majesty's Stationery Office, 1951.

Butler, J. R. M., *Grand Strategy, Volume II. September 1939–June, 1941.* London: Her Majesty's Stationery Office, 1957.

Carlyle, Margaret, ed., *Documents on International Affairs, 1939–1946. Volume II, Hitler's Europe.* London: Oxford University Press, 1954.

Churchill, Winston, *The Gathering Storm.* Boston: Houghton Mifflin Company, 1948.

Churchill, Winston, *The Hinge of Fate.* Boston: Houghton Mifflin Company, 1950.

Clark, Douglas, *Three Days to Catastrophe.* London: Hammond, Hammond & Company, 1966.

Cookridge, E. H., *Set Europe Ablaze*. New York: Thomas Y. Crowell Company, 1967.

Curtis, Monica, ed., *Norway and the War, Sept. 1939–Dec. 1940. Documents on International Affairs*. London: Oxford University Press, 1941.

De Jong, Louis, *The German Fifth Column in the Second World War*. Chicago: University of Chicago Press, 1956.

Derry, T. K., *The Campaign In Norway*. London: Her Majesty's Stationery Office, 1952.

Derry, T. K., *A Short History of Norway*. London: Allen & Unwin, 1957.

Donnison, F. S. V., *Civil Affairs and Military Government, North-West Europe, 1944–1946*. London: Her Majesty's Stationery Office, 1961.

Dove, Patrick, *I Was Graf Spee's Prisoner*. London: Withy Grove Press, 1940.

Dulles, Allen W., *Germany's Underground*. New York: Macmillan, 1947.

Eitinger, Leo, *Concentration Camp Survivors*. London: Allen & Unwin, 1964.

Embry, (Sir) Basil, *Mission Completed*. London: Methuen and Company, Ltd., 1957.

European Resistance Movements, 1939–45; First International Conference on the History of the Resistance Movements. New York: Pergamon Press, 1960.

European Resistance Movements, 1939–45, Proceedings of the Second International Conference on the History of the Resistance Movements. New York: Pergamon Press, 1964.

Fen, Ake, *Nazis in Norway*. Harmondsworth: Penguin Books, 1943.

Fjellbu, Arne, *Memoirs from the War Years*. Minneapolis, Minn.: Augsburg Publishing House, 1947.

Flender, Harold, *Rescue in Denmark*. New York: Simon and Schuster, 1963.

Foley, Thomas, *I Was An Altmark Prisoner*. London: Francis Aldor, 1940.

Frischauer, Willi, and Robert Jackson, *The Altmark Affair*. New York: Macmillan, 1955.

Groves, Leslie R., *Now It Can Be Told*. New York: Harper, 1962.

Gudme, Sten, *Denmark: Hitler's "Model Protectorate."* London: Victor Gollancz Ltd., 1942.

Gwyer, J. M. A., and J. R. M. Butler, *Grand Strategy*, Volume III. London: Her Majesty's Stationery Office, 1964.

Haestrup, Jorgen, *Panorama Denmark, From Occupied to Ally*. Copenhagen: Danish Ministry of Foreign Affairs, 1963.

Haines, C. Grove, and Ross J. S. Hoffman, *The Origins and Background of the Second World War.* New York: Oxford University Press, 1947.

Hansen, Poul, *Contemporary Danish Politicians.* Copenhagen: Det Danske Selskab, 1949.

Hansson, Per, *The Greatest Gamble.* London: Allen & Unwin, 1967.

Haukelid, Knut, *Skis Against the Atom.* London: William Kimber and Company, 1954.

Hewins, Ralph, *Quisling, Prophet Without Honor.* London: W. H. Allen, 1965.

Hilberg, Raul, *The Destruction of the European Jews.* New York: Quadrangle, 1961.

Hochhuth, Rolf, *The Deputy.* New York: Grove Press, 1964.

Hovelsen, Leif, *Out of the Evil Night.* London: Blandford Press, 1959.

Howarth, David, *The Shetland Bus.* London: Thomas Nelson and Sons Ltd., 1951.

Howarth, David, *We Die Alone.* New York: The Macmillan Company, 1955.

Hoye, Bjarne, and Trygve Ager, *Norwegian Church Against Nazism.* New York: Macmillan, 1943.

Ironside, Edmund, *The Ironside Diaries.* London: Constable and Company Ltd., 1962.

Irving, David, *The German Atomic Bomb.* New York: Simon and Schuster, 1967.

Ismay, *The Memoirs of General Lord Ismay.* New York: The Viking Press, 1960.

Jacobsen, Max, *The Diplomacy of the Winter War.* Cambridge: Harvard University Press, 1961.

Johnson, Amanda, *Norway, Her Invasion and Occupation.* Decatur, Georgia: Bowen Press, 1948.

Klefos, Brede, *They Came in the Night.* Greenlawn, New York: Harian Publications, 1959.

Knudsen, Harald Franklin, *I Was Quisling's Secretary.* London: Britons Publishing Company, 1967.

Koht, Halvdan, *Norway, Neutral and Invaded.* New York: Macmillan, 1941.

Lampe, David, *The Savage Canary.* London: Cassell and Company, Ltd., 1957.

Langer, William L. and S. Everett Gleason, *The Challenge to Isolation.* New York: Harper and Brothers, 1952.

Lapie, Pierre O., *With the Foreign Legion at Narvik.* London: John Murray, 1941.

Lauring, Palle, *History of the Kingdom of Denmark.* Los Angeles: Knud K. Mogensen, 1951.

Lehmkuhl, Dik, *Journey to London*. London: Hutchinson and Company, 1946.

Levin, Nora, *The Holocaust*. New York: Thomas Y. Crowell, 1968.

Macleod, Roderick and Denis Kelly, eds., *The Ironside Diaries*. Edinburgh: T. and A. Constable Ltd., 1962.

Manus, Max, *9 Lives Before Thirty*. New York: Doubleday, 1947.

Manus, Max, *Underwater Saboteur*. London: William Kimber, 1953.

Martienssen, Anthony, *Hitler and His Admirals*. New York: E. P. Dutton & Company, 1949.

Melchior, Dr. Marcus, *A Rabbi Remembers*. New York: Lyle Stuart, 1968.

Mentze, Ernst, *5 Years: The Occupation of Denmark in Pictures*. Malmo, Sweden: A. B. Allhems Forlag, 1946.

Midgaard, John, *A Brief History of Norway*. Oslo: Johan Grundt Tanum Forlag, 1963.

Mikes, H. George, *The Epic of Lofoten*. London: Hutchinson and Company, 1941.

Moen, Peter, *Peter Moen's Diary*. London: Faber and Faber Ltd., 1951.

Moulton, J. L., *A Study of Warfare in Three Dimensions*. Athens, Ohio: Ohio University Press, 1967.

Muus, Flemming, *The Spark and the Flame*. London: Museum Press Ltd., 1956.

Myklebost, Tor, *They Came as Friends*. Garden City, N.Y.: Doubleday, Doran and Company, 1943.

Nansen, Odd, *From Day to Day*. New York: G. P. Putnam's Sons, 1949.

Olsen, Oluf Reed, *Assignment: Spy*. New York: Scholastic Book Services, 1962.

Outze, Borge, ed., *Denmark During the German Occupation*. Copenhagen: Scandinavian Publishing Company, 1946.

Palmer, Paul, *Denmark in Nazi Chains*. London: Lindsay Drummon, 1942.

Palmstrom, Finn, and Rolf Normann Torgersen, *Preliminary Report on Germany's Crimes Against Norway*. Oslo: Official Norwegian Government document, 1945.

Paneth, Philip, *Haakon VII, Norway's Fighting King*. London: Alliance Press Ltd., 1944.

Peillard, Leonce, *Sink the Tirpitz!* New York: G. P. Putnam's Sons, 1968.

Reilly, Robin, *The Sixth Floor*. London: Leslie Frewin Ltd., 1969.

Reitlinger, Gerald, *The Final Solution*. New York: A. S. Barnes, 1961.

Riste, Olav, Magne Skodvin, and Johannes Andenaes, *Norway and the Second World War*. Oslo: Johan Grundt Tanum Forlag, 1966.

Riste, Olav, and Berit Nokleby, *Norway, 1940–1945; The Resistance Movement.* Oslo: Johan Grundt Tanum Forlag, 1970.

Roberts, Adam, ed., *Civilian Resistance As a National Defense.* Harrisburg, Pennsylvania: Stackpole Books, 1968.

Roskill, (Captain) S. W., *The War at Sea 1939–1945. Volume I.* London: Her Majesty's Stationery Office, 1954.

Royal Norwegian Government, *The Gestapo at Work in Norway.* London: 1942.

Royal Norwegian Government Information Office, *Norway's Schools in the Battle for Freedom.* London: Hodder and Stoughton, 1942.

Saelen, Frithjof, *None But the Brave.* London: Souvenir Press, 1955.

Salvesen, Sylvia, *Forgive—But Do Not Forget.* London: Hutchinson and Company, 1958.

Secret German Documents. London: His Majesty's Stationery Office, 1944.

Seth, Ronald, *How the Resistance Worked.* London: Geoffrey Bles, Ltd., 1961.

Shirer, William L., *The Challenge of Scandinavia.* Boston: Little, Brown and Company, 1955.

Shirer, William L., *The Rise and Fall of the Third Reich.* New York: Simon and Schuster, 1959.

Sonsteby, Gunnar, *Report from No. 24.* London: The New English Library, Limited, 1967.

Stevens, E. H., ed., *War Crimes Trials Series* (Volume VI). London: William Hodge and Company, Ltd., 1949.

Strabolgi, Joseph (Lord), *The Battle of the River Plate.* London: Hutchinson and Company, 1940.

Thompson, Laurence, *1940.* New York: William Morrow, 1966.

Thursfield, (Rear Admiral) H. G., ed., *Brassey's Naval Annual, 1948.* New York: Macmillan, 1948.

The Trial of the Major War Criminals, Proceedings of the International Tribunal. London: His Majesty's Stationery Office, 1947.

Uris, Leon M., *Exodus.* Garden City, New York: Doubleday, 1958.

Vian, Philip, *Action This Day.* London: Frederick Muller, Ltd., 1960.

Vigness, Paul C., *The German Occupation of Norway.* New York: Vantage, 1970.

Walker, Roy. *A People Who Loved Peace, The Norwegian Struggle Against Nazism.* London: Victor Gollancz Ltd., 1946.

Warbey, William, *Look to Norway.* London: Secker & Warburg, 1945.

Woodward, David, *The Tirpitz.* London: William Kimber, 1953.

Woodward, (Sir) Llewellyn, *British Foreign Policy in the Second World War.* London: Her Majesty's Stationery Office, 1962.

Worm-Muller, Jacob, *Norway Revolts Against the Nazis.* London: Lindsay Drummond, 1941.

Yahil, Leni, *The Rescue of Danish Jewry*. Philadelphia: Jewish Publication Society of America, 1969.

Ziemke, Earl F., *The German Northern Theater of Operations, 1940–1945*. Washington, D.C.: Department of the Army Pamphlet No. 20–271, 1959.

Articles and Pamphlets

After Three Years. Washington: The Royal Norwegian Information Service, 1943.

Anders, Georg, "The Liberation of Denmark." *Denmark During the Occupation*, Borge Outze, ed. Scandinavian Publishing Company, 1946.

Bennett, Jeremy, "The Resistance Against the German Occupation of Denmark." *Civilian Resistance as a National Defense*, Adam Roberts, ed. Stackpole Books, 1968.

"Blitzkrieg with Music." *The Reader's Digest*, September, 1940.

Borschsenius, Poul, "Aspects of the Rescue of Danish Jews." *Wiener Library Bulletin*, fall, 1968.

British Ministry of Economic Warfare, *Denmark Basic Handbook*. October, 1943.

Cohen, S. Ralph, "Scandinavia's Jewish Communities." *American Scandinavian Review*, summer, 1968.

Cranston, Maurice, *Non-Violence and Germany*. London: Peace News Ltd., 1945.

Denmark During the Occupation. Copenhagen: Danish Allied Committee.

Gathorne-Hardy, G. M., *Norway and the War*. London: Oxford University Press, 1941. Oxford Pamphlets on World Affairs No. 51.

Gubbins, (Major General Sir) Colin, "The Danish Resistance, 1940–45." Oxford: December, 1962.

Gubbins, (Major General Sir) Colin, "Resistance Movements in the War." *Journal of the Royal United Service Institution*. London: May, 1948.

Haestrup, Jorgen, "Denmark's Connection with the Allied Powers During the Occupation." *European Resistance Movements, 1939–45; Proceedings of the Second International Conference on the History of the Resistance Movements*. New York: Pergamon Press, 1964.

Haestrup, Jorgen, "Expose." *European Resistance Movements, 1939–45; First International Conference on the History of the Resistance Movements*. New York: Pergamon Press, 1960.

Hoge, Bjarne, and Trygve Age, *The Fight of the Norwegian Church Against Nazism*. London: Macmillan, 1943.

Hubatsch, Walter, "Problems of the Norwegian Campaign." *Royal United Service Institution Journal*. London: August, 1958.

"Jews in Scandinavia." New York: American Jewish Committee Library.

Joesten, Joachim, "Denmark's Costly Revolt." *The Virginia Quarterly Review,* winter, 1944.

Johanssen, Hagbard, *Resistance in Denmark.* War Resisters League Pamphlet.

Kjestadli, Sverre, "The Resistance Movement in Norway and the Allies, 1940–45." *European Resistance Movements, 1939–45; Proceedings of the Second International Conference on the History of the Resistance Movements.* New York: Pergamon Press, 1964.

Levin, Marcus, "The Norwegian Jews During the German Occupation." New York: American Jewish Committee Library.

Lund, Diderich, "The Revival of Northern Norway." *The Geographical Review,* October, 1947.

Mikkelsen, Colonel R., "The Danish Army on April 9,1940." *Denmark During the Occupation,* Borge Outze, ed. Copenhagen: Scandinavian Publishing Company, 1946.

Miles, Lion T., "Three Cases of International Law." *U.S. Naval Institute Proceedings,* August, 1941.

Munk, Kaj, *Four Sermons.* Blair, Nebraska: Lutheran Publishing House, 1944.

Nytrup, Per, *An Outline of the German Occupation of Denmark.* Copenhagen: Museum of the Danish Resistance Movement, 1968.

Sharp, Gene, *Tyranny Could Not Quell Them.* London: Peace News Pamphlet.

Terkelsen, Terkel M., *Denmark: Fight Follows Surrender.* London: The Information Office of the Danish Council, 1942.

Terkelsen, Terkel M., *Front Line in Denmark.* London: 1944.

"Thanks to Scandinavia." *National Jewish Monthly,* May, 1966.

Thaulow, (Lieutenant Colonel) Th., *Denmark During the Occupation,* Borge Outze, ed. Copenhagen: Scandinavian Publishing Company, 1946.

Toksvig, Signe, "Denmark's Resistance." *Atlantic Monthly,* August, 1942.

Tolischus, Otto D., "How Hitler Prepared." *New York Times Magazine,* June 16, 23 and 30, 1940.

Wigan, Anthony, "Quisling on Trial." *The Norseman,* November-December, 1945.

Wilson, (Colonel) J. S., *The Heavy Water Operations in Norway, 1942–1944.*

Scandinavian Sources

Backer, (Dr.) Julie, "*Statistisk Oversikt Over Krigsdodsfallene,* 1940-1945." Oslo, 1948.

Forhandlinger i Foketinget (Official Reports of Proceedings in Parliament)

Haestrup, Jorgen, *Hemmelig Alliance; Besaettelsestidens Fakta.* Copenhagen, 1959.

Haestrup, Jorgen, *Kontakt med England.* Copenhagen, 1954.

Haestrup, Jorgen, *Tyske Samlinger.* Copenhagen, 1961.

Haestrup, Jorgen, *Til Landets Bedste.* Copenhagen, 1966.

Jensen, Stig, *Sandfaerdige Lognehistorier fra Besaettelsen.* Copenhagen, 1970.

Jakobsen, Frode, *Standpunkter.* Copenhagen, 1966.

la Cour, Vilhelm, *Danmarks Historie, 1900–1945.* Copenhagen, 1950.

la Cour, Vilhelm, ed., *Danmark Under Besaettelsen.* Copenhagen, 1946.

Madsen, Carl, *Proces mod Politiet.* Copenhagen, 1969.

Munck, Ebbe, *Doren til den Frie Verden.* Copenhagen, 1967.

Omang, Reidar, *Altmark Saken, 1940.* Oslo: Gyldendal Norsk Forlag, 1953.

Politiken, *Besaettelsens Hvem-Hvad-Hvor.* Copenhagen, 1966.

Scavenius, Erik, *Forhandlingspolitiken under Besaettelsen.* 1948.

Stemann, Peter Christian von, *En Dansk Embedsmands Odysee.*

Wendt, Frantz, *Besaettelsen og Atomtid.* Copenhagen, 1966.

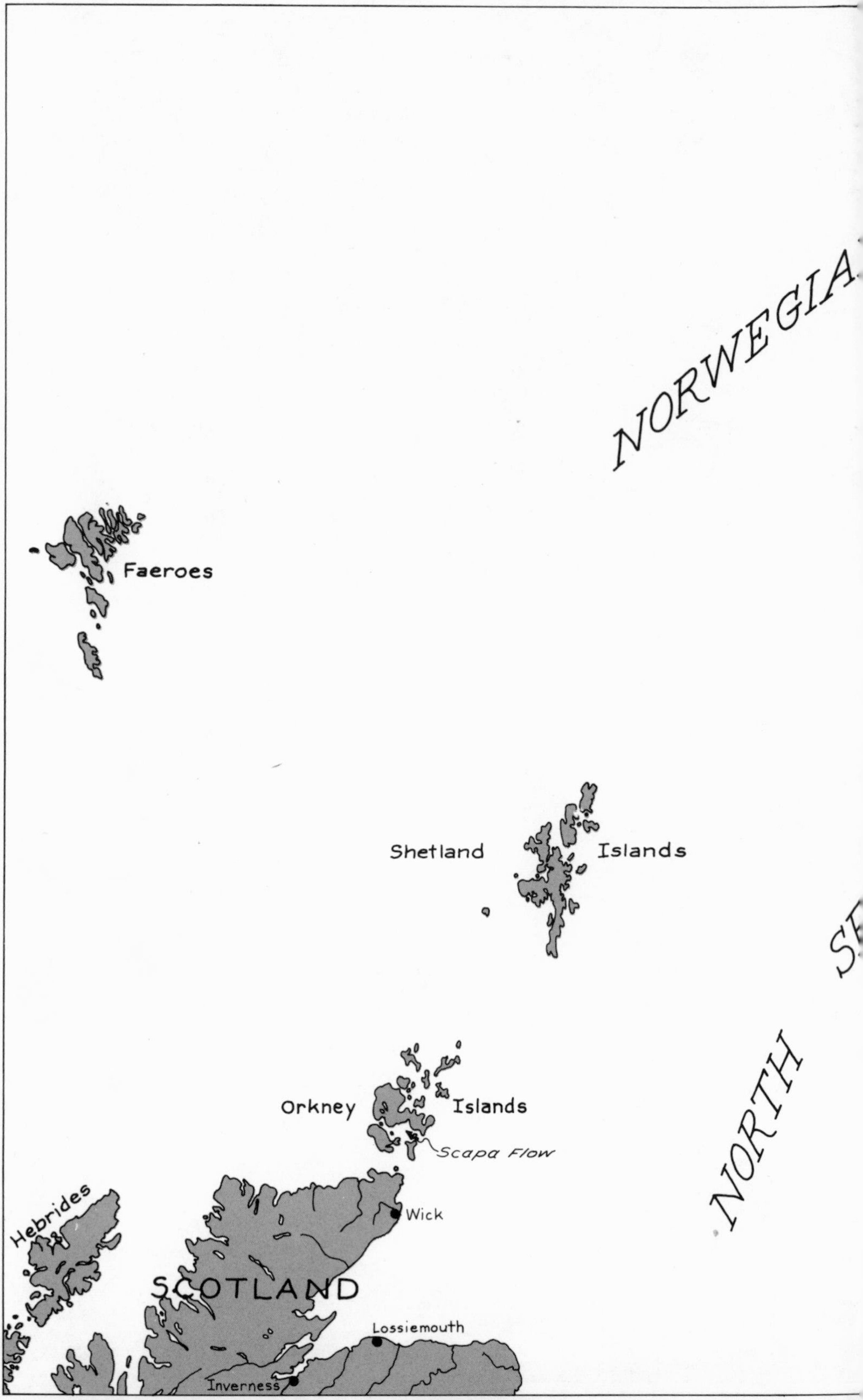

NORWEGIA

Faeroes

Shetland   Islands

SE

NORTH

Orkney   Islands

Scapa Flow

Hebrides

Wick

SCOTLAND

Lossiemouth

Inverness

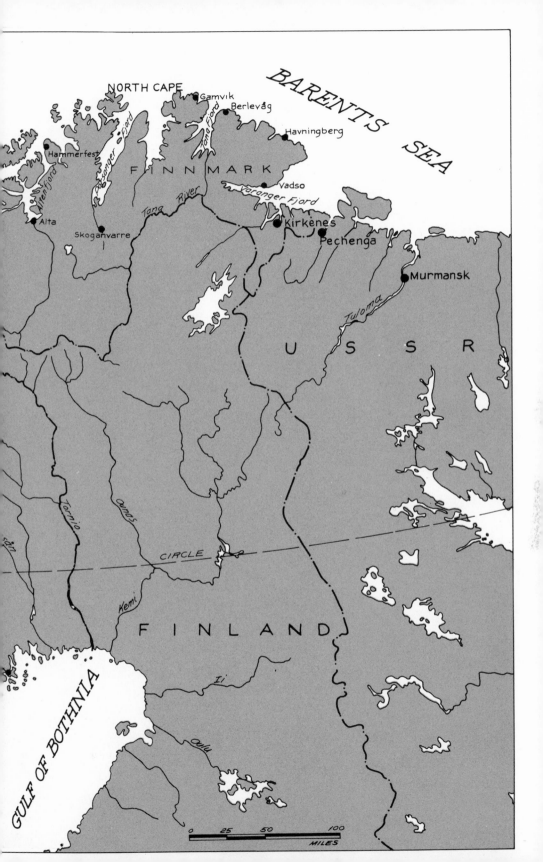

Index